Living and Working
in
Canada

A Survival Handbook

edited by
Graeme Chesters

SURVIVAL BOOKS • LONDON • ENGLAND

First published 1999
Reprinted 2001
Second Edition 2003

Survival Books Limited, 1st Floor,
60 St James's Street, London SW1A 1ZN, United Kingdom
☎ +44 (0)20-7493 4244, 🖷 +44 (0)20-7491 0605
✉ info@survivalbooks.net
🖳 www.survivalbooks.net
To order books, please refer to page 444.

British Library Cataloguing in Publication Data.
A CIP record for this book is available
from the British Library.
ISBN 1 901130 37 1

Printed and bound in Finland by WS Bookwell Ltd

ACKNOWLEDGEMENTS

My sincere thanks to those who contributed to the successful publication of the second edition of this book, in particular Michelle Snow, for her excellent local research and Canadian perspective, and Louise Cockburn, for the many hours she spent researching on the Internet. Also a special mention to the many people who assisted with the first edition – written by Janet Macdonald – including Ken Maxwell-Jones, Frank Berto, Bill Burnett, Diane Compton, Leslie Daniels, Marshall E. Drukarsh, Dan Hoffman, Diane Kerne, Brian Kilgore, Ian Nicholson, Brenda McManus and all the members of Compuserve's 'Canada' forums. Finally I would like to thank Jim Watson for the superb cover, cartoons and map.

OTHER TITLES BY SURVIVAL BOOKS

Living and Working Series

Abroad; America; Australia; Britain; France; Germany; the Gulf States & Saudi Arabia; Holland, Belgium & Luxembourg; Ireland; Italy; London; New Zealand; Spain; Switzerland

Buying a Home Series

Abroad; Britain; Florida; France; Greece & Cyprus; Ireland; Italy; Portugal; Spain

Other Titles

The Alien's Guide to Britain; The Alien's Guide to France; The Best Places to Live in France; The Best Places to Live in Spain; How to Avoid Holiday & Travel Disasters; Retiring Abroad; Rioja and its Wines; The Wines of Spain

Order forms are on page 444.

WHAT READERS & REVIEWERS

When you buy a model plane for your child, a video recorder, or some new computer gizmo, you get with it a leaflet or booklet pleading 'Read Me First', or bearing large friendly letters or bold type saying 'IMPORTANT – follow the instructions carefully'. This book should be similarly supplied to all those entering France with anything more durable than a 5-day return ticket. It is worth reading even if you are just visiting briefly, or if you have lived here for years and feel totally knowledgeable and secure. But if you need to find out how France works then it is indispensable. Native French people probably have a less thorough understanding of how their country functions. – Where it is most essential, the book is most up to the minute.

LIVING FRANCE

Rarely has a 'survival guide' contained such useful advice. This book dispels doubts for first-time travellers, yet is also useful for seasoned globetrotters – In a word, if you're planning to move to the USA or go there for a long-term stay, then buy this book both for general reading and as a ready-reference.

AMERICAN CITIZENS ABROAD

It is everything you always wanted to ask but didn't for fear of the contemptuous put down – The best English-language guide – Its pages are stuffed with practical information on everyday subjects and are designed to complement the traditional guidebook.

SWISS NEWS

A complete revelation to me – I found it both enlightening and interesting, not to mention amusing.

CAROLE CLARK

Let's say it at once. David Hampshire's *Living and Working in France* is the best handbook ever produced for visitors and foreign residents in this country; indeed, my discussion with locals showed that it has much to teach even those born and bred in l'Hexagone. – It is Hampshire's meticulous detail which lifts his work way beyond the range of other books with similar titles. Often you think of a supplementary question and search for the answer in vain. With Hampshire this is rarely the case. – He writes with great clarity (and gives French equivalents of all key terms), a touch of humour and a ready eye for the odd (and often illuminating) fact. – This book is absolutely indispensable.

THE RIVIERA REPORTER

A mine of information – I may have avoided some embarrassments and frights if I had read it prior to my first Swiss encounters – Deserves an honoured place on any newcomer's bookshelf.

ENGLISH TEACHERS ASSOCIATION, SWITZERLAND

HAVE SAID ABOUT SURVIVAL BOOKS

What a great work, wealth of useful information, well-balanced wording and accuracy in details. My compliments!

THOMAS MÜLLER

This handbook has all the practical information one needs to set up home in the UK – The sheer volume of information is almost daunting – Highly recommended for anyone moving to the UK.

AMERICAN CITIZENS ABROAD

A very good book which has answered so many questions and even some I hadn't thought of – I would certainly recommend it.

BRIAN FAIRMAN

We would like to congratulate you on this work: it is really super! We hand it out to our expatriates and they read it with great interest and pleasure.

ICI (SWITZERLAND) AG

Covers just about all the things you want to know on the subject – In answer to the desert island question about the one how-to book on France, this book would be it – Almost 500 pages of solid accurate reading – This book is about enjoyment as much as survival.

THE RECORDER

It's so funny – I love it and definitely need a copy of my own – Thanks very much for having written such a humorous and helpful book.

HEIDI GUILIANI

A must for all foreigners coming to Switzerland.

ANTOINETTE O'DONOGHUE

A comprehensive guide to all things French, written in a highly readable and amusing style, for anyone planning to live, work or retire in France.

THE TIMES

A concise, thorough account of the DOs and DON'Ts for a foreigner in Switzerland – Crammed with useful information and lightened with humorous quips which make the facts more readable.

AMERICAN CITIZENS ABROAD

Covers every conceivable question that may be asked concerning everyday life – I know of no other book that could take the place of this one.

FRANCE IN PRINT

Hats off to *Living and Working in Switzerland*!

RONNIE ALMEIDA

CONTENTS

1. FINDING A JOB   19

Employment & Job Services	22
Training & Education	23
Employment Agencies	23
Contract Jobs	25
Part-Time Jobs	26
Temporary & Casual Work	26
Holiday & Short-Term Jobs	27
Voluntary Work	27
Trainees & Work Experience	29
Nannies & Au Pairs	29
Working Women	30
Job Seeking	31
Salary	33
Self-Employment & Starting A Business	34
Illegal Working	37
Language	38

2. EMPLOYMENT CONDITIONS   41

Employment Contract	43
Place Of Work	44
Salary & Benefits	44
Travel & Relocation Expenses	47
Working Hours	48
Holidays & Leave	48
Insurance	53
Retirement & Pensions	55
Union Membership	55
Other Conditions	56
Checklists	60

3. PERMITS & VISAS   67

Immigrant Visas	69
Quebec	77
Non-Immigrant Visas	79

4. ARRIVAL   87

Arrival/Departure Record   88
Immigration   88
Customs   89
Finding Help   95
Checklists   97

5. ACCOMMODATION   101

Temporary Accommodation   102
Relocation Consultants   109
Canadian Homes   110
Buying A Home   112
Estate Agents   115
Rental Accommodation   117
Moving House   119
Keys & Security   121
Utilities   122
Heating & Air-Conditioning   126

6. POST OFFICE SERVICES   129

Business Hours   131
Letters & Letter Packages   131
Parcels & Packages   135
Valuables & Important Documents   136
Change of Address   138

7. TELEPHONE   141

Installation & Registration   142
Choosing A Telephone   143
Using The Telephone   143
Toll-Free Numbers   145
Information & Entertainment Numbers   145
Custom & Optional Services   146
Operator Services   146
Charges   147
Billing & Payment   148
International Calls   148

Public Telephones   149
Directories   151
Mobile Phones   152
Telegrams, Telex & Fax   153
Internet   154
Emergency Numbers   155
Public Service Numbers   155

8. TELEVISION & RADIO   157

Standards   158
Stations & Programmes   159
Cable Television   160
Satellite Television   161
Videos   162
Radio   163

9. EDUCATION   167

Public Or Private School?   169
Public Schools   171
Private Schools   177
Higher Education   179
Adult & Further Education   182
Language Schools   183

10. PUBLIC TRANSPORT   187

Travellers with Disabilities   188
Trains   189
Urban Transit Systems   193
Long-Distance Buses   195
Taxis   197
Airline Services   198
Ferries   203

11. MOTORING   207

Vehicle Importation   208
Vehicle Registration   210
Buying A Car   211

Safety & Emission Inspection 215
Driving Licence 216
Car Insurance 218
Speed Limits 220
General Road Rules 220
Canadian Roads 224
Winter Driving 225
Traffic Police 226
Motorcycles 227
Accidents 228
Drinking & Driving 230
Car Theft 231
Fuel 232
Automobile Clubs 233
Car Rental 233
Parking 235

12. HEALTH 239

Health Service 241
Emergencies 242
Doctors 243
Medicines & Pharmacies 245
Hospitals & Clinics 246
Childbirth 247
Dentists 248
Opticians 249
Counselling 250
Smoking 251
Drugs 252
Sexually Transmitted Diseases 253
Death 253

13. INSURANCE 257

Insurance Companies & Agents 258
Insurance Contracts 259
Social Insurance 260
Employment Insurance 265
Medicare 266

Private Health Insurance 266
Dental Insurance 269
Long-Term Health Care Insurance 270
Disability Insurance 271
Private Pension Plans 272
Household Insurance 272
Contents Insurance 276
Liability Insurance 277
Holiday & Travel Insurance 277

14. FINANCE 281

Canadian Currency 283
Importing & Exporting Money 284
Credit Rating 286
Banks 287
Mortgages 295
Income Tax 297
Property Tax 305
Capital Gains Tax 306
Inheritance & Gift Tax 307
Wills 307
Cost Of Living 309

15. LEISURE 311

Tourist Information 313
Parks 314
Camping & Caravanning 316
Amusement Parks 317
Museums & Art Galleries 318
Cinema 319
Theatre 320
Music & Ballet 321
Social Clubs 322
Night-Life 323
Gambling 323
Bars 325
Restaurants 326
Libraries 327

16. SPORTS 329

Aerial Sports 331
Baseball 332
Canadian Football 333
Climbing 334
Cycling 334
Fishing 336
Golf 336
Hiking 337
Hunting 339
Ice Hockey 339
Jogging & Running 341
Lacrosse 341
Motor Sports 342
Racquet Sports 342
Skiing & Other Snow Sports 343
Swimming 347
Watersports 348
Other Sports 350

17. SHOPPING 353

Sales Taxes 358
Shopping Hours 360
Shopping Centres 360
Markets 361
Department & Chain Stores 361
Food Shops & Supermarkets 362
Clothing 364
Furniture & Furnishings 365
Household Goods 366
Newspapers, Magazines & Books 367
Alcohol & Tobacco 369
Laundry & Dry Cleaning 370
Mail-Order Shopping 370
Duty-Free Allowances 372
Receipts & Warranties 374
Consumer Associations 375

18. ODDS & ENDS 377

Canadian Citizenship 378
Climate 379
Crime 381
Geography 382
Government 385
Legal System 387
Marriage & Divorce 389
Military Service 390
Pets 390
Police 392
Population 392
Religion 393
Social Customs 394
Time Difference 396
Tipping 397
Toilets 398

19. THE CANADIANS 401

20. MOVING HOUSE
OR LEAVING CANADA 409

Moving House 410
Leaving Canada 411

APPENDICES 416

Appendix A: Useful Addresses 416
Appendix B: Further Reading 420
Appendix C: Useful Websites 425
Appendix D: Weights & Measures 430
Appendix E: Map 434

INDEX 437

ORDER FORMS 444

IMPORTANT NOTE

Canada is a diverse country with many faces, a variety of ethnic groups, religions and customs, and continuously changing rules, regulations (particularly regarding social insurance, Medicare, education and taxes), interest rates and prices. **I cannot recommend too strongly that you check with an official and reliable source (not always the same) before making any major decisions or taking an irreversible course of action. However, don't believe everything you're told or read (even, dare I say it, herein).**

Useful addresses and references to other sources of information have been included in all chapters and in **Appendices A to C** to help you to obtain further information and verify details with official sources. Important points have been emphasised, **in bold print**, some of which it would be expensive, or even dangerous, to disregard. **Ignore them at your peril or cost.** Unless specifically stated, the reference to any company, organisation or product in this book doesn't constitute an endorsement or recommendation.

EDITOR'S NOTES

- Times are shown using am for before noon and pm for after noon. Most Canadians don't use the 24-hour clock. All times are local, so you should check the time difference when making inter-province or international phone calls (see page 396).

- Unless otherwise stated, prices quoted don't include goods and services tax or provincial sales tax, which are both added when you pay or order goods and services in Canada (see **Sales Taxes** on page 358). Prices are shown in Canadian dollars (prefixed by $) unless otherwise specified and should be taken as guides only (although they were correct at the time of publication).

- His/he/him also means her/she/her (please forgive me ladies). This is done to make life easier for both the reader and (in particular) the author, and **isn't** intended to be sexist.

- British English is used in this book, although Canadian words that differ significantly from British words are indicated in brackets. Canadian spelling is a mixture of British and American English – all spelling in this book is (or should be) British English.

- Warnings and important points are shown in **bold** type.

- Lists of **Useful Addresses**, **Further Reading** and **Useful Websites** are contained in **Appendices A, B** and **C** respectively.

- For those unfamiliar with the metric system of weights and measures, conversion tables are included in **Appendix D**.

- A map of Canada showing the provinces and territories is included in **Appendix E**.

INTRODUCTION

W hether you're already living or working in Canada or just thinking about it, this is **THE BOOK** for you. Forget about all those glossy guide books, excellent though they are for tourists; this amazing book was written especially with you in mind and is worth its weight in maple syrup. *Living and Working in Canada* is designed to meet the needs of anyone wishing to know the essentials of Canadian life, including immigrants, temporary workers, businessmen, students, retirees, long-stay tourists, holiday homeowners and even extra-terrestrials. However long your intended stay in Canada, you'll find the information contained in this book invaluable.

General information isn't difficult to find in Canada, where a multitude of books are published on every conceivable subject. However, reliable and up-to-date information specifically intended for foreigners living and working in Canada isn't so easy to find, least of all in a single volume. Our aim in publishing this book was to fill this void and provide the comprehensive **practical** information necessary for a relatively trouble-free life.

You may have visited Canada as a tourist, but living and working there is a different matter altogether. Adjusting to a different environment and culture and making a home in any foreign country can be a traumatic and stressful experience, and Canada is no exception. You need to adapt to new customs and traditions and discover the Canadian way of doing things: for example, finding a home, paying bills and obtaining insurance. For most foreigners in Canada, finding out how to overcome the everyday obstacles of life has previously been a case of pot luck. **But no more!** With a copy of *Living and Working in Canada* to hand you will have a wealth of information at your fingertips – information derived from a variety of sources, both official and unofficial, not least the hard won personal experiences of the author and editor and their family, friends, colleagues and acquaintances.

Living and Working in Canada is a comprehensive handbook on a wide range of everyday subjects and represents the most up-to-date source of general information available to foreigners in Canada. It isn't, however, simply a monologue of dry facts and figures, but a readable and entertaining look at life in Canada.

Adapting to life in a new country is a continuous process and, although this book will help reduce your beginner's phase and minimise the frustrations, it doesn't contain all the answers (most of us don't even know the right questions!). What it **will** do is help you to make informed decisions and calculated judgements, instead of uneducated guesses and costly mistakes. **Most importantly, it will save you time, trouble and money, and repay your investment many times over.**

Although you may find some of the information a bit daunting, don't be discouraged. Most problems occur once only and fade into insignificance after a short time (as you face the next half a dozen!). The majority of foreigners in

Canada would agree that, all things considered, they relish living there. A period spent in Canada is a wonderful way to enrich your life, broaden your horizons and (hopefully) please your bank manager. I trust that this book will help you to avoid the pitfalls of life in Canada and smooth your way to a happy and rewarding future in your new home.

Good luck!

1.

FINDING A JOB

The main problem facing those wishing to work in Canada isn't usually finding a job, but obtaining a work permit (employment authorisation) or being accepted for immigration. Described by the United Nations as 'the best country in the world in which to live', due to its high standard of living and quality of life, Canada wants to stay that way and is therefore fairly selective regarding immigrants. In addition to requiring them to be in good health and of good character (i.e. with no criminal record), Canada wants people who are hard-working and well educated, with training and experience. The largest class of immigrants, described as 'skilled workers', is decided by a points system that's heavily weighted towards those with high-level qualifications and work experience in jobs deemed to be in demand by the federal government.

Canada is a nation of immigrants and most Canadians can trace their ancestors back to foreign settlers within five or six generations. Some 30 per cent of the over 30 million population has British or Irish ancestry and around 25 per cent French ancestry (a figure that's steadily decreasing). Successive waves of immigration in the first half of the 20th century brought large numbers of Chinese, Ukrainians, Dutch, Scandinavians, Portuguese, Greek, Scots, Italians and Poles. The second half of the century saw an influx of immigrants from Asia (particularly Hong Kong, India, China and Taiwan – over 800,000 Canadians are of Chinese decent), with as many as two-thirds of Canada's immigrants coming from Asia. In the early 21st century, immigration from Iran, Iraq, Syria and Egypt is growing rapidly. Early immigrants tended to head for the wide open spaces of the prairies, but most now go to Toronto and the other large cosmopolitan cities. Major Canadian cities have the largest Chinese communities outside China and over 40 per cent of Toronto's population and 35 per cent of Vancouver's are immigrants.

Immigration: Total immigration is around 250,000 annually, mostly independent immigrants. Canada's birth-rate is falling and immigration is necessary to maintain the population at its current level, and therefore immigration targets are rising rather than falling (as in some other countries such as Australia). Those in favour of continued widespread immigration emphasise the cultural wealth and diversity of talents that immigrants have brought to Canada since its foundation. Like most other western countries, Canada has a problem with illegal immigrants, but it isn't nearly as severe as in the US.

Job Market: Manufacturing's share of the job market has been shrinking for decades and now only some 15 per cent of Canadian workers are employed in the manufacturing sector, the most important part of which is the automotive industry. The federal government estimates that by the end of 2003, 75 per cent of the workforce will be employed in service industries such as banking, insurance, education and a vast civil service. Among the occupations most in demand (in addition to those listed above) are information technology experts, health care specialists such as occupational therapists and physiotherapists, technical sales staff for computers, semi-conductors and instrumentation, and communications experts. Industries that are expected to show no growth in the next decade include clothing, pulp and paper, textiles, fishing and tobacco, while slow-to-moderate growth is predicted for the retail and wholesale trades and the printing and publishing industries.

Working conditions in Canada are governed by legislation designed to ensure that employees are treated fairly and equitably. The federal Employment Equity Act ensures that employers take concrete steps to improve the employment situation of women, those with disabilities, aboriginal peoples and members of visible minorities. The federal government operates a Federal Contractors Programme to ensure that employment equity programmes are implemented by employers wishing to do business with the federal government, and also ensures that provincial and municipal governments comply by enforcing equity programmes within their workforces. The three levels of government employ over 1.5 million Canadians or around 10 per cent of Canada's total workforce.

Recession & Recovery: Like most of the western world, Canada experienced a crippling recession in the early 1990s, triggering a huge increase in unemployment across the board, including previously immune groups such as middle class and white-collar employees, executives, professionals and managers. However, there was a strong recovery in the Canadian economy in the late 1990s and the federal budget balanced for three consecutive years from 1997 to 1999. Canada has been increasing its exports and changing from its previous pattern of exporting raw materials to selling high-value finished products such as telecommunications equipment, car parts and other transport equipment. Some 80 per cent of exports go to the US. At the end of the 20th century, the World Economic Forum in its 'Global Competitiveness Report' listed Canada as the fifth most competitive nation in the world, after Hong Kong, Singapore, the US and the United Kingdom.

The greatest growth has been in the western provinces, particularly in oil and gas rich Alberta, which has finally shaken off the long-term effects of a national energy programme in the 1980s that siphoned off $60 billion from Alberta to provide cheap energy for Ontario and Quebec. Calgary, once thought of as a cow town, has become a boom-town housing the headquarters of some of the leading players in high-tech industries plus several oil companies. British Columbia, richly endowed with natural resources including mineral reserves and timber, has benefited from the Pacific Rim economies, aided by the influx of wealthy Asian immigrants (one-third of BC's exports go to Asian markets). Vancouver has been dubbed 'Hollywood North' because US studios film there all year round (due to the mild weather) and because it's cheaper and has lower taxes (Toronto is also a popular film venue). British Columbia, Manitoba and Quebec also have thriving aerospace industries. The provincial government of Quebec is pumping money into Montreal to develop a multimedia complex, which should employ around 10,000 people by the end of 2008, and Ottawa is becoming known as Canada's 'Silicon valley'. The rich new Hibernian oil field off Newfoundland also promises a boom in the eastern maritime provinces.

Unemployment: The unemployment rate was 7.4 per cent (around 1.25 million people) in January 2003. However, although it has been falling in recent years, unemployment is more likely to result in permanent job loss than previously and many white-collar workers, particularly those seeking middle management positions, have made dozens of job applications without success. Increasing world-wide competition is squeezing everyone and Canadian companies are keen to reduce costs and increase productivity in order to survive.

Specialisation: Although specialisation has brought many Canadians greater rewards, it has seriously inhibited their freedom to change jobs. Over the next decade it's estimated that 80 per cent of new jobs will require more than a high school education, and most employers will require workers with a high degree of specialisation and training. Increasing specialisation and unemployment has encouraged (or forced) many people to turn to self-employment and start up small businesses.

Work Ethic: Canadians work hard, but less frenetically than Americans. Work is seen as an important part of life, but not the only thing life has to offer. However, the higher you rise, the harder you're expected to work, and burn-out is common among managers and executives who often work very long days. Key employees routinely give up breaks and take work home, and it isn't unusual for them to be called at home or even when on holiday (vacation). Don't be misled by the informality and casual atmosphere or dress in many companies, as most Canadian employers are ruthless when it comes to the bottom line.

Further Information: Human Resources Development Canada (HRDC), publishes an abundance of information about employment trends and job prospects in Canada. Their booklet, *Job Futures*, provides general information about over 200 occupational groups, including specific information on labour market conditions and projections of how these may change in the coming years. It also provides projections of job prospects in the next five years for graduates of trade and vocational schools, community colleges and universities. Provincial and local job market and career information is available from provincial agencies of the HRDC. *Job Futures* is available free on the Internet (🖳 www.hrdc-drhc.gc.ca/jobfutures/ english/index.html) and you can contact the HRDC at Job Futures, Applied Research Branch, HRDC, 7th Floor, 165 Hôtel de Ville, Hull, ON K1A OJ2 (☎ 1-800-935-5555). *Canada Prospects*, an annual guide to career information, is available from Career Awareness, Human Resources Partnership Directorate, HRDC, 140 Promenade du Portage, Phase 1V, Hull, Quebec K1A 0J9 (☎ 819-953-7260). The internet also provides a wealth of information (e.g. 🖳 www.escapeartist.com/ jobs10/canada.htm).

EMPLOYMENT & JOB SERVICES

Human Resource Centres of Canada (HRCC) provide free counselling and job placement in over 400 centres in towns and cities across the country (look under 'Human Resource Centre' in the 'Provincial Government' listings section). Self-help kiosks located in HRCCs provide updates on the job market and allow you to find out which occupations and job categories are in demand, the skills required and the training opportunities or services available to help you find work. HRCCs also operate computerised Job Banks containing listings of job vacancies in the local geographic area and across the nation, to help you match your skills and experience to specific jobs. You select the jobs that are of interest and can obtain more information from staff, who can also arrange interviews.

HRCCS employ counsellors who can test an applicant's occupational aptitudes and interests, help him make career decisions, and channel him into an appropriate training programme through screening and referral services. Many non-profit, community agencies offer counselling, career development, skills training and job placement services, generally targeted at 'disadvantaged' groups such as women, youths, minorities, the disabled, ex-offenders and older workers. Many communities have career counselling, training, placement and support services for both the employed and unemployed. Programmes are sponsored by a range of organisations, including unions, churches, social service agencies, non-profit organisations, local businesses and vocational rehabilitation agencies.

HRDC provides a wealth of information on the Internet (⌨ www.hrdc-drhc.gc.ca) including Worksearch, National Job Bank, National Labour Market Information, Electronic Labour Exchange (ELE), Youth – a Jobs Strategy Priority, Youth Resource Network of Canada and the Labour Programme. Government vacancies are also listed on the Internet (⌨ www.psc-cfp.gc.ca).

TRAINING & EDUCATION

Canadian employers respond well to job applicants who are in the process of improving their skills by undergoing training and further education. Many adult Canadians attend night school to gain additional qualifications and enhance their job prospects. Training and Development Canada, The Public Service Commission of Canada, Ottawa ON K1A 0M7 (⌨ www.edu.psc-cfp.gc.ca) provides training and career consulting at its regional offices. A good source of assistance in finding occupational training for new immigrants is Employment and Immigration Canada, Public Enquiries Centre, 140 Promenade du Portage, Phase IV, Hull PQ K1A 0JA or the HRCCs mentioned above. HRCCs can match job seekers with a vast array of local sources of career development training available from colleges, universities, school boards, private trainers and other community agencies. Provinces have primary responsibility for the direction, monitoring and administration of training programmes. Each province has a government body responsible for training, education and apprenticeships. For example, British Columbia pledged $36 million in 1998 to create 17,000 new jobs for young people and Ontario has passed new laws designed to double the number of apprentices entering the workforce, to 11,000 a year.

EMPLOYMENT AGENCIES

Employment agencies flourish in major cities and towns in Canada. Most large companies engage agencies to recruit staff, particularly executives, managers, professional employees and temporary office staff (temps). Most agencies specialise in particular trades, professions or fields, e.g. computing, accounting, publishing, advertising, banking, insurance, sales staff, secretarial and office staff, bilingual people, catering, teaching, health professionals, engineering and technical, nursing, industrial recruitment, construction, temporary workers and domestics, while others deal with a range of industries and positions. Agencies may handle permanent or temporary (e.g. less than 90 days) jobs or both.

Many agencies, often calling themselves 'executive counsellors' or 'executive search' consultants (head-hunters), cater for the lucrative executive market. Head-hunters are extremely influential and although many companies and managers consider it unethical to lure away a competitor's top staff, most are happy to use their services. Critics claim that this encourages job-hopping, forces up salary levels and diminishes corporate loyalty. You may be required to pay a fee by some executive counselling or search companies, in which case you should make sure that you know exactly what you receive for your money, as some make claims about what they can do for you which are over-optimistic.

Employment agencies must usually be licensed by provincial or municipal authorities. In Ontario, for example, three classes of licence are granted by the Ministry of Labour: Class A is for recruitment services that charge fees to employers, Class B for employment services that charge the individual job-seeker, and Class C which applies to employment services for domestic help only. Check whether you're required to pay a fee in advance and if you are, keep it to yourself, as some employers are sceptical of applicants who need to pay someone else to find them a job. This isn't to say that all such agencies are charlatans as there are many situations when an individual needs guidance in finding a suitable job, how to conduct himself at an interview or help in the early stages of job-searching from outside Canada.

Agency fees for permanent positions are usually equal to three months' gross salary or 25 per cent of the gross annual salary and are usually paid by employers. Many agencies state in their ads. that their services are 'fee paid', meaning that the employer pays for the agency's services, not the applicant. Some agencies act as employers, hiring workers and contracting them out to companies for an hourly rate. Employees are paid either an hourly rate (with weekly wages) or receive a monthly salary, possibly including paid federal and provincial holidays and annual holiday after a qualifying period (like a regular job), but receive no benefits such as medical insurance. Temporary employment agencies usually take a percentage of employees' wages, e.g. 10 per cent, or charge as much as your first two or three weeks' salary. Wages are usually negotiable, therefore you should drive a hard bargain and ask for more than you're willing to accept. In cities, good temps are hard to find, so you may have a lot of bargaining power. Shop around different agencies to get an idea of the usual rates of pay and fees.

Temporary agencies traditionally deal with workers such as office staff, domestic help, nurses and other medical services, security guards, cleaners, labourers and industrial workers. More recently, some agencies have begun to specialise in finding work for self-employed people on a contract basis, e.g. computer professionals, nurses, technical authors, technicians and engineers. Before you sign on with an agency, check that they're 'ISO 9002 approved' and therefore 'certified' to provide staff for lucrative short-term government contracts, which are common in Canada. Typical of such agencies is Spherion, whose Canadian HQ is at 5450 Explorer Drive, Suite 102, Mississauga, ON L4W 5W1 (☎ 905-361-1550, ▣ www.spherion.ca).

For the larger picture, you can obtain a copy of the *Canadian Directory of Search Firms* (Mediacorp Canada Inc.) that lists nearly 5,000 search firms and recruitment specialists in Canada listed by occupation, geographical area and those with offices in the US, Europe and Asia (as well as Canada). This book is available through *Canada Employment Weekly* (see **Appendix A** for the address) or alternatively you can contact the Association of Canadian Search, Employment and Staffing Services, 2121 Argentia Rd, Suite 404, Mississauga ON L5N 2X4 (☎ 905-826-6869, ▣ www.acsess. org) and ask for a list of agencies specialising in your field. An agency that specialises in finding jobs for migrant workers is Canada US Employment, 620 Wilson Avenue, Suite 502, Toronto ON M3K 1Z3, (▣ www.canadausemployment.com). Websites worth visiting to look for jobs before you come to Canada include ▣ www.work opolis.com and ▣ www.monster.com.

CONTRACT JOBS

It's possible to find contract work in Canada in many occupations, particularly in computers, aerospace and electronics. Contractors are usually employed on the same general terms as permanent employees, but at higher salaries. Contracts are usually for a minimum of one year (although open-ended contracts are also common) and may be extended for up to six years. If you wish to withdraw from a contract you should note that penalties can be severe and may include repayment of relocation expenses, visa charges and air fares. Teacher exchange positions are available (usually for an academic year from August to August) through the League for the Exchange of Commonwealth Teachers, LECT, 7 Lion Yard, Tremadoc Road, London SW4 7NQ, UK (☎ +44 (0)870-770 2636, ▣ www.lect.org.uk) or through the Society for Educational Visits and Exchanges in Canada. 57 Auriga Drive, Suite 201, Nepean, ON K2E 8B2 (☎ 613-998-3760, ▣ www.sevec.ca). You shouldn't experience difficulty in obtaining the necessary visas if you have skills that can provide an economic benefit to Canada, but you need a firm job offer before applying for a visa.

Contract jobs are available through employment agencies, some of which specialise in providing contract workers. Many contract jobs are for technical specialists, although there's also a strong market in providing cleaning, catering, maintenance and manual workers. Some companies specialise in supplying contract staff to major companies, many of whom are increasingly contracting out non-core support work, from cleaning to computing, rather than hiring full-time employees.

Professional contractors (or freelancers) often work from home. The potential for home-based work in Canada is huge, particularly within the computer industry, which is keen to capitalise on the number of people (particularly women) wishing to work part-time from home. The International Homeworkers Alliance (IHA), 143 Main St E, Hamilton ON L8N 1G4 (☎ 905-521-9888, 🖳 www.homeworkers.org) provides listings of work-at-home opportunities. You pay a membership fee to join and a small monthly maintenance fee to view the lists of companies, which you contact directly to arrange work. You should be aware that there are many scams posing under the umbrella of offering jobs to homeworkers, typical of which is one claiming that you can earn $1 a time for putting a piece of paper in an envelope ('stuffing'). You pay around $50 for the 'kit' that consists of a booklet listing various companies who may need envelope stuffers, only one of which pays $1 a time, but expects you to buy the envelope and get the piece of paper printed out of your fee. If in doubt, check offers with a Better Business Bureau.

PART-TIME JOBS

Part-time jobs are available in most industries and professions and are common in offices, bars, stores, factories, cafes and restaurants. Often part-time workers are poorly paid and rates are usually around (or below) the minimum wage (set by the province) for non-skilled workers, depending on the local unemployment rate and labour market. Part-time employees often have no protection from exploitation by employers, although some large companies provide part-time employees with the same benefits as full-time employees. Some companies operate a job-share scheme, where two or more people share the same job. Part-time jobs are also available through Human Resource Centres (see page 22) and employment agencies.

TEMPORARY & CASUAL WORK

Temporary and casual work, both legal and illegal, is available throughout Canada. However, visitors (or anyone without a work visa) should be wary of working illegally (see page 37). One of the big attractions for itinerants is that casual workers are often paid cash in hand at the end of each day's work. There are temporary employment agencies in most towns and cities. If you're looking for full-time work, a temporary job can often be a stepping-stone to a permanent position as many employers use them as trial periods. A temporary job also allows you to get your 'foot in the door' and to learn about other openings within a company that you may prefer or that you're better suited for. Short-term contract jobs include temporary office jobs available through specialist agencies and the usual range of menial jobs such as gardening or farm work, bar and restaurant jobs, and commission-only selling. There are some lucrative possibilities such as tree planting, where it's reported that you can earn as much as $10,000 for three months' work if you plant enough trees. For more details on this and other temporary jobs, contact Canadian Search, Employment and Staffing Services, 2121 Argentia Road, Suite 404, Mississauga ON L5N 2X4 (☎ 905-826-6869, 💻 www.acsess.org).

HOLIDAY & SHORT-TERM JOBS

In view of the necessity for potential employers to prove that there's no unemployed Canadian citizen or immigrant visa holder available to fill a job (see **Chapter 3**), it isn't possible (legally) to enter Canada on a visitor's visa and then seek work, whether full or part-time. Young people wishing to take holiday jobs or longer temporary employment in Canada find it easier to do so through organisations that specialise in 'gap' employment between secondary school and university or after university but before taking a full-time job. The book *Summer Jobs USA* (published annually by Peterson's) also contains some jobs in Canada. Most jobs listed are in summer camps and are for unskilled jobs such as waiting-staff, cleaners and gas jockeys. Many specify non-smokers only and prefer college students, while some require certified skills in first-aid and life saving. Where the job is for the whole summer season, training is usually provided at the beginning of the season.

VOLUNTARY WORK

The minimum age limit for voluntary (volunteer) work in Canada is 15 to 18 (depending on the province) and most organisations require fluent spoken English or French. Special qualifications aren't usually required and the minimum length of service varies from one month to one year (often there's no maximum length of service). Handicapped volunteers are also welcomed by many organisations. Voluntary work is (not surprisingly) unpaid, although meals and accommodation is usually provided and some organisations also pay a small amount of pocket money. However, this is usually insufficient for out-of-pocket living expenses (entertainment, drinks, etc.), therefore make sure that you bring enough money with you.

It's essential before travelling to Canada for any voluntary work that you check whether you're eligible and whether you're permitted to enter the country under the existing immigration and employment regulations. You may be required to obtain a visa (see **Chapter 3**), so check the documentation required with a Canadian embassy or consulate well in advance of your planned visit. The usual visa regulations apply to voluntary workers and your passport must be valid for at least one year.

International workcamps provide an opportunity for people from many countries to live and work together on a range of projects, such as building, conservation, gardening and community projects. Camps are usually run for two to four weeks between April and October. Normally workers are required to work an eight-hour, five-day week and work can be physically demanding. Accommodation is usually shared with your fellow slaves and are basic. Most workcamps consist of 10 to 20 volunteers from several countries, with English and/or French the common languages. Volunteers generally pay a registration fee and their own travelling costs to and from the workcamp, and may also be expected to contribute towards the cost of their board and lodging. An application to join a workcamp should be made through the appropriate recruiting agency in your home country.

There are many organisations that can help you find voluntary work in Canada, including the following:

- **Volunteer Canada**, 1 Nicholas Street, Suite 302, Ottawa ON K1N 7B7 (☎ 1-800-670-0401 or 613-241-4371, ▣ www.volunteer.ca) acts as a national umbrella organisation on behalf of volunteer bureaux and centres in all provinces and territories. They maintain a list of local volunteer bureaux and centres that match volunteers with opportunities.

- **The Canadian Red Cross Society**, 170 Metcalfe Street, Suite 300, Ottawa ON K2P 2P2 (☎ 613-740-1900, ▣ www.redcross.ca).

- **Bridges,** 453 Bank St (at Gladstone), Ottawa ON K2P 1Y9 (☎ 613-238-8182) seeks volunteers for a variety of social service positions.

- **Peace Brigades International,** 201-427 Bloor St W, Toronto ON M5S 1X7 (☎ 416-324-9737, ✉ pbinap@web.ca) seeks volunteers willing to help with promoting non-violence and protecting human rights.

- **British Universities North America Club (BUNAC)**, 16 Bowling Green Lane, London EC1R 0QH, UK (☎ +44 (0)20-7251 3472, ▣ www.bunac.org) operates a reciprocal exchange system called SWAP. They help you obtain the necessary work permits, but won't find you a job (although they provide lists of suitable jobs).

- **The Council on International Educational Exchange (CIEE)** runs a programme called Internship Canada with the Canadian Student Federation for undergraduates or 'gap' year students with a firm offer from a university. CIEE has offices in Australia, China, France, Germany, Italy, Japan, Spain, Taiwan and the UK, although you should inquire first through CIEE, 633 Third Avenue, 20th Floor, New York NY 10017-6706, USA (☎ 1-800-40-STUDY, ▣ www.ciee.org).

- **GAP,** GAP House, 44 Queen's Road, Reading, Berkshire RG1 4BB, UK (☎ +44 (1)18-959 4914) also places gap year students with volunteer projects in Canada.

- **Centre for International Mobility,** PO Box 343, Hakaniemenkatu 2 FIN-00531 Helsinki, Finland (☎ +358-9-7747-7033, ✉ cimoinfo@cimo.fi) has a few exchange places in conjunction with the International Association for the Exchange of Students for Technical Experience (IAESTE) in Canada.

- **IAESTE,** The Central Bureau, 10 Spring Gardens, London SW1A 2BN, UK (☎ +44 (0)20-7389 4771, 💻 www.iaste.org) organises exchange schemes with other countries.

- **United Nations Association (Wales) International Youth Service** operates student volunteer work exchanges in conjunction with the Canadian Federation of Students. Temple of Peace, Cathays Park, Cardiff CF1 3AP, UK (☎ +44 (0)1222-223088).

- **The Central Bureau for Educational Visits and Exchanges,** c/o The British Council, 10 Spring Gardens, London SW1A 2BN, UK (☎ +44 (0)20-7930 8466, 💻 www.britishcouncil.org) publishes a number of books including *Working Holidays, Volunteer Work* and *Teach Abroad,* and works in co-operation with IAESTE (see below).

TRAINEES & WORK EXPERIENCE

A number of countries have organised career development programmes with the International Association for the Exchange of Students for Technical Experience (IAESTE). The aim of the programme is to enable participants to gain practical experience for a maximum of 18 months in Canada and other participating countries. IAESTE also provides on-the-job training in Canada to full-time foreign university/college students in technical fields such as agriculture, architecture, computer science, engineering, mathematics, and natural and physical sciences. Applicants should be aged 19 to 30 and have completed two or preferably three years in a technical major. Applications must be made by 10th December in your country of citizenship to gain acceptance for the following summer. Training periods are up to 18 months, although the majority are for 8 to 12 weeks during the summer. The IAESTE programme is also available to Canadian students in over 50 countries. For further information ask your college or university for the address of IAESTE in your home country or contact them at the address above. In most countries there are government agencies handling educational exchanges and training in Canada, e.g. in the UK it's the Central Bureau for Educational Visits and Exchanges (see address above).

NANNIES & AU PAIRS

Canada has no schemes for au pairs. However, nannies are in high demand as are other domestic staff such as housekeepers, chauffeurs and butlers, particularly in the larger cities. Payment is usually in the form of accommodation, board and pocket money. Classed as temporary work, you need a work permit (see page 81) and are required to stay for a minimum of 12 months. There's also a government sponsored scheme called the 'Live-In Caregiver Programme' (LCP) and as the name of the scheme implies, it covers only those who live at the establishment or home where they work. It requires the equivalent of Canada secondary school education, minimum levels of professional training or professional work experience, and sufficient English or French to work unsupervised. You can obtain details from your local Canadian embassy, consulate or high commission (enclose a self-addressed envelope with the local equivalent of US$2 postage).

WORKING WOMEN

For many years, discrimination in Canada prevented women from competing equally with men and from entering male-dominated professions. However, in the last few decades women have succeeded in breaking down the barriers and now officially compete on equal terms with men for education, professional training, employment, leadership positions and political power. Women still encounter some prejudice, however, and resistance and some inequalities exist, not least in salaries. Despite laws prohibiting job discrimination on the basis of sex and requiring equal pay for equal work, women's pay is still only between 70 to 85 per cent of men's for some full-time jobs. But the situation is changing rapidly and there are ever more women in high-ranking professional jobs.

Professional women are common in Canada and have more equality than their counterparts in other countries, although some find it difficult (or impossible) to reach the top ranks of their professions. The main discrimination against professional women isn't salary but promotion prospects, as some companies and organisations are reluctant to elevate women to important positions. Generally the closer women get to the top, the more they're resented, although as mentioned, this is changing. Around 40 per cent of corporate managers are women, with most of those holding high positions employed in federal and provincial government jobs, although many are also self-employed or work in the health sciences. Nevertheless, you're likely to come across women in top positions in all walks of life in Canada.

There are increasing pressures on women to seek employment to supplement the family income and women constitute around 45 per cent of the labour force. Some 60 per cent of women work full or part-time and they make up around 65 per cent of part-time workers (although many would prefer full-time work). Status of Women Canada (SWC) is the federal government agency responsible for promoting gender equality and the full participation of women in Canada's economic, social, cultural and political life. SWC can be contacted at MacDonald Building, 123 Slater Street, 10th Floor, Ottawa ON K1P 1H9 (☎ 613-995-7835, 💻 www.swccfc.gc.ca/pubs/pubsorder_e.html) and provide information and fact sheets on their programmes and services for women.

As a means of circumventing prejudice and low wages, many women have turned to self-employment and around 30 per cent of the 700,000 businesses started between 1990 and 1995 are owned by women. Women-owned businesses have increased at twice the rate of male-owned businesses in recent years and provide employment for over 1.7m Canadians and create new jobs at a faster rate than the national average.

The federal government recognises this and provides a website (🖥 www.info export.gc.ca/businesswomen/menu-e.asp) for Canadian businesswomen that's billed as 'a unique way to link women entrepreneurs with each other and with the world in order to promote their business interests'. The site provides a broad range of business information in Canada and around the world and is also used by officials for policy and programme planning. The Canadian Women's Business Network, #105-3270 Ross Rd, Nanaimo, BC V9T 5J1 (☎ 250-751-2133, 🖥 www.cdnbiz women.com) is an Internet-based organisation that provides information for business women in Canada.

JOB SEEKING

When looking for a job in Canada, you should contact as many prospective employers as possible, either by writing, telephoning or just dropping off a curriculum vitae (résumé). Whatever job you're seeking, it's important to market yourself appropriately for the kind of job you're after. For example, the recruitment of executives and senior managers is handled almost exclusively by consultants who advertise in the national newspapers such as *The Globe & Mail* and interview all applicants before presenting clients with a shortlist. At the other end of the scale, jobs requiring little or no previous experience (such as store clerks) may be advertised in local newspapers or in store windows and the first able-bodied applicant may be offered the job on the spot.

When writing for a job, address your letter to the Human Resources Department and include your curriculum vitae and copies of references and qualifications. Writing for jobs from abroad is usually the least successful method of securing employment in Canada, as Canadian employers aren't allowed to employ people from outside the country unless they can prove that there's no Canadian citizen or immigrant visa holder available for the job. As well as the usual methods of job seeking, there are many Canada-specific resources for job seekers, some of which are listed below.

- HRCCs mainly handle non-professional skilled and unskilled jobs, particularly in industry, retailing and catering. HRCCs are a tremendous resource for job-seekers as they provide counselling and publications on job search techniques, interviewing tips, curriculum vitae writing and many other topics. They can also direct job-seekers to local job finding clubs that provide a free, three-week programme to assist people with their job search, including facilitators and coaches and the use of computers, faxes and photocopiers. Some clubs provide services for those aged 16 to 24 only.

- HRDC has dozens of work information websites that can be accessed through their main page (🖥 www.hrdc-drhc.gc.ca/common/work. shtml). Pages include the Job Bank and other job listings, work search assistance, labour laws, workers' support, and career and development information.

- Canadian Career Development Foundation, 119 Ross, Suite 202 (at Wellington), Ottawa ON K1Y ON6 (☎ 613-729-6164, 🖳 http://ccdf.ca/). A charitable foundation which is 'committed to advancing the understanding and practice of career development'. It aims to improve access for Canadians to quality career services.

- Canadian local and major city newspapers have 'Job Opportunities' or 'Help Wanted' sections on most days, although most advertisements appear on Sundays. Most local and national newspapers are available in reading rooms of local libraries in Canada, so you don't need to buy them. Jobs are also advertised in professional journals and trade magazines. Outside Canada, some Canadian newspapers are available from international news agencies, Canadian embassies and consulates, Canadian trade and commercial centres, and Canadian social clubs (although they don't always contain the 'Help Wanted' advertisements). To obtain Canadian newspapers from outside Canada, see page 368.

- International and national recruiting agencies who act for Canadian companies. These companies chiefly recruit executives and key managerial and technical staff, and many of them have offices world-wide and throughout Canada. Some Canadian companies appoint consultants to handle overseas recruitment in certain countries such as Commonwealth Jobsearch (Canada) Ltd, 2292 140th Street, Surrey, BC V4A 9R7 (☎ 604-541-8221, ✉ jbsearch@cdnimmigration.com).

- If your professional qualifications are recognised in Canada, you can write to Canadian professional associations for information and advice (addresses can be obtained from Canadian Chambers of Commerce). **Most professionals, e.g. in medicine and the law, must be licensed by individual provinces.**

- Subscribe to job newsletters and digests such as *Canada Employment Weekly*, Mediacorp Canada Inc., 21 New Street, Toronto ON M5R 1P7 (☎ 1-800-361-2580, 🖳 www.mediacorp2.com).

- The Canadian government maintains a list of government jobs on the Internet (🖳 www.psc-cfp.gc.ca/centres/emp/_e.htm).

- Other Internet job search engines include Canada Jobs (🖳 www.canadajobs.com).

- Many provinces also publish civil service 'job opportunities' newspapers. If you're in Canada and have a computer, many job opportunities are advertised on computer networks. Look for 'Community Nets' and 'Freenets' in major cities.

- Networking (getting together with like-minded people to discuss business) is a popular way to make business and professional contacts in Canada.

- Many good business contacts can be made among expatriate groups. Newcomers to Canada frequently find that ethnic business and professional associations are a good source of job information.

Many books are written for those seeking employment in Canada, including *Who's Hiring* (Mediacorp Canada Inc.), which lists Canada's top employers in 23 major occupations. *Where the Jobs Are: Career Survival for Canadians in the New Global Economy* by Colin Campbell details the companies and industries in Canada that are growing and which ones to avoid when looking for a career, as does *Canada's Best Careers Guide* by Frank Feather. *The Career Directory* lists 750 of Canada's largest employers and details what they look for in employees and what they pay, while *The Canadian Job Directory* concentrates on 'hidden' (unadvertised) jobs. Others books include *The Better Book For Getting Hired* by Robert P. Downe (Self Counsel Press Inc.), *The Canada Student Employment Guide* by Ann Rohmer, which lists over 800 Canadian employers and is geared towards those looking for an entry-level position, and *Get Wired – You're Hired*, which concentrates on job hunting online. All the above books are available from Canadian bookstores or can be ordered from the Career Bookstore, Canada Employment Weekly, 21 New Street, Toronto ON M5R 1P7 (☎ 1-800-361-2580, 🖥 www.mediacorp2.com).

SALARY

It can be difficult to determine the level of salary you should receive in Canada, particularly for professional and executive appointments, where salaries and benefits are rarely quoted in job advertisements (except for sales appointments, when the fanciful salaries quoted can be ignored). On the other hand, 'Help Wanted' small advertisements in local newspapers may state salaries. HRCCs (see page 22) can also provide information on local wage rates. Usually salaries are negotiable and it's up to you to ensure that you receive the level of salary and benefits commensurate with your qualifications and experience (or as much as you can get).

If you have friends or acquaintances working in Canada, ask them what an average or good salary is for your particular trade or profession. Minimum hourly wages, which apply to full-time and part-time workers are fixed by each province, and vary considerably:

Alberta	$5.90
British Columbia	$8.00
Manitoba	$6.75
New Brunswick	$6.00
Newfoundland	$6.00
Northwest Territories	$7.20
Nova Scotia	$6.00
Nunavut	$8.50
Ontario	$6.85

Prince Edward Island	$6.50
Quebec	$7.30
Saskatchewan	$6.65
Yukon	$7.20

Salaries in some companies and professions (particularly for government employees) are decided by national pay agreements between unions and employers. Salary reviews vary from every 6 to 18 months, depending on the employer. When negotiating your salary, bear in mind that benefits and employment protection provided by Canadian employers are less than in many other western countries. Canadian jobs come with fewer fringe benefits than those in most European countries and may not include a company pension, although more and more Canadian companies now offer pensions.

Salaries vary considerably for the same job in different regions of Canada, generally being higher in the major cities such as Toronto and Montreal and in remote areas such as the north of Canada (you need some incentive to spend most of the year buried under snow). Remember also to consider the local cost of living. For example, although salaries are much higher in Toronto and Vancouver than they are in Newfoundland, so is the cost of living and the extra salary might not compensate sufficiently (even though a secretarial job in Newfoundland may pay around $16,000, while a big city secretary can earn over $25,000). Salaries and conditions provided by multinational companies are fairly standard, although it's wise to obtain expert advice before accepting a job offer. The average weekly family income (net, i.e. take-home pay) in 2003 was $750, although this figure varies considerably from province to province. With the exception of executives, salary raises in recent years have barely matched inflation and wage growth is non-existent for many low-paid workers. Most salary increases for blue-collar workers came from working longer hours and salaries for non-executive staff have actually fallen (relative to the cost of living) in the last few decades.

SELF-EMPLOYMENT & STARTING A BUSINESS

Many Canadians and immigrants have an ambition to start their own business. Entrepreneurs are respected and encouraged in Canada and no stigma is attached to business failure, which often spurs people to even greater efforts. Even during the bleakest years of the recession in the early 1990s, over 700,000 new businesses opened their doors, more than half of which were sole proprietorships or small businesses with no more than two employees. Although many self-employed people come from the ranks of the unemployed, the majority leave secure and well-paid jobs to go it alone. As employers have increasingly been replacing full-time employees with freelancers, consultants and outside contractors in recent years, self-employment has become a necessity for many people, rather than an option. HRDC produces a list of business opportunities expected to expand in the next decade that currently includes retirement homes in small towns, personal and home security systems, home office products and services, health foods and specialist travel for the elderly.

Whatever people may tell you, starting your own business isn't easy (otherwise most of us would be doing it) and it requires a lot of hard work (self-employed people generally work much longer hours than employees), a sizeable investment and operating funds (most businesses fail due to lack of capital), good organisation (e.g. bookkeeping and planning), excellent customer relations (in Canada the customer is always right, even when he is wrong!), and a measure of luck (although generally the harder you work, the more 'luck' you have). Bear in mind that around two out of three new businesses fail within three to five years and that the self-employed must provide their own pension plans, and don't qualify for employment insurance and workers' compensation.

The key to buying or starting a successful business is exhaustive research, research and yet more research (plus innovation, value and service). Bear in mind that choosing the location for a business is even more important than the location for a home. Many business consultants advertise in the Canadian and foreign press (see **Appendix A**) and offer everything from sandwich bars to motels, and launderettes (Laundromats) to restaurants. **Always thoroughly investigate an existing or proposed business before investing a cent.**

Business Visas

For foreigners, one of the main attractions of buying a business in Canada is that it offers an easier method of obtaining a visa as the Canadian government is keen to encourage foreign entrepreneurs. There's no fixed minimum investment figure, but you must demonstrate that you have sufficient funds available to start a business and provide for your family for a reasonable period. In practice this usually means at least $250,000. It isn't mandatory to use a specialist business immigration lawyer, but doing so helps smooth the process. Always obtain a quotation in writing and shop around a number of immigration lawyers (but check their credentials and references), as fees can run into thousands of dollars depending on the amount of work involved. If you invest in a suitable business before you arrive in Canada, you're usually given an unconditional visa, otherwise you receive a conditional visa that requires you to have a business in operation (with at least one Canadian employee) within two years. For further information see page 72.

Business Structures

There are four types of business structure you can choose if you're self-employed: a sole proprietorship, partnership (general and limited), joint-venture or corporation. Due to the ever-changing and complex tax laws, you should consult a tax expert before deciding on the best type for you. You must also decide whether to buy an established business, a franchise or start a new business from scratch. When buying an existing business, always employ a licensed business broker (buyer's broker) to advise you on the purchase.

Franchises have a much higher success rate than other start-up businesses. For information contact the Canadian Franchise Association, 2585 Skymark Avenue, Suite 300, Mississauga ON L4W 4L5 (☎ 1-800-665-4232, 🖳 www.cfa.ca), which sets voluntary standards for members operating in Canada. The CFA provides an information package of franchise opportunities entitled *Investigate before Investing*, and holds regular information seminars for potential franchisees. *Canadian Business Franchise Magazine,* CGB Publishing Limited, 3060 Cedar Hill Road, Suite 300 A, Victoria BC V8T 3J5 (☎ 1-800-454-1662, 🖳 www.cgb.ca) focuses on particular franchises and contains articles that answer many of the usual questions from potential franchisees (it also lists franchises for sale). Blenheim Expositions Inc., 1133 Louisiana Avenue, Suite 210, Winter Park, Florida 32789, USA (☎ 407-647-8521) organises franchise shows at various locations throughout Canada. Shows that are held in conjunction with the International Franchise Association feature franchise opportunities only, while others include franchises and other business opportunities, and are promoted as 'be your own boss' shows.

Professional Advice

Before investing in a business in Canada it's essential to obtain appropriate professional and legal advice. If you aren't prepared to do this you shouldn't even think about starting a business in Canada (or anywhere else for that matter). Engaging the services of a business and investment consultant is usually the wisest course, although the quality of advice and service varies. Few foreigners are capable of finding their way through the web of legal requirements and regulations without expert advice (not to mention federal, provincial and local laws and regulations). The purchase of a business must be conditional on obtaining visas, licences, permits and any loans or other funding required. While it's much easier to buy an existing business than start a new one, you must investigate thoroughly the financial status, turnover and value of a business (obtain an independent valuation). It's also important to engage an accountant at the earliest opportunity.

Information

There are many local, provincial and federal government agencies and departments that provide information and advice about starting and running a business. The best place to start is the local provincial office of the Canada Business Service Centre (CBSC), which is a co-operative of 37 federal business departments, provincial government associations, and academic and research organisations. The CBSC provides a wide variety of business counselling on finance, accounting, record keeping, business start-up and management, taxes, marketing, sales promotion, advertising, retailing, manufacturing, and sales and service businesses. You can find their local address in the blue section of white pages or refer to their website (🖳 www.cbsc.org). Note that in some provinces the name of the organisation includes the name of the province, e.g. Canada-Ontario Business Service Centre (COBSC). The Business Development Bank of Canada provides not only loans and venture (or 'vulture' if you're a cynic) capital, but also provides counselling services for existing and proposed small businesses through its Counselling Assistance to Small Enterprises (CASE) programme. It has branches in every province, listed in the yellow pages under 'business', or you can phone ☎ 1-888-463-6232 for details of the nearest office.

There are many business and professional organisations in Canada for those of certain ethnic origins including the following:

- **Canadian Ethnocultural Council,** 176 Rue Gloucester Street, Suite 400, Ottawa ON K2P OA6 (☎ 613-230-3867, 🖳 www.ethnocultural.ca).

- **Canadian Arab Federation,** 5298 Dundas Street West, Toronto ON M9B 1B2 (☎ 416-231-7524).

- **Africa-Canada Development and Information Services Association,** 141-6200 McKay Avenue, Burnaby BC V5H 4M9 (☎ 604-431-9503).

- **Association of Filipino Entrepreneurs and Professionals,** 1061 McNicoll Avenue, Scarborough ON M1W 3W6 (☎ 416-502-9383).

- **Canadian-Italian Business and Professional Association Inc.,** 6020 Jean Talon Street East, Suite 830, St Leonard PQ H1S 3B1 (☎ 514-254-4929).

- **Ismaili Business Information Centre,** 60 Columbia Way, Suite 720, Markham ON L3R 7R2 (☎ 416-477-8434).

Most international accountants have offices throughout Canada and are an invaluable source of information (in English and other languages) on subjects such as forming a company, company law, taxation and social insurance. Most publish free booklets about business in Canada, including *Doing Business in Canada,* available from Ernst & Young, Beckett House, 1 Lambeth Palace Road, London SE1 7EU, UK (☎ +44 (0)20-7951 2000), *Doing Business in Canada* and *Canada, A Guide for Foreign Investors,* the latter two available from Price WaterhouseCoopers LLP, Southwark Towers, 32 London Bridge Street, London SE1 9SY, UK (☎ +44 (0)20-7583 5000). Most Canadian bookstores also stock a selection of books on starting and running a business in Canada.

ILLEGAL WORKING

There are thousands of people working illegally in Canada, most in 'transient' occupations such as bartenders, waiters and waitresses, nannies and servants, farmworkers (particularly during fruit and vegetable harvests), the fishing industry, and construction, where workers are often paid partly or wholly in cash. In order to get a job in Canada, an employee must have a social insurance number (SIN) that's issued to Canadians and legal immigrants. **It's strictly illegal for foreigners to work in Canada without a visa or official permission, and if you work illegally with false documents the consequences are even more serious if you're discovered.** If you're tempted to work illegally you should be aware of the pitfalls, as the black economy is a risky business for both employers and employees. Harbouring or employing alien labour, e.g. a housekeeper, isn't an offence under the criminal code of Canada, but you're charged under the Immigration Act and face a stiff fine. Foreigners caught working illegally are fined and deported, and refused entry into Canada for five years. Illegal immigrants have no entitlement to federal or company pensions, no employment insurance, no accident insurance and no benefits.

LANGUAGE

One of the most important qualifications for anyone planning to live or work in Canada is a good command of one (or both) of the two 'official' languages, English and French (although some ethnic groups seem to get along fine without speaking either). Around 65 per cent of the population are native English speakers and some 20 per cent French speakers. Despite the efforts of the federal government to encourage everyone to learn and use both languages, barely 15 per cent of Canadians speak both English and French, and one in six (around five million) Canadian residents grew up speaking a language other than English or French. English is by far the most important language and you usually need to speak, read and write it well in order to find your way in Canada, e.g. dealing with government officials, motoring, using public transport and shopping, and to understand and hold conversations with the people you meet. English proficiency is particularly important if you have a job requiring a lot of contact with others or speaking on the phone and dealing with other foreigners, many of whom speak their own 'dialect' of English.

French is mostly spoken in Quebec, where it's the first language, although there are also large numbers of French speakers in New Brunswick, which is officially bilingual, Ontario and Manitoba. French proficiency is essential in Quebec, where many people (particularly government officials) refuse to speak anything other than French and may refuse to speak to you if you don't speak French to them (although they're more accommodating with Americans and Britons than with Canadians). If you already speak fluent French as it's understood in France, you may take a while to adjust to the Canadian version, although they won't have any difficulty understanding you. Canadian French (called *Québécois* in Quebec, where it's also known as *joual*) isn't, for the most part, the French spoken in France and can be unintelligible, even to a Parisian.

It's important for foreign students to have a good command of English or French (as applicable), as they must be able to follow lectures and take part in discussions in the course of their studies. This may also require a wider and more technical or specialised vocabulary. For this reason, most colleges and universities won't accept students who aren't fluent in English (French in Quebec), and most require prospective students to take a Test of English/French as a Foreign Language (TOEFL/TOFFL). If you wish to improve your English or French before starting work or commencing a course of study in Canada, there are language schools throughout the country (see page 183).

If you already speak English fluently, you probably won't have too much trouble understanding Canadians, although if you don't speak with a Canadian, American or BBC accent, they may have trouble understanding you. Those who speak English with a European, Australian, New Zealand or South African accent find that most Canadians are incapable of distinguishing between their accents. Most Canadians and Britons understand each other most of the time, although there are inevitably occasions, particularly during your first few months in Canada, when small misunderstandings may cause bewilderment, amusement and even embarrassment. Most differences are found in the rich assortment of slang and colloquialisms, and most cities, regions and ethnic groups have their own idioms. Written Canadian English is closer to British English than American English and the differences are usually less obvious in the written word.

Around 15 per cent of Canadians speak neither English or French as their first language, including many immigrants, groups of native Americans (e.g. Cree, Ojibwa, Iroquois) and the Inuit (Inuktitut). Canadians use many words adapted from the various 'First Nations' (e.g. Inuit and Indian) languages such as igloo, parka, muskeg (a level swamp or bog) and kayak (Canada itself is a corruption of the word *kanata*, a Huron-Iroquois word for village or small community). Canada has also given the world many words and phrases including kerosene, puck, bushed, toque and black ice. For more information consult the *Gage Canadian Dictionary* and *A Concise Dictionary of Canadianisms*.

2.

EMPLOYMENT CONDITIONS

Employment conditions in Canada are largely dependent on individual contracts and an employer's general employment terms. Most are negotiated between employers and employees through collective bargaining agreements (e.g. with unions), civil service rules and industry practices, although federal and provincial laws govern certain aspects of employment conditions.

Government employees (around 10 per cent of the total workforce of 15.5 million) usually have considerably better job protection and legal rights than the employees of private companies. Employees in the private sector can lose their jobs with as little as two weeks' notice and, unless you've been working for an employer for at least three months, you won't be entitled to any redundancy (severance) pay. Even after five years' service, you're entitled to a paltry ten days' pay. Consequently, Canadian employers and are more likely to lay off workers when business is bad. On the other hand, you may also quit your job at any time for any reason, although it's usual to give two weeks' notice.

Job titles are important in Canada, as they define an employee's status and the perks that go with a job. All large Canadian corporations and employers have a strict hierarchy, including the federal civil service, which, despite attempts to simplify it, has over 4,000 job classifications, each with its own pay range. Employee benefits provided by medium and large firms are generally much better than those provided by small businesses.

Although it rarely happens, an employer may ask a credit bureau (see **Credit Rating** on page 286) for a report on an employee, but must inform him of this. Private employers are permitted to have dress or 'grooming' codes, although public employers have less freedom to limit their employees' freedom of expression. Employers are, within limits, entitled to ask about an employee's lifestyle; however, this mustn't conflict with federal and provincial laws regarding discrimination (see below).

There are a number of books about employment conditions in Canada, including a series published by Self Counsel Press on employer/employee rights in different provinces, covering hours of work and rest periods, maternity and parental leave, holidays, special employment situations (such as those for youths and apprentices), filing a complaint, human rights protection, dismissal and redundancy and labour standards.

When negotiating your terms of employment for a job in Canada, the checklists at the end of this chapter will prove useful.

Discrimination

It's illegal to discriminate against employees in Canada on grounds of sex, race, national origin, skin colour, pregnancy, age (except in Yukon), religion, marital status, sexual orientation, physical handicap or weight. It's also illegal for employers or trade unions to discriminate against or retaliate against anyone who wants to join, not join or quit a trade union (see **Union Membership** on page 55). Job advertisements are permitted to specify such characteristics of applicants only when they're an essential requirement – called a 'bona fide occupational qualification' – e.g. for a job as a female fashion model.

Women doing identical jobs as men, with equal skill, effort and responsibility and similar working conditions, are legally entitled to the same salaries and terms of employment. Employers cannot offer better benefits to male employees. For example, they aren't permitted to have different pension plans for each sex.

There's also protection from discrimination against the elderly and companies are prohibited from forcing active workers aged 65 and over to retire. In fact, there's no longer a mandatory retirement age in Canada.

Due to the threat of legal action by employees and rejected job applicants, large employers are careful not to discriminate against prospective employees. Despite the strict legislation, however, it's widely acknowledged that discrimination is widespread and it's often almost impossible to prove discrimination on the grounds of sex and extremely difficult on the grounds of race or other factors. If you believe that you've been the victim of employer discrimination, you should contact your provincial Human Rights Commission or the Canadian Human Rights Commission, National Office, 344 Slater Street, 8th Floor, Ottawa ON K1A 1E1 (☎ 613-995-1151, 💻 www.chrc-ccdp.ca). As with most issues in Canada, there are lawyers who specialise in discrimination and employee-employer disputes.

Not only are there laws against discrimination, there's also a federal Employment Equity Act, which requires employers to take steps to improve the employment situation of women, the disabled, native Americans and other minority groups. Federal and provincial government departments and other large 'public' employers such as police forces have taken the lead, operating what's known as a policy of 'affirmative action' (imported from the US). Furthermore, the Federal Contractors Programme requires that all employers who do business with the government operate their employment policies on the same basis. This policy has caused resentment among non-minorities, who see themselves as victims of 'reverse discrimination'.

EMPLOYMENT CONTRACT

If you're offered a job in Canada, it's wise to have a comprehensive and legally water-tight written contract detailing your terms of employment. However, foreigners are often dismayed to find that most Canadian employers don't automatically provide contracts, except for executives, professionals (such as university professors), engineers and professional athletes. A written contract of employment should contain all the terms and conditions that have been agreed between you and the employer, including those discussed in the remainder of this chapter. Before signing a contract, you should know exactly what it contains. If your knowledge of English (or French) is imperfect, you should ask for a translation.

Your employment is usually subject to satisfactory references being received from your previous employer(s) and/or character references. In the case of a school-leaver or student, a reference is usually required from the principal of your last school, college or university. For certain jobs, a pre-employment medical examination is required and periodical examinations may be a condition of employment, e.g. when good health is vital to the safe performance of your duties. If you require a permit to work in Canada, your contract may contain a clause stating that 'the job contract is subject to a permit being granted by the Canadian authorities'. For all jobs, you must have a Social Insurance Number (see page 262).

Employees with a contract must be notified in writing of any changes in their terms and conditions of employment.

If you don't receive a written copy of your employer's general terms and conditions, which apply to all employees, generally the federal and provincial minimum legal requirements apply. Employment conditions should include the date from which they take effect and state to whom they apply.

PLACE OF WORK

Unless your employment contract states otherwise, your employer can change your place of work (whether you like it or not) but must provide you with accommodation close to the new workplace. Some companies warn you that you may occasionally be required to work at other company locations, but you should ask before accepting a position.

SALARY & BENEFITS

Negotiating an appropriate salary is just one aspect of your remuneration package, which may consist of much more than what you receive in your pay cheque. Many companies offer a range of fringe benefits for executives, managers and key personnel, and it isn't unusual for executives to dramatically increase their annual salaries through profit-sharing, stock options and bonuses. When discussing salary with a prospective employer, take into account the total salary package, including commission, bonuses and benefits.

Your starting salary should be stated and overtime rates, bonus rates, planned increases and cost of living rises should also be included.

Salaries are usually paid by cheque (but can be paid in cash, by money order or by direct deposit to your bank account) every two weeks for hourly-paid workers and bimonthly or monthly for salaried workers. You must receive an itemised pay statement (or wage slip) detailing all deductions, either with your pay cheque or, when your salary is paid into a bank account, separately.

Minimum hourly wages that apply to both full and part-time workers are fixed by each province and vary considerably, e.g. $6 per hour in Newfoundland and $7.20 per hour in the Yukon (for a full list, see page 33). Under certain conditions, lower than minimum wage rates can be paid, e.g. to apprentices, disabled workers and full-time students. Minimum wages aren't applicable certain categories of worker, e.g. sales personnel working on commission, many farm workers, casual baby-sitters and employees of seasonal amusement and recreational establishments.

Salaries are usually reviewed once or twice per year, depending on your position and the industry. Annual increases may be negotiated individually by employees, by an independent pay review board or by a union (called collective bargaining). Generally you're better off negotiating your own salary increases.

Commission & Bonuses

Your salary may include commission or bonus payments, calculated on your individual performance (e.g. based on sales) or your employer's profits. Bonuses may be paid regularly (e.g. monthly or annually) or irregularly. Some employers in Canada pay employees an annual bonus (usually in December) and some limited companies may offer employees free shares. When a bonus is paid, it may be stated in your offer of employment, in which case it's obligatory. In your first and last years of employment, an annual bonus is usually paid pro rata if you don't work a full calendar year.

Some employers operate an annual voluntary bonus scheme, based on an employee's individual performance or the company's profits (a profit-sharing scheme). If you're employed on a contract or freelance basis for a fixed period, you may be paid an end-of-contract bonus.

Overtime

Hourly paid employees who work more than the following hours **must** be paid at not less than the overtime rate which is 1.5 times the regular hourly rate ('time-and-a-half'):

Province	Applicability
Alberta	Over 8 hours per day or 44 hours per week
British Columbia	Over 8 hours per day or 40 hours per week
Manitoba	Over 8 hours per day or 40 hours per week
New Brunswick	Over 44 hours per week
Newfoundland	Over 40 hours per week
Nova Scotia	Over 48 hours per week
Northwest Territories	Over 8 hours per day or 40 hours per week
Nunavut	Over 8 hours per day or 40 hours per week
Ontario	Over 44 hours per week

Prince Edward Island	Over 48 hours per week
Quebec	Over 40 hours per week
Saskatchewan	Over 8 hours per day or 40 hours per week
Yukon Territory	Over 8 hours per day or 40 hours per week

For daily overtime you receive time-and-a-half for the first three hours and double time for hours worked in excess of 11. When overtime is calculated weekly, you receive time-and-a-half for the first eight hours in excess of the above limits and double time for the ninth and any subsequent hours.

You must have 32 consecutive hours free from work each week, but your employer can ask you to work during this time provided that he pays you double time, i.e. twice the regular hourly rate.

An employer can give employees time off in lieu (called 'banking time' in Canada) instead of paying overtime, by mutual agreement. This compensatory time is on a 'one for one' basis, e.g. if you work five extra hours this week, you can work five hours less next week. As a cost-cutting move, some companies are starting to require time off in lieu and eliminating overtime altogether.

Employees who aren't covered by the overtime rules include agricultural workers, live-in household workers, taxi drivers and employees of bus and coach companies, railways and airlines. Many white-collar employees, e.g. executives, managers, administrators and professionals who earn 'ample' salaries, aren't covered by overtime laws, even when they're employed in covered industries. Employees who earn at least half of their salary in commission are also excluded from overtime pay rules, although they must receive a minimum level of pay. **Overtime work is voluntary and you cannot be forced to do it.**

Expenses

Expenses paid by your employer may be listed in your employment conditions. These may include travel costs from your home to your place of work, when travelling on company business or for training or education. Most companies pay a mileage allowance to staff who are authorised to use their private cars on company business (but make sure that business use is covered by your car insurance). Companies without a company restaurant or canteen may pay employees a lunch allowance.

Education & Training

If you need to improve your English or French, language classes may be paid for by your employer. If it's necessary for you to learn a foreign language (other than English or French) to do your job, the cost of language study should be paid by your employer. The education and training provided by your employer may be stated in your employment conditions.

It's in your interest to investigate courses of study, seminars and lectures that you feel would be of benefit to you and your employer. Some employers give reasonable consideration to a request to attend a part-time course during working hours, provided that you don't make it a full-time occupation. In addition to relevant education and training, employers must provide the essential tools and equipment for a job (although this is open to interpretation). It's compulsory for companies to provide relevant and adequate safety and health training for all employees (see **Health & Safety** on page 58).

Company Cars

Few Canadian employers provide company cars as fringe benefits. Even when a car is essential for your job, your employer will expect you to provide your own car, for which you're paid a mileage allowance when using it on company business. If a company car is provided, check what sort of car it is, whether you're permitted to use it privately, who pays for the fuel for private mileage and whether private use affects your tax position.

TRAVEL & RELOCATION EXPENSES

Your relocation expenses to Canada (or to a new job in another region of Canada) depend on your agreement with your employer, and may be detailed in an employment contract or your employment conditions. If you're hired from outside Canada, your air ticket (or other travel expenses) to Canada are usually booked and paid for by your employer or his agent. You can usually also claim any additional travel costs, e.g. the cost of transport to and from airports. If you change jobs within Canada, your new employer may pay your relocation expenses when it's necessary for you to move house. Don't forget to ask, as they may not offer to pay (it may depend on how desperate they are to employ you).

An employer may pay a fixed relocation allowance based on your salary, position and size of family (e.g. $10,000), or may pay the total cost of moving house irrespective of the amount. The allowance should be sufficient to move the contents of an average house and you must normally pay any excess costs yourself. Your employer may ask you to obtain two or three removal estimates when he's liable for the total cost of removal. Generally you're required to organise and pay for the removal yourself. Your employer usually reimburses the equivalent amount in Canadian dollars after you've paid the bill, although it may be possible to get him to pay the bill directly or make an advance payment.

Ensure that the relocation package is adequate and ask whether, if you leave the employer before a certain period elapses, you're required to repay a percentage of the cost (or the full cost if you break a contract).

Relocation expenses paid by your employer aren't considered to be a taxable benefit. However, you can no longer claim increased housing costs following a transfer as a deductible expense. See also **Relocation Consultants** on page 109.

WORKING HOURS

With some variations (depending on the type of industry in which you're employed), the standard working day is eight hours and the standard working week 40 hours. Where collective agreements exist, additional hours are paid at overtime rates (see page 45). In manufacturing, the average working week (with paid overtime) is 50 hours. Many Canadian executives and managers work long hours, which are essential if they want to succeed (generally the higher the position a person holds, the longer the hours he works).

Typical office hours are 8 or 9am to 4 or 5pm with a lunch break of between 30 and 60 minutes. Under federal law, employees must have a meal break of at least 30 minutes for every five hours worked and the time between starting and finishing work mustn't be more than 12 hours.

When you're paid by the hour, if you arrive at work and find there's nothing to do, your employer must pay you for at least two hours and, if there's less than a full day's work to do you, must be paid for at least four hours.

Most Canadian employers allow paid time off during working hours to visit a doctor or dentist.

Flexible Hours

Many Canadian companies operate flexible working hours, which are becoming more popular because of the different time zones (see page 396), particularly among office workers. (Phone calls to distant offices need to be carefully planned; for example, someone in Montreal has to wait until 11am to call someone in Vancouver at 8am, and the person in Vancouver has to call the person in Montreal before 2pm local time to be sure of catching him before he leaves.)

A flexible working schedule normally requires employees to be present between certain hours, e.g. 10am to noon and 2pm to 4pm. Employees may make up their required working hours by starting earlier than the required 'core' time, reducing their lunch break or by working later. Smaller companies may allow employees to work as late as they like, provided they don't exceed the legal maximum permitted daily working hours (see above).

HOLIDAYS & LEAVE

Annual Holiday

All workers must receive (and take) at least two weeks' paid holiday (vacation) per year, and those who leave a job before taking their holiday must receive payment in lieu. You may not be allowed the full two weeks if you join a company after their 'vacation year' has started, but you're usually allowed some days pro rata after you've worked for a few months. Holiday entitlement is calculated on a pro rata basis (per completed calendar month of service) when you don't work a full calendar year.

This miserly holiday allowance comes as a severe blow to Europeans and other foreigners who are used to receiving four to six weeks' paid annual leave (the average in Canada is 12 days per year compared with 25 in France and 30 in Germany). Teachers and others employed in educational establishments will be dismayed to discover that there's no paid Easter holiday of one or two weeks and the long summer holiday period is often unpaid, so that it may be necessary to find work in summer school.

After three years' consecutive employment, your official paid holiday entitlement usually rises to three weeks. Thereafter, each year of employment normally raises your annual holiday entitlement by one or two days, so it can take you eight years before you're entitled to four weeks' paid holiday per year. Many companies provide anniversary-year bonus holidays, such as an extra week after 10 or 20 years' service (yippee!).

Your annual holiday entitlement usually depends on your profession, position and employer, and some employers have more generous schemes based on your length of service. White-collar employees usually become eligible for longer holidays after a shorter term of service than blue-collar workers. Top managers may be entitled to additional annual holiday (but have no time to take it!).

Most employers require annual holiday to be taken within the year in which it's earned, but some allow some of it to be carried over to the next year.

Employees also receive holiday pay of 4 per cent of their wages (calculated on their wages received during the preceding year) in their first four years of employment and 6 per cent in the fifth and following years.

Before starting a new job, check that any planned holidays will be approved by your new employer. This is particularly important if they fall within your first 6 or 12 months. Holidays may usually be taken only with the prior permission of your manager or boss and in many companies must be booked up to a year in advance.

If you resign your position or are given notice, employers must usually pay you in lieu of outstanding holiday.

National & Provincial Holidays

When Canadians talk about a 'holiday' they mean a national (federal or provincial) holiday and not an annual or school holiday, which is called a vacation. The federal government designates seven days as national holidays. These are shown in the list below preceded by an asterisk (*). You're entitled to be paid for these days provided that you earn wages on 15 of the 30 days prior to the holiday (unless you're paid the minimum wage, in which case this doesn't apply). Individual provinces designate their own additional holidays, as shown below.

Banks, post offices, public schools, offices and most businesses are usually closed on national and provincial holidays.

Employees who must work on national holidays are entitled to be paid time-and-a-half for the first 11 hours and double time for hours worked in excess of 11 plus a day off in lieu. There are exceptions to this rule for certain employees, including those in petrol stations, hospitals, restaurants, continuously operating plants, amusement parks, seasonal industries (excluding the construction industry) and domestic services, who are paid the normal rate but must be given another (paid) day off in lieu.

The three main national holidays are Canada Day (which celebrates Canada's creation as a dominion), Labour Day (which honours Canadian workers) and Thanksgiving (which commemorates the first harvest of European settlers). Many holidays are celebrated by federal law on Mondays in order to create three-day weekends for federal employees and many provinces also hold provincial holidays on Mondays. When a holiday falls on a Saturday or Sunday, another day is usually granted to employees. If a holiday, such as Christmas Day, falls on a Sunday, banks and most shops close the following day.

Other holidays may include extended holiday plans, such as the period between Christmas and New Year's Day, local holidays (e.g. provincial national days), 'floating' holidays (e.g. your birthday, which some employers grant as a holiday) and days off for sickness, funerals, etc. (see **Compassionate & Special Leave** on page 52). Floating holidays may be decided by the employer or individual employees. Other holidays don't need to be paid days, but most employers pay for them. For example, many companies give employees a full paid holiday on Christmas Eve and some also on New Year's Eve.

Foreign embassies and consulates in Canada usually observe all Canadian national and local holidays **in addition to** their own national holidays.

The following days are national holidays and are observed by most Canadians, although only those marked with an asterisk are statutory holidays:

Date	Holiday
*1st January	New Year's Day
*March/April	Good Friday
March/April	Easter Monday
*Monday before 25th May	Victoria Day – Queen Victoria's birthday (not observed in Quebec)
*1st July	Canada Day (previously Dominion Day), the anniversary of the creation of the Dominion of Canada in 1867
*first Sunday in September	Labour Day (usually marks the 'end of summer')
*second Monday in October	Thanksgiving Day

11th November	Remembrance Day – The signing of the armistice of World War I, in which many Canadian soldiers fell in Flanders. As in the UK, people wear poppies and observe a two-minute silence at 11am. Not a full-day holiday for all Canadians.
*25th December	Christmas Day
26th December	Boxing Day

In addition to national holidays, there are the following provincial holidays:

Province	Holiday
Alberta	Third Monday in February – Alberta (or Family) Day
	First Monday in August – Heritage Day
British Columbia	First Monday in August – British Columbia Day
Manitoba	First Monday in August – Civic Holiday
New Brunswick	First Monday in August – New Brunswick Day
Newfoundland	First Monday in March – Commonwealth Day
	Nearest Monday to 17th March – St Patrick's Day
	Nearest Monday to 23rd April – St George's Day
	Nearest Monday to 27th June – Discovery Day
	Nearest Monday to 7th July – Memorial Day
	Nearest Monday to 10th July – Orangemen's Day
Northwest Territories	First Monday in August – Civic Holiday
Nunavut	1st April – Nunavut Day
Ontario	First Monday in August – Civic Holiday

Quebec	6th January – Epiphany
	40 days after Easter
	– Ash Wednesday/Ascension
	24th June – Saint-Jean-Baptiste Day
	1st November – All Saints' Day
	8th December – Immaculate Conception
Saskatchewan	First Monday in August – Civic Holiday
Yukon	Third Monday in August – Discovery Day

Compassionate & Special Leave

Most Canadian companies provide paid leave on certain occasions only, e.g. military leave, leave to attend the funeral of a family member ('bereavement days') and leave for jury duty, although smaller companies are generally more flexible. An employer must allow an employee time off for jury duty but isn't required to pay him (and the amount paid to jurors by the courts is derisory). A person selected for jury duty cannot be fired. Other special leave is usually limited to a number of days per year, e.g. three. The grounds for compassionate leave may be listed in your employment conditions. An employer isn't required to allow employees time off work for religious observance, although he's required to accommodate religious beliefs to a certain extent.

Whether or not you're paid for time off work or time lost through unavoidable circumstances (e.g. public transport strikes, car breakdowns and bad weather) depends on your employer and whether you're an hourly-paid or a salaried employee. The attitude to paid time off in Canada also depends on your status and position. Executives and managers, who often work much longer hours than officially required, usually have more leeway than blue-collar workers. Some public sector employers allow employees to take sabbaticals and may even continue to pay them a percentage of their salary (this is exceptional).

Pregnancy

Time off work for sickness in the early stages of pregnancy is usually given without question but usually isn't paid or is deemed to be sickness (see below). Pregnant women are entitled by law to 17 weeks' unpaid pregnancy leave. After giving birth, the mother is entitled to 35 weeks of unpaid maternity leave. Fathers are entitled to 27 weeks' unpaid paternity leave. Parents aren't allowed to take their leave simultaneously.

An employer cannot refuse to employ or fire a woman because of a pregnancy (or for any reason connected with pregnancy or childbirth), force her to take maternity leave or fail to honour her reinstatement rights after a pregnancy. A mother is entitled to her previous job (or a similar job) with no loss of wages, fringe benefits or seniority – as is a father after paternity leave. The law requires employers to treat pregnancy and childbirth as a temporary disability, and health insurance plans must cover these conditions if they include temporary disabilities. A pregnant or nursing mother cannot be required to work overtime.

Sickness Or Accident

You're usually required to notify your employer as soon as possible (i.e. within a few hours of your normal starting time) of sickness or an accident that prevents you from working. Failure to do so may result in loss of pay. You're required to keep your boss or manager informed about your illness and when you expect to return to work. For periods of up to seven days, you must usually provide a written statement of why you were absent on your return to work, although some employers require a doctor's certificate. If you're away from work for more than seven days, you must obtain a doctor's certificate.

INSURANCE

Social Insurance

Social insurance includes benefits for the unemployed, the aged, the disabled and those with very low incomes. Social insurance contributions are compulsory for most Canadian residents and are deducted from salaries by employers. See **Social Insurance** on page 260.

Health Insurance

Canada has a national health insurance scheme (Medicare) that's funded by the Ministry of Health and administered by provincial governments. Health cover is free in most provinces, although in some, members must make a monthly contribution. Medicare doesn't cover all health services and many people take out private insurance (called extended health cover), which may be provided by your employer, to cover non-insured hospital and other medical expenses. Newcomers aren't eligible for Medicare for their first three months in Canada and should purchase private health insurance to cover their families during this period. For more information see **Health Service** on page 241 and **Health Insurance** on page 270.

Compensation Insurance

Canada provides state benefits to workers for work-related injuries and illnesses through the Workplace Compensation Board (WCB). Payments are 85 per cent of your net pay before the injury or illness, less any earnings after the injury/illness, up to an annual maximum (which varies with the province and is amended annually but is generally in the region of $50,000). The WCB also pays other costs related to a workplace injury or illness, including healthcare costs, transport and clothing. Workers are entitled to compensation for job-related injuries, irrespective of whether they were at fault. If a worker dies as a result of an accident, his dependants receive the benefits. During the first two years, benefits are paid every two weeks, after which they're paid monthly. After six years, a benefit is made permanent and you may be entitled to a lump sum payment of up to 10 per cent of the annual benefit. A worker claiming such benefits is required to co-operate fully with the WCB in his rehabilitation and is expected to return to work as soon as possible.

Employment Insurance

State employment insurance provides workers and their families with a weekly income for a limited period when they're unemployed through no fault of their own, e.g. due to sickness, layoffs, plant closures or natural disasters. There's a mandatory employer and employee contribution towards the employment insurance fund. For further information see **Employment Insurance** on page 265.

Sick Pay & Disability Benefits

Sick leave is usually paid in full for a fixed number of days a year (annual sick leave plans) and employees are often permitted to carry over and accumulate unused sick leave from year to year (usually there's a maximum). Sick pay is more commonly available to white-collar employees than to blue-collar workers.

Short-term benefits in the event of an illness or accident are covered under the employment insurance scheme (see above). Long-term disability insurance (LTD) is provided under the Canada Pension Plan (CPP). However, workers are eligible for this benefit only if they've been contributing to the CPP for four of the last six years and in any case benefits are rarely sufficient to meet your financial commitments. Private LTD insurance typically replaces 50 to 60 per cent of income and usually begins after six months of disability and continues for a specified number of months or until retirement age, depending on your age at the time of the disability. Private LTD insurance is more commonly provided for white-collar workers than blue-collar workers. Employees are usually required to contribute towards the cost of private LTD insurance and there are normally service requirements of between a month and a year before you become eligible.

You should therefore find out whether you're covered under a private disability plan through your employer. Private sickness plans commonly have a service requirement, e.g. three months, before new employees become eligible for benefits. Short-term sickness and accident benefits usually continue for a maximum of 26 weeks (six months) and pay around two-thirds of your previous salary.

Some employees are eligible for an immediate disability pension under their company pension plan (see below). For more information about disability benefits and insurance, see **Disability Insurance** on page 271.

RETIREMENT & PENSIONS

The Human Rights Code prohibits employers from fixing a mandatory retirement age and makes compulsory retirement illegal. Therefore, anyone who wishes to continue working into his dotage can do so (provided he's still capable), although an employer can always decide to make you redundant! Nevertheless, 65 is the normal retirement age, and a gold watch the usual retirement gift.

Many Canadian companies provide an employee pension plan that tops up the federal pension scheme, Canada Pension Plan/CPP (called the Quebec Pension Plan or QPP in Quebec) – see page 263. Your contributions for both CPP and a company top-up scheme are deducted from your gross salary and vary according to your age and your employer's pension fund. Some employers don't operate their own pension scheme, but contribute to a private Registered Retirement Savings Plan (RRSP) or Life Income Retirement Account (LIRA). See **Private Pension Plans** on page 272 for more information.

UNION MEMBERSHIP

Around 4 million workers in Canada are union members; most of them are employed in government, education, manufacturing, and health and social services. There are over 900 unions in Canada, many of which are affiliated to the Canadian Labour Congress (CLC), 2841 Riverside Drive, Ottawa ON KIV 8X7 (☎ 613-521-3400, 💻 www.clc-ctc.ca). Around a quarter of unionised workers belong to unions that are affiliated to the American Federation of Labour and the Congress of Industrial Organisations (AFL-CIO). The CLC and AFL-CIO have a combined membership of around 3 million, while a further million workers belong to non-affiliated organisations. The two public sector unions, the Canadian Union of Public Employees (CUPE) and the National Union of Public and General Employees (NUPGE) are the largest unions in Canada. Unions remain strong in traditional industries such as manufacturing and transport, but have little influence in industries such as services, finance and retailing.

Under the Labour Code administered by the Ministry of Labour, employees have the right to form, join or assist labour unions, to bargain collectively through representatives of their own choosing on wages, hours and other terms of employment, and to engage in concerted activities for the purpose of collective bargaining or other mutual aid or protection, such as striking to secure better working conditions. However, employees also have the right **not** to join a union if they don't wish to do so.

Collective bargaining systems operate under the Industrial Relations and Disputes Investigation Act, one of the provisions being that a union that gains the support of a majority of the workers in a bargaining unit can obtain federal or provincial certification making it the legal bargaining agent for that unit. Employers must agree to collective bargaining once certification has been obtained. Some provinces have supplementary rules on unions and collective agreements. Certain employees such as farm workers, domestic employees of a family and managers have no rights to collective bargaining. Where union contracts are in place, the law prohibits work stoppages during the term of a collective agreement and if any disputes arise they must be settled through an established grievance procedure or arbitration.

Information about Canadian unions is published in the *Directory of Labour Organisations in Canada* available from Human Resources Development Canada, 140 Promenade du Portage, Phase lV, Hull, Quebec K1A 0J9 (☎ 819-953-7260).

OTHER CONDITIONS

Acceptance of Gifts

With the exception of those employed in the public sector, employees are normally permitted to accept gifts of a limited value from customers or suppliers, e.g. bottles of whisky or small gifts at Christmas. Generally any small gifts given and received openly aren't considered a bribe or unlawful (although, if you give your business to someone else in the following year, don't expect a gift next Christmas). Most Canadian companies forbid the acceptance of any gifts of substance and cash payments are totally out of the question (if you accept a real bribe, make sure it's a large one and that you have a secret bank account!). You should declare any gifts received to your immediate superior, who decides what should be done with them. Some Canadian bosses pool gifts and share them among all employees.

Confidentiality & Changing Jobs

If you disclose confidential company information, either in Canada or overseas (particularly to a competitor), you're liable to instant dismissal and may also have legal action taken against you. You may not take any secrets or confidential information (e.g. customer mailing lists) from a previous employer, but you may usually use any skills, knowledge and contacts acquired during his employ. You may not compete against a former employer if there's a valid, binding restraint clause in an employment contract. An employment contract may contain a clause defining the sort of information that the employer considers to be confidential, such as customer and supplier relationships and details of business plans.

If there's a confidentiality or restraint clause in an employment contract that's unfair, e.g. it inhibits you from changing jobs, it's probably invalid in law.

If you're in doubt, consult a lawyer who specialises in company law about your rights. If you're a key employee, you may have a legal binding contract preventing you from joining a competitor or starting a company in the same line of business as your employer (and in particular enticing former colleagues to join your company), although this will be valid for a limited period only.

Discipline & Dismissal

Some large and medium-size companies have comprehensive grievance and disciplinary procedures that must be followed before an employee can be suspended or dismissed. Some employers have disciplinary procedures whereby employees can be suspended with or without pay, e.g. for breaches of contract. Employees can also be suspended (usually with pay) pending investigation into an alleged offence or impropriety. Disciplinary procedures usually include both verbal and official written warnings, and are both to protect employees from unfair dismissal and to ensure that dismissed employees cannot (successfully) sue their employers. If you have a grievance or complaint against a colleague or your boss, there may be an official procedure to be followed in order to obtain redress. If an official grievance procedure exists, it may be detailed in your employment conditions.

In general, employers can terminate an employee's employment at any time without justification and, unless the employee has a contract, he's entitled to little or no compensation. Unlike those in most European countries, Canadian employers aren't liable for high redundancy payments and are more likely to lay off workers when business is bad. Dismissal is common among executives and managers, particularly for older employees, and is generally accepted as a fact of life. Companies often have a high turnover in senior executives and a shake-up at the top often works its way down the management ladder.

Many provinces have exceptions to the 'instant dismissal' rule for private employees, e.g. in cases where employees refuse to perform an act that violates public policy or where dismissal violated an oral assurance of job security or a 'just cause' policy. In these cases, employees can sue for wrongful dismissal. Employees of federal, provincial and local governments are covered by civil service laws and can be dismissed for 'just cause' only. In Canada, you cannot be fired within a certain period of falling ill or before or after giving birth, provided that you intend to return to work.

Where formal discharge and disciplinary procedures exist, company policy may state that an employee be given notice before he can be fired, in which case he may have a legal right to notice (see **Probationary & Notice Periods** below).

If you've worked at a job for over one year that isn't subject to a collective bargaining agreement and you believe you've been unlawfully dismissed, you should contact the Provincial Ministry of Labour or a labour law attorney to find out whether you have grounds for a wrongful dismissal lawsuit. An employee can file a complaint with a government inspector if he feels his dismissal was unjust, and an adjudicator from the Ministry of Labour will investigate the complaint. If the dismissal is found to be unjust, the employee is entitled to reinstatement with back pay.

If you're temporarily laid off, your employer must tell you two weeks before the job ends or pay you extra money if you've been employed for longer than six months. Although it varies with the province, you can usually be laid off for up to 13 weeks in any 20-week period without having your employment terminated.

When you leave a full-time job, your employer must give you a 'record of employment', without which you cannot apply for employment insurance.

Health & Safety

Work-related injuries are a major problem in Canada (there were 172,103 in 2001). The commonest causes of industrial injuries are motor vehicles, electrical hazards such as power lines, ladders, scaffolding and roofs (particularly on construction sites), toxic chemicals, and violent crime in the retail sector.

Canada has strict laws regarding worker safety and health, and in some provinces you have the right to refuse to do unsafe work without fear of being fired. Unsafe work may include working without proper protective clothing and equipment such as helmets or boots, or working with tools on which you haven't been trained. For more information on what work you can refuse to do and the procedures you must go through (stating why you think the task is unsafe, inspecting what you think is unsafe with your supervisor, calling a Health and Safety inspector, etc.), contact your local HRDC labour office or the HRDC Headquarters Library (☎ 819-997-3540), the Canadian Centre for Occupational Health and Safety at their local office or 250 Main Street East, Hamilton, ON L8N 1H6 (☎ 1-800-668-4284 or 905-570-8094, 🖳 www.ccohs.ca). Canadian law also requires (since the 1990 Smoking in the Workplace Act) that employers designate a particular area for smoking or ban it altogether.

Long-Service Awards

Most large companies present their employees with long-service awards after a number of years, e.g. 15, 20 or 25 years. These are usually in the form of a gift such as a clock presented to employees by senior management. Periods of absence, e.g. maternity leave, usually count as continuous employment when calculating your length of service.

Medical Examination

Canadian employers rarely require prospective employees to have a pre-employment medical examination. A medical may, however, be required for employees over a certain age (e.g. 40) or for employees in particular jobs (e.g. where good health is of paramount importance for reasons of safety). Thereafter a medical examination may be necessary periodically, e.g. every one or two years, or may be requested at any time by your employer. Medical examinations may also be required as a condition of membership of a company health, pension or life insurance scheme. Some companies insist on employees having regular health screening, particularly senior managers and executives. Employers are usually required to pay for mandatory medical exams.

Federal law allows employers to require applicants to take medical exams or drug tests, provided that they keep the results confidential, although many provinces regulate drug testing. It's very rare for employers to require existing and prospective employees to take a drug test; if they do, this cannot be administered until a conditional offer of employment has been made. Although uncommon, another test that can be required for jobs related to government work and national or company security is a lie detector test.

Part-Time Job Restrictions

Many Canadian companies don't mind full-time employees working part-time (i.e. moonlighting) for another employer, unless it's one in the same line of business or the work interferes with your full-time job. Any restrictions should be included in your employment contract.

Probationary & Notice Periods

For some jobs there's an official probationary period, varying from one or two weeks for hourly-paid employees to three months for salaried employees. Unless your contract or your employer's terms and conditions states otherwise, once you've been employed for more than three months your notice period is two weeks. If your contract or employer's terms and conditions specifies a different notice period, its length may depend on your method of payment, your job and your length of service.

Employees in the private sector who have worked for less than three months may lose their job without notice and for any reason or none at all; employees with less than three months' service may also quit a job without notice and for any reason. Once you've worked for three months, two weeks' notice is required by either party. Exceptions are employees covered by a collective bargaining agreement and those with contracts that contain other conditions.

Where formal discharge and disciplinary procedures exist, company policy may state that an employee be given notice before he can be fired, in which case he may have a legal right to notice. If you're fired and your employer insists that you leave right away, he must pay you for the notice period, plus any outstanding holiday and sick leave. See also **Discipline & Dismissal** on page 57.

Redundancy Pay

If you're employed in a volatile business, particularly in an executive or managerial position, it's important to have adequate financial compensation in the event of redundancy (severance) or dismissal written into your contract or, at the very least, to have a good understanding of what you're entitled to. Executives may have a clause in their contracts whereby they receive a generous 'golden handshake' if they're made redundant, e.g. after a take-over. Without a compensation clause , you're entitled to your normal notice period only, i.e. two weeks or one month, or payment in lieu of notice. An employer must pay redundancy pay if there are collective bargaining agreements or contracts that provide redundancy benefits. The law in some provinces requires redundancy pay under certain conditions, in others employees must usually rely on their employer's benevolence. Some companies wishing to reduce their workforce may offer employees voluntary redundancy payments (pay-outs) or early retirement. Minimum redundancy terms vary, but the following usually applies:

Period of Employment	Entitlement
Up to three months	None
Between 3 and 12 months less one day	One week's pay
Between 12 and 36 months less one day	Two weeks' pay

In British Columbia, employees receive one week's pay after three months' employment, two weeks' pay after one year and three weeks' pay after three years' employment, plus one week's pay for each additional year of employment up to a maximum of eight years. In all provinces, you may also be entitled to be paid in lieu of any holiday and days off for sickness or compassionate leave owed you, plus a refund of your contributions to company pension plans.

Many companies provide counselling for people who are made redundant, e.g. on job prospects and job hunting, benefits, retirement, retraining and self-employment. Redundancy pay doesn't affect your eligibility to claim employment benefit (see page 265). If possible, you should ensure that you receive a cheque for the total redundancy package and all paperwork before you leave.

CHECKLISTS

When negotiating your terms of employment for a job in Canada, the checklists below will prove useful. The points listed under **General Positions** below apply to most jobs, while those listed under **Managerial & Executive Positions** on page 65 may apply to executive and top managerial appointments only.

General Positions

Salary

- Is the total amount of the salary adequate, taking into account the cost of living (see page 309).

- Is it linked to inflation?
- Does it include an allowance for working (and living) in an expensive region or city (e.g. Toronto) or a remote area (e.g. in the Yukon, where workers often receive a 'hardship' allowance)?
- How often is the salary reviewed?
- Does the salary include commission or bonuses (see page 45)?
- Is overtime paid or time off granted in lieu of any extra hours worked (see page 45)?
- Is the total salary (including expenses) paid in Canadian dollars or is the salary paid in another country (in a different currency) with expenses for living in Canada?

Relocation Expenses

- Are relocation expenses or a relocation allowance paid?
- Do relocation expenses include travelling expenses for all family members?
- Is there a maximum limit and, if so, is it adequate?
- Are you required to repay your relocation expenses (or a percentage) if you resign before a certain period has elapsed?
- Are you required to pay for your relocation in advance (this may run into thousands of dollars)?
- If employment is for a fixed period, will your relocation expenses be paid when you leave Canada?
- If you aren't shipping household goods and furniture to Canada, is an allowance paid to buy furniture locally?
- Do relocation expenses include the legal and estate agent's fees incurred when moving home?
- Does the employer engage the services of a relocation consultant (see page 109)?

Accommodation

- Will the employer pay for temporary accommodation (or pay a lodging allowance) until you find permanent accommodation?
- Is subsidised or free, temporary or permanent accommodation provided? If so, is it furnished or unfurnished?
- Must you pay for utilities such as electricity, gas and water?
- What will accommodation cost?

- If accommodation isn't provided by the employer, is assistance in finding suitable accommodation given? What does it consist of?
- While you're living in temporary accommodation, will your employer pay your travelling expenses to your permanent home? How far is it from the place of employment?
- Are your expenses paid while looking for local accommodation?

Working Hours

- What are the weekly working hours?
- Does the employer operate a flexible working hours system (see page 48)? If so, what are the fixed (core) working hours?
- How early must you start? Can you carry forward any extra hours worked and take time off at a later date (or carry forward a deficit and make it up later)?
- Are you required to clock in and out of work?
- Can you choose to be paid or take time off in lieu of overtime worked?

Part-Time Or Seasonal Work

- Is part-time or seasonal work (e.g. during school terms) possible?
- Are flexible working hours or part-time hours working from home permitted?
- Does the employer have a job-sharing scheme?
- Are extended career breaks permitted with no loss of seniority, grade or salary?

Holiday Entitlement

- What's the annual holiday (vacation) entitlement? Does it increase with service? See page 48
- What are the paid national and provincial holidays (see page 49)?
- Is free air travel to your home country or elsewhere provided for you and your family and, if so, how often? Are other holiday travel discounts provided?
- Is paid or unpaid maternity/paternity leave provided (see page 52)?

Insurance

- Is health insurance provided for you and your family? What does it include (see pages 53 and 270)? It's important to ensure that all members of your family are fully insured before you set foot in Canada.
- Is free life insurance provided?
- Is accident or any special insurance provided by your employer?
- For how long is your salary paid if you're ill or have an accident (see **Disability Insurance** on page 271 and **Sick Pay & Disability Benefits** on page 54)?

Company Pension

- Is there a company pension scheme and, if so, what's your contribution (see page 55)?
- Are you required or permitted to pay a lump sum into the pension plan in order to receive a full or higher pension?
- What are the rules regarding early retirement?
- Is the pension transferable and do you receive the company's contributions in addition to your own if you resign? If not, does the employer contribute to a private pension plan?
- Is the pension linked to the inflation rate?
- Do the pension rules apply equally to full and part-time employees?

Employer

- What are the employer's prospects?
- Is his profitability and growth rate favourable?
- Does he have a good reputation?
- Does he have a high staff turnover and has he laid off a high percentage of workers in recent years?

Women

- What's the employer's policy regarding equal promotion opportunities for women?
- Is paid maternity leave provided?

- How many women hold positions in middle and senior management or at board level?

Education & Training

- What initial or career training does the employer provide?
- Is training provided in-house or externally and does the employer pay for training or education abroad, if necessary?
- Does the employer have a training programme for employees in your profession (e.g. technical, management, language)? Is the employer's training recognised for its excellence (or otherwise)?
- Are free or subsidised English or French lessons provided for you and your spouse (if necessary)?
- Does the employer pay for a part or the total cost of non-essential education, e.g. a computer or language course?
- Does the employer pay for day release to attend a degree course or other study?

Other Conditions

- What are the promotion prospects?
- Does the employer provide a free nursery (creche) for children below school age or a day care centre for the elderly?
- Is a free or subsidised employee restaurant provided? If not, is a lunch allowance paid? Is any provision made for shift workers, e.g. breakfast or evening meals?
- Is a travelling allowance paid from your Canadian home to your place of work?
- Is free or subsidised parking provided at your workplace?
- Are free work clothes, overalls or a uniform provided? Does the employer pay for the cleaning of work clothes (both factory and office)?
- Does the employer provide perks such as inexpensive home loans, interest-free loans or mortgage assistance? **An inexpensive home loan can be worth thousands of dollars per year.**
- Is a company car provided? What sort of car? Can it be used privately and, if so, does the employer pay for the fuel? Who pays for insurance, servicing and repairs?

- Does the employer provide fringe benefits or subsidised services such as in-house banking, credit union membership, car discount scheme, travel discounts, employees' discount shop or product discounts, sports and social facilities or club membership, fitness centre, subsidised theatre tickets, shopping services, shoe repairs, laundry or cleaning service, car servicing, on-site kindergarten or elementary school, and adult education?
- Do you have a written list of your job responsibilities?
- Have your employment conditions been confirmed in writing?
- If a dispute arises over your salary or working conditions, under the law of which country is your contract (if applicable) interpreted?

Managerial & Executive Positions

- Is private schooling for your children paid for or subsidised? Does the employer pay for a boarding school in Canada or another country?
- Is the salary indexed to inflation or protected against devaluation and cost of living increases? This is particularly important if you're paid in a foreign currency that fluctuates wildly or could be devalued.
- Are you paid an overseas allowance for working in Canada?
- Is a rent-free house or apartment provided?
- Are paid holidays provided (perhaps in a company-owned house or apartment) or 'business' conferences in exotic places?
- Are all costs incurred by a move to Canada reimbursed? For example, the cost of selling your home, employing an agent to let it for you or storing personal effects.
- Does the employer pay for domestic help or contribute to the cost of a cleaner or cook?
- Does the employer provide profit-sharing or stock options (which may be worth more than your annual salary)?
- Is a car provided, perhaps with a chauffeur?
- Are you entitled to any miscellaneous benefits, such as club memberships, free credit cards or tickets for sports events and shows?
- Is there an entertainment allowance?
- Is extra compensation (e.g. a 'golden handshake') paid if you're laid off or dismissed? This could be important in Canada's volatile job market!

3.

PERMITS & VISAS

A round 9 per cent of Canadian residents are foreign-born, which puts the country ahead of its neighbour, the US (around 8 per cent), in this respect. Countries with a higher immigrant share of the population include Switzerland (17 per cent) and Australia (20 per cent). Official immigration is over 250,000 per year. With the exception of certain visitors, all non-resident foreigners wishing to enter Canada require a visa. Canada issues a range of visas, that are broadly divided into immigrant visas (permanent residents) and work permits (employment authorisation). A work permit allows you to enter and remain in Canada on a temporary basis, usually for a six-month period, although in certain circumstances this can be extended.

Canadian immigration and naturalisation laws are enforced by the Federal Immigration Department of the Government of Canada, which is responsible for the processing of foreigners entering Canada and those seeking permanent residence. The Department maintains offices throughout Canada and in Canadian High Commissions, embassies and consulates throughout the world. Entry into the country is strictly controlled and anyone who doesn't comply with visa requirements can be fined, jailed or deported. Canada restricts entry of undesirables and misfits and anyone who's a threat to the health, welfare and security of Canada, by requiring applicants to undergo a medical and produce a police certificate declaring that they don't have a criminal record.

Unlike the US, where possession of a visa isn't a guarantee of entry into the country, it's unusual for anyone with a visa or work permit (with the attached 'record of landing') to be turned away unless their circumstances have changed since it was issued. For example, the holder of a visa may have got married or divorced since it was granted. The authorities don't mind you changing your circumstances, but they expect you to inform them in plenty of time. Only holders of permanent resident visas and work permits may work in Canada, including informal work in a household as a nanny, au pair or mother's helper. You need a full passport to enter Canada and if it's close to its expiry date, it's advisable to renew it before leaving for Canada.

An immigrant visa gives you the right to live and work in Canada (and change jobs freely) on a permanent basis and to apply for Canadian citizenship after three years' residence. Work permits (known as 'employment authorisation') are normally valid for six months, but are issued for specific jobs only and aren't transferable between jobs. In certain circumstances they can be extended to allow a maximum stay of three years. The key to obtaining a work permit, apart from having a genuine job offer in writing, is that a prospective employer must prove that there are no unemployed Canadian nationals or immigrant visa holders who can do the job. This requires employers to obtain a certificate from a Human Resource Centre in Canada to this effect, which can take several months. The information you provide in support of your application to enter Canada for any purpose is collected under the authority of the Immigration Act and protected and accessible only under the provisions of the Privacy Act and the Access to Information Act.

Canada doesn't have an annual immigration quota, but sets annual targets that can be exceeded if there are many high-quality applicants, and in years when there are fewer applicants officials may be more lenient regarding marginal applications. **Note that, as in many areas of life in Canada, the immigration rules for the province of Quebec (see page 77) are different from the rest of Canada.** Immigration to Canada is dealt with under the terms of the 1976 Immigration Act by Citizenship and Immigration Canada (📟 http://cicnet.ci.gc.ca) and general information, including links to immigration lawyers, is also available on the Internet (e.g. 📟 www.escapeartist.com). Serious immigrants (you must be serious to pay around $1,500 in application processing fees for one person!) may wish to obtain a copy of *Migrating To Canada* by M. J. Bjarnason (How To Books) or *Immigrating To Canada* by Gary Segal (Self Counsel Press Inc.).

Note that immigration is a complex subject and that the information contained in this chapter is intended as a general guide only. You shouldn't base any decisions or actions on the information contained herein without first confirming it with an official and reliable source, such as a Canadian High Commission, embassy or consulate. See also **Canadian Citizenship** on page 378.

IMMIGRANT VISAS

An immigrant visa bestows upon the holder the status known as 'permanent resident'. It consists of a piece of paper with the headings 'Immigrant Visa' and 'Record of Landing', which is attached to your passport after you've been processed by Canadian immigration at your port of arrival. Your passport is also stamped 'permanent resident' at this time. Immigrant visas grant holders and their dependants (spouse and children under the age of 19) the right to live, work and study in Canada (and change jobs freely) on a permanent basis, and confer eligibility for Canadian citizenship after three years. The main difference between the rights of a permanent resident and those of a Canadian citizen is that a permanent resident cannot vote in certain elections, hold public office or be employed in certain jobs, e.g. the police.

Permanent resident status cannot be withdrawn after landing, provided that the holder doesn't abandon his Canadian residence or commit certain crimes. However, you may lose your status if you spend too long outside Canada. You may not be outside Canada for more than 183 days in any 12-month period unless you obtain a 'returning resident permit' from a Canadian immigrant office. Ideally you should obtain this before you leave Canada, but you can get one outside Canada if necessary, e.g. if a short trip has to be extended unavoidably. These permits are normally valid for one year only, but can be issued or extended for up to two years. You must return to Canada before the expiry date or you may lose your immigrant status. Once you've obtained Canadian citizenship you can leave Canada for as long as you like and still have the right to return.

You shouldn't delay too long after your visa has been granted and must arrive in Canada no more than one year after passing your medical, even though the actual visa may not have been issued until several months after this. If you delay beyond this time, you must start the whole procedure again.

Visa Applications

When applying for an immigrant visa it's sometimes wise to employ the services of an experienced immigration attorney (lawyer) or immigration consultant, although it isn't always necessary. It depends on each individual case, although the procedure can be complicated and the rules and regulations change frequently. Many visa applications are rejected because the paperwork was incorrect, e.g. the wrong information was provided, a form wasn't completed correctly or the wrong visa application was made. If someone makes an application on your behalf, you should check that the information provided is correct in every detail. If an application is rejected (for any reason), the chances of being granted a visa by appealing or reapplying are less likely, so it's vital to get it right first time. There are many immigration attorneys and consultants in Canada and abroad, some of whom specialise in certain categories of immigrants only. Attorneys' fees depend on the complexity of the case and range from $250 for a simple consultation to $5,000 to $10,000 for a complex application involving a lot of work.

You should engage an attorney or consultant who's a member of their professional organisation, the Organisation of Professional Immigration Consultants, PO Box 63563, Woodside Square, 1571 Sandhurst Circle, Toronto, Ontario, Canada M1V 1VO (☎ 416-483-7044, 🖳 http://opic.org), who has been highly recommended or who has a good reputation, because incompetent and dishonest attorneys aren't unknown. **Bear in mind that nobody, however much you pay him, can guarantee that your application will be approved.** Always ensure that you know exactly how much you must pay and the exact services you receive in return. If you wish to appeal successfully against a refusal to grant a visa, you probably need to engage the services of an immigration attorney. Attorneys have the right to attend immigration interviews with you, but consultants don't.

Categories

People immigrating to Canada are divided into three basic categories: family reunification, refugee and humanitarian, and independent. Most applicants come under the independent category, which includes skilled workers, business entrepreneurs, investors and self-employed people. The categories for retired people and assisted relatives have been abolished. There's no category that gives an automatic right to a visa without going through the normal full application procedure, which includes assessment under a points system. There are two requirements for all immigrant applicants, irrespective of the category under which you apply: you must be of good character (no criminal record) and good health (i.e. no illnesses or diseases that could be a risk to other citizens or a burden on the health service). If you think that you may have a problem under either of these requirements but still want to apply, you should engage an immigration attorney to argue your case for you.

Family Reunification

There's now just one category available under family reunification, that of sponsored dependant. This means a close relative (husband or wife, dependent children, fiancé(e) with accompanying dependent children, father or mother, grandparent, or unmarried orphaned brothers, sisters, nephews, nieces or grandchildren under 22) sponsored by a Canadian citizen or a permanent resident aged at least 22. The Canadian government accepts around 80,000 people annually in this category.

If you fall into this category, you must ask your relative in Canada to start the process by obtaining the relevant forms from their nearest immigration centre, which include an 'undertaking of assistance' form. By sponsoring you, your relative and his spouse (if applicable) take on the responsibility of providing for your accommodation, food and general welfare for a period of up to ten years. This doesn't mean that you must live with the relative, but that they must provide for you if you need financial support during this period. In order to satisfy the immigration authorities that your relatives are able to do this, they must complete a 'financial evaluation' form detailing their income and assets. A certain level of income is required, depending on the number of people being sponsored. They must also provide a copy of their Canadian citizenship card or their immigrant visa, record of landing and documentary evidence of their relationship with you.

Provided that the documentation is acceptable, an 'undertaking of assistance' notification is issued and the Canadian High Commission, embassy or consulate in your home country is notified. You're then required to submit an 'application for permanent residence' and invited to attend an interview where you must present certain documents, e.g. your passport and marriage certificate (you're told what's required). As a sponsored dependant, your educational and occupational situation isn't taken into account, although you may be asked about these and whether you plan to work in Canada. Basically all you need do is prove your relationship with your sponsor, pass a medical (if required) and produce a police certificate to show that you don't have a criminal record.

Refugees & Humanitarian

This category is defined as people who can demonstrate a well-founded fear of persecution in their native land. To apply under this category you must first contact a Canadian High Commission, embassy or consulate in your home country or any other country to which you have access. The Canadian government accepts around 40,000 refugees per year.

Independent

This is the largest immigration category and the most likely to succeed, as over 90 per cent of applications are successful. The Canadian government accepts over 110,000 independent immigrants per year, who are divided into four sub-categories: skilled workers, business entrepreneurs, investors and the self-employed. All applicants must have an adequate command of either English or French, a good education and employment skills that are appropriate in the Canadian labour market, all of which are judged under a points system (see page 75).

Skilled Workers

You require a total of 70 points for eligibility under this category, including at least one point under 'occupational demand', i.e. your occupation must be on the official list of required occupations.

Business Entrepreneurs

Canada is a good place to start a business. Energy is cheap, there's a sophisticated transport network which makes the acquisition and distribution of goods easy, and Canada is a member of the North American Free Trade Agreement (NAFTA), with a trading bloc of over 360 million potential customers in the US and Mexico. The Canadian government is keen for foreign entrepreneurs to start businesses in Canada and provides various incentives including loans and counselling services, and favourable tax treatment of investment in research and development. However, taking advantage of incentives involves a high degree of red tape and bureaucratic scrutiny, including instructions on how to keep your books. Business taxation is high and you need to hire a good tax accountant.

You're expected to take an active part in running a business and must be able to prove your ability to do this from past experience. Your business should be capable of providing work for at least one Canadian citizen and make a significant contribution to the Canadian economy. If you've invested in a business before you arrive in Canada, you may be awarded an **unconditional visa**, but you will probably be required to provide a detailed business proposal. It's best to use a professional consultant, accountant or business attorney to draw up this proposal, as the legal aspects of setting up a business must be correct. If you aren't able to invest in a business before your arrival in Canada, you're granted a **conditional visa** that requires you to have the business up and running (with at least one Canadian employee) within two years. You must provide evidence of this to a Canadian Immigration Centre within this period.

To be accepted, you must prove that you have a successful business or managerial background, and that you have sufficient funds to set up a business and support yourself and your dependants for a reasonable time. There's no specific amount laid down for this, but you should have at least $250,000 of transferable funds and expect to invest at least $100,000 of this in your business. It's best to seek help from established Canadian organisations rather than rely on members of your own ethnic group when you arrive. It isn't uncommon for unscrupulous members of ethnic communities to take advantage of newcomers who rush into business without allowing sufficient time to familiarise themselves with local conditions. You should start by approaching the Economic Development Department in the province where you plan to settle, which provides information, seminars and counselling services for business migrants.

Financial assistance can be obtained from the Federal Business Development Bank (☎ 1-877-BDC-BANX), a government agency formed to assist small businesses. The Ministry of Canadian Heritage publishes a directory, *Multiculturalism Means Business*, that lists ethno-cultural organisations devoted to business. *Report on Business* magazine published a report in 1995 that identified five Canadian cities (St John, New Brunswick; Lethbridge, Alberta; Winnipeg, Manitoba; Ottawa-Carleton, Ontario; and Missassauga, Ontario) as 'the best in which to do business'. Criteria included a dedicated, trainable workforce, low labour costs and taxation, easy access to markets through good transportation routes, universities with top research programmes, and a pro-business attitude.

Investor

This category requires you to make a substantial passive investment to a Canadian business in which you won't be actively involved. This doesn't mean that you can invest your money in any business you choose and you must invest in a fund administered by an approved body (usually one of the provincial governments). This often means a venture capital fund. The minimum investment is $400,000 for a minimum period of five years, which must be made before you apply for a visa and you must meet the usual immigrant requirements. In addition, you must prove that you've successfully operated, controlled or directed a commercial undertaking or business and have amassed (not inherited) a minimum net worth of $800,000. It's wise to seek the assistance of an immigration attorney or consultant when applying in this category.

Self-Employed

Few people are considered under the self-employed category and most should apply under the business entrepreneur category. The criteria for this category is that you buy or set up a small business that creates employment for yourself and makes a significant contribution to the economy or the cultural or artistic life of the country. Successful artists, musicians, writers or sports personalities are favourably considered in this category. You aren't required to make a specified minimum investment, but must be able to satisfy immigration officials that you have enough money to set up your business and maintain yourself and your dependants.

Forms & Documentation

Application forms are available in most countries from the Immigration Division of a Canadian High Commission, embassy or consulate. You can write, phone or call at these offices to obtain a set of forms and also to check your occupation for eligibility. You're issued with a complete set of forms, a comprehensive guide to completing them, a form for requesting a police clearance certificate and a list of approved doctors for the medical examination. You can photocopy the forms if you need extra copies for your spouse and dependants. You must submit a form for each of your dependent children (i.e. those aged under 22 and unmarried), even though they may not intend to accompany you at this stage (the assumption is that they may decide to follow you later). You don't pay a fee for non-accompanying dependants at this stage.

When completing the forms, bear in mind that you're more likely to be refused a visa if you're discovered to have lied than if your circumstances aren't perfect. On the same premise, you may be refused entry when you arrive in Canada if any of your circumstances (such as getting married or divorced or having additional children) have changed since you applied. The immigration authorities don't mind these changes, but they do mind you concealing them.

You need to provide proof of your identity, marital status, education and employment through documents such as your passport, marriage or divorce papers, birth certificates for all family members, military records, examination passes and professional memberships, and a record of employment. You shouldn't send the originals of these with the application forms, but send photocopies instead. However, you should be prepared to produce the originals if requested. If there's insufficient space on the forms to provide full details of the information required, you should attach separate sheets of paper. This applies particularly to information about you and your spouse's occupations, as the more detail you give the easier it is for the immigration officials to compare these against the thousands of occupations listed in the 'Canadian Classification and Dictionary of Occupations' (CCDO). Of the 70 points you need for acceptance, up to 28 may come from your occupation.

Fees

Applicants are required to pay 'visa processing' and 'right of permanent residence' fees when they lodge their visa applications. The following fees were correct at the time of publication, although they change frequently:

- Principal applicant who's an independent skilled worker – $475; investor, entrepreneur or a self-employed person – $1,050.

- Accompanying spouse and each accompanying dependant aged 22 or over on the date of application – $550.

- Accompanying dependants aged under 22 on the date of application – $150.

- In addition to the above, all applicants (except dependants under 22 on the date of the application) must pay a 'right of permanent residence' fee of $975.

If non-accompanying dependants change their mind and decide to join you, their fees must be paid at that time. Refunds of visa fees aren't made should someone decide not to go, but the right of permanent residence fee is refundable for someone who decides against immigration or whose application is refused. All fees are payable when an application is submitted and must be made by banker's draft or cashier's cheque (personal cheques aren't accepted). Some immigration offices accept cash (check in advance), when you should take your application to the office in person and obtain a receipt. Fees should generally be paid in Canadian dollars, although some offices may accept local currency (check in advance and inquire what the procedure is regarding the exchange rate).

Points System

Immigration into Canada is decided on a points system, whereby points are awarded for various categories (listed below). It's advisable to make a self-assessment before completing the forms, as if you fall well short of the required 70 points you may need to re-think your application category or hire a professional attorney or consultant. Self-Assessment Guides (SAG) are available for independent/skilled workers and business applicants from immigration offices in most countries. Points are awarded as follows:

- **Occupation** – Maximum ten points, with a minimum of one point necessary. You need to consult the CCDO to identify your occupation.

- **Specific Vocational Preparation** – Maximum 18 points with a minimum of two points necessary. Points relate to the amount of training you've had in your trade or profession. Consult the CCDO or extracts for information.

- **Age** – The maximum of ten points is awarded to those aged between 21 and 44 years, above which two points are deducted for each year until you reach age 49 or older, when you receive no points. At age 18 you receive four points, at 19 six points and at age 20, eight points.

- **Education** – Maximum 16 points. This is calculated on a rising scale, where you receive no points if you haven't completed secondary school and 16 points for a post-graduate degree.

- **Pre-Arranged Employment** — Maximum ten points. You must prove that you have a job arranged in Canada and that the employer has official approval for employing you rather than an unemployed Canadian citizen or immigrant visa holder. The prospective employer must contact his nearest Human Resource Centre and complete form EMP5056. The process of obtaining approval can take several weeks and few employers bother to go through it unless they really need you.

- **Work Experience** — Maximum eight points. Points are awarded for the number of years experience you have in your trade or profession.

- **Demographic Factor** — Maximum eight points. Points are awarded by immigration officials to limit or boost the number of immigrants from a particular country or region.

- **Language Ability** — Maximum 15 points. To obtain the maximum number of points you must be able to speak, read and write both English and French fluently, i.e. without requiring language tuition after your arrival. If you're fluent in one language only you receive nine points, otherwise you receive two points for speaking, reading and writing respectively, provided that you can demonstrate that you're capable, or one point if you can cope with a few words only.

- **Personal Suitability** — Maximum ten points. Points are awarded by an immigration officer, usually after an interview, based on his judgement of how well he thinks you will adapt to living in Canada and integrate into the community. The average applicant is awarded between five and seven points.

- **Relatives In Canada** — Five bonus points are available if you have a relative closer than a cousin who's already living in Canada and who's willing to declare that he will help you to settle in.

Priority System

Immigration officials deal with visa applications under a priority system in the following sequence:

1. Sponsored applications for husbands, wives, children under 22 and orphans.
2. Applicants with a job offer in Canada validated by a Human Resource Centre.
3. Entrepreneurs, investors and self-employed people.
4. Qualified people willing to work in designated occupations.
5. Sponsored applications for parents and grandparents and all other sponsored applicants that don't come under category 1.
6. All others including independent applications from those who will be seeking work in Canada on their arrival.

Interviews

An interview isn't always necessary and if you're called for one you shouldn't assume that it means you're going to be turned down (immigration officials are far too busy to be bothered with applications that they feel must be refused). The main purpose of an interview is to decide how many points to award under the personal suitability and language categories, and even then only if your points total is marginal. Your spouse and dependent children must attend the interview with you and although interviews are informal, you must be able to demonstrate a mature approach to immigration. You should expect to be asked about your education and your current job, as well as how you intend to find somewhere to live, find a job, educate your children and other matters. It helps to mention that you've made contingency plans in case it takes longer than expected to find a job and also that you've been reading Canadian newspapers and books on the Canadian way of life. You may be tested on your language ability if neither English or French is your mother tongue. You should take with you the originals of all your supporting documents (e.g. passport, education certificates, job references, etc.) and evidence of your financial situation (e.g. bank statements).

QUEBEC

The procedure for applying to immigrate to Quebec is much the same as for the rest of Canada, with a few differences. You begin the process by obtaining a preliminary questionnaire from the Quebec Immigration Service (☎ 514-864-9191, 🖳 www.immigration-quebec.gouv.qc.ca/anglais/index.html), which has offices in certain countries such as Belgium and France. Provided that your replies to the preliminary questionnaire are satisfactory, you're sent a second, more detailed, questionnaire. If your answers to this are also satisfactory, you're invited to an interview during which, among other things, you need to show that you're deeply interested in Quebec, its history and culture. If that's satisfactory you're given a *Certificat de Sélection de Québec* and accepted into the normal processing system and must complete the usual legal and medical requirements. No fees are payable until you've obtained this certificate and join the normal system. This process takes at least six months and sometimes as long as a year. Immigrating to Quebec costs more than it does to other parts of Canada because, in addition to the regular federal immigration fees, those applying under the Quebec system are required to pay extra processing fees for the *Certificat de Sélection de Québec*, as follows:

- **Independent/Skilled Worker:** $300 (principal applicant) and $100 per accompanying person.
- **Entrepreneur and Self-Employed:** $700 (principal applicant) and $100 per accompanying person.
- **Investor:** $850 (principal applicant) and $100 per accompanying person.

A points system is designed for those seeking employment or business opportunities in the province of Quebec. For employed status you require 60 points and for entrepreneur, investor or self-employed status 50 points. Entrepreneurs and investors are awarded a bonus of 25 points and the self-employed a bonus of 20 points. Points are gained as follows:

- **Education** — A maximum of 11 points are awarded, one for each completed year of primary and secondary school.
- **Specific Vocational Training** — A maximum of 19 points are awarded.
- **Adaptability** — A maximum of 22 points can be awarded of which 15 are for personal skills, five for motivation and two for your knowledge of Quebec. A minimum of 15 points is required from this category.
- **Occupational Demand** — A maximum of 15 points are awarded.
- **Experience In Occupation** — A maximum of 10 points are awarded.
- **Age** — Up to the age of 35 years you receive ten points, at age 36 nine points, at 37 six points, at 39 two points and at age 40, one point.
- **Spouse** — If your spouse has a desirable occupation, four points are awarded.
- **Children** — One point for one child, two points for two children and four points for three or more children.
- **Relative Or Close Friend In Quebec** — Five points are awarded if you have a relative or close friend in the 'immediate area' where you plan to settle and two points for elsewhere in Quebec.
- **Language** — You receive up to 15 points for French, of which six are for understanding, five for speaking, three for reading and one for writing. You receive an additional five more points if your spouse has fluent French. You also receive a maximum of two points for English.

Investors: Investors planning to invest in Quebec must arrange their investment through a broker in the province.

Entrepreneurs: Entrepreneurs are welcomed by Quebec but must have a knowledge of the province gained through a preliminary visit, at least three years' business experience, of which at least one must have been in a management capacity, produce a detailed business plan, and intend to employ at least three Quebec residents.

Self-Employed: Self-employed applicants need to have experience, at least $250,000 and a good knowledge of Quebec. Special consideration is given to those who will make a positive contribution to the artistic and cultural development of the province.

Unless you speak and understand a fairly good amount of French, you shouldn't think about settling in Quebec. Most business and governmental affairs in the province are conducted in French and many *Québécois* refuse to speak any other language, particularly when they think you speak just English. You certainly need to be bilingual if you hope to obtain a job in government or public service, and some private companies hire only bilingual applicants. Your children must attend a French-language school. However, you're free to relocate elsewhere in Canada after you've settled in Quebec.

NON-IMMIGRANT VISAS

Visitor Visas

In the words of its brochures, 'Canada welcomes visitors to share its unique history, culture and magnificent scenery'. A visitor is defined as 'a person who enters Canada for a temporary purpose, such as a tourist', but he must still be of good health and have no (major) criminal convictions. You must also have documentary evidence to prove that you're able to return home. The immigration officer at your port of entry will want to see either a return ticket or a ticket for onward travel.

Citizens of the following countries don't require a visa to visit Canada: Andorra, Antigua and Barbuda, Australia, Austria, Bahamas, Barbados, Belgium, Botswana, Brunei, Costa Rica, Cyprus, Denmark, Dominica, Finland, France, Germany, Greece, Grenada, Hong Kong, Hungary, Iceland, Ireland, Israel (blue passports), Italy, Japan, Kiribati, Liechtenstein, Luxembourg, Malaysia, Malta, Mexico, Monaco, Namibia, Nauru, the Netherlands, New Zealand, Norway, Papua New Guinea, Portugal, St. Kitts and Nevis, St. Lucia, St. Vincent, San Marino, Saudi Arabia, Singapore, Slovenia, Solomon Islands, South Korea, Spain, Swaziland, Sweden, Switzerland, Tuvalu, United Kingdom, US, Vanuatu, the Vatican, Western Samoa and Zimbabwe.

To enter Canada as a visitor, whether or not you require a visa, you need to have the following:

- A passport valid for the length of your stay;
- Sufficient money to support yourself and your dependants during your stay;
- Private medical insurance for the duration of your stay.

As a visitor, in addition to the above you also need to be aware of the following:

- You must only be in Canada for a temporary period only;
- You must not work while you're in Canada.

Some nationals require a visitor visa, even when they're in transit to somewhere outside Canada. Application forms for visitor visas are available from Canadian High Commissions, embassies and consulates abroad. The completed form must be returned with two passport-size photographs, a passport valid for the length of your stay, evidence of your immigration status in your country of residence (if it isn't the country of your birth), details of your travel plans, proof of funds available for your visit and evidence that you're employed. All documentation must be in English or French or be accompanied by a certified translation into either of these languages.

The processing fee for visitor visas is $75 (single entry) or $150 (multiple entry) per person, up to a maximum of $400 per family. Fees must be submitted with the completed application form and be in the form of a banker's draft in Canadian dollars drawn on a bank in Canada (and which will clear there). The draft must be made payable to The Receiver General for Canada.

In some countries, applications can be submitted in person to the immigration section of a Canadian High Commission, embassy or consulate, and a visa issued while you wait. Applications are processed on a first come, first served basis, therefore it's wise to arrive early (check opening times in advance). Routine applications submitted by post or courier should take six working days to process. On the rare occasion when an interview is necessary, you receive notification within six working days. It's recommended that postal applications are sent by registered post and that the self-addressed return envelope is also registered. Applications may be submitted by private courier, in which case the courier should be paid in advance for the return of your documents.

Student Authorisation

If you're attending an English or French-language course of no more than six months' duration, you don't require student authorisation. For longer courses you must complete an application form to apply for student authorisation and require the following:

- A letter of acceptance from the educational institution in Canada at which you plan to pursue a full-time course of study. This should provide details of the course title, its duration, level of study, tuition fees and the start date.

- A passport valid for the duration of your study period and two additional passport-size photographs of yourself and any accompanying family members.

- Evidence of sufficient funds to cover your tuition fees, living expenses and return transportation costs. This should be either a copy of your most recent bank statement or a letter from your parents stating that they will be financially responsible for you during your stay in Canada. General letters of reference from your bank aren't sufficient. The minimum requirement is $10,000 per year and more is required if your spouse and/or children accompany you ($40,000 for a family).

- Medical insurance to cover the duration of your study period.

Students under 18 years of age who won't be accompanied by a parent require a custodian in Canada and you must supply proof in the form of notarised declarations (one signed by the parent or legal guardian in the country of origin, the other by the custodian in Canada) stating that arrangements have been made for the custodian to act in place of a parent in emergencies.

The student authorisation processing fee is $125, which must be submitted with the completed application form by bankers draft in Canadian dollars drawn on a bank in Canada (and which will clear there). The draft must be made payable to The Receiver General for Canada. Correctly completed student authorisation applications take up to four weeks to process. Unless you're a citizen of one of the countries that don't require a visitor visa (see page 79), you require a visa as well as student authorisation. An accompanying spouse and children may also need visitor visas and must pay the appropriate fees.

You may need to pass an immigration medical or attend an interview. If you intend to study in Quebec, you also require a *Certificat d'acceptance du Québec* from Quebec immigration before you arrive in Canada. The educational institution in Quebec can advise you how to obtain this certificate.

The spouses of authorised students are eligible for an open work permit (unless they're full-time students), which can be obtained after arrival. Children of authorised students are also eligible for open student authorisation to enable them to study at primary or secondary school for the duration of their parent's study. You must return to your home country after completing your studies.

Work Permits

You may not work permanently in Canada unless you have permanent resident status or are a Canadian citizen. In order to do temporary work in Canada, you must have a valid work permit (employment authorisation) that must be obtained from a visa office before you enter the country. Before applying, you require a job offer from an employer who has obtained the necessary validation from a Human Resource Centre by demonstrating that there are no unemployed Canadian citizens or immigrant visa holders available to take the job. You cannot obtain a work permit for a job if you're already in Canada. There are some exceptions to the requirement for jobs to be validated (although they still require a work permit), which include the following:

- Senior managers or executives planning to enter as inter-company transferees;
- Exchange teachers or professors or post-doctoral fellows;
- Engineers or technicians going to supervise the installation of equipment sold by their company to a Canadian purchaser or going to repair or service such equipment;
- Volunteers who have been offered work with a registered Canadian religious or charitable organisation;
- Film crews planning to film documentaries or travelogues in Canada;
- Some musicians or performers with a contract to perform in Canada.

Unless you're a citizen of one of the countries that doesn't require a visitor visa, you also require a visa in addition to a work permit. In any case, you must return to your own country after completing your temporary work. To apply for a work permit you must complete an application form and have the following:

- A letter offering temporary employment in Canada and a copy of the form that your prospective employer has had validated at a Human Resource Centre.

- Evidence of your qualifications to do the job being offered. This could be a copy of your degree or other diplomas, trade qualification papers or a letter from your present or recent employers.

- A passport that's valid for the duration of your work period and two additional passport-size photographs of yourself and any accompanying family members.

- Medical insurance to cover the duration of your work period.

The processing fee for a work permit is $150 and must be submitted with the completed application form by banker's draft in Canadian dollars drawn on a bank in Canada (and which will clear there). The draft must be made payable to The Receiver General for Canada. An accompanying spouse and children may need visitor visas and must pay the appropriate fee for these. Groups of 4 to 15 performing artists pay a maximum group fee of $450. You may need to pass an immigration medical or attend an interview. Correctly completed work permit applications take from four to six weeks to process between May to September and two to four weeks during the rest of the year.

The spouse of an authorised employee may apply for a work permit after his arrival in Canada, but must obtain a validated job offer before applying or meet one of the exemption categories listed above. The children of an authorised employee are also eligible for open student authorisation to enable them to study at primary or secondary school in Canada for the duration of their parent's employment. There are a number of people that don't require a work permit, including the following:

- Accredited diplomats, consular officers, representatives and officials of foreign countries, and employees of the United Nations or any of its agencies, inter-governmental organisations (in which Canada participates), plus members of staff of any of the foregoing.

- Members of the armed forces of a country that's a designated state for the purposes of The Visiting Forces Act, including those who are designated as civilian components of a visiting force.

- Clergymen, members of religious orders or lay people visiting Canada to assist congregations or groups in their spiritual goals, where the duties consist of preaching, presiding at liturgical functions or spiritual counselling.

- Performing artists, members of the staff of such artists or groups of artists, where the whole group numbers not less than 15 people.

- Members of the crew of ships or aircraft of non-Canadian ownership engaged predominantly in the international transportation of goods or passengers.

- Employees of non-Canadian news companies visiting Canada for the purpose of reporting on Canadian events.

- Representatives of businesses carrying on activities outside Canada or representatives of foreign governments visiting Canada for the purpose of purchasing Canadian goods or services (including inspection of the quality of the goods and training, or familiarisation with the goods or services purchased). Representatives selling goods and services in Canada, provided that selling isn't to the general public.

- People entering Canada to provide emergency medical or other services for the preservation of life or property.

- People who are members of a non-Canadian-based sports team or individuals who are visiting Canada to engage or assist in sports activities or events. This includes judges, referees and other officials in international sports events organised by an international amateur sports association and hosted by a Canadian organisation.

- Judges at animal show competitions.

- External examiners of degree-level theses or projects.

- Guest speakers entering Canada for the sole purpose of making a speech or delivering a paper at a dinner, graduation, convention or similar function.

- Expert witnesses entering Canada for the sole purpose of testifying in proceedings before a court, tribunal or regulatory board.

- Permanently employed personal servants entering Canada for a period of less than 90 days to perform their regular duties with their employer, during the employer's sojourn in Canada.

- Officers of foreign governments sent by that government to take up duties with a federal or provincial agency pursuant to an exchange agreement with the Canadian government.

- Medical electives or clinical clerks at a Canadian medical teaching institution to observe clinical or medical procedures.

- Trainees of Canadian parent or subsidiary corporations, where the trainee won't be actively engaged in the production of goods or services.

- Executives of the organising committee of a convention or meeting, or members of the administrative support staff of such a committee who are permanently employed by the organisation staging the convention or meeting.

- People exempted by the Canadian-United States Free Trade Agreement Implementation Act.
- People who hold student authorisation and during the period of full-time study are employed on the campus of their university or college.

Work Programmes for Students

Canada has a number of student work programmes for citizens of the UK, Ireland, Sweden and Finland. To qualify you must be a full-time student at a university or similar recognised post-secondary institution in your country of citizenship, be aged between 18 and 30, and provide an unconditional letter of acceptance or a letter confirming that you've recently graduated.

UK & Ireland: Two programmes are currently available. *Programme A* is a student general working holiday (vacation) programme. Students must obtain a written job offer from a Canadian employer stating the salary, period of employment, type of work involved and that the employment is full-time. If the job is an unpaid traineeship, you must provide proof of sufficient funds to cover the work period. You must also provide written confirmation of your return to studies at the end of the period of employment in Canada. You won't normally require a medical examination unless the employment is in health services, child care or a related occupation. No fee is payable for authorisation. The number of places on this programme is limited and applications are dealt with on a first come, first served basis. *Programme B* is operated in conjunction with the British Universities North American Club (BUNAC) and Union of Students in Ireland Travel (USIT). An offer of employment isn't required under this programme, but you must provide evidence of $1,000 to take with you ($600 if you have a relative in Canada) and evidence of return transportation home. In the UK you should contact BUNAC, 16 Bowling Green Lane, London EC1R 0BD (☎ +44 (2)07-251 3472, 🖳 www.bunac.org/uk/) and in Ireland contact USIT, 19-21 Aston Quay, O'Connell Bridge, Dublin 2 (☎ +353-1-602-1600, 🖳 www.usitnow.ie).

Finland & Sweden: For information regarding Finland you should contact CIMO, PO Box 343, Hakaniemenkatu 2, SF 00531 Helsinki (☎ +358-9-7747-7033). In Sweden, only the general working holiday programme is available and places are limited, so you should apply early. For details contact the International Employment Office, Box 7763, S-103 96 Stockholm (☎ +46-8-4065700). There's no student working programme for Denmark or Norway.

4.

ARRIVAL

On arrival in Canada your first task is to get through immigration and customs. Fortunately this presents few problems for most people. If you're a US citizen or permanent US resident you don't require a passport or visa to enter Canada, but you should carry identification papers that establish your status (if not a passport, your driver's licence or an ID card with your photograph, or if you're a naturalised US citizen, your naturalisation certificate). Permanent residents should carry their green card. You will find that US dollars are perfectly acceptable in most Canadian shops, hotels or restaurants. With the exception of certain visitors, most people wishing to enter Canada require a passport with a visa (see **Chapter 3** for information). **If you stop in Canada in transit to another country, you may be required to go through Canadian immigration and customs at your first port of entry.**

It's wise to obtain some Canadian dollars before arriving in Canada, as this saves you having to change money on arrival. You may find it more convenient to arrive on a weekday rather than during the weekend, when offices, banks and stores may be closed. In addition to information about immigration and customs, this chapter also contains a list of tasks that must be completed before or soon after arrival in Canada, and includes suggestions for finding local help and information.

ARRIVAL/DEPARTURE RECORD

Before you arrive in Canada by air or sea, the airline or shipping company gives you a landing card (officially called a 'traveller declaration card') to complete. You must complete it in pen in block capitals and in English or French. If you don't have an address in Canada, it's often wise to enter the name of a hotel in an area or city where you're heading or write 'touring', rather than leave it blank. If you enter Canada by road from the US there's no form to complete, but you're questioned as to where you've come from, your destination in Canada, how long you're planning to stay and whether you have anything to declare.

Many non-immigrant visas are of the multiple-entry kind that allow you to enter and leave Canada as often as you wish during its validation period. However, the period that you're allowed to remain also depends on the expiration date of your passport. If you have a valid multiple-entry, non-immigrant visa and obtain a new passport, retain your old passport and take it with you when travelling to Canada, as the visa remains valid. You must *never* remove a visa from your old passport, as this invalidates it.

IMMIGRATION

When you arrive in Canada, the first thing you need to do is go through Canadian Immigration. This is divided into two sections, 'Canadian Residents' and 'Non-Residents'; make sure you join the correct line. Canadian immigration officials are usually friendly and polite, but if you encounter one who isn't, you should remain polite and answer any questions in a direct and courteous manner, however personal or irrelevant you may think they are. It never pays to antagonise immigration officials, e.g. by questioning the relevance of certain questions.

Although they're nowhere near as aggressive as their counterparts in the US, Canadian immigration officials are trained to suspect that anyone who doesn't have the right to live and work in Canada could be a potential illegal immigrant. Nationals of some countries may be singled out for 'special treatment', e.g. people from a country that's hostile towards Canada or which has a reputation for illegal immigrants. It's an unfortunate fact of life that some immigration officials (like some people) are prejudiced against certain groups. Immigration officers have the task of deciding whether you're permitted to enter Canada and have the necessary documentation, including a visa if required. Present the following to the immigration officer, as applicable:

- your passport (plus an old passport if it contains an unexpired visa);
- your completed 'traveller declaration card';
- evidence of private medical insurance to cover the duration of your stay;
- evidence that you have sufficient money to support yourself and your family for the duration of your stay.

You should also have any documents or letters to hand that support your reason for visiting Canada. After entering Canada with an immigrant visa, your passport is stamped to show that you're a permanent resident. You're permitted to travel abroad and re-enter Canada by showing this passport stamp until you become a Canadian citizen (see page 378). If you enter Canada from certain countries, you may be required to have an immunisation certificate. Check the requirements in advance at a Canadian High Commission, embassy or consulate before travelling. An immigration officer can decide to send you for a routine health check before allowing you to enter Canada.

Clearing immigration during a busy period can take a number of hours, so it's advisable to be prepared and take a book. Among the most notorious entry points for delays are Toronto and Vancouver airports. Immigration lines are shorter at smaller airports, although you may have little choice of entry point.

CUSTOMS

If you travel to Canada by air or sea, you're given a *Customs Declaration* form to complete by the airline or shipping line. Hand the completed form to the customs officer at your port or frontier of entry. The head of a family may make a joint declaration for all members residing in the same household and travelling together. There are no restrictions on the amount of money you may take into Canada, in either Canadian or foreign currency (or take out when you leave).

Canadian ports and international airports operate a system of red and green 'channels' as is common in Europe. Red means you have something to declare and green means that you have nothing to declare (i.e. no more than the customs allowances, no goods to sell, and no prohibited or restricted goods). If you're certain you have nothing to declare, go through the 'green channel', otherwise go through the red channel. Even when you go through the green channel you may be stopped, your customs declaration form inspected and you may be asked to open your bags. **There are stiff penalties for smuggling.**

A list of items you're bringing in is useful for short-stay visitors and essential for long-stay visitors or migrants, although the customs officer may still want to examine your bags. If you're required to pay duty, it must be paid at the time goods are brought into the country. Import duty may be paid:

- in cash in Canadian dollars only;
- by Canadian dollar travellers' cheques;
- if you have the proper identification, by personal cheque for amounts of $500 or less, drawn on a bank in Canada and made payable to 'Canada Customs and Revenue Agency';
- with major credit cards, e.g. MasterCard and Visa.

If you're unable to pay on the spot, customs keep your belongings until you pay the sum due. This must be paid within a certain period, noted on the back of your receipt. Postage or freight charges must be paid if you want your belongings sent on to you.

If you're discovered trying to smuggle goods into Canada, customs may confiscate them, and if you hide them in a vehicle, boat or plane, they can confiscate that also! If you attempt to import prohibited items, you may also be liable to criminal charges or deportation. If you have any questions regarding the importation of anything into Canada, contact the customs representative at a Canadian High Commission, embassy or consulate. For information about personal exemptions, see **Duty-Free Allowances** on page 372. Temporary visitors driving across the Canadian border from the US should be aware that although you don't need to pay any import duty on the vehicle, you may not lend it to a Canadian while you're there, unless it's to share the driving on a long trip.

Canada Customs and Revenue Agency publishes various brochures, including *I Declare* and *Settling in Canada*, that are available from Canada Customs and Revenue Agency, Connaught Building, 2nd Floor, McKenzie Avenue, Ottawa, ON K1A 0L5 (☎ 613-957-0251).

Permanent & Temporary Residents

When you enter Canada to take up permanent or temporary residence, you can usually import your personal belongings duty and tax free. This applies to one shipment only and you cannot go back to your country of origin and bring or ship in another load of duty-free belongings. Any duty or tax payable depends on where you've come from, where you purchased the goods, how long you've owned them, and whether duty and tax has already been paid in another country. The requirement is that goods should have been 'owned, possessed and used' (if they haven't been used, you may need to pay duty unless they're wedding gifts for a wedding within three months after your arrival) before your arrival in Canada and it's advisable to have sales receipts and registration documents.

Items defined as 'personal and household effects' include antiques and family heirlooms, appliances, boats and their trailers, books, furniture, furnishings and linen, hobby tools and other hobby items, jewellery, musical instruments, private collections of coins, stamps or art, silverware, private aircraft, and holiday (vacation) trailers (but not trailers for permanent residence). They also include vehicles, provided that they will be used for non-commercial purposes only.

If you're coming to live in Canada and are sending your household goods unaccompanied, you must provide customs with a detailed list of everything brought into the country and its value. Items of high individual value, such as works of art, antiques or jewellery, should have a recent valuation certificate. A person emigrating to Canada may bring professional equipment such as books, tools of trade, occupation or employment. Canadian High Commissions, embassies and consulates provide a free information package and sample inventory list.

You must produce two copies (preferably typed) of a list of the goods you plan to bring in as settler's effects, showing their value, make, model and serial number (where applicable). Keep another copy for yourself. This list should be divided into two parts: one marked 'Annexe A, Goods in Possession' (those that you have with you) and the other marked 'Annexe B, Goods to Follow'. The customs officer completes form B4, *Personal Effects Accounting Document*, based on the list that you provide, and gives the form a file number and a receipt copy that you must produce when you collect any unaccompanied goods.

You will be asked by customs officials whether you packed the goods yourself or had them packed for you and whether anyone else may have had access to them since they were packed. Where relevant, removal companies provide documentation certifying that your goods were sealed by them, but you should be aware that if you admit that anyone other than a removal company packed or had access to your belongings, they will be subject to a full customs inspection for which you must pay. Copies of form B4 can be obtained from customs offices and completed in advance to speed up the process. It's unnecessary to employ a broker or agent to clear your belongings through customs, as you can do this yourself after you arrive in Canada or you can authorise someone to represent you.

There's no time limit on receiving 'goods to follow', but you must collect them up to 40 days after the completion of form B4 (see above). This means that you can tell the carrier to hold shipment until you've arranged permanent accommodation for it and know where you want the goods sent; they're held in bond until you produce the forms to clear them. Imported goods mustn't be sold, lent, rented or otherwise disposed of in Canada within one year of their importation or of your arrival (whichever is later) without customs authorisation.

Seasonal Residents

If you're a non-resident of Canada and inherit, receive, buy or rent (on a minimum three-year lease) a permanent structure in Canada for use as a seasonal residence, you may claim certain items as duty-free imports for the purpose of furnishing that residence. Portable or mobile homes don't qualify for these exemptions, nor do certain 'construction' items such as electrical or plumbing fixtures, windows, doors and other items designed for permanent fixture to a building.

Visitors

If you're a visitor, you can bring your personal belongings to Canada free of duty and tax without declaring them to customs provided that:

- they're brought in with you and are for your personal use only;
- they're kept in Canada for no longer than six months in a 12-month period;
- you don't sell, lend, rent or otherwise dispose of them in Canada;
- they're exported either when you leave Canada or before they've been in Canada for more than six months, whichever occurs first.

Returning Residents

If you're a Canadian resident returning from abroad, you must complete form E24, *Returning Persons Declaration*, on which you declare articles acquired abroad and in your possession at the time of your return, including:

- articles that you've purchased abroad;
- any gifts that were given to you while abroad, including wedding or birthday presents;
- articles purchased in duty-free stores;
- repairs or alterations made to any articles taken abroad and returned;
- items you're bringing into Canada for another person;
- goods you intend to sell or use in your business.

Returning residents may bring into Canada personal belongings of Canadian origin free of duty without proof, provided that they're clearly marked as made in Canada (they will be labelled in both English and French). Foreign-made personal articles taken abroad are dutiable when they're brought into Canada, unless you have proof of prior possession, such as a receipt of purchase. Items such as watches, cameras, tape recorders, computers and other articles that can be readily identified by a serial number or permanent markings, can be registered with customs before leaving Canada. Customs officers list your valuables and their serial numbers on a wallet-sized card, *Identification of Articles for Temporary Exportation* (form Y38), provided that you show them to a customs officer and attest that you acquired them in Canada or lawfully imported them. They won't register jewellery on this form and suggest that you carry an appraisal report with a signed and dated photograph of each item together with the bill of sale and, if relevant, proof that duty has been paid. If you take an item of jewellery out of Canada and change it in a way that increases its value, it's no longer considered the same item and duty must be paid on it. (The same applies to motor vehicles.)

Household effects and tools of a trade or occupation taken out of Canada are allowed in duty-free when you return, provided that they're properly declared and registered. All furniture, carpets, paintings, tableware, linens and similar household furnishings acquired abroad may be imported free of duty, provided that they've been used abroad by you for not less than one year, or were available for use in a household where you were resident for one year. The year of use needn't be continuous nor does it need to be the year immediately preceding the date of importation. Items such as clothes, jewellery, photographic equipment, tape recorders, stereo components and vehicles are considered to be personal articles, and cannot be imported free of duty as household effects. The exemption doesn't include articles placed in storage outside the home or articles imported for another person or for sale.

Drugs & Syringes

If you have any prescription drugs they should be clearly identified and carried in the original packaging with a label stating what they are and that they're being used under prescription. It's advisable also to carry a copy of your prescription and the phone number of your doctor. Diabetics and others who need to bring syringes with them should also carry some evidence of their medical condition. Even if you feel you have no need to declare these items and have nothing else to declare, it's advisable to go through the red channel and declare them to customs officials.

Restricted Goods

Some items may not be imported into Canada or are subject to restrictions, including the following:

- All weapons must be registered when they arrive in Canada. Restricted items are: modified weapons of any kind, semi-automatic and automatic weapons (although some semi-automatic weapons with short barrels are allowed), sawn-off guns and rifles, switchblades, some martial arts weapons, mace and pepper spray (pepper spray isn't actually illegal, but it's illegal to bring it into the country), blowguns, crossbows, replica firearms and replacement ammunition magazines. Be warned that if you include firearms of any sort in your household effects, the whole shipment is likely to be held for inspection on arrival. For more information, contact the Security Programmes Division, 2881 Nanaimo Street, Victoria BC V8V 1X4 (☎ 1-800-731-4000 ext. 119501) and obtain a copy of the brochure *Importing a Firearm or Weapon into Canada*.

- Explosives, ammunition and fireworks all require authorisation and permits. For more details contact the Chief Inspector of Explosives Division, Natural Resources Canada, 580 Booth Street, 15th Floor, Ottawa ON K1A 0E4 (☎ 613-995-8415).

- Automobiles, motorcycles and boats are all permissible import items, but vehicles must conform to regulations on safety standards and emissions, and must bear a compliance label to that effect. For full details contact the Road Safety and Motor Vehicles Directorate, Transport Canada, 330 Sparks Street, Tower C, Place de Ville, Ottawa ON K1A 0N5 (☎ 613-990 2309).

- Goods subject to import controls such as certain clothing, handbags and textiles. For more information contact the Export and Import Permits Bureau, Department of Foreign Affairs and International Trade, PO Box 481, Station 'A', Ottawa L1A 0G2 (☎ 613-996-3711, 🖳 www.dfait-maeci.gc.ca).

- Meat, dairy products, and fresh fruit and vegetables. Certain food items may be imported from the US, although the limits are low (usually around two days' worth of edibles).

- Agricultural and horticultural products, including seeds, fertilisers, pest control products and plants (see also endangered species below).

- Some animals and plants that are classified as endangered species may not be imported dead or alive, nor any product made from their fur, feathers, skin or bone (not to mention internal organs sold in some countries as medicine).

- You're allowed to take your domestic pets into Canada with you, but they must be accompanied by a certificate of good health. Dogs and cats require proof of vaccination against rabies. For details applying to your own country of origin, the best place to start is with organisations that specialise in shipping animals abroad. See also **Pets** on page 390.

- Although they aren't restricted, video cassettes can arouse suspicion in customs officials, who may think they contain pornographic material.

Even if you have a permit, all restricted goods must be declared and presented to a customs officer.

FINDING HELP

One of the biggest difficulties facing new arrivals in any country is how and where to obtain help with day-to-day problems, e.g. finding a home, schools, insurance requirements and so on. This book was written in response to that need (and also because the author needs to earn a living!).However, in addition to the comprehensive information provided in this book, you also require detailed *local* information. **Although the general principles of the law and many other aspects of daily life in Canada are more or less the same throughout the country, each province has its own laws and ways of doing things.**

Migrants who don't have a job or relatives in Canada may wish to be met on arrival by a friendly face and there are number of organisations and individuals who perform this service for a fee, some of which advertise in publications such as *Canada News* (see page 420) in the UK. Another option is a volunteer-run organisation called the 'Host Program' that's funded by Citizenship and Immigration Canada to provide friendship to new immigrants. Volunteers are carefully matched to immigrants and share their time and friendship during their critical first few months, helping with banking, grocery shopping, finding services, schools, and showing newcomers how to use the transit systems and unfamiliar household appliances. You can contact the local host programme via the following addresses:

Alberta: Calgary Catholic Immigration, 3rd Floor, 120–17 Avenue SW, Calgary AB T2S 2T2 (☎ 403-262-2006, 🖳 www.ccis-calgary.ab.ca).

British Columbia: Immigrant Services Society, # 501, 333 Terminal Avenue, Vancouver BC V6A 2L7 (☎ 604-684-2561, 🖳 www.issbc.org).

Manitoba: Citizenship Council of Manitoba, 2nd Floor, 406 Edmonton Street, Winnipeg MB R3B 2M2 (☎ 204-943-9158).

Newfoundland: Association for New Canadians, PO Box 2031, St John's NFA1C 5R6.

Nova Scotia: Metropolitan Immigration Settlement Association, Suite 200, 2131 Goltingen St, Halifax NS B3K 5Z7 (☎ 902-423-3607, 🖳 www.misa.ns.ca).

New Brunswick: Multicultural Association of Fredericton, 123 York Street, Fredericton, NB E3B 3N6 (☎ 506-454-8292).

Ontario: Catholic Immigration Centre, 219 Argyle Avenue, Ottawa ON K2P 2H4 (☎ 613-232-9634, 🖳 www.cic.ca), Culturelink, 160 Springhurst Avenue, 3rd Floor, Toronto ON M6K 1C2 (☎ 416-588-6288, 🖳 www.culturelink.net) or the Social Development Council of Ajax/Pickering, 134 Commercial Avenue, Ajax ON L1S 2H5 (☎ 905-686-2661).

Prince Edward Island: The Immigrant Settlement Adaptation Program, Suite 301, 129 Kent Street, Charlottetown, Prince Edward Island C1A 1N4 (✉ settle@isn.net) provides assistance to government-sponsored refugees.

Saskatchewan: Regina Open Door Society, 1855 Smith Street, Regina SK S4P 2N5 (☎ 306-352-3500).

Obtaining information isn't usually a problem as there's a wealth of information available in Canada on every conceivable subject. However, without these services you may discover that finding up-to-date information, sorting the truths from the half truths, comparing the options available, and making the correct decisions are difficult, particularly as most information isn't intended for foreigners and their particular needs. You may find that your friends, colleagues and acquaintances can help, as they're often able to proffer advice based on their own experiences and mistakes. But take care! Although they mean well, you may receive as much false and conflicting information as accurate (not always wrong, but possibly invalid for your particular province, community or situation). Canadians are renowned for their friendliness and you should have no trouble getting to know your neighbours and colleagues, who are usually pleased to help you settle in. In most communities there are local volunteer services designed to meet a range of local needs, that can usually also direct you to a range of free or inexpensive local services.

Libraries (see page 327) are a mine of local information. Besides keeping reference works, phone directories, local guidebooks, maps, magazines and community newspapers, they distribute useful leaflets and brochures regarding local clubs and organisations of every description. Library staff are helpful at providing information and answering queries, and may even make phone calls for you. Town halls, police headquarters (the police are usually helpful), visitors bureaux, tourist offices and chambers of commerce, some of which have multilingual staff, are also good sources of free maps and local information. Some large companies have a department or staff dedicated to assisting new arrivals or use a relocation company (see page 109) to perform this task. Relocation magazines are published in many areas (contact local chambers of commerce or estate agents for information).

There are expatriate and ethnic clubs and organisations in most areas. These may provide members with detailed local information regarding all aspects of living in Canada, including housing costs, schools, names of doctors and dentists, shopping information and much more. Many clubs produce fact sheets, booklets, newsletters and run libraries, and most also organise a variety of social events including day and evening classes, ranging from cooking to English or French-language classes. There are also numerous social clubs in most towns, whose members can help you find your way around (see page 323). Many countries have consulates in the main cities, most of which maintain a wealth of local information about everything from doctors to social organisations. Many businesses (e.g. banks) produce books and leaflets containing valuable information for newcomers, and local libraries and bookstores usually have books about the local area (see also **Appendix B**). Other ways to meet people include enrolling in a day or evening class, joining a local church or temple and, if you have school age children, taking part in the activities of the local Parents Advisory Council.

CHECKLISTS

Before Arrival

The following checklist contains a summary of the tasks that should (if possible) be completed before your family's arrival in Canada:

- Obtain a visa, if necessary, for yourself and all your family members (see **Chapter 3**). Obviously this *must* be done before your arrival in Canada.

- Make sure that you have any necessary permits for yourself and your personal and household effects (e.g. car, firearms, pets).

- Visit Canada prior to your move to compare communities and schools, and arrange schooling for your children (see **Chapter 9**).

- Find temporary or permanent accommodations and buy a car. If you purchase a car, arrange insurance (see page 218) and register it in the province where you will be resident (see page 210).

- Arrange for shipment of your personal and household effects.

- Arrange travel insurance for yourself and your family. **Note that ordinary travel insurance won't cover you for a one-way trip (see page 277).**

- Arrange health insurance for your family (see page 270). This is essential if you aren't covered by Medicare or your Canadian employer.

- Open a bank account in Canada and transfer funds in dollars (you can open an account with many Canadian banks from abroad).

- Obtain an international driver's permit (if your current licence isn't written in English or French).

- Obtain an international credit card, which will be invaluable in Canada.

- Obtain as many credit references as possible, e.g. from banks, mortgage companies, credit card companies, credit agencies, companies with which you've had accounts, and references from professionals such as lawyers and accountants. In fact anything that will help you establish a credit rating.

Collect and take with you all your family's official documents, including birth certificates, driver's licences, marriage certificate, divorce papers, death certificate (if a widow or widower), educational diplomas, professional certificates, school records, student ID cards, employment references, curriculum vitae, medical and dental records, bank account and credit card details, insurance policies (plus records of no-claims' allowances) and receipts for any valuables. You also need a number of passport-size photographs, particularly for school-age children.

After Arrival

The following checklist contains a summary of the tasks to be completed after arrival in Canada (if not done before arrival):

- On arrival at a Canadian airport or port, hand your passport, record of landing and other documents to the immigration official.

- Hand your Traveller Declaration Card (provided on the ship or aeroplane) or, if your goods are being shipped separately, a *Personal Exemption Customs Declaration* (form E24) to the customs officer and if you're importing more than your personal exemption (see page 372), provide a list.

- If you haven't bought a car in advance you may wish to rent one (see page 233) for a week or two, as it's almost impossible to get around in Canada without one (**note that renting a car at an airport is the most expensive option**).

- Register immediately for Provincial Health Insurance (Medicare), because cover isn't backdated to when you arrive in the country, but begins from when you apply (see page 266).

- Do the following within the few weeks following your arrival (if not done before):

  - apply for a social insurance card (SIN) from your local social insurance office (see page 262);

  - open a cheque account at a local bank (they print cheques while you wait) and give the details to your employer (see page 289);

  - arrange schooling for your children (see **Chapter 9**);

  - find a local doctor and dentist (see **Chapter 12**);

  - arrange whatever insurance is necessary, such as health, car, household and third party liability (see **Chapter 13**).

5.

ACCOMMODATION

In most areas of Canada, accommodation (*accommodations* — the plural is always used in Canadian English) isn't difficult to find, depending of course on what you're looking for and whether you wish to rent or buy. There are, however, a few exceptions such as large cities (e.g. Toronto, Montreal and Vancouver) and their suburbs, where accommodation is in high demand and short supply, and rents can be astronomical. Rents and the cost of property in different regions and cities vary enormously, with property in the most expensive areas costing up to ten times as much as in the cheapest. Accommodation usually accounts for around 25 per cent of the average Canadian family's budget, but can easily rise to 30 or 40 per cent in high cost areas. A quarter of households spend 30 per cent or more of their income on housing and half of those who rent spend 25 per cent or more. On average, homeowners pay around $800 per month in mortgage costs, while those renting pay an average of $600 per month. The average cost of a single-family house in Canada is $150,000. British Columbia has by far the most expensive housing, averaging $240,000, followed by Ontario at $180,000; Newfoundland is the least expensive at an average of just $70,000.

Three-quarters of Canadians live in urban areas with over 400 people to the square kilometre, most in a bungalow, house or a flat (apartment). Some two-thirds of Canadian families own their own homes, compared with around 70 per cent in Britain, 55 per cent in France, and 50 per cent in Germany and Spain. It's estimated that around two million Canadians live in mobile home units, which are popular with first-time buyers. In addition, many well-off Canadians own a second (vacation) home, usually a cabin in the back-country where they can hunt or fish in the summer. Skiing enthusiasts may own a property (or a time-share) in one of the top ski resorts such as Banff, while those who cannot bear Canada's harsh winters (particularly retirees) often have apartments or mobile homes in the warm southern US states such as Florida.

Canadians are extremely mobile, moving home on average every 2.5 years. Not surprisingly, many are anxious that buying a home won't restrict their mobility (companies often want staff to move from one end of the country to the other) and that they will be able to sell for a profit when they move on. During the recession of the early to mid 1990s, the value of housing plunged, although values have since recovered. In 2003, house prices were stable throughout Canada.

TEMPORARY ACCOMMODATION

On arrival in Canada you may find it necessary to stay in temporary accommodation for a period before moving into a permanent home or while waiting for your furniture to arrive. Choosing where to live is an important decision. You want to choose a neighbourhood where you feel comfortable, which depends on whether you're single or married with a family, drive or rely on public transport, and how close you want to live to work, schools, bus routes, stores and other local amenities. If friends or relatives haven't made arrangements for you, it's best to book into monthly furnished accommodation (which includes everything except a washing machine and tumble-dryer, which are available communally) when you first arrive. This gives you time to talk to the locals and explore the various local communities before making a long-term commitment. In most medium-size cities you can expect to pay around $900 per month for a small apartment, $1,100 for a townhouse and well over $1,500 for a detached home. In the central areas of major cities (e.g. Toronto, Vancouver and Montreal) you can pay over $2,000 per month just for an apartment.

Some companies provide rooms, self-contained apartments or hostels for employees and their families, although this is usually for a limited period only. If you're hired from abroad or your company is transferring you to Canada, you're usually provided with temporary accommodation until you find a permanent home. In many cities and suburbs there are 'corporate' hotels, which are hotels that have been renovated and converted to serviced apartments and are rented on a weekly basis. In most major cities there are long-stay hotels, such as the Glen Grove Suites in Toronto, that usually provide leisure and sports facilities for guests. In most areas, particularly in large cities, self-contained furnished apartments are available with their own bathrooms and kitchens. Although expensive, they're more convenient and usually less expensive than a hotel or motel room, particularly for families (considerable savings can be made by preparing your own meals). Another advantage is that you can usually rent an apartment on a daily, weekly or monthly basis and you aren't required to commit yourself to a long period.

Single people and married couples (without children) may be able to find temporary accommodation in hostels, such as those provided by the Young Men's Christian Association (YMCA) and Young Women's Christian Association (YWCA), both of which have hostels throughout Canada. Alternatively, in most areas it's possible to rent a furnished room or bed & breakfast accommodation for a short period. Information about hotels, motels, bed and breakfast, self-catering, hostels, dormitories and YMCA/YWCAs is provided on the following pages (see also ▣ www.caa.ca, the website of the Canadian Automobile Association, which has a list of hostels in Canada and other countries).

Hotels

The quality and standard of Canadian hotels vary considerably, from superb international luxury establishments (some with hundreds of rooms) to seedy and rundown back street hovels (called flophouses), where you're unlikely to find a bedtime mint on your pillow. Canada doesn't have as many private family hotels as Europe, although delightful 18th and 19th century inns, lodges and historic hotels can be found, particularly in the area around the St Lawrence seaway and the maritime provinces. A full listing of these can be found in Fodor's *Canada's Great Country Inns*.

Advertised room rates don't include goods and services tax (GST) and provincial taxes (PST — see page 358), so ask for the room rate inclusive of taxes. Many hotels have reduced rates at weekends (during the week they're full of business people) or lower Sunday through Thursday rates if they're in popular weekend resorts; some have reduced rates in winter during the off season. Many hotels in summer resorts, particularly the small eastern maritime provinces, are closed during the winter, i.e. from October to May, and those that remain open usually have greatly reduced rates.

The following table provides a *rough* guide to the minimum rates for a double room in Canada, although in the major cities and resorts during the high season you can pay easily double the rates shown:

Class	Stars	Price Range
Luxury	4/5	$200++
First class	3	$150+
Mid-range	2	$100+
Economy	none/1	$50+

During off-peak periods, or at any time when room-occupancy is low, you can usually haggle over room rates, which are often fluid and based on what the market can bear. Always ask about discounts and special rates. Among the many discount categories that may be available are family, group, foreign visitor, students, senior citizens, youth hostel members, YMCA/YWCA members, plane/train/bus pass holders, rental car users, CAA or other auto club members, government or airline employees, and military and corporate rates (which may be granted to anyone with a company identification or business card). If you're from outer space, ask about special rates for extraterrestrials.

Many hotel chains have periodic special offers, such as a four-for-one programme, where up to four people can stay in a double room for the price of a single. The major hotel chains usually allow children under 12 to stay free when sharing their parents' room, plus free continental breakfast. If you're seeking a low-cost bed, look for accommodation described as student, budget, economy, no frills, rustic, basic or European-style rooms, all of which are euphemisms for inexpensive and basic. In major cities such as Toronto there are long-stay hotels, some of which cater for women only. Rates vary and may be under $20 per night or even lower for weekly rates, depending on the facilities available. You can also find budget hotels on the Internet (e.g. 🖳 http://budget hotels.com).

Most hotel chains have toll-free reservation numbers (listed in the yellow pages) and any hotel in a chain can make reservations for you at other hotels in the chain. Some hotel chains provide free phones at airports (and free shuttle buses) and main railway stations. When booking a hotel, it pays to have a reservation confirmed in writing either by post, fax or telegram, and obtain a reservation number (which allows a booking to be easily traced). A deposit may be required when booking if you don't use a credit card. A reservation guaranteed by a major credit card will be kept all night; otherwise a room is usually held until 6pm only (4pm in major resorts). If you plan to arrive later than this, inform the hotel in advance. You must usually cancel a reservation held with a credit card guarantee or an advance deposit 48 hours prior to your confirmed arrival date. However, it's often unnecessary to make a reservation unless you're planning to stay in a popular resort area or a major city. You can usually check in as late as you wish and check out is usually by 11am or noon. You aren't required to produce your passport or any ID when registering at a hotel in Canada.

Resort hotels are common in Canada, many of which are owned and operated by the Canadian Pacific Railway, although some of these, particularly those in busy tourist resorts, can be very expensive. Resort hotels provide a range of private facilities including golf courses, tennis courts, horseback riding trails, bike and hiking paths, swimming pools and ocean or lake beaches. Always check whether the use of sports facilities and other activities is included in room rates, otherwise it can add around $50 per day to the cost. If you plan to stay at a resort hotel for a number of days, you may be quoted 'American Plan' (AP), which includes all meals (full board), 'Modified American Plan' (MAP), which includes breakfast and lunch or dinner (half-board) or 'European plan' (no meals). With AP and MAP you're expected to pay for meals whether you take them or not, although out of high season you can usually haggle over this.

Motels

Motels (motor-hotels, also called 'motel lodges' and 'motor inns') can be found on highways throughout the country. They offer guests a clean and comfortable no-frills room at a reasonable price, and chains generally offer standard rates and facilities throughout the country (although some offer facilities such as swimming pools and saunas). Motels generally provide better, cleaner and safer accommodation for your money than do inexpensive downtown hotels. Rates are quoted per room rather than per person and are usually quoted for single occupancy with a charge for each additional person. This means that for families and other groups willing or able to share rooms, costs are reduced considerably. Motel room rates range from $45 to $100 per night, with the higher prices being in resorts or remote areas in high season. Motels offer a range of discounts (see above under hotels).

The motel business is highly competitive and rates vary depending on local competition. Most motels have neon signs outside stating 'vacancy' or 'no vacancy' and often quote their rates on billboards, although those *without* neon signs or on roads bypassed by new freeways are often cheaper, particularly during mid-week. Motels don't usually have restaurants, room service or provide breakfast, although family restaurants, fast food outlets, cafes and bars are usually located nearby (and may offer discounts to motel guests). Sometimes breakfast is available through room service, although it's generally expensive. If a motel has a restaurant, it's usual to pay for each meal separately, rather than charge them to your bill (as is usual in hotels). It's normal to pay in advance when you check in at a motel and you must usually pay a key deposit of around $5 and possibly a deposit for a TV remote control (called a converter).

Many motels furnish all their rooms with two double beds (queen or king size) or a double bed and two singles (twin beds). Additional fold-up camp beds (cots) can usually be provided. Some motels have suites with more than one bedroom sharing the same facilities (intended for families or groups), which are self-catering rooms with a small kitchenette. If you're travelling as a family or group, ask how many people a room accommodates and whether there's a surcharge for additional people. Most motels (and hotels) don't charge for children under 12 sharing their parents' room or provide a cot in the parents' room for a small extra charge.

Motel rooms are usually fairly similar with little individuality or character. On busy highways most motels are well appointed, but in remote areas they can be run-down, pretty sleazy and on the 'wrong' side of town, as they're often used for adulterous or financial assignations. All rooms have TV (often with cable TV and pay-per-view films), a private bathroom (with towels and washcloths/flannels), phone, air-conditioning and heating, and possibly a fridge. Motels often provide washing machines and dryers, and vending machines for drinks and sweets. Ice is usually available from a machine in the lobby. **Always ask to see a room before paying.**

Unlike the US, most motels in Canada are independently owned and run, although there are a number of franchises and chains. The largest and cheapest nation-wide chains of motels include Days Inn with around 65 locations and Comfort Inns with over 50 locations, plus smaller chains such as Stay'n Save Inns (which have five motels in British Columbia). If you're staying at a chain motel, the receptionist will be glad to book you a room at other motels in the chain. Most motel chains also have a toll-free booking number. To find the toll-free reservation number, call the toll-free information directory (1-800-555-1212). The Canadian Automobile Association (🖳 www.caa.ca) publishes booklets containing a list of approved motels and their rates, and all motel chains publish directories containing directions, maps, facilities, addresses and telephone numbers.

Bed & Breakfast (B&B)

Bed and breakfast (called *Gîte du Passant* in Quebec) accommodation, often referred to as 'inns', is becoming increasingly popular in Canada, particularly in small towns and holiday (vacation) centres. Standards and prices vary considerably, from a reasonable $35 for a single to $250 (on a par with a luxury hotel) for a double, depending on the location and the season. A private bath isn't always included, so check when booking. In Toronto and other major cities, B&B helps tenants and owners pay their mortgages and rents, and is a reasonably affordable way of staying downtown. B&Bs in Canada can be rented via official agencies or reservation organisations, or you can make a booking yourself by telephoning the numbers shown in brochures, B&B guide books and yellow pages. Be wary of scams at international airports run by what look like tourist information centres, but which are actually private businesses that make their money by charging a commission on booking people into expensive hotels and B&Bs. The warning sign is that they ask for a 'booking deposit' (their commission) in advance on a daily rate; if you don't like the place the only way you can get a refund is to go back to the airport for it.

The breakfast part of B&B may vary from a roll and coffee or tea (i.e. continental breakfast), to a full cooked meal with many courses (in some parts of Canada they take breakfast *very* seriously), so check in advance. Many B&Bs offer other meals, picnic baskets, transportation, tours and worthwhile free services ranging from bike loans to the use of libraries, saunas, Jacuzzis/hot tubs, gardens, tennis courts and swimming pools.

There are some regional bed and breakfast associations that inspect and approve B&Bs, but mostly it's a buyer beware situation. A wealth of B&B guides have been published in recent years including *The Annual Directory of American and Canadian Bed & Breakfasts* by Tracey Menges (Rutledge Hill Press), *The Canadian Bed & Breakfast Guide* by Gerda Pantel (Penguin Books), *The Western Canada Bed & Breakfast Guide* by Sarah Bell (Gordon Soules Book Publishers) and *Atlantic Canada Bed and Breakfast* (Formac Publishing). There are several B&B 'guides' on the Internet, including Bed and Breakfast Online Canada (🖳 www. bbcanada.com) and the Western Canada Bed and Breakfast Innkeepers Association (🖳 http://bcbandb.com). Most B&B associations also have websites that list B&Bs in their area. If you don't have access to the Internet, contact the Bed and Breakfast Registry (☎ 604-859-0082).

Self-Catering

Self-catering apartments, houses, bungalows and condominium (condo) apartments are common throughout Canada, particularly in cities and mountain (e.g. ski) resorts. However, they don't always accept children, so check in advance. Apartment hotels are usually owned by a company and designed for short-term rentals, whereas condominium apartments usually have individual private owners who let their apartments through management companies. Accommodation usually consists of a studio or a one or two-bedroom apartment, with a fully-equipped kitchen or kitchenette and a private bathroom with a shower.

Some condo complexes provide the same facilities as hotels, such as a lobby, lounge, coffee shop and restaurant, while others provide no services. Condos usually have double beds, fully-equipped kitchens with a dishwasher, all linen, a washer and drier (or shared facilities), TVs, and often air-conditioning and room telephones. Most resorts have a daily maid service. Other amenities may include swimming pools, tennis courts, golf courses, saunas, barbecue grills, and grocery and other stores within the complex. When choosing self-catering accommodation, check the minimum and maximum rental periods, furnishings and equipment level, whether pets are allowed, sports and social facilities, local beaches, public transport, nearby stores, maid and baby-sitting services, and anything else of importance to you. Apart from serviced condos and hotel apartments, most self-catering accommodation doesn't provide a maid or cleaning service, although local services can usually be arranged.

The cost of a one-bedroom condo in a first class complex starts at around $100 per night for two adults and may be no more than $150 per night for four adults. Children under 12 may be accommodated free of charge when sharing an apartment with their parents. A quality two-bedroom apartment costs between $125 and $150 per night and accommodates up to six people. Weekly and monthly rates considerably reduce the cost per night. An apartment is often a good choice for a family; it's cheaper than hotel rooms, provides more privacy and freedom, and you're able to prepare your own meals when you please.

Condo apartments can be rented through travel agents and are often included as part of fly-drive packages. Some discount travel organisations (plus the CAA and credit card companies) provide savings of up to 50 per cent on hotels, condos and other rental accommodation. Book as early as possible, particularly during holiday (vacation) periods, and avoid national events when everything is booked up months in advance. Most guide books list agencies and organisations providing self-catering accommodation, and many establishments advertise in the travel and property sections of newspapers. In the metropolitan Toronto area, Econo Lodging Service provides a free reservation service for short-term furnished apartments (☎ 416-494-0541).

Hostels, Dormitories & YMCAs/YWCAs

For those travelling on a tight budget, one way to stretch limited financial resources is to stay in hostels, which may be located in anything from a historic city building to an old lighthouse or log cabin. Most hostels recognise International Youth Hostel Federation (IYHF) membership, although there are far fewer hostels in Canada than, for example, in Europe. Hostelling International-Canada is affiliated to the IYHF and has around 70 locations. While everyone is welcome, members pay a reduced rate for accommodation and other programmes available through individual hostels. Non-Canadian guests must be members of the youth hostel association in their own country or purchase a 'welcome stamp' for each night's stay. Contact Hostelling International-Canada, 205 Catherine Street, Suite 400, Ottawa ON K2P 1C3 (☎ 1-800-663-5777 or 613-237-7884, 🖳 www.hihostels.ca) for a list of hostels and membership details. Hostelling International members receive discounts for restaurants, museums and transportation (which includes rental cars, buses, ferries and airlines). Rates are between $10 and $25 per night, usually for a bunk in a single-sex dormitory, although private rooms are also sometimes available.

Other Canadian hostelling organisations include the Canadian Hostelling Association, 1600 James Naismith Drive, Gloucester ON K1B 5N4 (☎ 613-748-

5638) and Backpackers Hostels Canada, which has hostels, retreat centres, residences, homes, inns and hotels, costing between $15 and $20 per person, per night. Backpackers Hostels publish a guidebook to hostels in Canada available from Thunder Bay International Hostel, Longhouse Village, RR13, Thunder Bay ON P7B 5E4 (☎ 807-983-2042, 💻 www.backpackers.ca).

Some hostels limit stays, e.g. to three nights, and it's advisable to book in advance, particularly during holiday periods or in large cities. Some allow non-members to stay for a small extra charge so that they can experience hostel life before becoming members. Youth hostels provide separate dormitories (e.g. 8 to 16 beds) for males and females. All hostels require guests to buy or rent (for around $1) a sheet sleeping bag (sleep sack) consisting of two sheets sewn together or provide their own. Most require guests to share light domestic duties and don't provide meals, but usually have cooking facilities. There's often a curfew after 10pm and alcohol, smoking and drugs are prohibited. However, Canadian hostels are generally more relaxed than their European counterparts. A variation on youth hostels is the home hostel, which is a private residence with the same rates as a hostel.

Other inexpensive city accommodation can be found at Young Men's Christian Association (YMCA) and Young Women's Christian Association (YWCA) hostels. Two-thirds of Ys' lodgings are mixed (coed) and accept both women and families, while the rest are for men only. Room rates for Ys located in cities range from around $45 to $55 for a single and $50 to over $100 for a double room with a bathroom. It's usually necessary to reserve a room and pay in advance, for which there's a reservation fee. Most Ys offer cheaper weekly rates and some offer economy packages that include room, half-board (breakfast and evening meal) and excursions. Many Ys have swimming pools, gyms and other sports facilities. For information contact YMCA Canada, 42 Charles Street East, 6th Floor, Toronto ON M4Y 1T4 (☎ 416-925-5462, 💻 www.ymca.ca).

Another place to stay in university cities during holiday times is on a university campus. Rooms are open to all, although bona fide students are given preference, with prices around $35 per room. The major drawback is that campuses may be quite a way from the city centre and the rooms are fairly basic, although you can use the university's sports facilities. It's advisable to book rooms in advance through a university's accommodation office.

RELOCATION CONSULTANTS

If you're fortunate enough to have your move to (or within) Canada paid for by your employer, he may arrange for a relocation consultant to handle the details. Services provided by relocation companies usually include house hunting (rent or purchase), shipment of furniture and personal effects, reports on schools, area information dossiers, orientation tours, plus miscellaneous services such as financial counselling, home marketing, spouse counselling and assistance after arrival. Relocation consultants' services are expensive and can run in to thousands of dollars per day, although most people consider it money well spent (particularly if their employer is footing the bill!). Fees can vary considerably, so if you're paying the bill obtain a number of quotations and compare exactly what services are included. Most large property companies have relocation divisions and many offer a free relocation service to individuals.

If you just wish to look at properties for rent or sale in a particular area, you can make appointments to view properties through estate agents (see page 115) in the area where you plan to live and arrange your own trip to Canada. However, make *absolutely certain* that agents know exactly what you're looking for and obtain property lists in advance. Relocation guides are published in many areas and cities, and contain house prices, guides to neighbourhoods, employment prospects, school scores, maps, entertainment information and public services. Information is also available from local chambers of commerce and estate agents. A series of regularly updated relocation guides for various Canadian cities and provinces are available from Moving To Magazines Limited, 178 Main Street, Unionville, ON L3R 2G9 (☎ 905-479-0641, 💻 www.movingto.com).

CANADIAN HOMES

Depending on the province, Canadian homes are built in a range of architectural styles including ranch, contemporary, Victorian, French manor and English Tudor. In addition to single-family detached homes and apartments, you can choose from a wide range of townhouses. Homes include single and two-storey, and split and multi-level houses. The average size of a detached single-family home is around 1,500ft² (139m²) for owner-occupiers and the average size of new single-family homes is over 1,800ft² (167m²). Whereas land values constitute a large part of the cost of a home in many countries, building plots in Canada are inexpensive in comparison and extensive prefabrication helps reduce building costs.

Kitchens in modern Canadian homes are usually large with an eat-in dining area, plenty of counter space, built-in cupboards (cabinets), dishwashers, waste disposal units, and possibly laundry facilities and/or a pantry. Kitchens in older homes may not have been modernised, although most Canadian homes contain a profusion of labour-saving devices. Cookers or stoves, which may be electric or gas, don't usually have grills but broilers, which are larger than European grills and are located in the top of the oven, and therefore you cannot bake or roast and grill at the same time unless you have a double-oven stove. Most Canadians use a separate toaster. There's usually no facility for warming plates on Canadian ranges. Canadian refrigerators are frost-free, huge (big enough to withstand a supermarket strike for at least a year) and modern models usually have ice-cube dispensers.

Most Canadian bathrooms contain baths (tubs) with a diverter valve on the taps to allow you to switch to a shower attachment; many homes also have a separate shower room or a shower or bathroom attached (en suite) to the master bedroom. Most modern two or three-bedroom family homes have two full bathrooms. Canadian baths tend to be small, uncomfortable and not very deep (but then most Canadians prefer to shower), and bathrooms seldom contain a bidet. Canadians also have what are called half-bathrooms (or a half-bath), which isn't a bath for babies, but a room *without* a bath. It usually contains a toilet and wash basin, and possibly a shower. Modern homes usually have a downstairs toilet. Canadian showers supply water in torrents, rather than the trickle common in many countries.

In many parts of Canada, particularly the affluent middle class suburbs of the major cities, many homes have outdoor or indoor heated swimming pools. If you have a pool it will need a lot of attention, such as filling, emptying, cleaning, filtering, chlorinating, etc., although there are companies that can look after it for you (you can pay someone to do anything in Canada). Many homes also have hot tubs or Jacuzzis. A hot tub is usually located outside the house where the climate is favourable (such as southern British Columbia) and consists of a large, usually square-shaped, wooden tub (or wood-covered fibreglass) containing hot water, the temperature of which is thermostatically controlled. Hot tubs usually accommodate a number of people and are intended as a relaxation rather than a bath. A Jacuzzi is usually installed inside a home and has jets like a whirlpool bath.

Both houses and apartments have light fittings in all rooms and these are included in the sale, together with window and floor coverings. Few homes have curtains (drapes) as windows are fitted with shades or blinds to keep out the sun. Modern houses are usually carpeted, but polished wooden floors are common in older homes. Most have large fitted wardrobes (closets), plus other standard features such as smoke and security alarms. Most modern houses have ultra-efficient heating and new houses usually include thermal insulation and double or treble glazing. Older houses may have single glazing with detachable storm windows. Windows and doors in all areas usually have screens to keep out flies, mosquitoes and other insects during summer, although storm windows may need to be removed to fit them. Modern Canadian homes usually have separate living, dining and family rooms (often used as a play room for children), a study (den), bar, cellar or basement (useful for storage), and maybe a utility or laundry room, which tends to be in the basement.

The area at the back of the house is called the yard, rather than garden, and as well as plants and a place for children to play, it almost certainly has a barbecue. Most Canadian houses have a paved or covered outdoor area such as a terrace, patio, deck or porch (often screened to keep out bugs). Homes are built either of brick or a wooden (or more recently, steel) frame with an outer surface that may consist of wood, brick, stucco, cedar shingles or a 'siding' of wood, aluminium (plain or painted) or vinyl, which is popular because it's maintenance-free. Roofs are made of 'shakes' (overlapping thin slices of wood) or tiles (shingles) made of asphalt, cedar, pine or other wood.

BUYING A HOME

If you're staying for less than two years you're usually better off renting a home than buying. For those staying longer than two years, buying should be the better option, as it's generally no more expensive than renting. As elsewhere, what you need to pay depends on the region and the actual suburb in a city. Property values vary considerably from region to region. A house of 1,500ft^2 (139m^2) costs around $170,000 in Calgary, $85,000 in Halifax, $140,000 in Montreal, $45,000 on Prince Edward Island, $250,000 in Toronto, $220,000 in Vancouver and $110,000 in Winnipeg. The nation-wide property company Royal Le Page publishes a regular survey of house prices on the Internet (🖳 www.royallepage.ca). Most new detached homes in Canada are built to order by developers who are also the builders. Townhouses and apartments are part of large complexes and are often ready to move into (although if you buy while they're being built you can choose the porcelain, paint, carpet and fixtures and fittings). Whether you're buying a new or used property, you can usually haggle over the price, but be careful how you do it. People who come from countries where haggling involves making disparaging remarks about the property can have a hard time when dealing with Canadians, who may take it as a personal insult.

The 'experts' (i.e. inspectors) say that you should always have a house inspection (survey) on a resale house, although most people don't bother with houses under around 15 years old. Some experts even recommend an inspection on a new property with a warranty, as some builders use short cuts and inferior products that can lead to problems later. Before buying a new condo you should speak to people who have already purchased one, as problems are commonplace (owners are usually happy to share their problems!). Before buying an older condo, you're strongly advised to approach the condominium committee and request the minutes from their last two years' of meetings, their budget and any other records they will let you see. In this way, you can see if there are any regular complaints (e.g. about noise), how much money is in the contingency fund (if any) and whether there are any structural problems or renovations that you will be required to pay towards. You may also be advised to have a radon test if a property is located in an area susceptible to high levels of radon (a naturally occurring radioactive gas which can cause lung cancer). The average home inspection costs $200 to $250; for a little more, some inspectors produce a video film of their findings, in addition to a written report. In some provinces an owner must disclose any significant defects when selling a property and if he fails to do so you have a good chance of receiving damages if you sue. **All claims must be made within a limited period.** Always use a certified and licensed professional inspector who's a member of the Canadian Association of Home Inspectors, PO Box 507, 64 Reddick Road, Brighton ON K0K 1H0 (☎ 613-475-5699, 🖳 www.cahi.ca) or another professional organisation.

The following are the types of property available in Canada:

- **Condominium** — A flat (apartment), usually located in a city or resort where building land is expensive and rare. May be relatively low-rise, e.g. four floors, in small towns or suburbs, or high-rise in the downtown area of major cities.

- **Townhouse** — A terraced house style home on two or more levels (sometimes also called 'split-level'), attached to the next unit, with private entrances and often an integral garage. Townhouses are sometimes part of a condominium-type development.

- **Duplex** — One building split into two separate houses with private entrances, either side-by-side (called 'semi-detached' in the UK) or top and bottom.

- **Bungalow and Bi-Level** — Although a bungalow normally has only one floor, these also have a basement, part of which is often used as a family recreation room. In a bi-level the main floor is raised so that the basement area has some windows above ground level.

- **One and One-Half Storey** — A bungalow with a high pitched roof which has one or more rooms in it (called a 'chalet bungalow' in some other countries).

- **Standard Two Storey** — Detached, possibly with a garage, standing on its own plot of land. Normally has a small basement and two or three bedrooms.

- **Executive Home** — A detached house on its own (usually large) plot of land, with at least four bedrooms, two bathrooms, study, laundry room, recreation room, attached two-car garage, and possibly a swimming pool and/or tennis court and anything else you fancy if you're prepared to pay for it.

- **Mobile Home** — The other end of the scale from an executive home, a mobile home is anything from a small to large single-level home, designed to be transported on a trailer. They're normally found in special 'mobile home' sites on blocks and are connected to the utility services and mains sewerage. They're a cheap option for homebuyers or people renting.

There's also the classic log cabin in the country on its own piece of land ('acreage'), which is the typical dream home for many immigrants. Estate agents love people who want to buy one of these – they know they will be screaming to sell it and move into the city after a couple of winters of being snowed in and having their sewerage system back up because it's minus 40 degrees and everything has frozen solid! It's advisable to postpone this dream home until you've spent a couple of winters in Canada in a town in the wilderness.

Fees

In addition to the cost of a property, there are also other costs which you should be aware of:

- Property purchase tax or land transfer fees of from 0.5 to 2 per cent of a property's total value (not applicable in Alberta, rural Nova Scotia or Saskatchewan);

- Goods and services tax (GST) is payable on new homes and in some provinces provincial sales tax (PST) is also payable (see page 358). Both taxes are normally included in the quoted price. Depending on the cost of the home, this may be refundable to first-time buyers in some provinces;

- Inspection and survey fees;

- Legal fees;

- Registration fees for the deed and mortgage;

- Property insurance (you must have fire insurance to obtain a mortgage, see page 272);

- Property tax (see page 305);

- Mortgage application fees and possibly legal fees associated with the mortgage. If you don't have the standard 25 per cent deposit and qualify for a 'CMHC-insured' mortgage (see page 295), you also need to pay for an insurance policy to cover the risk to the lender. If the mortgage company wants an appraisal (survey and price) on the property, you must also pay for this;

- Vendor's adjustments. This is the 'unused' portion of pre-paid expenses such as real estate tax, utilities and annual maintenance fees for condominiums and other 'community' homes;

- Utility connection fees.

Further Reading

There are many books published about buying and selling property in Canada, including the following (all from Self-Counsel Press): *For Sale By Owner* by Edward M. Walsh, *Real Estate Buying/Selling Guide for BC* by Ebbe Syberg-Olsen, *Real Estate Buying/Selling Guide for Alberta* by George C. Stewart, and the *Real Estate Buying/Selling Guide for Ontario* by Stanley M. Rose. Free property booklets and magazines listing properties for sale are published in most regions (many are available in local editions) and distributed via local estate agents, stores, restaurants, supermarkets, bookstores and libraries.

Holiday Homes

Every weekend during the summer, southern Ontarians depart in droves from Toronto to their second homes in what's known as 'cottage country' – usually Muskoka (don't call it 'the Muskokas' as only outsiders do this), while those from southern Quebec go to the Laurentians, Vermont, or Lake Champlain or

Plattsburgh (a small city is upstate New York's Lake Champlain Valley). During the winter, they still go to their country cottage to snowmobile, when local gas stations are as likely to be filling snowmobiles as cars. The most popular areas for holiday (vacation) homes are the country areas of Ontario and Quebec, and the mountains of Alberta and British Columbia. Canadians who enjoy the outdoor life often buy or rent a cabin, trailer or houseboat somewhere in the backwoods for the summer or an apartment, condominium or time-share in one of the popular ski resorts in the winter. Renting is usually done through an agency and, depending on the size of the property, can range from $50 to $250 per day. Monthly rates are usually available at a discount over weekly rates.

From a legal viewpoint, Canada is one of the safest countries in the world in which to buy a holiday home. There are few traps for the unwary and property and planning laws are much stricter than in most European countries. Non-residents' rights as property owners are the same as those of Canadian citizens. For safety, however, you should always do business with an established company or a real estate agent with a good reputation. If you're a foreign resident, bear in mind that with a visitor's visa you can only remain in Canada for a maximum of six months per year (see **Chapter 3**). However, if you buy or inherit a seasonal residence in Canada, you can bring furniture and personal effects into the country duty free.

Many builders offer a furnishing package (or 'turn key' service) that includes all furniture, electrical apparatus, linen and miscellaneous items for an inclusive special price. This is particularly designed for buyers who are planning to let their homes. A typical furniture package for a 3-bedroom property costs $12,000 to $15,000 and is generally better value than buying items individually (but check, as value varies). Furnishings must be financed separately and cannot be included in a mortgage.

Part-Ownership Schemes: If you don't wish to invest in buying a property outright, you may wish to investigate part or holiday ownership schemes such as shared ownership, where a consortium of buyers own shares in a property-owning company, part-ownership between family, friends or even strangers (some companies offer this option), a holiday property bond, or even timesharing. Timesharing in Canada doesn't have the dreadful reputation that it has earned in Europe, although it isn't as good value as part-ownership.

ESTATE AGENTS

Some 90 per cent of people in Canada buy and sell their homes through estate agents (realtors), who must be licensed by local property boards. Many estate agents are doing more and more of their business via the Internet. In most provinces, real estate brokers and their sales people must be registered under the province's Real Estate and Business Brokers Act (REBBA). A typical example is Ontario, which requires sales people to be permanent residents of Canada over 18 years of age, to be employed by a registered broker and to have passed written examinations. Registration must be renewed every two years. Most estate agents belong to three bodies: the national Canadian Real Estate Association (CREA), Suite 1600, 344 Slater Street, Canada Building, Ottawa ON K1R 7Y3 (☎ 613-237-7111, 🖳 http:/crea.ca/), the provincial association and a local board (e.g. in a city).

Unlike other countries, where most agents are engaged by the seller, estate agents in Canada act for the buyer as often as the seller and can, in some circumstances, act for both. Under CREA rules, members are required to disclose in writing (to all parties concerned) who they're working for. There are three possible types of agency:

- Vendor's agent, where the estate agent works for the vendor and must disclose to him anything known about a buyer (like the maximum price you're prepared to pay for a property – so don't mention this if you hope to do a deal);
- Purchaser's agent, where the estate agent works exclusively for the buyer and must disclose anything known about the vendor;
- Dual agent, when the estate agent works for both parties.

Most agents are self-employed and pay a percentage of their commissions and a desk fee to the agent where their licence is held. There are no fixed commissions in Canada as there are in some other countries and they're always negotiable (agents usually receive anywhere between 3 and 7 per cent commission, and the figure is invariably negotiable). Where a buying and selling agent are involved, they split the commission.

The other main difference between estate agents in Canada and many other countries is that in Canada there's a computerised Multiple Listing System (MLS) that holds details of all properties for sale. Therefore it isn't necessary to traipse around a number of estate agents to see what properties they have for sale and you can simply engage an agent to act for you as a purchaser and find suitable properties on the MLS. Many agents are either mortgage brokers or affiliated to mortgage providers, and it's normal practice for them to pre-qualify you for a mortgage before they start showing you properties.

When an agent has shown you a home that you wish to buy, he immediately writes up a purchase contract. He then contacts the seller's agent and asks when he can present an offer. The purchase contract is drawn up with the time usually left open until an hour or two after the agreed presentation time, after which it becomes void. The buyer's agent then goes to the seller's home and presents his offer to the seller and the seller's agent. He then usually waits in his car while the owners discuss the offer with their agent; if acceptable, the deal is signed and a deposit cheque paid into the trust (escrow) account of the seller's agent. Trust accounts are protected through an insurance scheme approved by the local real estate board. If the offer is unacceptable, the buyer may make a counter-offer which is re-presented to the purchaser. In theory you can go back and forth indefinitely, but in practice it's usually no more than once or twice.

There may be conditions in an offer that must be satisfied by a set date, otherwise the contract is void. The most common conditions are being subject to satisfactory home inspection or financing, but there can be others, e.g. subject to the vendor finding another house by a set date or to the buyer selling his home. These conditions are usually valid for a limited period only and once waived, the contract is legally binding on both parties. Therefore within a few hours of finding a home you like, it can legally be yours.

Less than 10 per cent of homes sold in Canada are sold directly by owners to buyers without using an agent or broker. When an owner is selling his own home, he usually holds an 'open house' at weekends when the public can inspect it without making an appointment. If successful, an owner is likely to save thousands of dollars in agent's fees, part or all of which he may pass on to the buyer. It's particularly recommended when you're selling an attractive home at a *realistic* price. However, if you're buying directly from a vendor, you should always use the services of a lawyer, an appraiser and a home inspector before going ahead with a deal. Some people (mostly lawyers) say you should use a lawyer to check the contract even if you're dealing through a licensed estate agent. Most estate agents use standard contracts that have been approved by their provincial associations in which there's a clause stating that the agent must use due diligence, honesty and integrity. If you wish, you can have a 'subject to lawyer's approval' clause added to a contract for safety.

RENTAL ACCOMMODATION

Rental accommodation is are freely available in most areas, although the choice and cost of rental property varies considerably depending on the city or region. Renting is generally the best solution for anyone planning to remain in Canada for a limited period, say less than two years. Rental property can be found within a few weeks in most areas, while in others it can take much longer and you may have to compromise on what you're looking for. In major metropolitan areas, finding an apartment or house that suits both your needs *and* your budget may be difficult, and you may be forced to live out of town and commute. In many cities, old warehouses are being converted into huge studio apartments (known as 'artist studios') consisting of a single vast room up to 1,000ft^2 (over 90m^2), possibly with a loft.

Most property in Canada is rented unfurnished and you may have difficulty in finding a furnished apartment or house. Furnished apartments in Canada are usually equipped with the basic essentials only, which include a stove (range), refrigerator (or fridge/freezer), and basic furniture. Some linen (e.g. bed, bath and table) may also be supplied. Unfurnished apartments usually have a stove and a refrigerator or fridge/freezer. Most property is centrally heated; with apartments, this may be from a communal boiler and the rent includes your share of the heating costs. Most modern apartment blocks have a communal laundry room with coin-operated washing and drying machines. Apartments and houses in modern urban developments usually have their own washing machine and dryer. Luxury apartment developments often have swimming pools, Jacuzzis, saunas, heated spas, racquetball and tennis courts, and a fully-equipped health club or fitness centre, all of which are 'free' to tenants. Cable TV is usually included in the price of the rent.

Single people, particularly the young and students, may find it difficult to secure affordable accommodation. Studio, bachelor and efficiency apartments are all fancy names for a one-room apartment in which you live, sleep and eat, with a separate kitchen and tiny 'bathroom'. Single people can save money by sharing accommodation. This is common in all areas and costs between $300 and $500 per month in metropolitan areas. Advertisements ('room to share') for roommates are found in most newspapers and in free 'singles' newspapers and magazines. It's also possible to rent furniture (a student package starts at around $50 per month).

Rental Costs

Rental costs vary considerably depending on the size (number of bedrooms) and quality of a property, its age and the facilities provided. Most importantly, rents depend on the neighbourhood and the region of Canada. The rent for similar properties in different parts of the country can vary by as much as 1,000 per cent. As a general rule, the further a property is from a large city or town, public transport or other facilities, the less expensive it is. Average rental costs for unfurnished apartments and houses range from $450 per month for a bachelor studio, $550 to $700 for a one to two-bedroom apartment, $650 to $950 for a two to three-bedroom townhouse and $850 to $1,600 for a three to four-bedroom detached house, with an overall average of around $650 per month.

Leases are usually for a fixed period of 12 months, so unless you're sure you want to stay that long it's better to remain in temporary accommodation until you've found a place you really want. Many immigrants commit themselves to a year's rental and then regret it when they find a property they want to buy, feeling they've wasted what could have been part of the deposit on a purchased home. Bear in mind that if you want to be able to leave at short notice you should sign an agreement that allows you to give 30 days notice, otherwise you must find someone to sub-let from you (if it's permitted). Furnished rentals range from $1,200 per month for a small apartment, $1,600 for a two-bedroom apartment with a full kitchen, $1,800 for a two to three-bedroom townhouse and in excess of $2,000 for a detached family home. In metropolitan areas such as Toronto and Vancouver and even their outer suburbs, you can expect to pay $3,000 or more per month just for an apartment, while in backwater towns and villages you pay much less than the rates stated above.

It's possible to find less expensive, older apartments and houses for rent, but these are generally small and don't offer the conveniences of a new property. You can also find 'heritage' houses and apartment buildings that are old restored properties, although these are sought after and therefore are more expensive than modern homes. If you like a property but think the rent is too high, you should try to negotiate a reduction or ask the agent to put your offer to the owner. Check the cost of extras such as maintenance, which may include grass-cutting, window-washing, leaf-removal and snow removal (if a house has a sidewalk, you're normally responsible for clearing it of snow). Sometimes rents may include heating, air-conditioning, gas cooking and hot water, but not electricity.

The laws concerning rental accommodation vary considerably from province to province and even from city to city. To check on your rights, contact the non-criminal division of the local legal aid society, which may be able to put you in touch with a tenants' rights coalition or association in your area. There are also a number of books available, including *Landlord/Tenant Rights in British Columbia* by David Lane & Roneen Marcoux, *Rental Form Kit for BC*, and *Landlord/Tenant Rights in Ontario* by Ron McInnes (all published by Self Counsel Press Inc.).

MOVING HOUSE

If you're moving to Canada from abroad, it usually takes from four to eight weeks to have your personal effects shipped, depending on the distance and route. It's wise to obtain at least three written quotations and (if possible) obtain some recommendations before committing yourself. Moving companies (or movers) usually send a representative to carry out a detailed estimate. Most international companies charge by the cubic foot or metre, while local companies may charge by the number of boxes and their weight. Most pack your belongings and provide packing cases and special containers, although this is naturally more expensive than packing them yourself. Ask how they pack fragile and valuable items, and whether the costs of packing cases, materials and insurance (see below) are included in the quotation. If you're packing yourself, most shipping companies provide packing crates and boxes. Whenever possible, it's best to have your own container rather than share one. There are enough potential hazards (one immigrant's most sentimental possessions were smashed when a car was put into the container on top of their box) without adding the unpacking and re-packing of the container as each family's possessions are loaded and unloaded.

For international moves, it's best to use a shipping company that's a member of a professional association such as the International Federation of Furniture Removers (FIDI), the Overseas Moving Network International (OMNI) or the Association of International Removers Ltd. Members usually subscribe to an advance payment scheme that provides a guarantee. When a member company fails to fulfil its commitments to a customer, the contract is completed at the agreed cost by another company or your money is refunded. Make a complete list of everything to be shipped and give a copy to the shipping company. Don't include anything illegal (e.g. guns, bombs, drugs or pornographic material) with your belongings as customs checks can be rigorous and penalties severe. Give your shipping company a phone number and an address in Canada through which you can be contacted.

You should fully insure your belongings with a well-established insurance company during shipment or while in storage (warehouses have been known to burn down!). Around 50 per cent of all moves result in some damage to possessions (water damage is common during international moves). Don't use the moving company's insurance policy as this may limit their liability to a paltry sum. It's advisable to make a photographic or video record of any valuables shipped for insurance purposes.

If your stay in Canada is for a limited period only, it may be wise to leave your most valued possessions at home (e.g. with relatives or friends), particularly if their insured value wouldn't provide adequate compensation for their loss. If you bring them, it's wise to take them with you or ship them by air. If there are any breakages or damaged items, these must be noted and listed before you sign the delivery bill. If you need to make a claim, be sure to read the small print as they must usually be made within a limited period, sometimes within a few days. Always send claims by registered post.

For house moves within Canada you can rent a van or lorry (truck) by the hour, half-day or day. Many transport companies also sell packing boxes in various sizes and rent or sell removal equipment (trolleys, straps, etc.) for those who feel up to doing their own move. See also the checklists in **Chapter 20** and **Customs** on page 89.

What to Take With You?

If you're staying in Canada for a prolonged period or plan to become a permanent resident, you need to decide what personal and household items to take and how to ship them. What you actually take is a personal matter, but in many cases it's better to abandon (or sell) many items in your home country and buy replacements when you arrive in Canada. For example:

- Clothing. If you come from a warm or hot country, bear in mind that Canada has long, very cold winters (except in Vancouver, where it's mild but wet). While you need some summer clothes, taking too many may mean that most languish in a wardrobe for nine months of the year, so there's little point in paying to ship them.

- TVs and videos made for any country other than Canada and the US won't work in Canada as the transmission standards are different (see page 158), although they can be converted.

- Electrical items that operate on a 220-240V system, rather than Canada's 110V system (see page 123).

- Furniture can easily be replaced in Canada, either new or secondhand. Take into account the cost of shipping and insurance (and possibly storage while you look for somewhere to live) versus the cost of replacement.

- Beds and bedding. Bed sizes are different in Canada from those in Europe and many other countries. When your bed linen needs replacing you won't be able to replace it locally and may need to buy new beds, therefore you may as well do it at the start and save the cost of shipping them.

- Cars and other motor vehicles. Canadian safety and exhaust emission standards are high and you must bring any imported vehicles up to these standards before you can use them on Canadian roads. If you're coming from the UK or another country where you drive on the left, your vehicles won't be suitable for Canada where they drive on the right.

In the end it comes down to whether you can bear to be without certain possessions and to the cost of buying replacements compared with the cost of shipping and storing them (possibly less what you can gain by selling them before you go). Bear in mind that the main bulk of your effects may not arrive until several weeks after you do and then may be held for customs checks, so ensure that the things you need to survive for the first few weeks or months are sent by air (including your children's favourite toys).

KEYS & SECURITY

When moving into a new home, particularly in a burglary-prone urban area, it's often wise to replace the locks (or lock barrels) as soon as possible and fit high security (double cylinder or deadbolt) locks, as you have no idea how many keys are in circulation for the existing locks. However, if you're renting, you need to obtain the permission of the owner or landlord, who may forbid it (he will certainly want a key). If you own your home, you may wish to have an alarm system fitted, as this is usually the best way to scare off thieves and may also reduce your homeowner's insurance premium (see page 272).

Most outside doors, particularly apartment doors in major cities, are fitted with a peep-hole and chains so that you can check the identity of a visitor before opening the door. Inside doors often have locks that are operated by pressing and/or twisting a button on the centre of the door knob or by pushing or twisting the knob itself (these locks should be replaced if found on outside doors, as they aren't secure). All external doors should be lockable from the inside as well as the outside.

No matter how secure your door and window locks, a thief can usually obtain entry if he is determined enough, often by simply smashing a window (although you can fit external steel security blinds). You can, however, deter thieves by ensuring that your house is well lit, even (or particularly) when no one is at home, when it's often wise to leave a TV or radio on (a timer switch can be used to switch radios, TVs and lights on and off randomly). Most security companies provide home security systems connected to a central monitoring station. When a sensor, e.g. smoke or forced entry, detects an emergency or a panic button is pushed, a signal is sent to a 24-hour monitoring station. Remember, prevention is better than cure, as those who are burgled rarely recover their belongings. Police recommend that you display alarm/security company stickers even if you have no alarm.

If you lock yourself out of your apartment (or car) there's usually a local locksmith on emergency call day and night to help you. A locksmith's services are expensive and it may be more economical to break a window to gain entry to your home (but difficult if you live on the 39th floor). If you vacate a rented house or apartment for an extended period, it may be obligatory to notify your building superintendent, agent or insurance company, and to leave a key with the superintendent or agent in case of emergencies. Fire prevention is also an important aspect of home security and it's advisable to install smoke detectors in all rooms and keep a fire extinguisher handy.

UTILITIES

Electricity, gas and water companies in Canada are called 'utility' companies, and are owned by private companies, local municipalities or the provincial government (there are also co-operatives in some rural areas). Canada produces around 14 per cent of its energy from nuclear power plants in Ontario, Quebec and New Brunswick. As utility companies are monopolies, provincial governments have established public utility or public service commissions (PUCs or PSCs) to set rates and regulate their operation in accordance with provincial law. In some regions you may be billed for both electricity and gas (and/or water) by the same utility company on one bill, although each utility is itemised separately.

If you're renting a property, your water may be included in your rent. You should apply in person to utility companies to have your electricity, gas or water service switched on (take with you proof of ownership or a lease plus a photo ID, such as a driver's licence, and a bill addressed to you at that address). A security deposit is necessary if you're a new customer, which is usually equal to an average monthly bill (based on the previous owner's/tenant's usage). A deposit may be returned (without interest) when you've been billed for a number of consecutive billing cycles, e.g. eight, or have paid most bills before the penalty due date in the past year or so. When moving into a property there's a 'start-up' fee (usually $25) to switch on the service and read the meter, which is included in your first bill. You must contact your electricity, gas and water companies (usually at least 48 hours in advance) to get a final meter reading and bill when vacating a property.

Electricity and gas meters are read and customers billed monthly in most areas, although in some areas bills may be sent every two or three months; the number of billing days is shown on the bill. If the meter reader is unable to read your meter, you receive an estimated bill, which is usually annotated with 'EST', 'Avg' or 'A'. A utility company may send a revised bill based on a meter reading provided by the householder. You're usually given 30 days to pay a bill before it becomes overdue. If you miss paying a bill (or your payment arrives after the due date) it's added to your next bill and you may be charged a late payment penalty, e.g. 5 per cent of the outstanding amount. If you don't pay a utility bill, you eventually receive a 'notice of discontinuation of service', when you should pay the bill within the period specified, e.g. 15 days, even if you dispute the amount. Utility companies offer an 'equal payment plan', where your annual energy costs are spread evenly throughout the year.

Most utility companies publish a number of useful booklets explaining how to conserve energy, e.g. through improved insulation, and thus reduce your bills. Most utility companies perform a free home energy conservation survey of your home and private companies conduct a more in-depth audit for around $200 (most utilities also offer rebates and financing for the purchase of new energy-efficient appliances). Some provinces have proposed deregulation of electricity supplies, which has led to a scam where people calling themselves 'energy brokers' or 'energy aggregators' approach residents and offer future discounts for signing up with them. Contracts appoint the broker as the resident's agent in purchasing electricity at unspecified prices for a period (e.g. five years or longer), which isn't advisable.

Most provinces have 'utility consumer advocates' who are public officials who handle consumer problems concerning utilities. To find out whether your province has one, write to the Consumers Council of Canada, 35 Madison Avenue, Suite 100, Toronto, ON M5R 2S2 (☎ 416-961-3487, 🖳 www.consumers council.com).

Electricity

The electricity supply in Canada is 110/120 volts AC, with a frequency of 60 hertz (cycles). Every resident, whether in an apartment or a house, has his own electricity meter. This is usually located either in the basement of an apartment block or outside a house, where it can be read when the occupants aren't at home. When you buy a new property there's a 'new meter charge' (connection fee) of around $10. In many areas electricity is charged at peak and slack period (off-peak) rates at different times of the day and different seasons (usually summer and winter). Electricity costs vary depending on the area, e.g. from 5¢ to 8¢ per kilowatt-hour (KWH or KWHR). There's also a 'supply fee' (service fee) every two months, e.g. BC Hydro charges around $7.

It's possible to operate electrical equipment rated at 240 volts AC with a converter or a step-up transformer to convert it to 110 volts AC, although generally it isn't worth bringing electrical appliances to Canada that aren't rated at 110 volts AC. Some electrical appliances (e.g. electric razors and hair dryers) are dual-voltage and are fitted with a 110/240 volt switch. Check for the switch, which may be inside the casing, and make sure it's switched to 110 volts *before* connecting it to the power supply. Most people buy new electrical appliances in Canada, which are of good quality and reasonably priced. Shop around before buying electrical appliances as prices vary considerably (also check comparison tests in consumer magazines).

An additional problem with some electrical equipment that isn't made for the North American market is that the frequency rating is designed to run at 50 hertz (Hz) and not Canada's 60Hz. Electrical equipment *without* a motor is generally unaffected by the increase in frequency to 60Hz (except TVs). Some equipment with a synchronous motor may run okay with a 20 per cent increase in speed; however, automatic washing machines, ranges, electric clocks, record players and reel-to-reel tape recorders are unusable in Canada unless they're designed for 60Hz operation. To find out, look at the label on the back of the equipment; if it says 50/60Hz, it should be okay. If it says 50Hz, you might try it anyway, but first ensure that the voltage is correct as outlined above. If the equipment runs too slowly, seek advice from the manufacturer or the retailer. For example, you may be able to obtain a special pulley for a reel-to-reel tape deck or record turntable to compensate for the increase in speed.

The standard Canadian mains plug has two flat pins (live and neutral) plus an optional third pin (neutral). It's possible to buy adapters for many foreign plugs, but it's more economical to change plugs. All appliances sold in Canada are fitted with a moulded two-pin plug that runs off any outlet in the country. Some electrical appliances are earthed, which means they have a three-core wire and are fitted with a three-pin plug. If you need to fit a plug, the colour coding is usually white (neutral), black (live) and green (earth). **Always make sure that a plug is correctly and securely wired, as bad wiring can prove fatal. Never fit a two-pin plug to a three-core flex.**

In some Canadian homes there are no switches on wall sockets, so electrical appliances should be fitted with their own on/off switches. Light switches usually operate in the opposite way to some other countries, where the UP position is ON and the DOWN position is OFF (some switches may operate from left to right). The ON position may be indicated by a red spot on the switch. Standard and other lamps often have two or three-way bulbs that provide two or three levels of brightness (e.g. bright, medium and dim). Often lamp switches (or knobs) must be turned in a clockwise direction or pushed and pulled. Electric light bulbs have a standard size screw fitting for all lamps and sockets, that may be different from other countries. Bulbs for older appliances or foreign appliances (e.g. sewing machines) may not be available in Canada, so you should bring a few spares with you.

Most Canadian apartments and all houses have their own fuse boxes. If a fuse blows, first turn off the mains switch. This may be on the consumer unit or on a separate switch box nearby. Fuses in modern homes and homes with modern wiring are usually of the circuit breaker type; when a circuit is overloaded it trips to the OFF position. Switch off the main switch and open the circuit breaker box. After locating and remedying the cause of the failure (if possible), just switch the circuit breaker to the ON position. Close the circuit breaker box and switch on the main switch. Most electricity companies service your major electrical appliances, e.g. heating or air-conditioning system, and some provide service contracts.

If you have a suitable roof for solar panels or live away from the centre of a town and have room for a wind generator or have a nearby stream, then you may be able to generate some of your own electricity. **These are intended as supplementary systems as they won't generate sufficient power to run the heavy-duty appliances installed in most modern homes.** They can, however, provide back-up systems in times of power outages and can considerably reduce your electricity bills.

Gas

Gas (usually natural) is available in most Canadian cities. The same company may supply you with both gas and electricity, when you receive one bill for both, with gas and electricity costs itemised separately. Gas is available in all but the remotest areas of Canada, although most modern houses are all electric and aren't connected to the gas supply. When you buy a new property there's a 'new meter charge' (connection fee) of around $25. Outside cities and in remote areas, gas may be supplied in bottles. Gas is usually billed by the gigajoule and usually costs $4 to $6 per gigajoule. **If you rent an apartment, your gas consumption may be included in your rent.** Gas leaks are extremely rare and explosions caused by leaks even rarer (although often devastating and therefore widely reported). It's wise to install a carbon dioxide gas detector that activates an alarm when a gas leak is detected.

Water

In many areas, you don't receive a water bill as the cost is included in local property taxes. In other areas there's a charge and each building or apartment has its own water meter, where you're billed each month or quarter for the water you use. Bills may include a meter charge, e.g. $10 per month. Water rates are typically 30¢ to 60¢ per cubic metre and typical monthly water bills are $25 per month for a one-bedroom apartment, $70 for a 2,000ft^2 (186m^2) house and around $225 for a four-bedroom, four-bathroom house with a hot tub.

Some provinces occasionally have restrictions on the use of water during the summer months, e.g. for swimming pools, washing motor vehicles or watering gardens, when there may be bans between sunrise and sunset. Canadians usually drink water straight from their house supply, although some people find the taste of the water or the purifying (e.g. chlorination) chemicals unpleasant and prefer to drink bottled spring or mineral water. Householders in many areas fit filters to cold-water taps used to provide water for drinking or cooking. It's generally safe to drink water from rivers, lakes, wells and streams in both rural and country areas.

Canadian taps can be complicated for the uninitiated and may be fitted with a variety of strange controls, e.g. one common design is operated by a handle that works on a universal joint arrangement, where an up-and-down movement controls the flow and a left-to-right movement the temperature; in Canada the left tap is generally for hot water. When there are separate hot and cold water taps in a shower, both taps may turn in the same direction or in opposite directions; **check them before scalding or freezing yourself.** Where a shower and bath are combined, a lever or knob is commonly used to convert the flow from bath to shower and vice versa. Most Canadian baths and washbasins have a single mixer spout. Sometimes taps must be pulled or pushed rather than turned and a lever may also control the plug.

Before moving into a new home in Canada you should inquire where the main stop-valve or stopcock is, so that you can turn off the water supply in an emergency. **If the water stops flowing for any reason, you should ensure that all taps are closed to prevent flooding from an open tap when the supply starts again.**

HEATING & AIR-CONDITIONING

In most of Canada the winters are very cold and Canadians look upon central heating as absolutely essential. However, it can also get very hot in the summer, so all modern office buildings and around a third of private homes also have air-conditioning. Around half of Canadian homes are heated by piped natural gas and another third by electricity. The rest have oil storage tanks or wood stoves (mostly in rural areas where there are no utility lines). Heating bills in the winter are usually between $150 and $200 per month. Modern homes often have a combined heating and cooling (air-conditioning) system that's thermostatically controlled. Many homes are also fitted with ceiling fans. When using air-conditioning, all windows and outside doors should obviously be closed. You may find that some air-conditioners are noisy and you may need to switch them off at night to get to sleep. Air-conditioners can be rented during the hottest months of the year.

If you live in an apartment block, heating is usually centrally controlled and is turned on in the autumn and off in the spring. Apartment buildings in some cities must, by law, be heated to specified minimum temperatures during the coldest months. If you live in an apartment in a building with a centrally-controlled heating system, you may have no control over room temperatures, apart from turning individual radiators on or off, although most radiators are fitted with a gauge with low, medium and high settings. In some apartment buildings the cost of heating and air-conditioning is included in your rent. If you're required to pay for heating/cooling separately, check the average monthly cost.

Central heating dries the air and may cause your family to develop coughs and other ailments. Those who find the dry air unpleasant can increase the indoor relative humidity by adding moisture to the air with a humidifier, vaporiser, steam generator or even a water container made of porous ceramic. Humidifiers that don't generate steam should be disinfected occasionally.

6.

POST OFFICE SERVICES

Canada Post is a crown corporation operating some 20,000 post offices and postal outlets and delivering to over 13 million addresses. Post offices and post boxes in Canada are denoted by a red sign bearing the words 'CANADA POST – *POSTE CANADA*' and the logo of a white wing motif on a red background. Around 20 per cent of post offices are operated by Canada Post, while the rest are run by private individuals (called postal outlets) from businesses such as convenience stores, gift stores, pharmacies, and university book and stationery stores. Many post offices also offer fax, electronic mail and telegram services. In Canada, letters and parcels are called *mail* (post), which is *mailed* (posted) in a *mailbox* (which also refers to the box outside a home where letters are deposited) and delivered by a *mail carrier* (postman).

The Canadian postal service is reliable, but neither cheap nor fast. Canada Post's delivery standards for letter post are three days for local letters, three days within a province and four days between provinces. Unless you pay for special services, next day delivery is rare (even within a city) and it isn't uncommon for ordinary letters to take five or six business days to get from a rural collection point to their destination. Canada Post says this is because post has to go to a main sorting office and they don't seem to think it odd that US Mail, which covers the same vast distances, manages to deliver 75 per cent of 'over 600 miles' (965km) post within its target of three days. Delivery between major cities is generally faster than to small towns and a letter travelling between major cities (e.g. Toronto and Vancouver) is usually delivered faster than a letter posted to a small town in a neighbouring province – but don't bank on it! Not surprisingly, fax and electronic mail (e-mail) are *very* popular in Canada.

The post office operates a domestic guaranteed express post service (priority post), as do private companies such as DHL, Emery World-wide, Federal Express, Greyhound Courier Express, Loomis, Purolator and UPS (who also provide express international parcel services). Companies guarantee next day delivery for domestic express items sent before a certain time of day and provide a money-back guarantee if the promised delivery times aren't met. Pick-up services are provided by the post office and private companies. As in the US there are several nation-wide companies such as Mail Boxes, Etc. that offer all post services except letter delivery. Services include a post box service, post-hold, post forwarding, stamps, envelopes, postcards, packing supplies, air shipping/receiving, postal metering, postal money orders, telegrams, cablegrams, fax, copy service and other business services.

If you have a complaint about any aspect of the postal service or post fraud, you should contact your local post office or postal outlet and complete a complaints form. If you don't receive satisfaction you should contact Canada Post's Customer Service (☎ 1-800-267-1177) and if that fails, the Office of the Ombudsman, PO Box 90026, Ottawa ON K1V 1J8 (☎ 1-800-204-4198).

Information about Canada Post's services is provided in a range of leaflets available from post offices, the *Canada Postal Guide* (☎ 1-800-565-4362 to purchase a copy) and via the Internet (🖥 www.canadapost.ca). For information about telegrams, telex and fax, see page 153.

BUSINESS HOURS

Post office hours in Canada are usually from 10am to 5pm, Mondays to Fridays and main post offices in major towns don't close at lunch times. In rural areas and small towns, post offices may have restricted and varied business hours, and may open any time between 8 and 9.30am until between 2 and 5pm Mondays to Fridays, or may open for a few hours each morning only and perhaps a few hours on Saturdays (if located in a retail store that opens on Saturdays). Some central post offices in large cities provide 24-hour, self-service facilities, where you find stamp and change machines, scales, tables of postage rates and post boxes large enough to accept parcels. All post offices are closed on Sundays and national holidays. It's wise to avoid post offices at lunch times and after 4pm when offices send their post. On 30th April, the last day on which Canadians can file their tax returns, main post offices remain open until midnight to date stamp tax returns (if you owe tax and are a day late filing, you're charged interest!). Post offices should be avoided at all costs during the week leading up to this date!

LETTERS & LETTER PACKAGES

Canada Post operates just one class of post, dividing it into letter post, other letter post and international post, as shown below.

Letter Post

With maximum dimensions of 245mm x 150mm x 5mm (postcards 235mm x 120mm) and a maximum weight of 50g:

- Within Canada: up to 30g = 48¢; 30 to 50g = 77¢.
- To the US: up to 30g = 65¢; 30 to 50g = 90¢.

Other Letter Post

Includes non-standard and ove4rsize letters with maximum dimensions of 380mm x 270mm x 20mm and a maximum weight of 500g:

- Within Canada: up to 100g = 96¢; 100 to 200g = $1.60; 200 to 500g = $2.10.
- To the US: oversize letters up to 100g = $1.40; 100 to 200g = $2.60; 200 to 500g = $4.60.

International Post

Post within Canada or to the US that weighs over 1kg goes by surface parcel post. International letter packages up to a maximum of 2kg can be sent by air.

- Airmail: up to 30g = $1.25; 30 to 50g = $1.75; 50 to 100g = $3; 100 to 200g = $5.20; 200 to 500g = $10.
- Small Packets: up to 100g = $2.65 surface/$4 airmail; 100 to 250g = $3.55/$5.45; 250 to 500g = $5.40/$10.65; 500g to 1kg = $9.50/$21.30; 1 to 2kg = $13.55/$35.55.

General Information

Note the following when sending letters and parcels in Canada:

- The post office operates a domestic **Priority Post Service** (letter post) or **Expedited Parcel Service** for parcels, both providing next day delivery for post between certain destinations. To check whether the pickup and delivery destination for your post allows this service, call ☎ 1-888-550-6333. A less expensive option providing delivery within two days is **Xpresspost**. Pre-paid envelopes are available for priority courier and xpresspost, and prepaid bubble packs and boxes for xpresspost.
- Affix airmail labels (available free from post offices) to all international airmail. Alternatively you can write or stamp '*PAR AVION* – BY AIRMAIL' in the top left corner.
- You can collect post from any post office in Canada through General Delivery (called *Poste Restante* in most other countries). Post should be addressed as follows: Name, c/o General Delivery, town, province and postal code (if known). General delivery post is kept at a town's main post office (if there's more than one) and is returned to the sender if it's unclaimed after 14 days. Therefore when sending post via general delivery always put a return address on the envelope. Identification is necessary for collection and some post offices ask for two forms of identification, e.g. passport, social insurance card, driver's licence or a credit card.
- If you have an American Express (Amex) card or use Amex travellers' cheques, you can have post sent to an Amex office. Standard letters are held free of charge (registered letters and packages aren't accepted). Post addressed to an Amex office should be marked 'client mail service' and is kept for 30 days before being returned to the sender. Post can be forwarded to another Amex office or address, but there's a charge. Other organisations also provide post holding services for members.
- If you have post sent to you at a temporary private address in Canada, you should have it addressed c/o the regular occupants. Otherwise the postman may return it to the sender (he *knows* you don't live there). If a letter cannot be delivered, it's returned stamped 'return to sender', 'not deliverable as addressed', 'moved not forwardable' or something similar. All post sent in

Canada should have a return address in case it cannot be delivered (you can have a name and address stamp made).

- Post boxes are red, with white lettering and look like dustbins on legs. Most post boxes have a flap with a handle (which may be invisible from the top of the box) that you pull back to open the slot where post is deposited. There are also post boxes at railway stations, airports and in hotel lobbies. These are often simply a slot in a wall marked 'CANADA POST'. Post is also collected from private homes, post offices and businesses.

  In some suburbs and rural areas there may be no post boxes, as post is collected by the postman when he does his rounds. In some areas, particularly where there are large houses with long driveways, houses have delivery/collection boxes situated at the end of the drive. These have a small flag (a metal arm) that's raised to indicate to the postman that there's post to be collected. In apartment blocks there are usually rows of post boxes in the foyer or entrance hall. In the suburbs there's one delivery/collection per day only, while in city centres there may be a number of collections per day, with the last at around 6pm or earlier at weekends. In most areas there's one delivery per day, either in the morning or mid-afternoon, excluding Sundays and holidays. In some remote rural areas there's no post delivery service and all post must be collected from the local postal outlets. In new suburban subdivisions there may be no door-to-door post delivery service. Instead there's what's called a 'superbox' (although there's nothing 'super' about it) at the end of the street with locked boxes to which all post is delivered.

- In most areas (over 4,600 locations) you can rent a postal box (PO box), which is a locked compartment within a post office or postal outlet. Postal boxes come in five sizes with rents from $72 to $460 per year.

- When you receive post from overseas on which duty is payable, the duty may be collected by the postal service, along with customs clearance and delivery fees on dutiable items. For packages containing dutiable articles, the customs officer will attach a *Customs Invoice* (E14) showing the rate of duty and the amount to be paid. For further information, obtain a copy of *Importing Non-Commercial Goods by Mail* (form RC 4051E) from a customs office.

- Most post in Canada is sorted by machine, which is expedited by the use of full and correct postal addresses and codes. Each character of the postal code has its own significance. The first three characters of the postal code (known as the forward sortation area/FSA) identify a particular geographical area. The first character (always a letter) designates a province or a territory within a province. The second character (always a number) denotes whether the post is to go to an urban or rural location. The third character of the code (always a letter) further defines the destination, e.g. in an urban code it identifies a postal station or city post office and in a rural code a group of post offices within a geographic area. The last three characters of the code (known as the local delivery unit/LDU) help to direct post to a specific location such as a city block, a large business, an office building or a community in a rural destination. The postal code follows the province name or initials (and doesn't precede it as in many other countries), as shown in the example below:

> René le Phew
> 9753 Gold Rush Avenue, Apt 999
> Noname City YT T7F 6R4
> Canada

Addresses in rural areas may be of a different sort, either a post office box address, where people have their own locked box in the lobby of a post office, or a 'rural route' address such as RR#3, S45 C67. These consist of a number of locked boxes at the side of the road, where the RR number refers to a route taken by the postman, the S refers to the site of the block of boxes and the C refers to the individual box (compartment) belonging to a person. Delivering to boxes reduces the travelling done by postmen, but not by those to whom the post is addressed!

If you don't know your postal code or want to find someone else's, you can consult the *Postal Code Directory*, available at all main post offices or you can buy a copy for $21.95 (plus taxes) from the National Philatelic Centre, Canada Post, 75 St Ninian Street, Antigonish NS B2G 2R8 (☎ 1-800-565-4362). You can also find postal codes on the Internet (🖳 www.canadapost.ca/tools/pcl/bin/default-e.asp). Postal codes are also available by phone (☎ 1-900-565-2633) at a cost of 75¢ per call for a maximum of three postal codes.

● When postal codes were established, the following two and three-letter province and territory abbreviations were also introduced and are the beginning of the code:

Alberta	AB
British Columbia	BC
Manitoba	MB
New Brunswick	NB
Newfoundland and Labrador	NL
Northwest Territories	NWT
Nova Scotia	NS
Nunavut	NU
Ontario	ON
Prince Edward Island	PE
Quebec	QC
Saskatchewan	SK
Yukon Territory	YT

- Stamps can be purchased in booklets of 10, 25 and 50, or in rolls of 100 from vending machines located in or outside post offices, airports, bus and railway stations, drugstores, banks, news-stands and hotels. Many post offices have self-service machines where stamps, stamp booklets, express post stamps, postcards, stamped envelopes and stamp pins are available, some of which may accept up to $20 bills. Stamp machines accept ATM 'cash' cards.

- If you send an item of post with insufficient postage it's returned to you for the collection of postage. When there's no return address on the item (which is written in the front top left corner in Canada) it's forwarded to the addressee for the collection of postage due plus an administrative charge (called a 'deficient postage fee').

- Domestic money orders can be purchased from post offices for any value from 1¢ to $999.99 for a flat fee of $2.75. International money orders can also be purchased for certain countries (the fee varies depending on the amount and the destination country) in Canadian dollars, US dollars and British pounds. Costs vary, e.g. $3.75 to the US and $4.75 to the UK. The maximum value available to the latter is £100.

- Literature for the blind weighing up to 7kg can be sent free within Canada, to the US and to other international destinations. You must write 'Literature for the Blind' where the stamp is normally affixed (in the top right-hand corner on the front of the envelope or parcel).

- Like many countries, Canada provides special services for philatelists. Post offices sell first-day covers, stamp collecting kits, *The Postal Service Guide to Canadian Stamps*, and sets of commemorative and special stamps. A free catalogue of philatelic services is available from the National Philatelic Centre, Station 1, 75 St Ninian Street, Antigonish NS B2G 2R8. (☎ 1-800-565-4362).

- Canada Post replies to letters addressed to Santa Claus (how sweet), although they're unlikely to send you a Ferrari. The address is Santa Claus, North Pole, Hoh Oho, Canada (🖳 www.canadapost.ca/holiday).

PARCELS & PACKAGES

Parcel rates vary widely depending on the size, weight and destination. The rates depend on the originating post office and the destination. Enquire at a post office or use the parcel rate calculator on the Canada Post website (🖳 www. canadapost.ca). There's only one class for regular parcels, delivery of which takes from three to ten days. If you want a faster service you can choose Xpresspost, which delivers within one to two days, or Priority Post which delivers overnight (by noon the next day) or within one day.

International letter packages weighing up to 2kg can be sent by airmail. International parcels containing personal hand-written or typewritten communications 'having the character of current correspondence', *must* be sent as letters or letter packages. Unless prohibited by the country of destination, merchandise or other items contained in letters (within the applicable weight and size limits) may also be sent at letter postage rates. Domestic parcels and parcels to the US and certain other countries can be insured. There are two services for international parcels: air and ground (surface). The maximum weight of parcels to most countries is 20kg, although it's only 10kg or 14kg to some countries. Parcels weighing over 10kg can be sent by surface only, although you can send them by courier. The maximum size limit for length, width and girth is a total of 1.05m (3.55ft) and the maximum length plus girth is 2m (6.56ft).

Parcels sent to addresses outside Canada must be accompanied by a customs declaration form. Requirements in most countries are met by using an adhesive form C1, which is a combined customs and dispatch note. If the item being sent is of 'no commercial value' (NCV), you should write this on the customs form under 'value'. Forms are available from post offices. When sending such things as drawings, large photographs or paintings through the post, you should sandwich them between cardboard or put them inside a cardboard tube to prevent them being damaged. All parcels must be securely wrapped. Postal outlets sell a variety of packaging products including tape, envelopes, padded envelopes, boxes, tubes, wrapping paper and cushioning material.

Urgent international parcels can be sent by Canada Post's SkyPak International Courier to the US, Europe, the Pacific Rim and other international destinations (a total of over 200 countries). It provides a next business day or two-day service to many destinations. Private parcel delivery services are operated by companies such as Federal Express, Loomis, Purolator and United Parcel Service (UPS). These companies provide a next day air parcel service within Canada, second day domestic air services, and international document and parcel services to over 180 countries and territories world-wide. Parcels can also be sent via postal, business and communication services, which have offices nation-wide.

VALUABLES & IMPORTANT DOCUMENTS

Canada Post provides a number of services for the delivery of valuables and important documents and letters:

- **Registered Post:** If you need verification that an item was received or require proof of posting, domestic post can be registered, which is often used to send legal documents, financial statements and important letters. Proof of posting, delivery confirmation (an official stamped receipt is provided at the time of posting) and information on the delivery status of the item are available by calling a toll-free number. Registered post costs $4.50 plus postage and includes indemnity against loss of up to $100 in value.

- **Security Registered Post:** If you need additional security or insurance you can use security registered post, which is available for domestic post, US post, international letters and parcels, and literature for the blind. This service provides proof of posting and delivery confirmation (the addressee's signature is obtained on delivery and may be returned to the customer with an acknowledgement of receipt card if this option is chosen). Added security is provided by special handling and insurance of up to $5,000 in Canada (costing 55¢ per $100 insurance), plus a toll-free number (☎ 1-888-550-6333) to check the delivery status (this can also be done via the Internet). The weight limit for domestic security registered post is 30kg and the cost is determined by the weight, size and destination of the item.

- **Insurance:** Insurance can be purchased in conjunction with COD, Priority Courier, Xpresspost, Expedited Parcel Service, Regular Parcel Service, Registered and Delivery Confirmation. Fragile and perishable items can be insured for loss but not against damage. The insurance limit depends on the destination, e.g. $5,000 for registered post within Canada and $1,000 for surface and air parcels to the US.

- **Money Packets:** For high-security processing of valuables such as banknotes, lottery tickets and jewellery, you should use the money packets service. Money packets may be only sent within Canada and (for security reasons) this service is only available at main city post offices. Indemnity is limited to $100 for loss or damage, although you can arrange for additional insurance through a private insurer. The cost is $10.71 up to 250g, $16.09 from 250g to 500g, and $6.20 for each additional 500g or fraction thereof above 500g, up to the maximum weight of 30kg.

- **Collect on Delivery (COD):** COD (called 'cash on delivery' in some other countries) is a domestic service for post for which an amount is due to the sender up to $1,000. COD items can be insured for up to $1,000.

- **Advice of Receipt:** The advice of receipt (AR) service provides you with the signature of the addressee. An AR card or label is purchased at the time of posting or (in some cases) up to two years after an item has been sent. When purchased at the time of posting, the AR card or label is attached to the item. A signature is obtained from the addressee on delivery and the card is returned to the sender, thus providing delivery confirmation. When purchased after posting, the card is sent to the postmaster, superintendent or manager of the delivery office, where the addressee's signature is obtained from the AR card. Acknowledgement of receipt costs 95¢ at the time of posting. To the US and other international destinations, AR can be used only with registered post at the time of posting.

- **Special Delivery:** A special delivery service is available to the US and selected international destinations and provides for expedited handling in Canada and delivery abroad. Special delivery costs $4.75 plus postage.

CHANGE OF ADDRESS

Before you move home you should complete a 'request for redirection of post' form available at postal outlets. You receive a free change of address kit including free postcards (as many as you want) to notify correspondents of your new address. Whenever possible, notify your post office at least one month before you move and be sure the effective date is entered on notification forms (the change of address actually takes 10 to 14 days to become effective, but it's wise to allow longer). The service is available for a six-month period for both residential and business addresses and can be extended provided that the extension is requested before the expiry date. There's no limit to the number of times it can be extended, but the current rate must be paid each time.

Redirection of post within Canada costs $30 for each six-month period and $60 to the US and other international addresses. When the period expires, post is returned to the sender (including international post), therefore you should remember to give all your correspondents your new address well in advance. Publishers of periodicals usually need at least six weeks' notice to effect a change of address. **If you complete a change of address form, your junk post (which earns Canada Post some $8 billion per year) automatically follows you as Canada Post sells its mailing list (including redirection of post forms) to companies.**

You can also request a 'temporary redirection of post' for up to three months for a fee of $9 per month (total $27) within Canada and $18 per month (total $54) to the US and other international addresses. Temporary redirection can be renewed for up to six months for an additional monthly fee. If you're going to be away from your home for a period, you can also have the post office hold your post until you return. You must complete a 'post-hold' form and pay the fee of $3 per week (there's a minimum 2-week period). Delivery is made on the 'resume service' date indicated on the card.

If you receive post that isn't addressed to you, you have two choices what to do with it (the third is to throw it away, which is illegal!). You can send it on to the addressee by crossing out your address, writing the correct address and dropping it in a post box without a stamp. Or, if you don't know the new address, you can cross out the address and write 'address unknown' and drop it in a post box (it's returned to the sender).

7.

TELEPHONE

Canadians are among the most habitual telephone users in the world, making more calls than people in almost any other country. Almost all Canadian households have at least one fixed-line phone and around 30 per cent also have a mobile phone (that's one for around every 1.5 people, compared with 1.9 in the US and 2.1 in Australia), and the country has over 14 million residential and 8.4 million business lines. Since the telecommunications industry was deregulated in 1994, increased competition in the long-distance market has resulted in greatly reduced call rates and Canada has one of the most modern and cheapest (for both local and long-distance calls) telephone systems in the world.

The major phone companies in Canada are AGT Alberta (Alberta), Telus (British Columbia), Bell Atlantic (Nova Scotia, New Brunswick, Newfoundland and Prince Edward Island), Bell Canada (Ontario and Quebec) and MTN (Manitoba). Canadian phone companies are expanding (and even buying or merging with US companies) and diverging into other areas; they've recently been permitted to send news and advertising over their lines and are lobbying to be allowed to transmit TV signals.

Emergency numbers are listed in the front of telephone directories (for more information see also page 151).

INSTALLATION & REGISTRATION

Homes in Canada (both new and old) are invariably wired for telephone services and many homes have points (phone jacks) in almost every room, although you should check the number and type of points in advance. If you need additional wiring or points you can have it done by your phone company, a contractor or you can do it yourself. Installation of one point plus wiring should take around half an hour and cost around $40. There's a fee of around $100 for installing a line if a new property doesn't have one and a connection fee of around $45 if a property already has a line (plus the cost of any additional points). To have a phone connected, contact a local phone company (their numbers are listed in telephone directories). You usually need to provide:

- Your name, full address, social insurance number (if you have one, if not, your passport number) and your previous address;

- The type of monthly service you require, your choice of long-distance company, how you would like your directory listing to appear or whether you would like an ex-directory (unlisted) number (see page 152).

If you aren't a previous customer but have a credit history with Visa or MasterCard or can prove that you own your own home, no deposit is necessary. Otherwise you must pay a $200 deposit with your first bill, which is refunded with interest after one year, or alternatively find a co-signer with an account with the phone company who will be responsible if you abscond without paying the bill. You're given a number when you apply.

CHOOSING A TELEPHONE

There are basically two types of telephone, the old-fashioned pulse telephones and the newer 'touch-tone' system where each key emits a different musical tone when pressed. Most Canadian homes have touch-tone phones, which are essential for contacting most large businesses that provide automated answering, such as checking credit card balances remotely. Pulse phones are universal and work on either pulse or tone lines. You can also buy a tone adapter that converts a pulse tone phone to tone operation or a switchable pulse/tone phone. Old rotary-dial phones work on the pulse system. All phones used in Canada must be approved by the Canadian Radio-Television and Telecommunications Commission (CRTC), which is indicated by the 'CRTC registration number' shown on a label fixed to the base or back of a phone.

Renting phones from a phone company isn't expensive (e.g. from around $5 per month), although most Canadians buy their own phones (they can also be purchased from phone companies via monthly payments). The price of a phone usually depends on the quality of its construction (the most important attribute), country of origin, and, not least, its features. A standard one-piece pulse phone (with the keys on the handset) costs around $20, while an all-singing, all-dancing, multi-function model costs from $100 to $300. If possible you should test phones before buying or buy from a retailer who provides a money-back guarantee. It's also wise to check the warranty period (usually one year) and its terms before making a purchase. The latest phones include Bell Canada's Vista screenphone (the rental cost for a Vista 350 screenphone is around $9.95 per month), which has a cordless infrared keyboard and allows you to store names and numbers, access Bell's electronic phonebook, access telephone banking, send and receive e-mail, and access Bell Direct, Interactive and SmartTouch services.

Cordless phones are popular and consist of a base station and a handset. The handset can be operated from 100 feet (short range) up to 1,000 feet (long range) from the base, depending on where they're used. It's wise to choose a cordless phone with a battery backup (in case of power failures) and a lockout security feature that prevents other cordless users dialling into your base station. Consumer Report Books publish *The Phone Book* (Consumers Union), containing everything you need to know about buying and installing phone equipment.

USING THE TELEPHONE

All phone dials and push buttons in Canada are marked with letters and numbers, so you just dial the number or press the key corresponding to a letter. Using a telephone in Canada is much the same as in any other country, with a few Canadian idiosyncrasies. When you make a call you hear either a regularly repeated long buzzing tone, which indicates that the number is ringing, or a rapidly repeated series of short buzzes, which indicates that the phone is busy (in use). When you pick up the receiver you hear the dial tone or, if you have voicemail (the phone company's answering service) and have new messages, you hear a series of beeps (e.g. three) followed by a pause (repeated).

Telephone numbers consist of a three-digit area code (123), a three-digit exchange code (456) and a four-digit subscriber number (7890), usually written as 123-456-7890. An area code may cover a city, a portion of a province or an entire province. Canada uses the same code system as the US and area codes for Canada and the US are shown on maps in telephone directories. New codes are being introduced as existing numbers have been exhausted by the growth of mobile phones, fax machines, computer modems and pagers. The area codes in Canada are as follows:

Area	Code(s)
Alberta North	780
Alberta South	403
British Columbia	250
Labrador	709
Newfoundland	709
New Brunswick	506
Northwest Territories	867
Nova Scotia	902
Manitoba	204
Montreal	514
Nunavut	867
Ontario	519, 705, 807 and 905
Ottawa	613
Prince Edward Island	902
Quebec	418, 450 and 819
Saskatchewan	306
Toronto City	416
Vancouver	604
Yukon Territories	867

If you're making a call to a number within your local service area, you dial the seven-digit number only (except in British Columbia and Ontario, where you have to dial ten digits). When making a call to another area code, you dial 1 + area code + the seven-digit telephone number. Local calling and service areas are shown in telephone directories.

Provinces are served by local phone companies such as Bell Canada, which are regulated by provincial and federal agencies. For long distance, e.g. inter-province and international calls, there are completely independent long-distance phone companies such as AT&T, Intel and Sprint. Most areas are served by a number of long-distance companies, although some have one only. Your local provincial phone company is your long-distance carrier by default and if you want to use another company you must make arrangements with that company.

All phone companies provide special services for those with disabilities including hearing and speech impaired customers, who are exempt from certain charges. Special handsets are available for the blind (with a nodule on the figure 5) and extra large key pads for the partially sighted. Telephones fitted with a flashing light, loud ring, a built-in amplifier or an inductive coupler (for those with behind-the-ear hearing aids) are available for the hard of hearing. A number of companies and organisations provide a Telecommunications Device for the Deaf (TDD) or teletype (TTY) line. These are typewriter-like devices that permit hearing or speech-impaired people to communicate over phone lines. Ask your phone company about TDD services.

Most phone companies offer message-taking services (voicemail) that can be less expensive (around $3 per month) and more efficient than having your own answering machine (costing from around $50 to $125). Message features usually include timed messages, the ability to receive messages when you're on another call, and to save and erase messages selectively.

TOLL-FREE NUMBERS

Toll-free numbers are indicated by the codes 800, 888 and 877, and are provided by businesses, organisations and government agencies in Canada (and the US). Many organisations and businesses list these numbers in all correspondence, advertisements and on all documentation, and they're usually listed in directories alongside ordinary numbers. Most toll-free numbers are for long-distance callers only and must be prefixed with a '1' (a local number is usually provided for local callers). Many toll-free numbers can be accessed from outside North America, although calls aren't free. Sometimes toll-free numbers are given as letters to make them easier to remember, e.g. 1-888-VIA-PREFER for VIA Rail. For information about toll-free numbers, call the national toll-free directory assistance numbers (☎1-800-555-1212, 1-888-555-1212 or 1-877-555-1212).

INFORMATION & ENTERTAINMENT NUMBERS

Don't confuse toll-free numbers with 900 information or entertainment numbers, which are expensive. Information numbers provide information on a wide range of subjects, including health, weather, road conditions and sports, while entertainment numbers include music lines, chat lines, competitions, horoscope or dial-a-prayer lines. These numbers are often used by fraudsters who make offers which seem too good to be true (they are!), e.g. 'guaranteed' credit or cash loans at low rates. Bear in mind that companies with these numbers often make their living entirely from the income generated by calls. The longer they can keep you on the line and the more times they can induce you to call, the more money they make. **Be wary of any advertisements that fail to clearly disclose the cost of calls or make it difficult for you to determine the total cost.** Some information provided by information and entertainment numbers is also available free via public service numbers (see page 155).

The use of information/entertainment numbers is a multi-million dollar growth industry. Charges usually range from around $1.99 to $9.99 per minute (average around $4.99), although with some lines there's no upper limit. Children and guests often make calls to these numbers using someone else's phone and run up thousands of dollars in bills (psychic and sex lines are among the most popular). Most phone companies offer a blocking option that allows you to block calls to 900 and other numbers from your home or office number (you can also block long-distance calls). If you have a complaint about a 900 number you should contact the Canadian Radio-Television and Telecommunications Commission (☎ 877-249-2782, 🖥 www.crtc.gc.ca/eng) or write to the Secretary General, Ottawa ON K1A 0N2 (☎ 819-994-0218).

CUSTOM & OPTIONAL SERVICES

All phone companies provide a range of extra services, usually called custom calling or optional services, most of which require a touch-tone phone that provides faster dialling plus access to a range of computerised services. Custom calling or optional services include call answer, call waiting, three-way calling and call forwarding, which can usually be ordered individually or as part of a package deal. Services cost from around $4 a month for one service to $9.95 for three. Alternatively you can choose a package that includes the most popular custom calling services.

OPERATOR SERVICES

To obtain the operator you dial 0. All operators speak English and many also speak French (if you want a French-speaking operator you will be connected to one). The operator provides a number of services and can also help you in an emergency. If you're trying to make an urgent call and the number is continuously busy, you can ask the operator to interrupt the conversation (there's a fee, e.g. $5). When the operator is making a connection, you should ask whether you're connected rather than 'through' to your number, as through means finished in Canada (also a line is said to be 'busy' and not 'engaged'). Whenever possible you should dial direct, as operator assisted calls are expensive unless you're unable to obtain a number due to a fault. If you dial correctly and get the wrong number, report the fault (see your telephone book for the number). The faulty call should be credited to your bill or, if you're using a payphone, you should be allowed a free call. Operators don't give out telephone numbers and to find out a number, call Directory Assistance on 411. A charge of around 50¢ is added to your telephone bill. Certain types of call can be made only through the operator, including:

Collect Calls: A collect (reverse charge) call is where the person being called agrees to pay for the call. To make a collect call, dial '0' followed by the area code and the number you wish to call. When the operator answers, tell him you wish to make a collect call and give your name, and they put you through as soon as the party accepts the call.

Conference Calls: You can talk with several people in different locations simultaneously via a conference call, provided that the phone has a 'conference call' or 'link' button. Desktop video-conferencing (DVC) is also possible via personal computers, where the person talking can be seen by other parties (as with a videophone).

There's a special charge for the above services, depending on the area and the phone company.

Person-To-Person Calls: The operator will try to obtain the required person for you and you pay for the call only when you reach him – useful when making a long-distance or international call.

Third-Number Calls Or Bill-To-A-Third-Number: You can make a call from another phone and bill it to your own or another number (provided that there's someone at home to verify that the charges are acceptable).

Time And Charge: When making a long-distance call you can ask the operator to tell you its duration and cost.

CHARGES

Throughout Canada, you pay a flat service fee (around $25 per month) and all local calls are then free. You can make long-distance calls through your local phone company or choose another company for those calls. If you're going to be away from your home for at least one month, you can usually save on line rental by asking your phone company to temporarily suspend your service.

Rates for long-distance calls vary with the time of calls, the phone company and the 'call plan'. One company may be cheaper for long-distance domestic calls but more expensive for international calls. Most people have a choice of company such as Stentor Group, AT&T, Sprint or their cable TV supplier. If you have a choice, contact companies direct for information about their services, rates, billing, dialling arrangements and special services, before choosing a company. Competition has intensified in the last few years, with discounts and rewards for switching carriers (e.g. frequent-flier miles, merchandise or free calls); offers vary from week to week and with good timing you can get your calls practically free. For this reason, some people switch their long-distance company a number of times per year. Since deregulation, however, most local companies now offer long-distance calls at competitive rates, so there's little point in switching.

From mid-1998, Sprint, closely followed by all the other long-distance carriers, offered unlimited long-distance calls within Canada between 6pm and

8am (local time) daily and any time at weekends and on Christmas and New Year's Day for a flat fee of around $20 per month. After this was introduced the average Canadian long-distance call increased from 5 to 30 minutes and the volume of calls created technical problems, which the phone companies overcame by installing thousands of new circuits.

BILLING & PAYMENT

Telephone bills are sent out monthly. Bills are divided into a number of pages and include a list of itemised calls and monthly charges for special services and equipment rentals. At the bottom of the bill there's usually a perforated payment return portion that must be included with your payment. Both local and long-distance calls (if billed by the same company) are itemised with the date, time, place, area and number called, rate, number of minutes and cost. Bills are sent by your local phone company and don't include charges for long-distance calls if you use a separate company. If you have any questions about your bill, the appropriate phone number to call is shown.

In addition to call charges, bills may contain a subscriber line charge, goods and services tax (GST), provincial sales tax (PST), line maintenance fee, and long-distance charges. Service charges are billed one month in advance. Where applicable, telephone line installation and connection fees are included in your first bill. Payment can usually be made in person at a phone company office, at authorised payment agencies, via the Internet or by post (a return envelope is included with your bill).

Your regular monthly bill is usually sent on the same date each month and is overdue when payment isn't received by the 'due by' date printed on the bill. Payments received after the due date are shown as the balance on the next bill. If payment isn't received by the due date, you may be sent another bill advising suspension of your service if it isn't paid within a certain period, e.g. seven days. You may also be charged a 'late payment' fee, e.g. 1.5 per cent of the amount due. If your service is suspended you must pay the amount due plus a reconnection fee (e.g. $40) and it may also be necessary to pay a deposit.

INTERNATIONAL CALLS

Most private phones in Canada are on International Direct Dialling (IDD), which allows calls to be dialled to over 190 countries and collect (reverse charge) calls to be made to around 140 countries. To make an international call, you dial the international access code (011), the country code (e.g. 44 for Britain), the area code *without* the first zero, and finally the subscriber's number. For example, to call the number 123-4567 in central London, England (area code 0207) you dial 011-44-207-123-4567. The reason you don't get the operator after dialling the first 0 of 011 is that there's an automatic delay after you dial 0, during which time you can dial additional numbers.

When making a person-to-person, collect call (not accepted by all countries), calling card or billing to a third number international call, dial 01 instead of 011, followed by the country code, city code and number. The operator comes on the line and asks for details, such as the name of the person you're calling or your calling card number. If you cannot dial an international call directly, you must dial 00 and go through the international operator, when the cost is the same as dialling yourself. **If you ask the operator to connect you when it's possible to dial yourself, the call is much more expensive.** When using the operator, it saves time if you tell him the country code, the area code without the leading zero and the subscriber's number.

Calls to the US cost little more than domestic calls and substantial savings can be made by calling during off-peak periods. International calls have different times for off-peak calls, depending on the country called. Costs vary considerably and are constantly changing. In early 2003, Telus were quoting the following per minute rates on their website: Australia (87¢), France (70¢), Germany (88¢), Hong Kong (87¢), Ireland (92¢), Italy ($1.11), Japan ($1.18), New Zealand (99¢), South Africa ($1.51) and the UK (55¢), for off-peak calls made using their *Your Way Straight Savings* plan. Check with your long-distance carrier for information. For toll-free information regarding international calls, dial ☎ 1-800-874-4000. The codes for major international cities are listed in telephone directories.

Long distance phone companies compete vigorously for overseas customers and offer Canadian citizens and residents calling cards, which allow you to bill calls made in Canada and abroad to a credit card or your home or business phone bill. The benefits of calling cards are that they're fee-free, calls can be made in Canada and to/from most countries, calls can usually be made from any phone, including hotel phones, calls are made via an English-speaking operator in Canada (foreign-language operators are also available) and, most importantly of all, calls are charged at Canadian rates (based on the cost between Canada and the country you're calling from and to) and are usually much cheaper than calls made via local phone companies. With a 'Call-Me' card your family and friends can call you free of charge from anywhere at your expense **(so don't give them to telephone sales people)** by entering a personal four-digit number and the card number.

Canada subscribes to the Home Country Direct service that allows you to call a special number giving you direct and free access to a bi-lingual operator in Canada. The operator connects you to the number required and also accepts calling card and reverse charge (collect) calls. For information about the countries served by the Home Country Direct service call ☎ 1-800-CALL-ATT and ask them to send you a Canada Direct wallet card.

PUBLIC TELEPHONES

Public phones or payphones are plentiful in cities and towns (where they're usually located on street corners), airports, railway and bus stations, hotel and office building foyers, bars and restaurants (many provide cordless phones), post offices, libraries and other public buildings, shops, department stores and drugstores, launderettes (laundromats), shopping centres (malls), petrol stations, and at motorway service stations. Most are usually in working order. There are no public phone offices in Canada and all long-distance and international calls must be made from payphones, many of which provide little shelter from noise and the elements (some public phones have a 'LOUD' button to increase the volume). **Because local calls are free to subscribers, some shopkeepers allow you to make a local call from their phone.**

Before using a payphone, read the operating instructions, which may vary depending on the area. AT&T provide public phones in airports with a screen on which instructions can be displayed in English, French, German, Spanish and possibly other languages (e.g. Cantonese in Vancouver), called a 'public phone plus'. Some payphones are 'dial tone first', which means you get a dial tone before you insert any coins. Coins are inserted only after you've dialled and are connected to your number. These phones allow you to dial an emergency number (or the operator, directory assistance or a toll-free number) when you have no coins. With other payphones, you must insert the minimum call fee before you get a dial tone (even when calling an emergency service), although the fee is returned automatically if it's a free call. If you've inserted coins and there's no reply, you simply replace the receiver to get your money back.

The cost of a local call from a payphone is 25¢ for a three-minute call. Payphones usually accept nickels (5¢), dimes (10¢) and quarters (25¢) only and don't give change, so insert the correct amount. Some new payphones charge 25¢ per minute for calls anywhere within continental Canada. Off-peak rates also apply to payphones. You can also make toll-free calls from payphones. Direct dial calls from payphones also benefit from off-peak discounts, but are more expensive than calls from private phones.

Charges for long-distance calls from payphones are set by the company that services the phone. When you make a call from a payphone, check the dialling instruction card on the phone to see which long-distance company services the phone. If you wish to use a long-distance company other than the one assigned to the payphone, you must first dial the number 1 followed by the code for your preferred provider. Some payphones provide fast access to long-distance carriers by pushing a single button and allow you to bill calls to a credit card. After you've dialled the number and before the call is connected, the operator tells you the charge for connection (usually $2.50). Insert this amount and be prepared to pay more when requested. If you're making an international call, you require a huge pile of quarters. After you've deposited the correct amount, the call is connected. As with local calls, your coins are returned if there's no answer.

Payphones usually have directories that are attached in various ingenious ways to payphones. You can also obtain free directory assistance by dialling 411. For directory assistance for toll-free numbers dial ☎ 1-800-555-1212, 1-888-555-1212 or 1-887-555-1212. The costs of long-distance calls from hotel rooms, either direct-dialled or via the hotel switchboard, are usually expensive due to high surcharges (and a hotel's exclusive deal with a phone company). To save money, use a payphone in the lobby. Local calls usually cost around 75¢ from a hotel room, although they may be free from a motel (which may be indicated by a 'free local calls' sign).

Many phone companies issue payphone cards for various values such as $5, $10, $20 and $50, and some also issue long-distance calling cards. These include Cardcaller Canada (☎ 416-733-2163) long-distance calling cards that are sold in various outlets for $10, $20 or $50 (calls cost 60¢ per minute). AT&T (☎ 1-888-240-3295) have two kinds of card: one is prepaid while the other debits calls to a credit card. Bell Canada issues HELLO or ALLO debit cards (available from Bell Canada phone centres or Shopper's Drug Mart stores) with PIN numbers enabling them to be used from any phone in the country (Bell Canada's Quickchange or LaPuce smart cards can only be used in some payphones in Ontario and Quebec). Before buying a card, check to see whether it's restricted to domestic calls or allows you to make calls abroad. In major tourist or transport centres, payphones accept credit cards.

If you use a rotary dial phone, dial 0 followed by the area code and the seven-digit number only. When the operator answers, tell him you're placing a calling card call and give him your card number. Some companies make a surcharge for calling card calls. Cards can also be used to make international calls to Canada from overseas.

DIRECTORIES

Telephone directories (commonly referred to as phone books) contain a wealth of information about telephone services, using telephones, area codes and time zone map, international city codes, call rates, emergency numbers, service numbers, toll-free numbers, repair services, establishing or changing services, local service options, customer calling services, customer rights, phone safety, billing and payment, directory assistance, area and long-distance calling, dialling instructions and operator assistance. Other information often includes a calendar of events, local information and maps, public transportation, leisure and sports, parks, shopping, community services and postal codes. Emergency numbers are usually listed inside the front cover of both white and yellow pages, and some directories include nuclear emergency information, and a first aid and survival guide.

Directories are divided into sections, e.g. general information, white pages (subscribers' numbers), blue pages (local, provincial and federal government offices), yellow pages (business listings) and green pages (coupons). Yellow pages are indispensable in Canada and list subscribers under a business or service heading (in alphabetical order). Local 'yellow page' directories are also published in some areas. You can order extra copies of any white or yellow pages published by your local phone company by completing a pre-paid card in your local directory, but you may have to pay for them. Directories for provinces other than the one where you live can also be ordered (for a fee).

In most areas, white and yellow pages are published annually by Area Code, e.g. 416 (Toronto) or 604 (Vancouver). Telephone directories, including yellow pages, are available in bars, restaurants, hotel lobbies, main post offices and public reference libraries, some of which also keep foreign directories. National directories listing businesses, colleges and universities, associations and organisations, international organisations, and travel resources (resorts, car rental, hotels and motels, etc.) are also available.

With your basic telephone service you receive a listing in the white pages of your local telephone book and business customers also receive a free listing in the yellow pages. Two people with the same family name can have both their first names listed and you can purchase additional listings for around $1 per month. Anyone can get an ex-directory (non-listed) number in Canada for a fee of around $1 per month. This means that your number isn't included in the directory, but is available through directory assistance. For an additional fee (e.g. $2 per month), you can have a non-published number, which means your number is also unavailable through directory assistance. Bell Canada customers (and others) can include their e-mail and Internet addresses in the white pages for a small monthly fee.

In all areas you dial 411 for local directory assistance (inquiries) or information. Often numbers are given by recorded messages and repeated, so be ready to write them down. The operator will help you in an emergency (the emergency number is 911 in all cities). Residential customers pay for all calls to directory assistance, usually around 75¢ per call, while calls from payphones are free. White and yellow pages can also be accessed via the Internet (e.g. 🖥 www. yellowpages.ca) and with certain phones such as a Vista 350 or 450 screenphone, where you just press and key and speak the name of the person or company whose number you require (the number can also be dialled automatically).

MOBILE PHONES

Some 30 per cent of Canadians have a mobile phone (usually referred to as cell phones), a total of over six million, which are now relatively inexpensive. In recent years mobile phones have progressed from being an expensive yuppy status symbol to essential equipment for business people (and teenagers) and anyone who does a lot of travelling. In fact, due to their widespread use (and nuisance value) many restaurants, sporting venues, clubs and hotels have been forced to ban their use. Some businesses use jammers that can detect and jam every handset within 100 metres!

Until recently, all portable phones in Canada operated on the cellular system, where calls are made through designated radio frequencies that connect through 'cells'. This caused some problems with crossed lines because there are only 412 radio frequencies for cell-phones, which soon became saturated with calls. The most recent development is a new digital technology called Personal Communications Services (PCS), which offers increased capacity and a generally superior service. One advantage of PCS is that you can receive e-mail or faxes by plugging a PCS phone into a computer. It's also less vulnerable to crooks who use scanners to 'grab' a caller's phone and identification numbers and use them to make free long-distance and international calls. It's wise to lock your phone when it isn't in use and keep it and any documents in a safe place, eliminate international calling if you don't need it and report any bogus calls to your provider immediately.

Calls to and from mobile phones are expensive. Most are billed by the minute, and some start charging as soon as you're connected to the service company rather than to the person you want to talk to. The average cost per month depends on which plan you choose and varies from $19.95 to $59.95 per month (the average is around $35). Calls typically cost around 65¢ per minute during business hours, but are usually free on weekdays between 6pm and 6am, and at weekends. Options such as voicemail, call waiting and call forwarding usually cost around $4.95 per month. You must usually buy your own phone (they cost from around $100), although a new company may give you a phone as a bonus if you sign a contract for one or two years.

PCS calls are cheaper than with standard phones, for example FIDO (🖥 www.fido.ca) offers 400 minutes of local calls per month for $45, bills you by the second and provides a global service that allows you to use your phone in many other countries. You can also operate a phone with a phonecard instead of subscribing to one of the standard price plans. You simply buy vouchers (e.g. for $5, $25 or $50) and enter their numbers into your phone, thus 'loading' it with the relevant amount of call time.

You may also be interested in Bell Canada's Simply One service that combines a fixed line (home or business) and mobile phone with one phone number, one long-distance plan, one voicemail box and a single bill. Both phones can be used at the same time on the same line and a third party can be added for three-way conferencing. Simply One is available in selected areas only and costs from $25 per month depending on the package chosen.

TELEGRAMS, TELEX & FAX

To send telegrams, contact CN/CP Telecommunications (listed in the telephone directory) who operate a 'telepost' service with Canada Post that accepts messages 24 hours per day, seven days per week. Messages telephoned to the nearest CN/CP public message centre are delivered the next day anywhere in Canada or the US. The cost can be charged to a credit card. However, few people in Canada use telegrams nowadays as most have a phone. For the same reason, telex isn't much used, although it's still available through Western Union. Charged by the minute, not by the word, it's useful if you send a lot of international telegrams.

In addition to being home to the world's most frequent phone users, Canada also has a wealth of fax (facsimile) machines. Faxes can be sent from a payphone-type machine and credit card operated machines found in public places throughout Canada, e.g. airports and railway stations. There are public fax bureaux in most cities and most hotels provide fax services (e.g. fax machines in foyers and in-room in some hotels) for public use. You can also use Intelpost, a fax-type service for sending documents and photographs via satellite to North American and European cities. You can also obtain a fax pager that displays the name of the sender and his phone number, and allows you to redirect the fax to a laptop computer or a nearby fax machine.

INTERNET

The success of the Internet is built on the ability to view and collect information from computers around the world by connecting to a local Internet provider for the 'cost' of a local phone call (which is free in Canada). If you have correspondents or friends who are connected to the Internet, you can make long-distance and international 'calls' for the price of a local phone call. Internet users can buy software or use Internet services such as IDT Net2Phone (🖳 http://web.net2phone.com) and Creative WebPhone (🖳 www.adirtech.com) that effectively turn your personal computer into a voice-based telephone. All you need is a sound card, a microphone, a modem and access to an Internet Service Provider (ISP). Most systems work more like a sophisticated two-way radio than a phone and aren't as efficient as using a phone. However, as local calls are free this enables you also to make free long-distance and international calls (apart from your ISP fees). You can also use a sophisticated form of electronic mail such as ICQ (🖳 www.icq.com) where each party has a split screen and can see the other's message as it's typed.

Over a third of Canadian households have at least one person who uses a computer for communication (e.g. e-mail, Internet or ISDN) at home or at work. The greatest concentration is in Alberta and Ontario with 40 per cent and the smallest in Quebec with just 20 per cent. Internet use from home is more common in households with young people (at least one person accesses the Internet regularly in around 40 per cent of households where there's someone under 18, compared with just 25 per cent where there's nobody under 18).

To get onto the Internet you need to subscribe to an ISP (there are over 100 throughout the country) such as America Online (☎ 703-264-1184), Compuserve (☎ 1-800-336-6823) or the IBM Global network (☎ 1-800-426 4968, 🖳 www.ibm.com/globalnetwork). The most popular ISP is Sympatico (☎ 1-800-773-2121, 🖳 www.sympatico.ca) which is owned by Bell Canada and offers a series of plans, e.g. around $10 for five hours access per month, $20 for 40 hours per month and $25 for 150 hours per month (additional hours cost around $1.50). The top providers in each province are often the telephone and cable companies. They sell modems for between $59.95 and $69.95, and sometimes offer preferential rates for your first six months online, e.g. $24.95 per month for the first six months for IDSL (high speed Internet connection, which doesn't interfere with your telephone line), thereafter $34.96.

EMERGENCY NUMBERS

The national emergency number in Canada is 911 for police, fire and ambulance emergencies, plus coastguard, cave and mountain rescue services. Emergency phone numbers for all other emergency-type organisations (e.g. rape crisis, Samaritans, etc.) are listed inside the front cover of telephone directories. There are also local emergency numbers that you should make a note of and keep in a prominent place near your phone(s). If you're calling from a payphone the local emergency number is usually shown on the phone dial. Emergency 911 calls are free from all phones, including payphones (no money is required). If you don't know the number or get no reply from 911, call the operator (dial 0) and ask for the emergency service you require.

When making an emergency call, don't hang up but let the emergency person end the conversation, as they may have important questions or instructions about what you should do until help arrives. If you're unable to remain on the line, tell the operator the nature of the emergency, the exact location (address, town, etc.), where help is required and your phone number. If you have a shared line that's required for an emergency call, you will be informed by the operator and must hang up immediately.

In addition to the above emergency services, in most areas there are special local crisis hotlines for help and advice concerning missing children, youth crises and runaways, child abuse, battered women, deaf contact (or an emergency teletypewriter for the deaf), eye traumas, alcoholics anonymous, animal bites, poison advice, crime victims, gays and lesbians, health, rapes, suicide prevention, VD clinics, AIDS and drug abuse. These numbers are usually listed in local directories. See also **Emergencies** on page 242 and **Counselling** on page 250.

PUBLIC SERVICE NUMBERS

There are no national service numbers (e.g.for weather) in Canada, as provided in many other countries, although some private companies offer these services via 900 numbers. Public service numbers are listed in telephone directories, e.g. in a 'Self Help Guide'. There are also free 'talking yellow pages' at the front of yellow pages. They may include arts, leisure and recreation, consumer problems, children's services, disabled services, discrimination, education, elderly services, employment, financial services, health, information/referral services, landlord/tenant services, legal services, pollution, taxes, transportation, veterans' services, voter information, weather and welfare. In most areas there are consumer information services (often free) that may be provided by local Better Business Bureaux. All provinces provide a range of toll-free hotlines offering a wide range of information including education, health, consumer and welfare information. Bi-lingual (English/French) information specialists are often available to answer your questions. Some communities have a local 'special event telephone line', where residents can make community announcements.

8.

TELEVISION & RADIO

Most Canadian households have at least one TV and over 70 per cent have two or more. The average Canadian family watches around 23 hours of TV per week. Prime time viewing is from 7 to 11pm. A TV is an essential part of Canadian life and even the most modest motel or hotel boasts a colour TV in every room. Airports and bus stations have coin-operated TVs built into the arms of chairs, and bars, clubs, dance halls and even launderettes have TVs. The majority of programmes are produced in the US and are every bit as banal and senseless as you may have heard. In many homes, TV rivals family and religion as the dispenser of values and is often referred to as the 'plug-in drug' or the 'third parent'.

The pervasive influence of the US on Canadian TV has led the Canadian government to mandate that all Canadian TV stations must devote a certain percentage of time each day to Canadian-produced programmes. Private TV licensees must generally achieve an annual Canadian content level of 60 per cent, measured over the broadcast day, and 50 per cent overall during the peak evening hours. Stations owned by the Canadian Broadcasting Corporation (CBC) must have 60 per cent Canadian content at all times (it broadcasts 90 per cent Canadian content in prime time). Canadian speciality and pay-TV services also have Canadian programming requirements. The Canadian Radio-Television and Telecommunications Commission (CRTC) oversees Canadian TV and radio standards.

There's no TV licence fee in Canada and with the exception of some government grants received by CBC, Canadian TV is financed by advertising. The more people who watch a particular programme, the more advertising costs, which results in fierce competition between stations to produce programmes that increase their daily ratings. Programmes that receive poor ratings are often axed at the drop of a hat. Some programmes, particularly sports broadcasts, are actually produced by one or more advertisers.

Television programmes (broadcast and cable) are listed in daily newspapers, many of which provide free weekly programme guides. There are free TV guides in most areas and many more are available on news-stands. For information about **Radio** see page 163.

STANDARDS

The standards for TV reception in Canada aren't the same as in most other countries (except the US). The Canadian transmission standard is NTSC, which is broadcast on 525 lines rather than, for example, the 625-line PAL standard used in most of Europe. TVs and video recorders that aren't manufactured for the NTSC standard won't function in Canada, although dual-standard TVs are available. If you bring a TV to Canada from overseas you may get a picture or sound, but not both. Video recorders manufactured for non-Canadian markets cannot be used to record or play back NTSC-standard videos (however, PAL video recorders and TVs are useful for playing PAL videos in Canada). The cost of a TV varies considerably, depending on its make, screen size, features and, not least, the retailer. High-definition TVs (HDTVs) employing a wider screen are also available, but are expensive. **A TV remote control is called a converter in Canada.**

In most apartments there's no need to fit a private aerial (antenna) as all large buildings have a master aerial on the roof, although nowadays most Canadians receive their TV via cable.

STATIONS & PROGRAMMES

Canadians have four nation-wide TV networks: Canadian Broadcasting Corporation (CBC) - or as one wag famously put it, the Canadian Broadcorping Castration - Canadian Television Network (CTV), Global/Canwest, and *Société de Radio-Télévision du Canada (SRC)*, the French-language arm of CBC. CBC and SRC are government subsidised. In 1997, CBC, which includes 22 TV stations, celebrated 60 years of public broadcasting. There are also around 40 regional networks, including CHUM/CITY, Manitoba Television Network (MTN), Television Northern Canada (TVNC) and TeleQuébec that broadcast to a few provinces. Several provinces have government supported TV networks, such as TVOntario. Networks compete intensely for the 'best' (or rather, most popular) programmes and sports events. Toronto is the media capital of Canada and the major networks all have their head offices there. In addition to the national and regional networks, there are over 100 licensed commercial TV stations available on cable. Local stations also show their own local news, sports and other broadcasts, which are often surprisingly amateurish affairs.

Despite the high proportion of Canadian-made programmes, most are every bit as bad as programmes in the US, particularly those made by small stations with small budgets. Even the programmes made by CBC can be pretty bad, particularly the poorly disguised clones of popular US programmes, such as *Street Legal* (LA Law), *North of 60* (Northern Exposure), *Degrassi* (Saved by the Bell) and *Side Effects* (St. Elsewhere). However, not everything is rubbish and Canadian TV produces a big-business soap called *Traders* and also *Forever Knight*, where the Toronto homicide cop hero is an 800-year-old vampire. It also occasionally produces some comedy gems, such as *The Royal Canadian Air Farce*, *This Hour Has 22 Minutes* and *Due South*, which is billed as a 'wacky cop-come-comedy' about madcap Mounties (characters include a good-looking but incredibly dim Mountie hero, his ex-Chicago cop side-kick and a deaf, lip-reading husky dog masquerading as a wolf). Canadian TV has its own annual awards for the 'least worst' TV programmes, called a Gemini (TV's equivalent of the Oscar). Swearing isn't permitted on TV in Canada and pornography isn't available on terrestrial or cable TV.

One big difference between TV in Canada and the US is the news. Unlike the US, Canadian TV shows international news and doesn't descend into meaningless sensationalism (not much anyway). The Canadian Broadcasting Corporation is an excellent source of news, taking its lead from the BBC and doing a good job of living up to its standards.

Most TV stations are on the air 24 hours per day and most programmes (with the exception of sport and some political coverage) are broadcast at the same time each day, irrespective of the time zone. Because Newfoundland is half an hour ahead of the rest of Atlantic Canada (see page 396), the phrase 'half an hour later in Newfoundland' has become part of the Canadian lexicon. If a programme is shown at 8pm in Atlantic Canada, it's then broadcast an hour later in central Canada, where it's again 8pm, and so on across the country. Some British Columbia sports events may start early to hit prime time in Toronto or start at the normal time in British Columbia, which gets them on the air in the late evening in Ontario.

Canadians with cable can receive the US Public Broadcasting System (PBS), which offers a much better quality of programme. The PBS network of regional stations was developed as an antidote to the national networks, so that the 'few' discerning viewers (mostly foreigners) could watch some serious TV occasionally. PBS channels show some of the highest-quality programmes, many of which are foreign (e.g. British) imports. PBS output includes comedy (British sitcoms are popular), children's programmes (e.g. Sesame Street), drama, documentaries, discussion programmes, excellent science and nature features, live music and theatre, and anything that's generally too highbrow for national network viewers. However, as a result of its lack of funds, the PBS network is forced to broadcast many low-budget, narrow-interest programmes and must canvas incessantly for sponsorship and donations to stay on the air. They request donations of at least $50, or you can become a 'friend of the station' for $100 or $200. If you make a donation they send you gifts, such as a John Cleese T-shirt if they're running a Fawlty Towers marathon or a CD of a symphony if they're showing an orchestral performance.

CABLE TELEVISION

Around 75 per cent of Canadian households subscribe to cable TV, which has over 150 TV channels available. Most cable stations broadcast 24-hours per day and many subscribers can receive over 50 stations. Although there are some general entertainment cable TV channels, many are dedicated to a particular topic, including movies, sports, religion, comedy, local events, news, financial news, shopping, children's programmes, weather, health, music (rock, country) and foreign-language programmes (e.g. Italian or Mandarin).

English soccer-addicted expatriates will be glad to hear that The Sports Network (TSN) shows an English Premiership match every Saturday at 9.30am Eastern Standard Time. Cable TV isn't subject to the same federal laws as broadcast TV and therefore channels may show programmes that aren't permitted on network TV. In 1997, CRTC licensed Bell Canada and four other companies to provide video-on-demand (VOD) services that allow viewers to browse a computerised library of video programmes, mostly movies. Bell Canada also provides FM radio and Internet services over their phone lines.

The cable channels available in a city or locality depend on the franchise agreement with the local municipality, although the most popular channels are usually available throughout the country. Cable companies charge an installation fee of around $39.95 and provide a basic cable service for a flat fee of around $20 per month, plus premium subscription stations which average another $10 to $20 per month. The average subscriber pays around $35 per month. Some companies provide a preferred or plus service, which is an expanded basic service.

A typical popular cable package includes all the local terrestrial Canadian stations, ABC, NBC, CBS and Fox from the US, CBC and CTV dedicated news channels and the CNN and CNBC news channels from the US, some US-based cable channels such as Arts and Entertainment, Canadian cable stations such as Women's Television Network, and some cross-breeds such as Bravo, which shows some US Bravo shows and Canada-only Bravo programming. Canada has two cable sports channels that buy some programming from ESPN and other sports programmers in the US. Other programmes include Much Music, Much More Music, Musique Plus (French), the Nashville Network (TNN), Lifetime TV (LIF), Cable News Network (CNN), Financial News Network (FNN), Entertainment Sports Programming Network (ESPN), The Weather Channel (TWC), Home Shopping Network (HSN), The Turner Network (TNT), Arts and Entertainment (A&E), the Discovery Channel, Youth TV (YTV), Showcase (an arts channel), Teletoon (cartoons/classic comedies), and Prime TV (mostly old classic movies and TV shows).

Cable TV is standard in most large towns and cities, where most homes have access to more than one cable company. Ask your neighbours or estate agent which companies supply your cable TV service and call to ask them about their rates and options. Most apartments, condos and some townhouses have cable included in the rent or they have cable hooked up. All you need to do is call and tell the cable company your address and they switch it on within 15 minutes and send you a bill. Modern TVs are 'cable ready' and no cable converter box is required. To receive pay-per-view programmes you need to pay a deposit and obtain a descrambler from your cable company. When there's a programme you want to watch, such as a movie or sports event, you ring your cable company and they unscramble it for you.

Cable TV is usually available in hotels, motels and even in some YMCAs and youth hostels (although some hotel pay-per-view films are expensive). Cable TV programmes are listed in weekly TV magazines, such as the best-selling *TV Times*, and in daily newspapers, where they may be divided into standard and premium channels.

SATELLITE TELEVISION

It's only recently that satellite TV has become fully legal and regulated by the Canadian government, with point-multi-point microwave systems spreading across Canada. There are around 20 TV satellites positioned over North America serving both Canada and the US, each with a capacity to transmit up to 24 channels. The so-called independent superstations use the power of both cable and satellites to programme nation-wide. Most satellite transmissions are broadcast exclusively for local cable TV companies, who pass the satellite signal through their cable network to subscribers. Every hotel, bar and club has a satellite dish that's mainly used to receive sports events (some show a number of ballgames simultaneously on different TVs).

However, a growing number of people are buying satellite dishes to receive transmissions, particularly in remote rural areas where homes cannot be connected to a cable system. Digital dishes with a 1.5ft dish cost around $199 and can receive TV stations from around the world. Alternatively, some companies provide a 'free' dish if you sign up to view their selected programmes for a number of years. A cheaper alternative is the new microwave service that uses ground-based transmitters. Monthly costs are about the same as satellite, but the initial outlay is less. The biggest drawback is that CRTC rules force customers to buy a Canadian pay channel for every US channel purchased.

The contracts between the satellite owners, programmers and local cable TV companies are exclusive, so direct reception of the satellite signal is illegal. There has been some controversy in recent years concerning a dish owner's right to freely receive satellite signals, although it's virtually impossible to enforce the law about the way you convert the satellite signal after it has entered your home. Satellite owners' attempts to scramble signals have had little effect and plans for pirate descramblers are quickly on the market and sold through advertisements in magazines such as *Popular Mechanics* (although a new scrambling system may soon obstruct the pirates). If you have a large satellite dish you may be interested in the *World Radio TV Handbook* edited by David G. Bobbett (Watson-Guptil Publications).

VIDEOS

The Canadian video market is one of the largest in the world and over 70 per cent of Canadian homes have a VCR (video cameras are also popular). In the last decade there's been an explosion in the number of video rental stores in Canada (most towns have a few), although saturation point was reached some years ago in the major cities, where competition is intense. You can buy practically anything on video in Canada, where there's a huge market in educational, training and sports videos. New videos sell for $16.95 to $19.95 and previously viewed videos (old rentals) of recent releases cost around $6 to $12 (with a 14-day guarantee). Videos of movie classics cost between $6 and $9.99. One of the best places to buy videos is from a mail-order video club, most of which offer new members amazing introductory offers, e.g. six movies for 39¢ each (plus shipping and handling), in return for an agreement to buy six more over a period of three years at regular prices (around $20 each).

Many video stores are open from around 9am until midnight or even 2am, seven days per week. To rent a video you must be a member, for which stores require ID and proof of your address. If you're aged under 18, a parent is required to be a guarantor. Rental charges are usually around 99¢ to $4.99, depending on the movie rating (new top ten movies are the most expensive) and local competition. The standard rental period is usually one day for new releases and three days for regular movies. Most stores will rent you several old releases for a number of days for a single price, e.g. 'five flicks, five days, five bucks' or 'seven movies, seven days, $7'. Each of the major video franchises offers different incentives to keep its clientele coming back. Blockbuster boasts that any new release you want (selected titles of course) will be in stock, otherwise your next rental is free. Classic and educational videos can also be rented from public libraries.

The main video rental chains are Blockbuster, Rogers Video, Videoflicks and Jumbo Video. Rogers and Blockbuster don't stock 'blue' movies but what they term 'adult' movies, although some privately owned stores do (the minimum age limit for renting adult movies is 18). Movies are available on VHS videos, laser disk and DVD. Many video stores sell food such as ice-cream bars, ice-lollies, sweets and popcorn.

Some large chains also rent Nintendo and Sony playstations, with a large variety of games. The rental for this type of gaming station is usually around $12.99 for three days, plus the cost of the game rental, typically $5.99 for three days. You must also make a deposit of $150 to $200 in cash or with a credit card for the playstation. This is a relatively inexpensive way to find out whether a child will get good value from these games before forking out hundreds of dollars to buy one.

RADIO

Radio flourishes in Canada and has a growing audience, despite the competition from TV, cinema and videos (the average Canadian listens to the radio for around 14 hours per week). Radio reception is good in most parts of the country, including stereo reception, which is excellent in all but the most mountainous areas (where you're lucky to receive anything). Canada has around 500 local radio stations and in major cities you generally have a choice of around 50 stations, although in remote areas you may be able to receive a few stations only. Local stations generally stick to a bland commercial format with little originality, although they're a good source of information about local entertainment and for road and weather reports. Although most stations are commercial, advertising on radio is a lot less obtrusive than on TV. Many radio stations are highly specialised and these include a variety of foreign language stations and non-commercial stations operated by colleges, universities and public authorities. Stations are classified as AM (or medium wave) or FM (VHF, often stereo), and a few broadcast simultaneously on both wavebands; frequencies are quoted in kHz (AM) or MHz (FM). Canadian radio stations are identified by their call sign: a four letter designation that begins with 'C.'

Canadian mainstream commercial radio (like commercial TV) is of little interest if you're looking for serious discussion or education, but excellent if you're into music, news or religion. Music stations can be highly specialised, offering easy-listening, country and western, or rock. Interestingly, the mix is changing, as many listeners have abandoned music stations for talk radio. Part of the problem is poor sound quality on AM, therefore stations are turning to formats that don't require quality sound (three-quarters of Canadians have CD players in their homes or cars, which may have something to do with this). The situation may improve with digital technology, which gives better sound quality and is also immune to interference from static or echoes. Those with cable TV can subscribe to an FM stereo service in most areas, which improves FM reception on your stereo receiver.

If you're looking for serious radio, you need to tune to CBC (⌨ www.radio. cbc.ca). Government-subsidised at a cost of around 8¢ per day for every Canadian, CBC offers primarily news and public affairs programming (patterned on BBC Radio) in English and French, plus a 24-hour cable news service in both languages, a Northern service in eight Aboriginal languages, and Radio Canada International (RCI), a short-wave radio service broadcasting around the world in seven languages. CBC started broadcasting in 1937 and has been called the 'ribbon of reason' that holds Canada together (just as the railway was once the 'ribbon of steel'). However, the ribbon has become a little tattered in recent years and when CBC was faced with an estimated budget shortfall of over $400 million between 1994 and 1998, it was forced to cut over a thousand jobs.

CBC has two radio channels: Radio One and Radio Two. Other national radio networks include Radio Canada and the *Société de Radio-Télévision du Canada* (SRC), which are both in French. One of the most popular shows is the CBC's *This Morning*, which goes out between 9am and noon on weekdays; it's entertaining as well as educational and provides a well-rounded view of the nation's current opinions. Other popular shows include *As It Happens*, a nightly interview show which covers topics from major news events to minor fluff, *Quirks and Quarks*, a weekly science show, *Definitely NOT the Opera*, a weekly show about pop culture, and *'Madly Off In All Directions'*, half an hour of sketches and stand-up comedy.

9.

EDUCATION

Canada spends around 8 per cent of its gross domestic product on education and has a diversified education system, with public and private schools ('school' usually refers to everything from kindergarten to university) at all levels operating alongside each other. Around 14 per cent of Canadians have a university degree, over 25 per cent have a diploma from a post-secondary education institution and around 50 per cent graduate from high school. However, although very few Canadians are illiterate in the sense of not being able to read and write, almost 15 per cent have had only a primary education and a surprisingly high proportion (although most of these are new immigrants, with limited English or French-language skills) have only marginal literacy skills. For example, they cannot use a weather chart to calculate temperature differences, cannot decipher a simple graph or use a bus schedule. Perhaps not surprisingly, native Americans have lower levels of schooling than others and some 55 per cent have no high school diploma and fewer than 5 per cent are university graduates.

Full-time education is compulsory in all provinces and includes the children of foreign nationals permanently or temporarily resident in Canada. However, admission to a public school for foreign children is dependent on the type and duration of the visa granted to their parents, and free schooling may not be possible. Compulsory schooling in Canada usually commences at the age of five or six and continues until age 15 or 16, although the typical Canadian receives 13 years of education (the average is lower in rural areas and small towns, and higher in metropolitan areas).

Education in Canada is the responsibility of individual provinces and districts, therefore standards and requirements vary considerably from province to province and district to district. However, the federal government provides financial support for post-secondary education, adult occupational training and tuition in the two official languages. It's also responsible for educating native Americans, armed forces personnel and their families, and inmates of prisons and other penal institutions.

Education in public primary and secondary schools is free, but parents must pay 'student fees' of between $5 and $100 per term for extra-curricular classes such as music or art. Most students attend public schools, although some 5 per cent attend private fee-paying schools, some of which are church-sponsored, parochial schools (usually Roman Catholic, although in some cities there are others, such as Muslim schools). Most public schools are mixed (co-educational) day schools. Private schools include both day and boarding schools and are mostly mixed, although some are single sex. With the exception of some private schools, all education in Canada is non-denominational.

Formal education in Canada comprises three levels: elementary, secondary and higher education. Vocational training, adult education and special schools or classes (e.g. for gifted and handicapped children) also form part of the education programme in most provinces. Foreign families resident in Canada for a limited period may prefer to send their children to a private international school, where the organisation and curriculum are similar to that of public schools, although the administration differs. In recent years, many parents concerned about a decline in public education have turned to private schools. Although the cost of private education is high, many parents consider it an acceptable price to pay, particularly if the outcome is a bachelors or masters degree from a prestigious university. With the exception of most private and some parochial schools, school uniforms are rare in Canada.

The language of instruction in most of Canada is English, the exception being Quebec where it's primarily French, although in some communities classes are offered in both languages. For children of *Québécois* citizens who attend an English primary school there's a publicly supported English school system where English is the language of instruction. All other schools in Quebec teach in French and most children attend French schools irrespective of the language spoken at home. Each year some 30,000 migrant children enter Canada speaking neither English or French and must start their education in special language units or special schools. If your children don't speak English or French fluently, enquire whether English or French as a Second Language (ESL/FSL) classes are available or whether study is available in other languages. In some major cities children can be taught in foreign languages, e.g. in Vancouver some schools teach in Punjabi, Cantonese, Japanese and Korean.

Many provinces and communities provide schools or special classes for children with special educational needs, including those with emotional and behavioural problems, moderate and severe learning difficulties, communication problems, partial hearing or physical handicaps. There are also private schools in Canada catering for gifted and talented children, and most public schools have gifted and talented programmes.

PUBLIC OR PRIVATE SCHOOL?

Before making any major decisions about your children's education, it's important to consider their individual ability, character and requirements. This is of particular importance if you're able to choose between public and private education, when the following points should be considered:

- How long are you planning to stay in Canada? If you're uncertain, it's probably better to assume a long stay. Due to language and other integration problems, enrolling a child in a Canadian school (public or private) with a Canadian syllabus is recommended only for a minimum of one year, particularly for teenage children.

- Bear in mind that the area where you choose to live affects your choice of public schools. It's usually necessary to send your child to the public school that serves the area where you live, which is why homes within the catchment area of desirable schools are in demand and more expensive. It's difficult and may be impossible to get your child accepted at a public school in another area. In some cities (e.g. Edmonton) parents can send their children to any school in the city and in Manitoba parents can choose any school in the province, provided that space is available.

- Do you know where you're going after Canada? This may be an important consideration regarding your children's schooling. How old are your children and what age will they be when you plan to leave Canada? What future plans do you have for their education and in which country?

- What educational level are your children at now and how will they fit into the Canadian public school system or a private school? The younger they are, the easier it is to place them in a suitable school.

- If your children don't speak English or French, how do they view the thought of studying in one of these languages? Are they willing to take ESL or FSL classes? Does the school offer a good programme? Alternatively, is schooling available in Canada in their mother tongue?

- What are the school hours and the school holiday (vacation) periods? How will they affect your family's work and leisure activities?

- Is religion an important consideration in your choice of school? Around a quarter of public schools are Roman Catholic 'separate' (i.e. denominational) schools and many private schools are also maintained by religious organisations.

- Do you want your children to attend a mixed (co-educational) or a single-sex school? All public schools in Canada and the majority of private schools are mixed.

- Should you send your children to a boarding school? If so, should it be in Canada or in another country?

- What are the secondary and higher education prospects for your children in Canada or another country? Are Canadian examinations or qualifications recognised in your home country or the country where you plan to live after leaving Canada?

- Do the schools under consideration have a good academic record? What percentage of high school pupils go on to higher education? Other important indicators are the school dropout rate, the average daily attendance rate, the expenditure per pupil (including textbooks) and the average teacher salary.

- How large are the classes? What is the teacher-student ratio?

Obtain the opinions and advice of others who have been faced with the same decisions and problems as yourself and collect as much information from as many different sources as possible before making any decisions. Speak to the principals and teachers of schools on your shortlist. Finally, most parents find that it's beneficial to discuss the alternatives with their children before coming to a decision.

PUBLIC SCHOOLS

There isn't a federal government controlled or funded state school system in Canada. State-funded provincial schools are called public or separate schools (which are Roman Catholic public schools), and although anyone can attend either, they're generally split along religious denomination lines. Public schools are the responsibility of individual provincial departments of education and funded mainly from local and provincial taxes, with some federal funds. Practices and policies regarding education (both public and private) vary from province to province. Provincial departments of education determine education policy in accordance with provincial laws. The minister of education is responsible for setting policy relating to educational affairs, such as the allocation of provincial and federal funds, certification of teachers, textbooks and library services, provision of records and educational statistics, and setting and enforcing the term of compulsory education.

One of the unique aspects of the Canadian public school system is the amount of decentralisation and the degree to which schools are run by local school authorities. Each province is divided at the local level into school districts governed by a superintendent and a locally elected school board (or board of education) that decides instructional policies, hires teachers, purchases equipment and generally oversees the day-to-day running of schools. Most schools have Parents Advisory Councils (PACs) that mainly concern themselves with raising money to buy equipment such as computers, video surveillance, emergency lighting, playground equipment and school buses for children with special needs.

Teacher qualifications and standards vary from province to province. All provinces require teachers to have a licence or certificate to teach in public elementary and secondary schools, although the actual requirements for teacher certificates are set by provincial education departments. All provinces require a bachelor's degree for teaching elementary grades and most require a bachelor's degree as the *minimum* preparation for teaching in secondary schools, while a few insist on five years' study or a masters degree. The full-time teaching force at primary and secondary level is around 310,000, with another 40,000 at universities and colleges. Parents are encouraged to participate in their child's education and schools are constantly seeking volunteer 'teacher's assistants' to help with reading, art and special projects.

Choosing a Public School

For most Canadian parents, one of the most important (if not *the* most important) criterion when choosing a new neighbourhood is the reputation of its public schools. This is often measured by the number of students schools send to top Canadian universities (statistics are provided by all schools). In recent years there's been an ongoing debate about school choice, which varies considerably depending on the city or province, e.g. in Edmonton (Alberta) parents can send their children to any school in the city and in Manitoba parents can choose any school in the province, provided that there are spaces available there.

However, in most areas it's necessary to send your child to the public school that serves the area where you live and it's difficult to get your child accepted at a public school in another area. For this reason, homes within the catchment area of desirable schools are in demand and more expensive. If you intend to send your child to a public school, you should make enquiries about the quality of local schools before deciding where to live. Often the more expensive that property is in a neighbourhood, the better the local public schools. Relocation guides are published in many cities and regions, which usually include profiles of local schools and comparative scores for different grades. Many communities take pride in the quality of their local public school system, which is crucial in maintaining property values.

The quality of public schools varies considerably from province to province and community to community, and although some are poor, most are excellent. Where schools are well-run, well-supported and well-funded by the local community, the quality of public education rivals any in the world and can offer opportunities seldom available in many other countries. Even at schools where average standards are low, students who take full advantage of the opportunities afforded receive an excellent education.

Organisation

Most children start school before the age of six, when compulsory schooling usually begins, either in a nursery school or a kindergarten (see page 174). The maximum 13 years of formal elementary and secondary education covers education from the ages of 5 to 18, divided into increments called grades (kindergarten and grades 1 to 12). Children usually start in kindergarten at the age of five and advance one grade per year until reaching grade 12 at age 18. Occasionally a student must repeat a grade due to prolonged absence or low marks, but this is rare.

A child can legally quit (drop out of) school at 16, this is generally discouraged and the vast majority of students stay at high school until they reach the age of 18.

Age	Grade	School
2 to 5	-	Pre-School or Kindergarten
6 to 11	1 to 6	Elementary
12 to 14	7 to 9	Junior high
15 to 18	10 to 12	Senior high

Usually a student has one teacher for all major subjects during his first six years of schooling (elementary) and a different teacher for each subject during the last six grades in junior and senior high schools.

Registration

At elementary and secondary levels, students usually attend a public school close to their home. If you have a preference for a particular public school or school district, it's usually necessary to buy or rent a property in that area (see **Choosing a Public School** above), although you can request that your child attends a school outside your area (called 'cross-boundary'). It's quite normal for Canadians to ask an estate agent to find them a home in a particular school district. All schools prefer children to start at the beginning of a new term (semester), although this isn't necessary.

Parents should enquire at a school district's central office or Board of Education to find out which school their child will be assigned to and the documents required for registration. Usually you need to produce proof of residence, an immigration record of landing, a passport, a birth certificate (or a certified copy), and details of your child's medical history, including immunisations and tuberculin screening (see **Health** below). It's also necessary to provide past scholastic records, including a school report from your child's last school. This is used to assign students to a class or grade and should be as detailed as possible, with samples of essays, projects and examinations.

Many towns provide transport to school (buses), although it may be provided for certain schools or ages only, and may depend on the travelling distance to school, e.g. there may be a school bus only when the distance from home to school is over 2 or 2.5 miles. Some towns provide buses for children in special education only.

Terms & School Hours

The school year in Canada usually runs from the first week of September until the end of June (ten months) and is divided into periods or quarters (terms/semesters). There are a few year-round schools and some that have a year that runs from mid-August to the end of May. School holiday dates are published by schools well in advance, thus allowing parents plenty of time to schedule family holidays during official school holidays. It's not a good idea to take a child out of school when he should be taking examinations or during important course work assignments.

The school day in elementary schools is usually from 8.30am to 3 or 3.30pm, with an hour for lunch. There are also usually two 15-minute breaks (recesses) to allow students to let off steam between classes (and to allow teachers to find the aspirin). In high schools, hours are usually from 8.30am until 2.30pm. Extracurricular activities and sports are scheduled after school hours. Lessons in public schools are held from Mondays to Fridays and there are no lessons on Saturdays. Canada also has what it calls 'semestered high schools', where instead of the standard eight subjects being taught throughout the year, four subjects are taught each term, with one long lesson (usually 70 minutes) on each subject each day. This system is thought to give a better understanding of each subject and to be more suitable for pupils who find it difficult to cope with eight subjects each week.

Health

In most provinces, school children must be immunised against a range of diseases before starting school. These may include polio, DTP (diphtheria, tetanus and whooping cough) and MMR (measles, mumps and rubella or German measles). Tuberculosis screening may also be necessary. Most schools have full or part-time nurses (who may cover a number of schools) or at the very least staff trained in administering first-aid. Special medical checks (physicals) are necessary to take part in some sports activities. Dental checks aren't carried out at schools, but many schools promote a dental health week. Health education is provided in both elementary and secondary schools, including sex education and the perils of drugs and smoking (which are combined with community programmes). In many communities, volunteer ambulance corps members teach children about safety and accident prevention.

Pre-School Education

Pre-school education embraces all formal and informal education before the age of five (when compulsory schooling starts). It includes tots and toddler programmes, play school, nursery school and kindergarten. Attendance at school for children under five years of age isn't compulsory in Canada, where pre-schools and nursery schools are private. However, kindergarten is part of the public school system and is compulsory for children who are aged five on 1st September, when they will start at the beginning of the school year in September.

There are various types of pre-schools in Canada, including non-profit co-operative schools, church-affiliated schools, local community schools, private schools and Montessori schools. A co-operative school is usually the least expensive as parents work voluntarily as teachers' aides alongside professional teachers. Church-affiliated schools are usually attached to religious centres and may include religious education (**it isn't always necessary for children to follow the same religion as the school**). Private schools are the most expensive and vary considerably from small home-run set-ups to large custom-built schools. A number of private nursery schools in Canada use the Montessori method of teaching, developed by Dr. Maria Montessori in the early 1900s. Montessori is more a philosophy of life than a teaching method and is based on the firm belief that each child is an individual with unique needs, interests and patterns of growth. Some Montessori schools have both 'pre-school' (for children aged two and a half to six years) and elementary levels (ages 6 to 12).

Nursery school is highly recommended for all children, particularly those whose parents don't speak English or French as their mother tongue. After a few years in nursery school a child is integrated into the local community and well prepared for elementary school (particularly when English or French isn't spoken at home). Parents can also make friends in the community through pre-school contacts.

Elementary School

Children must start school on 1st September following their fifth birthday. The first years of compulsory schooling in Canada are called elementary or primary school. Elementary school is usually mixed and is usually attended until age 11 (grades 1 to 6), when students go on to a junior high school. In some districts, students attend elementary school until age 13 (up to grade 8) before attending a senior high school.

The elementary school curriculum varies with the organisation and educational aims of individual schools and local communities. Promotion from one grade to the next is based on student testing and a child whose performance is poor may be required to repeat a year, while a gifted child may be allowed to skip a year. Elementary schools provide instruction in the fundamental skills of reading, writing and maths, as well as history, geography, crafts, music, science, art, and physical education (phys ed. or gym). French and 'foreign' languages, which used to be taught only at high schools, are now being introduced during the last few years of elementary school in some areas and if you wish, your child can enter an 'early French immersion programme' at kindergarten or grade 1 level. For more information contact the local branch of the 'Canadian Parents for French' programme.

Secondary School

Secondary education in Canada is for children aged from 12 to 18 (grades 7 to 12). It generally takes place in a high school, that's often divided into junior and senior high (held in separate buildings or even at separate locations). Junior high is for those aged 12 to 14 (grades 7 to 9) and senior high for ages 15 to 17 (grades 10 to 12). In Quebec, students attend secondary school for three years only and then transfer to a general and vocational college (*collége d'enseignement général et professionnel/CEGEP*) for a further two or three years. Like elementary education, secondary education is mixed.

Secondary schools may specialise in academic or vocational streams or the arts; all include some kind of 'streaming' system that's designed to prepare students for a vocational or community college or university. Mandatory or 'core' curriculum subjects must be studied for a prescribed number of years or terms, as determined by each province. These generally include English, maths, general science, health, sport (physical education) and social studies or social sciences (which may include Canadian history and government, geography, world history and social problems). In addition to mandatory subjects, students choose optional subjects (electives) that will benefit them in the future.

Electives usually comprise around half of a student's work in grades 9 to 12. Around the ninth grade, students receive career guidance counselling as they begin to plan their careers and select subjects that will be useful in their chosen fields. Counselling continues throughout the senior high school years and into college. Larger schools may offer a selection of elective courses aimed at three or more levels: academic, vocational and general. Students planning to go on to college or university elect courses with an emphasis on academic sciences (biology, chemistry, physics), higher mathematics (algebra, geometry, trigonometry and calculus), advanced English or French literature, composition, social sciences or foreign languages.

The vocational programme may provide training in four fields: agricultural education which prepares students for farm management and operation, business education which trains students for the commercial field, home economics which prepares students for home management, child care and care of the sick, and trade and industrial education which provides training for jobs in mechanical, manufacturing, building and other trades. Students interested in entering business from high school may take typing, book-keeping, computer studies or 'business' English or French.

School sports are popular in Canada, although most take place outside school hours (extracurricular). Team sports have a high profile at high school and being 'on the school team' is more important to many students than being top of the class. Students who excel at sports are often referred to disparagingly as 'jocks', implying that they're too stupid or lazy to succeed at their academic work. However, if a student's grades don't reach the required level he is likely to be barred from taking part in team sports until his grades improve (and he is constantly monitored). High school sport is central to school activities and the ceremony that goes with college sport is also found at high-school level.

In addition to sports, many other school-sponsored activities take place outside school hours, including science and nature clubs, musical organisations (e.g. band and choir), art and drama groups, and language clubs. Nearly every high school has a student-run newspaper and a photographic darkroom is also usually available. Colleges and universities place considerable weight on the achievements of students in high school extracurricular activities, as do Canadian employers. High schools are also important social centres and participation in school-organised social events such as school dances and the first hockey game of the season is widespread.

Examinations & Grades

When a student enrols in a public school, a 'record file' is opened for him (which follows him throughout his school years) and there's a continuous evaluation system throughout all grades. Students are marked on each essay (paper), exam and course taken in each subject studied throughout their 13 years of education (grades K to 12). The following grading system is used in high schools throughout Canada:

Grade	Classification	Percentage
A	Excellent	90-100
B	Good	80-89
C	Average/fair	70-79
D	Poor	60-69
F (Fail)	Below	i60

All grades are internal and are in relation to the general standard achieved at a particular school, which usually makes it difficult to compare standards in different schools and provinces. Marks depend on a range of criteria, including a student's performance in tests given at intervals during the year, participation in class discussions, completion of homework assignments, and independent projects. Students receive a report card at least twice per year (in some districts it may be up to six times per year), which shows their grades in each subject they're studying.

High school students who need to make up lost time after illness (or idleness) can attend special 'cramming' courses at learning centres run by private companies such as the Sylvan Learning Centre, which has centres in most large towns in Canada (see your yellow pages or 🖥 www.educate.com). High schools divide their curriculum into 'advanced', which prepares students to go to university, or 'general', which prepare students to go to a community college or trade school.

High school students take the General Education Diploma (GED) before completing high school, which is the recognised entrance qualification for admission to a Canadian university (although mature students aged 25 or over can take GED 'equivalency exams' if they haven't passed the GED).

PRIVATE SCHOOLS

There are private fee-paying schools in all cities in Canada serving a wide range of needs and educating around 5 per cent of Canadian children. Private schools include single-sex schools, schools sponsored by religious groups, schools for students with learning or physical disabilities, and schools for gifted children. Some private schools place the emphasis on sports or cater for students with artistic talent in art, drama, dance or music. There are also schools emphasising activities such as outdoor living or which adhere to a particular educational philosophy, such as Montessori and Waldorf schools. Although most Canadian private schools prepare students for entry to a Canadian college or university, some international schools prepare students for the International Baccalaureate (IB) examination. Some private schools teach exclusively in a foreign language, e.g. Cantonese, follow traditional curricula and prepare students for examinations set by examining boards in their home country.

Private schools are organised like public schools (see page 171), although the curricula and approach differ considerably. They range from nursery schools to large day and boarding schools, from experimental and progressive schools to traditional institutions, and include progressive schools with a holistic approach to a child's development and schools with a strict traditional and conservative regime, and a rigid and competitive approach to learning. School work in private schools is usually rigorous and demanding, and students often have a great deal of homework and pressure. Many parents favour this competitive 'work ethic' approach and expect their offspring to work hard to justify the expense.

Fees vary considerably depending on a variety of factors, including the age of students, the reputation and quality of the school and its location (schools in major cities are usually the most expensive). Fees aren't all-inclusive and additional obligatory fees are payable, plus fees for optional services. Unless you're rich or someone else is paying, you usually need to start saving *before* you have any children, although there are some federal tax breaks (see **Registered Education Savings Plans** on page 180). Some schools offer payment plans to attract new students. In addition to tuition fees, most private schools solicit parents for contributions (**some schools are quite aggressive and verbal in their requests**). Most schools provide scholarships for gifted and talented students, although they may be reserved for children from poorer families or ethnic minorities. Some schools have large endowments, enabling them to accept any students they wish, irrespective of their parents' ability to pay.

Private schools provide a broad-based education and generally offer a varied approach to sport, music, drama, art and a wide choice of academic subjects, e.g. some schools offer horse-riding or skiing during school hours or unusual subjects such as speleology (the scientific study of caves). Due to their smaller classes, teachers in private schools are able to provide students with individually-tailored lessons and tuition, rather than teaching on a production-line system. Private schools employ specialist staff, e.g. reading specialists, tutors to help those with difficulties and specialists to assist students who wish to accelerate their learning or work independently. Most private schools also offer after-school programmes, sports teams, clubs, enrichment programs and tutorial classes.

When making applications you should do so as far in advance as possible. It's usually easier to gain entry to the first grade than to get your child into a later grade, where entry is strictly limited. Entry may be facilitated for foreign children as many schools consider it an advantage to have a wide selection of foreign students. Gaining entrance to a prominent private school is difficult, particularly in major cities, and you can never guarantee that a particular school will accept your child. Although many nursery and elementary schools accept children on a first-come, first-served basis, the best and most exclusive schools have a demanding selection procedure and many have waiting lists. Don't rely on enrolling your child in a particular school and neglect other alternatives.

Before enrolling your child in a private school, make sure that you understand the withdrawal conditions in the school contract, particularly if you expect to be in Canada for a limited time only. Before sending your child to a particular private school, irrespective of its reputation, you should consider carefully your child's needs, capabilities and maturity. For example, it's important to ensure that a school's curriculum and regime are neither too strict nor too liberal for your child.

Directories of private schools are available in most reference libraries in Canada, from the provincial Ministry of Education or from the Canadian Association of Independent Schools, 13425 Dufferin St., King City, ON L7B 1K5 (☎ 905-833-3385, 🖳 www.cais.ca).

HIGHER EDUCATION

Higher education in Canada is often referred to as post-secondary education, and refers to study beyond the secondary school level and usually assumes that a student has undertaken 13 years of study and has a General Education Diploma (GED). Students must usually take a University Transfer Course at a college for one year before attending a university. Mature students aged over 25 are also admitted to these courses, whether or not they have a GED, but must take GED 'equivalency exams'.

For those students who don't go to university, post-secondary education continues at community colleges, which are low-fee colleges with one to three-year programmes in a range of practical and para-professional skills, ranging from graphic design to nursing, taught under the broad categories of Arts, Business, Health Services, and Science and Technology. For information and a list of colleges contact the Association of Canadian Community Colleges, 200-1223 Michael Street N, Ottawa ON K1J 7T2 (☎ 613-746-2222, 🖳 www.accc.ca).

Over 40 per cent of Canadian high school graduates go on to some sort of higher education. There are three main levels of higher education in Canada: undergraduate studies (bachelor's degree), graduate studies (master's degree) and postgraduate studies (doctorate). Canada has 77 universities and 216 community colleges, with a wide variety of admission requirements and programmes. Of the total annual university enrolment of around 600,000 full-time and some 250,000 part-time students, over half are female and around 30,000 are overseas students. The academic standards of colleges and universities vary greatly, and some institutions are better known for the quality of their social life or sports teams than for their academic achievements. Establishments range from vast educational 'plants', offering the most advanced training available, to small intimate private academies emphasising personal instruction and a preference for the humanities or experimentation.

Tuition fees increased dramatically in the 1990s and have more than doubled since 1990. Some universities offer programmes that are completely funded by student fees, e.g. Queen's University in Kingston (Ontario) charges well over $50,000 for its two-year Master of Business Administration (MBA) programme. Studying at Canadian universities costs more for international students than for Canadian students. In the academic year 2002/2003 a foreign undergraduate studying engineering paid around $12,000, while a Canadian (or foreigner resident in Canada) student paid only $3,880; for an arts course the costs were around $9,500 for a foreign student against just $3,608 for a Canadian. In recent years, many students have become immigrants in order to reduce tuition fees. You can check the latest tuition fees in *MacLean's Guide to Canadian Universities*.

The cost of living also varies greatly from area to area and is, not surprisingly, highest in the major cities. Health insurance is essential and compulsory, although students may be automatically enrolled in the university health insurance plan. Many families participate in savings and investment schemes to finance their children's college education. In the 1998 budget, the Canadian government introduced several new schemes to help fund education, including enhancements to Registered Education Savings Plans, which are savings schemes to fund post-secondary education with tax-breaks. The money in a plan isn't taxed until a student starts to draw on it and because most students are on low incomes the tax payable is far less than it would otherwise have been. If the designated student doesn't go on to post-secondary education, another child can be named or the funds in the plan can be transferred to the parent/grandparent's own Registered Retirement Savings Plan (RRSP). Other plans include one that allows adults to withdraw money from their RRSPs without paying tax, provided that they spend the money on their own education, and a ten-year 'Canadian Millennium Scholarship' scheme to help needy students fund their higher education. A useful book describing these schemes is *Head Start – How To Save For Your Children's or Grandchildren's Education* by Gordon Pape & Frank Jones (Stoddart Publishing).

Many students obtain part-time employment to finance their studies, both during term-time and summer breaks (foreign students should check in advance whether their visa allows such employment), while others receive grants, scholarships and loans to help meet their living expenses. Scholarships are awarded directly by universities as well as by fraternal, civic, labour and management organisations. Although public universities don't usually provide financial aid to foreign students, it's possible to obtain a scholarship or partial scholarship for tuition fees from a private university. The federal government provides student loans and may also pay some of your fees and living expenses (see 🖳 www.hrdc-drhc.gc.ca/). There are also special opportunity grants, e.g. a grant of $3,000 per year for three years is available for female doctoral students. Ask the financial aid office of the college, institute or university that you plan to attend for information. The average debt for an undergraduate in the final year of study is around $15,000, and owing up to around $35,000 at the end of a four-year course isn't unusual; you can owe up to a daunting $80,000 at the end of a Masters degree course.

Entry qualifications for Canadian colleges and universities vary considerably; generally the better the university (or the better the reputation), the higher the entrance qualifications. Some specialist schools, such as law schools, have a standard entrance examination. Usually overseas qualifications that qualify students to enter a university in their own country are taken into consideration. It's also necessary for mature students returning to full or part-time college education to provide any diplomas or certificates showing the education level they've attained (otherwise they must take basic tests). Whatever your qualifications, each application is considered on its merits. All foreign students require a thorough knowledge of English (French in Quebec) and those who aren't of English (or French) mother tongue must take a TOEFL/TOFFL test (see page 183). Contact individual universities for details of their entrance requirements.

Applications must be made to the Director of Undergraduate Admissions at colleges and universities. If you plan to apply to highly popular colleges and universities, such as those in Toronto, you must apply in August (or autumn) for admission in the following autumn term (August/September), although it's advisable to start the process 18 months in advance. For less popular universities, the latest a foreign student can apply for September admission is March of the same year, as overseas applications usually take at least six months to process. The number of applicants each university receives per available place varies considerably depending on the university. You would be wise not to make all your applications to universities where competition for places is at its fiercest (unless you're a genius). It's best to apply to three universities of varying standards, e.g. speculative, attainable and safe.

All colleges and universities have a huge variety of societies and clubs, many organised by the students' union or council, which is the centre of campus social activities. Canadian universities usually have excellent sports facilities and some provide full academic scholarships to athletes.

There are many books providing information about Canadian universities and colleges, including *MacLean's Guide to Canadian Universities* (also available on the website ▣ www.macleans.ca/contents/universities.asp), *The Complete Guide To Canadian Universities* and *Your Guide To Canadian Colleges*, both by Kevin Paul (Self Counsel Press Inc.). Moving Publications (see Appendix A) publish a *Guide to Canadian Universities* and the *Student's Guide to Financial Survival*. Canadian college catalogues are available from high school guidance offices, libraries and bookstores.

There are also many Internet sites that provide information about Canadian universities and colleges, including ▣ www.schoolfinder.com, ▣ www.look smart.com (which includes a home page for college admissions with links to admissions offices, financial aid, scholarships, etc.), ▣ www.varsitylink.com (which specialises in athletic recruiting and provides free registration of online athletic profiles to university-bound athletes in all sports) and ▣ www. uwaterloo.ca/ canu/index.html for universities in Ontario. Many provincial departments of higher education have a toll-free 'education hotline' where you can obtain information about all aspects of higher and further (adult) education. You can also contact the Association of Universities and Colleges of Canada, 350 Albert Street, Suite 600, Ottawa ON K1R 1B1 (☎ 613-563-1236, 🖳 www.aucc.ca).

ADULT & FURTHER EDUCATION

Adult and further education generally refers to education undertaken by adults of all ages after leaving full-time study, and often after years or even decades of intervening occupation. It doesn't include degree courses taken at college or university directly after leaving high school, which come under higher education (see page 179). It also excludes short day and evening classes, e.g. those held at community colleges and usually termed 'continuing education' (although there's often a fine distinction between further and continuing education). Further education includes everything from basic reading and writing skills for the illiterate to full-time advanced, professional and doctorate degrees at university. On many university campuses, more students are enrolled in adult and further education courses than in regular degree programmes.

Adult education courses may be full or part-time and are provided by colleges, universities, community colleges, technical schools (which may use the facilities at elementary and high schools), trade schools, business schools, and elementary and high schools. Courses are also provided by private community organisations, government agencies, job training centres, labour and professional organisations, private tutors and instructors, business and industry, industrial training programmes, museums, clubs, private organisations and institutes, correspondence course schools and educational TV programmes. Typical of these classes are those offered under the auspices of the Forum for International Trade Training (FITT) for people who want training and a qualification (e.g. the Certified International Trade Professional/CITP) in import and export skills. FITT provides workshops for small and medium-sized businesses, and also sponsors and monitors training at universities and colleges throughout Canada. For more information, contact FITT, 30 Metcalfe Street, Ottawa ON K1P 5L4 (☎ 613-230-3553 or 1-800-561-3488, 🖳 www.fitt.ca).

Each year thousands of students attend further education courses at universities or community colleges, many of which are of short duration and job-related, and scheduled in the evenings, at weekends and during the summer recess. Lecturers may be full or part-time faculty members or professionals practising in the fields in which they lecture. Students generally aren't required to take a minimum number of courses per semester or to take courses in succeeding semesters. You can register in a formal vocational programme or simply take a course for pleasure. The most popular fields in adult education are accounting, business administration and management, education, engineering, health professions, fine and applied arts, physical education, language, literature, religion and psychology. The federal government underwrites the cost of basic adult education, so that older students, particularly members of minority groups, can go back to school for the rudiments of an education they failed to get as children, in reading, writing, maths, history and geography. Many cities and provinces also offer career, vocational and continuing education programmes in public schools, including English and French as a Second Language (ESL/FSL) classes. Adult education also gives students the opportunity to complete their high school studies, which in some cities can be undertaken in Cantonese and other languages.

Many further education courses are of the open learning variety, where students study mostly at home. Correspondence colleges, most of which are private commercial organisations, offer literally hundreds of academic, professional and vocational courses, and enrol many thousands of students per year. In 1997, New Brunswick introduced 'TeleEducation NB' and launched 'TeleCampus' on the Internet, which allow students to enrol, study and pay for courses on the Internet (the aim was to have 10,000 students on-line by the year 2000, although in spring 2003 it was difficult to find out exact numbers). Quebec operates a scheme called *Télé-Université* (☎ 514-843-2015), a subsidiary of the University of Quebec, for those wishing to pursue higher education at home using multimedia equipment (it provides 20,000 students per year with diplomas). A new initiative sponsored by Industry Canada, called Schoolnet (💻 www.schoolnet.ca), aims to encourage students to use interactive websites and plans to connect all of Canada's schools and public libraries to the Internet.

LANGUAGE SCHOOLS

If you don't speak English (or French if you're planning to live in Quebec) fluently or you wish to learn another language, you can enrol in a language course at numerous language schools in Canada. There are English-language schools in all cities and large towns, although the majority, particularly those offering intensive courses, are in the major cities. Many adult and further education institutions provide English courses and many Canadian universities offer summer and holiday English and French-language courses. Colleges and universities often run an English Language Programme, which is a pre-academic, English-as-a-Second-Language (ESL) programme for students whose native language isn't English.

Obtaining a working knowledge of or becoming fluent in English while living in Canada is 'relatively easy' (if learning any language can ever be called easy!), as you're constantly immersed in the English language (except in Quebec) and have the maximum opportunity to practise. However, if you wish to speak English fluently, you probably need to take lessons. It's usually necessary to have a recognised qualification in English or pass a Test of English as a Foreign Language (TOEFL) in order to be accepted at a college or university in Canada. Foreigners who wish to study English full-time can enrol at one of the many English-language centres at Canadian universities.

Most language schools offer a variety of classes depending on your current language ability, how many hours you wish to study per week, how much money you want to spend and how fast you wish to learn. Courses vary in length from one week to six months and cater for all ages. Full-time, part-time and evening courses are offered by most schools, and many also provide residential courses. Fees at a community college are around $250 to $350 for ten weeks (two classes per week of three to four hours). Residential courses (often with half-board, consisting of breakfast and an evening meal) usually offer excellent value for money. Bear in mind that if you need to find your own accommodation, particularly in a major city, it can be *very* expensive. Language classes generally fall into the following categories:

Category	No. hours per week
Compact	10 to 20
Intensive	20 to 30
Total immersion	30 to 40

Course fees vary considerably and are usually calculated on a weekly basis. Fees depend on the number of hours tuition per week, the type of course, and the location and reputation of the school. Expect to pay $125 to $175 per week for a compact course and around $225 per week for an intensive course providing 20 to 30 hours of language study. Half board accommodation usually costs around $175 to $225 extra per week (or more in large cities). It's possible to enrol at a good school for an all-inclusive (tuition plus half-board accommodation), four-week intensive course for as little as $450 per week. Total immersion or executive courses are offered by many schools and usually consist of private lessons for a minimum of 30 or 40 hours per week, with fees running to $2,200 or more per week. **Not everyone is suited to learning at such a fast rate (or has the financial resources!).**

Some immigrants are eligible for free federal government sponsored classes called Language Instruction for Newcomers to Canada (LINC). Other low-income students may have their fees paid or part-paid by provincial governments, although there's often a waiting list for classes. In some areas, immigrant settlement agencies, community groups and churches provide free or low-cost language classes.

Whatever language you're learning, don't expect to become fluent in a short period unless you have a particular flair for languages or already have a good command of a language. Unless you desperately need to learn a language quickly, it's better to space your lessons over a long period. Don't commit yourself to a long course of study (particularly an expensive one) before ensuring that it's the correct course for you. Most schools offer a free introductory lesson and free tests to help you find your appropriate level. Many language schools offer private and small group lessons. It's important to choose the right course, particularly if you're studying English to continue with full-time education in Canada and need to reach a minimum standard or gain a particular qualification.

You may prefer to have private lessons, which are a faster but more expensive way of learning a language. The main advantage of private lessons is that you learn at your own speed and aren't held back by slow learners or dragged along in the wake of the class genius. There are invariably advertisements from English teachers in local newspapers. You can also place an advertisement for a private teacher in local newspapers and magazines, on shopping mall notice boards, at town halls, libraries, universities and schools, and through your (or your spouse's) employer. Your friends, colleagues or neighbours may also be able to help you find a private teacher. For further information regarding languages in Canada, see **Language** on page 38.

10.

PUBLIC TRANSPORT

Like their neighbours in the US, Canadians aren't enthusiastic public transport users and when not flying prefer to drive. Public transport varies from excellent to adequate in the major cities, but is poor in country areas where you almost always need your own transport. In cities, modern integrated transport systems allow travellers to transfer from one kind of transport to another on a single ticket, completing their journeys quickly, inexpensively and safely.

With a few exceptions, such as the luxury express coach service between Calgary and Edmonton, the long-distance bus services leave much to be desired, and the train service is no longer what it was in the days before the airlines took over, when it was the only way to travel (unless you were prepared to use a horse, canoe or dog-sled). With over half the population living in the area round the Great Lakes and the St Lawrence lowlands, most of whom only venture beyond the urban areas for holidays (vacations), there isn't much call for train travel other than in the tourist season. Even the famous cross-Canada train, *The Canadian*, which used to leave Montreal for Vancouver every day, now starts from Toronto and runs only three days per week. The one area of public transport where Canada really excels is air travel, where Canadians enjoy among the most comprehensive and cheapest services in the world (only the US does better). Trains and cars just cannot compete over long distances, e.g. it takes around five days to drive from Toronto to Vancouver, but you can fly in just five hours.

There are reduced fares on public transport for children, youths, students and senior citizens in most areas, and some local services are subsidised by provincial and local governments. Regular travellers can save money by buying blocks of tickets or monthly passes. Many cities and towns provide park and ride services, where inexpensive or free parking is combined with low cost public transport into town centres. A restricted service is provided on federal holidays, including Christmas Day, and on New Years Eve most public transport in major cities is free after around 6pm until 2am, to discourage people from drinking and driving.

When you're booking a holiday you should be wary of travel and holiday deals that seem too good to be true, as they most likely are! **Don't give your credit card details or send any money in response to an advertisement until you know more about a company and have received written details of an offer.** Better still, book through a travel agent who's a member of the Association of Canadian Travel Agents, 130 Albert Street, Suite 1705, Ottawa ON K1P 5G4 (☎613-237-3657, 💻 www.acta.net), who can organise and book all your travel arrangements and save you both time and money.

TRAVELLERS WITH DISABILITIES

Canadian public carriers under federal jurisdiction (railways, ferries and airlines either based in Canada or other scheduled and chartered carriers using Canadian airports) must ensure that disabled travellers don't 'encounter undue obstacles' while travelling and that their staff have received 'awareness training'. Airlines operating planes with 30 or more seats must provide assistance with embarking and disembarking if given 48 hours notice (and ideally even if they aren't given notice). Some municipal and inter-city buses are equipped with wheelchair-lifts and other services. Travellers should contact individual carriers for information about their services or alternatively contact the Accessible Transportation Directorate (☎ 819-997-6828), TTY (☎ 819-953-9705) or the Canadian Paraplegic Association, 1101 prom Prince of Wales Drive, Suite 320, Ottawa ON K2C 3W7 (☎ 613-723-1033, 🖥 www.canparaplegic.org). The US-based Twin Peaks Press publishes a *Directory of Travel Agencies for the Disabled* that lists over 300 travel agents specialising in helping travellers with disabilities.

TRAINS

The railway was responsible for opening up Canada in the 19th century and played a major role in the development and exploitation of the whole North American continent, although it has been in decline since the 1950s and has lost much of its former business to the automobile, air travel and long-distance buses. Having said that, it has undergone something of a revival in recent years, particularly as a relaxed way to view some of the spectacular scenery in the west of the country. Canada's rail network is one of the largest in the world, with 31,000mi (50,000km) of tracks. However, in terms of passenger miles per head of population it rates well behind other industrialised nations. The fastest and best trains carry freight, which has priority over (and subsidises) the passenger service.

The passenger rail service in Canada is operated by VIA Rail (a federal crown corporation) and the rolling stock and lines are owned by Canadian Pacific and Canadian National. VIA Rail serves some 450 communities on a network of 8,700mi (14,000km), carrying around four million passengers per year and operating some 450 trains per week (around two-thirds in the Quebec City-Windsor corridor). Some 90 per cent of all rail transportation in Canada is on the two main transcontinental routes, with just 10 per cent on the 30 regional railways. Long distance trains have carriages with swivel chairs (parlour coaches), *couchettes*, bedrooms for two people and single bedrooms (roomettes), and some luxury trains, such as *The Canadian*, have carriages with panoramic windows (dome cars), elegant dining rooms and hot showers. Anxious to share in the new enthusiasm for trains from tourists, VIA Rail is looking at ways to bring its system and services up to date, including privatisation or franchising.

Rail is unable to compete with the low cost and speed of air travel (a 10-hour train journey can usually be accomplished in one hour by air) and the convenience of car travel. Canadian long-distance trains move painfully slowly compared with those in most European countries (but at least they give you a chance of seeing a bear or a moose as you crawl through the Rockies). On some routes there's just one train per day and late trains are so common on long-distance routes that timetables warn passengers not to book connecting transportation in advance. There are no passenger trains on the islands of Newfoundland and Prince Edward Island and on several routes you must travel part of the way by coach. The rail system is at its best in the Montreal-Windsor corridor, which is hardly surprising as almost half the population lives there (you can connect at Windsor for US Amtrak trains to Detroit and Chicago). Trains are frequent and relatively fast, particularly during the peak commuting hours.

The advantages of long-distance rail travel are the spaciousness of the carriages (cars) and the chance to relax and enjoy the changing landscape. Service is the equal of any railway in the world and you can eat and drink well at what are reasonable rates by international standards. As a means of travel for tourists with plenty of time and a wish to see some of the world's most spectacular scenery, trains provide the best opportunity in Canada for relaxed travel, isolated from the usual hectic pace of life (Canadian trains are God's way of telling Canadians to slow down).

VIA Rail provides special accommodation for wheelchair-bound passengers (indicated by a wheelchair symbol on the outside of carriages) on most trains, including specially designed sleeping accommodation and bathrooms on overnight trains. Wheelchair symbols in the timetable show which stations are accessible to passengers with special needs and have hydraulic wheelchair lifts and platforms at train level. Wheelchairs are available on request at most stations, although disabled, elderly and other passengers requiring special assistance should notify VIA Rail by phone 24 hours before their departure. Passengers requiring special meals should give 48 hours notice, as should those who require medications to be stored at low temperatures. Passengers who require assistance in attending to their personal needs (e.g. eating, medical care or personal hygiene) must travel with an escort, who's given a free seat.

Seeing eye and hearing-guide dogs may ride in passenger carriages, but other household pets (such as dogs and cats) must travel in baggage cars in cages that allow them to stand. Cages can be purchased at most stations and VIA Rail reserves the right to refuse to transport animals in unsuitable cages. Customers are responsible for feeding and exercising their animals, and there's a charge of between $10 and $40 per animal.

For information about VIA Rail services, write to Customer Relations, VIA Rail Canada Inc., PO Box 8116, Station 'A', Montreal PQ H3C 3N3 (☎ 1-800-681-2561, 💻 www.viarail.ca). The *National Timetable* booklet (available from any VIA Rail station) contains information about all VIA Rail's long-distance routes, sleeping accommodation and travel advice. VIA Rail stations, offices and approved travel agents also provide information about package tours, connections with other train services and buses, hotel reservations and car rental.

In addition to the VIA Rail system and local rail services, there are a number of scenic narrow gauge railways in Canada including the White Pass & Yukon Railway. Daily coaches leave Whitehorse for Fraser, where they transfer passengers to narrow-gauge trains for the scenic ride to Skagway. The one-way journey takes 4.5 hours and runs from mid-May until mid-September (☎ 1-800-

343-7373, 💻 www. whitepassrailroad.com). Several companies operate restored steam locomotives such as BC Rail's 'Royal Hudson', which runs between North Vancouver & Squamish and covers several other old routes (☎ 604-986-2012, 💻 www.bcrail.com). In the east, the South Simcoe Railway in Ontario uses 1920s carriages and an 1890s locomotive from the old Canadian Pacific Railway, while in Quebec the Hull-Chelsea-Wakefield line employs a 1907 steam locomotive that runs alongside the scenic Gatineau river (☎ 819-778-7246, 💻 www. steamtrain.ca/ discover). There are a number of books for rail lovers including *Rail Ventures: Comprehensive Guide to Train Travel in North America* by Jack Swanson (R. Rinehart Publishers), *The Trans-Canada Rail Guide* by Melissa Graham (Trailblazer) and *The Railways: Discovering Canada Series* by Robert Livesey & A. G. Smith (Stoddart).

Tickets

Train tickets in Canada are either one-way (singles) or round trip (return). You can buy long-distance tickets that allow you to break your journey, which is cheaper than buying separate tickets for each section. Tickets for VIA Rail services should be purchased from a ticket office or agent *before* commencing your journey; however, personnel on trains can issue tickets to extend your journey to any destination on that train's route. You can also buy upgrades for accommodation on board trains, such as sleeping cars, club service and custom class accommodation (subject to availability).

Paying: You can pay for tickets and accommodation at stations or on board trains in cash and with credit cards such as American Express (Amex), Diners Club, MasterCard and Visa (debit cards are also accepted at VIA Rail stations, but not on trains). Tickets can also be purchased from travel agents or over the Internet with a credit card.

Fares: Children under the age of two travel free (provided that they don't occupy a seat) and those aged under 15 receive a 50 per cent discount in economy class and a 25 per cent discount in VIA 1 (1st class) and sleeper classes. Children under eight aren't permitted to travel alone, but children aged from 8 to 11 may travel unaccompanied under certain conditions and with written permission from a parent or legal guardian. Senior citizens over 60 receive a discount of 10 per cent on all fares and up to 50 per cent on some routes subject to certain conditions (e.g. advance purchase, restricted periods, limited number of economy class seats, cancellation fees, etc.). Full-time students with an International Student Identity Card (ISIC) and youths aged under 18 receive a 40 per cent discount in economy class and up to 50 per cent subject to certain conditions (as above for seniors). Group discounts are also available for groups of 20 or more.

Other discounts are available on specific routes, e.g. Victoria–Nanaimo, and in northern regions you can obtain a 40 per cent reduction on economy class tickets year-round or sleeper class fares during super-saver periods, provided that you buy them at least seven days in advance. On the Toronto–Vancouver route you can obtain a 25 per cent reduction on economy class or 'Silver and Blue' class tickets during off-peak periods and a 40 per cent reduction during super-saver periods by purchasing your ticket at least seven days in advance. On the Montreal–Halifax/*Gaspé* route or the Quebec City–Windsor corridor, you can obtain a 40 per cent reduction on economy or sleeper class by buying a ticket at least seven days in advance. On all the above routes, the number of seats available at reduced rates is limited.

Reservations: VIA Rail advises passengers to arrive at a station 30 minutes before the departure time. This, however, is generally necessary only when you need to buy a ticket or have luggage (baggage) to check in. Although you can pay when making a reservation, it isn't necessary and if you don't you're given a date by which you must pay for tickets. Only the advance purchase of a ticket guarantees a seat. If you're planning to take a long-distance train during the summer or on a federal holiday, it's wise to book well in advance. You can make reservations up to six months in advance at city railway stations, VIA Rail ticket offices, at most travel agents, by phone or through VIA Rail's 'Reservnet' Internet booking service (⌨ www. viarail.ca). When you reserve a seat or sleeper via the Internet, you're given a reservation number and a date/time by which you must pay for your ticket or the reservation is cancelled. If you arrive at a station without a reservation and seats are still available, you're assigned a seat and sold a ticket on the spot.

Refunds: To obtain a refund of an unused ticket, you must submit the ticket with the receipt coupon. Refunds can usually be made at any VIA Rail sales office or at the travel agent that issued the ticket. Where refunds cannot be made immediately, a refund application must be made and the refund is sent to you. Refunds of a CANRAILPASS and reduced fare tickets are subject to certain conditions. For refunds by post, you must send the original tickets and receipt coupons (not photocopies) to VIA Rail Canada Inc., Ticket Refunds, Union Station, 65 Front Street West, Room 0119, Toronto ON M5J 1E7. Send tickets by registered post so that you have proof of their delivery.

Canrailpass: The Canrailpass provides 12 days of economy class travel within a 30-day period. Prices in spring 2003 were $448 for an adult and $403 for a youth, student or senior during the low season (October 16th to May 31st), and $719 for an adult and $647 for a youth, student or senior during the high season (June 1st to October 15th). You can buy a maximum of three extra days travel within the 30-day period for $39 for an adult (others $36) in the low season and $61 (others $53) in the high season. Canrailpass holders can also buy upgrades at special rates and receive a payphone pass with $15 of free calls, discounts on rooms in the Choice hotel and motel chains, 15 per cent discounts on sightseeing tours with Gray Line coaches and special rates with National Tilden car rental.

At some suburban stations, ticket outlets may be open during peak hours only, outside of which tickets must be purchased on trains. If you're in doubt check in advance. Rail ticket machines may be provided that accept all coins (except pennies) plus $5, $10 and $20 bills. Monthly tickets can usually also be purchased by post.

Accommodation

VIA Rail accommodation is offered in two classes: economy and first class. The cheapest 'accommodation' is economy class, where you must sleep in your seat on overnight trips. Blankets and pillows are distributed to passengers aboard the eastern overnight trains, but passengers on the western overnight must bring their own or you can buy them on trains. First class includes the overnight 'sleeper class', where you have a private 'bedroom' with a seat that converts to a bed and are provided with bedding and towels. First class passengers can choose their seat at the time of reservation and enjoy the use of payphones (payable by credit card), priority boarding, three-course meals, complementary aperitif, and a choice of wines with lunch and dinner.

First class is known by different names depending on the route. For example, it's called 'VIA 1' on the rail corridor between Quebec City and Windsor, 'Silver & Blue' class on trains from Toronto west (including *The Canadian*) and 'Easterly' class on the *Ocean* and *Chaleur* trains from Montreal east to the *Gaspé* Peninsula. Halifax Easterly and 'Silver & Blue' trains include a coach with a scenic dome, the Bullet Lounge (where breakfast is served), the Mural Lounge, an art-deco dining carriage and showers in each sleeping car. Not surprisingly, first class costs over twice that of economy class.

URBAN TRANSIT SYSTEMS

Canada's major cities have excellent urban and suburban transit systems, operated mainly for the benefit of commuters. Fast and frequent services are available on a mixture of buses, surface and underground (metro/subway) trains, monorails, and in some cities, ferries. Tickets are valid for the whole system or you receive a free transfer that allows you to change from one mode of transport to another. Tickets are singles or multiples or passes for one or more days. Smoking, eating, drinking and playing radios and cassette/CD recorders aren't usually permitted (except with headphones), and only guide dogs and pets enclosed in acceptable carrying cases are allowed. Bicycles can be taken on some trains, although usually outside commuting hours only. When a transit system includes buses and trains, fares are the same for both and there are usually discounts for children aged under 14, students, seniors and when tickets are purchased in blocks or 'books'. When paying cash you need the exact amount and should keep your ticket as proof of payment until you complete your journey. The choice of public transport in selected cities is shown below:

- **Calgary** has buses and the Calgary Light Rail Transit System known as the 'C-Train'. There are express buses during the morning rush hours, on which there's a supplement of 30¢ in addition to the standard fare of $1.60. You can travel for up to one hour in one direction for the basic fare, changing as often as necessary. Buses generally run around every 20 minutes and the C-Train every few minutes. Schedules and maps are available from the Calgary Transit office, 206-7 Avenue SW, Calgary (☎ 403-262-1000).

- **Edmonton** has a Light Rapid Transit (LRT) system with the same fares for both buses and trains. Schedules and maps are available from Customer Services Churchill LRT Station (☎ 780-496-1611).

- **Montreal** has a rapidly expanding underground (*métro*) system (there were 65 stations in 2002, with more scheduled to open), which is fast, clean and quiet, and an extensive network of buses. Underground tickets are available from booths at any station, which you insert into a slot in the turnstiles to gain access to platforms. Underground and bus tickets are valid on both modes of transport and if you want to transfer to a bus, you obtain a transfer (*correspondence*) ticket from the machine just inside the turnstile. A single journey costs $1.85 (you can buy a strip of six tickets for $8), a one-day tourist pass $5 and a three-day pass $12. Unlike some other underground networks, the Montreal underground is safe at almost any time of the day or night.

- **Ottawa** has only one form of public transport available which is a bus service, of which there are two systems: the Ottawa-Carleton Regional Transit Commission (☎ 613-741-4390) with 130 routes and the other in Hull operated by the *Societé de Transport l'Outaouais* (☎ 819-770-7900). Transfers between the two systems can be purchased on buses. Fares vary depending on the route (indicated by a colour code at bus stops) and are shown in the front window of buses. You can buy tickets at news-stands, Shoppers Drug Mart or Pharmaplus stores, or pay the driver in cash, when you must tender the exact fare.

- **Quebec** city has buses only. Maps are available from tourist information booths or from the Commission de Transporte (☎ 1-888-461-2433).

- **Toronto** has an interconnecting underground, bus and tram (streetcar) system operated by the Toronto Transit Commission (TTC). As in Montreal, the system is fast, safe, clean and relatively quiet, and operates from 6am until 1.30am the next day, from Mondays to Saturdays and from 9am to 1.30am on Sundays. There's cheap all-day parking at underground stations, but spaces (lots) are filled early by commuters. To use the network you need an underground or surface transport token, a ticket or the exact change. To transfer to a bus or tram, you need to ask for a 'transfer' when you buy your underground token. You can buy tickets or tokens at underground entrances or stores displaying the sign 'TTC tickets may be purchased here'. A single fare (one token) is $2.25 for adults ($9.50 for five tokens), $1.50 for students and seniors ($12.50 for ten tokens) and 50¢ for children aged under 12 ($4.25 for ten tokens). You can also buy a special $7.75 pass from underground ticket collectors that's valid for one person for unlimited travel after 9.30am on weekdays or for up to two adults and four children anytime on weekends or holidays. For further information, including a *Ride Guide*, ring ☎ 416-393-4636 or see the Internet (🖥 www. city.toronto.on.ca/ttc/fares.htm).

- **Vancouver** has electric and gas-powered buses run by the Vancouver Regional Transit System, SeaBus catamaran ferries and the SkyTrain monorail (which is an inexpensive way to get around urban and suburban Vancouver). Daily services on main routes operate from 5am until 2am the following day, with less frequent 'Owl' services running on some downtown-urban routes until after 4am. Most buses are wheelchair accessible. Fares are the same on all three systems with one-way, all-zone, off-peak fares of $2 ($4 during rush hours). Transfers are free and available on boarding and are valid for 90 minutes for travel in any direction on all modes of transport. Day passes cost $6 for adults and $4 for seniors, students and children. For further information call ☎ 604-953-3333.

- **Winnipeg** has several bus lines serving the metropolitan area and a '99 Flyer' shuttle service for the downtown shopping area (including Chinatown, the library and Forks Market) between 11am and 3.15pm for a standard fare of 25¢ (special blue signs apply to this service only). Discounts are available on all services for children under 17, students and seniors. Schedules and maps are provided in the back of the Winnipeg telephone directory or by phone (☎ 204-986-5700).

LONG-DISTANCE BUSES

In addition to the local buses that operate in Canadian cities and their suburbs, Canada also has an extensive network of long-distance buses (also called coaches). Long-distance buses are the cheapest form of public transport in Canada and to the US. Although there have been cutbacks in services in recent years caused by increased competition from domestic airlines, long-distance buses continue to survive and even to prosper. You can travel almost anywhere in Canada by bus on an extensive network of scheduled routes with good connections. Most small towns away from the major cities have some sort of bus service, but these tend to be infrequent and slow, so for convenience almost everybody drives.

A number of companies provide long-distance services, by far the largest of which is Greyhound Lines, which faced an uncertain future until the owners of Greyhound Canada (Laidlaw) purchased Greyhound America in late 1998 for almost $100 million. Greyhound Canada operates from Toronto westwards, while in the eastern provinces the major service provider is Voyageur Colonial. Greyhound carries over two million passengers some 40 million miles per year and travels to over 1,000 towns and cities in Canada. It provides the cheapest option for independent travellers seeking door-to-door transport to small towns and those that aren't served by Greyhound are usually covered by regional and local bus companies, many of which accept Greyhound bus passes. The largest of these is Acadian Lines (☎ 902-454-9321), which operates throughout the Maritime Provinces.

Bus terminals in major cities offer a host of services and usually have a restaurant, travel agent, ticket, luggage and parcel services, toilets and left luggage lockers. Bus passes often entitle you to discounts at bus terminal restaurants (although it's usually cheaper to eat away from terminals), nearby hotels, youth hostels and on sightseeing tours. Although bus terminals are usually safe places, they're sometimes located in run-down, inner-city areas and aren't the best places in which to spend a lot of time.

You must usually buy your ticket at a bus terminal or a central office before boarding a bus. Allow plenty of time as there are often long queues (lines). Tickets aren't generally sold on buses, except in some rural areas and on city (urban) routes. Obtain information about schedules, connections and fares, and confirm them by checking the posted schedules. Always ask for the cheapest available fare, which may not be advertised. Greyhound offers a variety of special fares including companion, family, seniors (60 and over) and a Canada pass. You can buy open-dated tickets from bus terminals or travel agents in advance, although usually it's unnecessary or even impossible to make a reservation. You can make as many stopovers as you wish, provided that the entire journey is completed before your ticket expires (although there may be restrictions on special fares and sightseeing tours). Bus pass coupons must be validated each time they're used, so you should arrive early at terminals to have your ticket stamped. In addition to boarding a bus at a bus terminal, buses also stop at designated 'flag stops'. When you see your bus approaching you must flag it down by waving at the driver to get his attention.

Fares depend on a number of considerations, including whether you're making a one-way or round-trip (return), the time of travel and when you're returning. One child under four travels free and other children under four travel at half price; children aged 5 to 11 travel for half fare when accompanied by an adult. In addition to standard fares, a range of discount and promotional fares is available, although these don't usually apply during holiday periods. The range of tickets available includes one-way, round-trip, supersaver, group discounts, discounts for senior citizens and handicapped travellers (10 per cent discount), excursion fares and promotional fares.

As with planes and trains, luggage is checked in before boarding a bus. Allow around 45 minutes in cities and 15 minutes in small towns. You should identify your luggage with a name tag and keep your claim check in a safe place. When two buses are running on the same service, make sure your luggage is put on the correct bus as it isn't unusual for it to end up on the wrong one. You can take a small to medium-sized bag (you can buy one with a cold pack to keep your lunch fresh) onto the bus, provided that it fits into the overhead luggage compartment. **Always keep any valuables with you on the bus.**

Most long-distance buses have air-conditioning, heating, toilets (absolutely essential when travelling with children), and reclining seats with headrests and reading lamps. The seats are comfortable, with the smoothest ride being in the middle of the bus away from the wheels (the best view, however, is at the front, where you also have the most leg room). Window seats are often cooler than aisle seats, particularly at night when drivers usually turn up the air-conditioning to keep themselves awake. Take a warm sweater, jacket or blanket inside the bus with you, as the powerful air-conditioning is freezing at anytime. If you plan to sleep on a bus, an inflatable pillow or sleeping bag (to use as a pillow, not to bed down in the aisle) is useful. Ear plugs are also recommended if you're a light sleeper.

If you use a radio or cassette player on a bus, you must wear earphones. Smoking and alcohol are prohibited on all buses and if you're caught having a puff in the restroom you're thrown off the bus and could be prosecuted by the bus company and the police (there's a fine of up to $500!). If you're travelling across Canada, bear in mind that distances are vast and a coast-to-coast trip takes seven or eight days, with only brief stops at fast food joints or bus terminals every few hours, and no overnight sleep stops or stops for showers (the main consolation is that you don't need to pay to sleep on the bus). **At rest stops, you may have just a few minutes to stretch your legs or grab some food and the driver may drive off without warning if you aren't on the bus.** Many people provide their own food and drink, so that they can eat at their leisure. On long journeys you may have to get off the bus occasionally for it to be cleaned.

For information about Greyhound services contact Greyhound Canada Transportation Corporation, 877 Greyhound Way SW, Calgary AB T3C 3V8 (☎ 1-800-661-8747, 🖳 www.greyhound.ca). For information about Voyageur contact Voyageur Colonial Ltd, 265 Catherine Street, Ottawa ON K1R 7S5 (☎ 613-238-5900, 🖳 www.voyageur.com/info.htm). The Brewster bus line, PO Box 1140, 100 Gopher Street, Banff AB T1L 1J3 (☎ 403-762-673, 🖳 www. brewster.ca) operates sight-seeing tours in the west, mainly in the Rockies.

TAXIS

Taxis are relatively inexpensive in Canada and are plentiful in most cities (except when it's raining, or you have lots of luggage). Taxis are usually easily distinguishable in major cities, e.g. the Yellow Cab Line cabs are painted (surprise, surprise) bright yellow, although there are several companies in most cities so you can expect taxis to come in a variety of colours and styles. The only common feature is a plastic 'Taxi' sign on the roof, which when illuminated means that the taxi is available. Taxis can be hailed on the street or you can pick one up at a cab rank outside hotels and railway stations.

There's a minimum charge of around $2 or $2.50 (flagdrop) after which the cost is around 25¢ for each 275m (300 yards). In addition to what's shown on the meter, you must also pay any additional costs such as bridge or ferry tolls and surcharges, e.g. for night and Sunday journeys. Special rates may apply to some destinations, which are usually posted in cabs. Most drivers don't like changing anything larger than a $10 or $20 bill, but don't mind keeping the change. With the exception of Quebec, where taxi drivers (like everybody else) may refuse to answer you if you don't speak French, most Canadian taxi drivers are courteous and helpful.

At Canadian airports and major rail stations there may be a taxi 'dispatcher'. His job is to get you a taxi, advise you on fares and help prevent you being cheated by cab drivers (or bogus cab drivers). At some airports and rail stations, fares to popular destinations are also posted on notice boards, while at smaller rail stations there may be special taxi phones. Minibus shuttle services are also available at most airports; like taxis, they take you exactly where you want to go, but the fare is lower as it's shared with your fellow passengers.

All taxi drivers must hold both a chauffeur's licence and a taxi licence from the municipal authority. If you have a complaint about a taxi, note the cab and driver's licence numbers and the name of the taxi company. This information should be listed on the receipt, which must be provided on request.

AIRLINE SERVICES

Canadians have excellent air links to most countries and around 100 airlines transport over 36 million passengers some 50 billion miles per year. The two most popular domestic routes, Montreal-Toronto, and Vancouver-Toronto, each carry over a million passengers per year and even the short route from Calgary to Edmonton (less than 200mi/320km) carries nearly half a million passengers per year.

Canada has one major international airline, Air Canada. It has a fleet of around 160 aircraft serving some 550 destinations world-wide and is a member of the Star Alliance that includes Air New Zealand, All Nippon Airways, Ansett Australia, Lufthansa, SAS, Thai, United and Varig. It's recognised as one of the world's top airlines and in 1999 was chosen as the 'Best Airline for Travel to Canada' by readers of *Business Traveler International* magazine and voted the 'Best Passenger Service Airline' in the world by *Air Transport World* magazine. Canada's smaller carriers include Canada 3000 and local carriers such as Air Alliance in Quebec, Air Atlantic and Air Nova in Atlantic Canada, AirBC in British Columbia and Air Ontario. In the north of the country the larger carriers use Boeing 737s (or similar planes) when flying into 'regular' airports, although in smaller towns and remote areas the smaller airlines operate float planes that land on lakes, using skids (rather than floats) when they're frozen.

You should check-in at least an hour before a domestic flight and two hours before an international flight, as some airlines may over-book. Check-in closes 30 minutes before departure and if you turn up later than this you will find you've been transferred to a later flight (bumped). Although there are occasionally delays in departure, in general flights are punctual and you don't spend 'hours' flying around in circles above busy airports waiting to land. Canada is one of the world's safest countries in which to fly and its major airlines have an excellent safety record that's second to none. **Smoking on aircraft is banned on all domestic and foreign flights in Canada and may also be prohibited in airport terminal buildings except for designated areas.**

Useful publications for frequent-fliers include the Official Airline Guides (OAG) *Worldwide Pocket Flight Guide, The Complete Sky Traveler* by David Beaty

(Methuen) and *The Round the World Air Guide* by Katie Wood and George McDonald (Fontana). Those interested in flying history will enjoy *Wingwalkers: The Story of Canadian Airlines* by Peter Piggott (Harbour Publishing).

Airports

Canada has international airports at Calgary, Edmonton, Gander (Newfoundland), Halifax, Montreal, Toronto, Vancouver and Winnipeg. These are termed 'gateway' airports and act as a hub for Canadian carriers and regional/commuter airlines that operate services to smaller airports. When taking a plane from an international airport in Canada, check in advance which terminal you require. With the exception of Montreal Mirabel airport, which is 34mi (55km) outside town and takes around one hour to reach from the city centre, and Edmonton which is 19mi (30km) outside town and takes 45 minutes to get to, all other major airports can be reached from the city centre in around 30 minutes. St John's, Winnipeg and Vancouver airports are less than 5mi (8km) outside town and can be reached in around 15 minutes. Most airports provide short and long-term parking lots.

Major airports are organised by airline, where each carrier has separate check-in desks, gates, lounges and even exclusive terminals at some airports. Signs at airports are in both English and French and most have information desks and centres with multilingual staff. If you have any problems inquire at the ticket booth of the airline with which you're travelling. Flight departures aren't announced but are displayed on information screens and departure boards, so keep an eye out for your flight.

You may have a long walk to the baggage reclaim area, although major airports have moving walkways. Luggage trolleys (carts) are free at some airports, but need to be rented at others for $1 (this means if you're a foreigner arriving in Canada, you cannot get a trolley unless you've got some Canadian coins!). Most international airports have banks, currency exchanges and cash machines (ATMs), and stamp and travel insurance machines. All international airports have executive and VIP passenger lounges, and publish free passenger information booklets. Major airports also have emergency clinics (and sometimes a dental service), restaurants, bars, gift stores, luggage storage, lost property offices, fax machines, photocopiers, computer rentals and other business services. Duty-free goods are available on cross-border flights with the exception of flights that are pre-cleared to US destinations.

Public transport to and from major airports includes buses, taxis, mini-buses, limousines and sometimes rail services. Often there's a dispatcher whose job is to find you a taxi and advise you about fares. Many hotels and motels provide a courtesy bus service at major airports, although smaller airports may have no bus services at all. A shuttle minibus or mini-van door-to-door 'taxi' service is often provided and can be booked to pick you up at home. Air taxis, both helicopters and light aircraft, are available at all major airports and many smaller regional airports. *The Airport Book: The Passenger's Guide to Major Airports in the United States & Canada* by Albert Diaz is a comprehensive guide to all major airports in Canada. Some airports levy an Airport Improvement Fee (AIF) for departing passengers of between $10 and $15.

International Fares

International air fares to and from Canada are among the lowest in the world and have been slashed even further in recent years. When travelling to Canada, particularly from Europe, it's cheaper to travel from a major city (e.g. London), where a wide choice of low-cost fares is available. If you're travelling from London, shop around travel agents and airlines for the lowest fares, and check the travel pages of *Time Out* magazine and British Sunday newspapers such as the *Sunday Times* and the *Observer*. Fares from London can be as low as around £180 Gatwick-Toronto or £300 Gatwick-Vancouver. One of the best companies for cheap flights from the UK is Canadian Affair (☎ +44 (2)07-616 9184, 🖳 www. canadian-affair.com). However, you may get the best deal from a travel agent.

With the exception of full-fare open tickets, fares depend on the number of restrictions and limitations you're willing (or able) to tolerate. These include minimum advance purchase periods, limitations on when you can fly, a minimum and maximum period between outward and return flights, and advance booking of both outward and return flights, with no changes permitted and no refunds (or high cancellation penalties). Apex (advanced purchase excursion) fares are generally the cheapest, particularly for midweek flights. Apex seats must usually be booked between seven and 21 days in advance and there are restrictions on the length of your stay, e.g. a minimum of seven and no more than 21 days. The main disadvantage with all discounted tickets is that they're non-refundable and cannot be used on other flights or airlines. Before buying a ticket, carefully check the restrictions. Many apex tickets carry 15 to 100 per cent penalties for reservation changes or cancellations. It pays to shop around before buying a ticket, as it's easy to pay a lot more than is necessary for an identical service. The cheapest round-trip ticket to/from Canada is usually cheaper than any one-way flight.

The cheapest international flights can usually be purchased from 'bucket shops' and 'consolidators' (both in Canada and abroad), which are companies selling surplus seats at large discounts. They deal mainly in international and transatlantic flights, and rarely offer domestic flights, on which discounts are insignificant. Fares change frequently, so if you're looking for the lowest fares, keep an eye on the travel and business sections of major newspapers (e.g. the Saturday edition of the *Toronto Globe & Mail*, where promotional flights are widely advertised) or contact a travel agent which specialises in low cost fares. Although it's easier to ask a travel agent than to call individual airlines, some travel agents won't always tell you about the cheapest fares because it lowers their commission. However, you can check directly with Air Canada (☎ 1-888-247-2262, 🖳 www.aircanada.ca), particularly on Wednesdays when they may offer heavily discounted flights for the following weekend. Generally, however, their fares tend to be quite high, sometimes double those of other airlines. Other websites with ticket saver plans include Trip.Com (🖳 www.thetrip.com), best for business travellers, and Epicurious Travel (🖳 www. travel.epicurious.com), who allow you to sign up for all available discount lists at the same time.

There are a number of Airpass schemes in Canada. Air Canada offers a variety, some of which are valid for travel throughout mainland North America, either on Air Canada flights only or combined with Continental or United Airlines' flights. Canadian regional airlines also offer unlimited flights in specified areas. The EastPass covers Manitoba, Nova Scotia, Ontario and Quebec, the WestPass covers Alberta, British Columbia, Manitoba, Saskatchewan, Northwest Territories and Nunavut, and the NationalPass covers the entire network. Horizon Air offers an unlimited flights pass for Calgary, Edmonton, Vancouver and Victoria.

Domestic Fares

Flying is the fastest and most convenient way of travelling in Canada and to the US, which together have the lowest air fares in the world (some even lower than Greyhound buses). Low-cost airlines offer 'no-frills' flights (bring your own sandwiches) and while the seat may not be as wide as on a major carrier, the fares are unbeatable. Like international fares, Canadian domestic fares vary depending on ticket restrictions (see above), and are heavily influenced by the time of day, the day of the week, how far in advance you book your ticket and the season.

There are generally three fare seasons in Canada: high (summer and holiday periods), shoulder (e.g. late November around Thanksgiving) and low or off-peak, which is most other times (particularly during school terms). The summer peak season runs from June 1st to September 1st. Christmas and New Year are peak periods for domestic flights, although not usually for international flights. The shoulder season is the Canadian term for a period that's less busy than the high season. It often includes the period immediately prior to a federal holiday. When planning a flight during a holiday period, book *well* in advance.

One-class economy seating is popular on short domestic flights and many airlines are replacing first class with a better business class. The most expensive fares are open return tickets, for which there are no advance booking requirements and flights can be booked or cancelled at any time. Open tickets are usually valid for one year, during which a full refund can be obtained at any time. Excursion and discount fares usually apply to round-trip flights only and must normally be purchased in advance, e.g. 7 or 14 days. Other common conditions are minimum and maximum stay requirements, such as 6 to 14 days or 1 to 6 days including at least one Saturday night.

With the exception of full-fare tickets, fares are usually non-refundable, although you may be able to change your flight for an additional fee (e.g. $25). On long-haul domestic flights (usually scheduled over one hour), services are much the same as on international flights, with meals, drinks and films (although you must usually pay for alcoholic drinks, films are usually free).

Short-haul flights are often economy (coach) class only, while long-haul flights usually have first and economy class compartments. Infants under two years of age travel free on most domestic flights provided that they don't occupy a seat. There's a 10 per cent discount for children aged two to 12 and seniors aged 65 or over, but youths (13 and over) must pay full fare. However, a discounted adult fare is often cheaper than a child fare. Many airlines also offer discounts for youths, students and senior citizens (over 60 or 65).

As a result of deregulation, special promotional fares can be offered at almost any time and there's usually at least one airline offering a promotional flight to where you want to go. Promotional fares or special offers on major routes can make a journey of a thousand miles cheaper than a short hop of a few hundred miles. Many smaller airlines are able to offer inexpensive domestic flights by using little-used airports and some offer all seats at the same low fare, which may be lower than the lowest fare offered by larger national airlines. Sometimes it's cheaper to buy a round-trip than a one-way ticket and leave the return trip unused. Charter flights are often the cheapest, but they don't provide the same security as a discounted seat on a scheduled flight. Other inexpensive flights are available through travel clubs, although members may be given little advance notice of flights or tour packages.

You should reserve a seat on a domestic flight. When you book your flight, you're usually allocated a seat number and can check in at the gate if you have carry-on luggage only. If you need to travel on a particular flight, book as early as possible. If you don't have a reservation you can go to an airport and wait for a flight, called 'flying stand-by', although some airlines restrict this to certain age groups, e.g. 12 to 24 with Air Canada (you must have ID). Many airlines routinely over-book flights (when not half-empty) as an insurance against passengers who don't turn up ('no-shows'). This sometimes results in passengers with reservations being 'bumped' (denied a seat) and being forced to travel on a later flight, for which they sometimes receive 'Denied Boarding Compensation' (DBC). Compensation, if offered, may be a sum of money equal to the price of your ticket, a ticket upgrade on the next flight or even a free return ticket to any destination on the airline's domestic network. Airlines sometimes ask for volunteers, who might be offered compensation, e.g. Air Canada sometimes pays up to $300 (although you might have to be pushy to get it), in addition to which you're offered a seat on the next flight (which may be just one hour later) or a free re-booking. Some people jump at the opportunity (if there's compensation) and therefore it's rare for someone to be bumped involuntarily. Compensation excludes charter flights and delays due to cancelled or delayed flights, e.g. as a result of an aircraft malfunction or bad weather.

To avoid being bumped, try to check in at least one hour before the scheduled departure time for a domestic flight and check in by the time specified. If you check in late and are bumped, you won't be entitled to claim DBC. One way to ensure you have a seat is to visit an airline office (or some travel agents) and obtain a boarding pass and seat number in advance. When the weather is bad in the local area or the area where your flight terminates, it's wise to confirm your flight before arriving at the airport. Some airlines recommend that you confirm your flight 48 to 72 hours in advance. Although the 'OK' under status on your ticket means that a reservation has been made, a confirmation may still be necessary.

The latest innovation is 'electronic ticketing' (introduced by the budget airlines), where you receive no ticket or boarding pass. Tickets are typically booked by phone with a credit card and you receive an itinerary by fax or post, or on the Internet and you receive an itinerary by email. If you have no luggage or only hand luggage you can go directly to the departure gate where they assign you a seat (if you have luggage to check in you may be assigned a seat then).

Most Canadian airlines operate a bonus 'frequent flyer' or 'mileage club' scheme for regular passengers, where passengers receive free tickets, bonus miles, free upgrades and discounts after travelling a number of miles, e.g. 25,000. Benefits may also include car rental and hotel discounts. Membership of these schemes is free, although you must join at the check-in counter before flying. Bonus miles can also be earned by using car rental companies, hotel chains and credit cards affiliated to frequent flyer schemes or by buying certain products (the 'Air Miles' schemes are run by organisations outside the airlines).

There are several sources of information on frequent flyer programmes including *The Official Frequent Flyer Guidebook* (☎ 1-800-209-2870 or 🖥 www. flyersguide.com for ordering information) containing 600 pages of detailed information including award charts on over 50 major frequent traveller programmes. It explains in-depth how the different programmes work and shows you how to earn more when you travel. *Frequent* magazine, Frequent Publications, 4714-C Town Centre Dr, Colorado Springs, CO 80916, USA (☎ 1-800-333-5937) and *Inside Flyer* magazine (☎ 1-800-767-8896, 🖥 www. insideflyer.com) are monthly magazines that report the latest news on frequent flyer programmes. Most Canadian airlines also operate airline clubs for travellers. Membership privileges include the use of private airport lounges, computers and fax facilities, ATMs, showers, cheque-cashing facilities and other special services.

FERRIES

All maritime provinces have ferry services to connect islands to the mainland and with each other. Ferries are a slow means of transportation, which ferry companies are starting to capitalise on by turning their boats into mini cruise ships with onboard dining and private cabins. Rates are per vehicle, inclusive of up to four passengers, or per passenger for those without a vehicle. Reservations are recommended as ferries often run only once per day and if you show up without a booking and the ship is full, you have to wait 24 hours for the next one. Make sure you plan to arrive at the ferry terminal in advance of your departure time, as ferries usually depart exactly on schedule. Attendants park your car on board ferries and you travel (ride) in the passenger compartments. Passengers without vehicles may check in their luggage, which is subject to limited liability. Smoking is permitted in designated areas of ships and terminals only and is strictly prohibited on vehicle decks.

In British Columbia, the BC Ferry Corporation provides a daily car and passenger service from Vancouver to Victoria and the Gulf Islands. The journey takes 2.5 hours and is on a turn-up-and-go basis (no bookings). The service between Port Hardy and Prince Rupert (summer only) is operated on alternate days in each direction, takes 15 hours and it's wise to book (☎ 1-888-724-5223 or 1-800-BCFERRY, 🖥 www.bc ferries.bc.ca). It costs $46 for an adult, $23 for a child and $95 for a standard vehicle up to 80in (2.03m) high and 20ft (6.09m) in length. *The FERRY Traveler*, 2250 York, Suite 301, Vancouver BC V6K 2C6 (☎ 604-733-9113) lists the dozen or so ferries that travel to Vancouver Island. The fare from Vancouver to Vancouver island is $10 one way for those aged over 12 and $5 for those aged 5 to 11 and seniors (65 and over) from Friday to Sunday. The trip is free for those aged under five and for seniors from Mondays to Thursdays. A motorcycle costs $17.50, a car $34.75 and a RV or oversize vehicle $56.50 (in addition to the above fares for occupants).

In New Brunswick, toll-free river ferries are part of the highway system and are located mainly on the Lower Saint John and Kennebecasis rivers. Other toll-free services operate between Deer Island and Letete on the mainland. Toll ferries operate between Blacks Harbour and Grand Manan, and between Deer Island and Campobello islands, the latter only in summer. The Marine Atlantic company (☎ 1-800-341-7981) operates a daily ferry service from North Sydney (Nova Scotia) to Port Aux Basques (Newfoundland) costing $25 per person or $146 for a car (more for buses and trucks). Marine Atlantic also operates ferry services throughout the Atlantic Maritime provinces and also provides a 'Cruising Labrador' service.

In Ontario, Northland Ferries' (☎ 519-596-2510) ChiCheemaun service connects Tobermory on Bruce Peninsula with South Baymouth on Manitoulin Island from May to October. In Greater Toronto, the Metro Parks Department operates ferries to the Toronto islands (Centre Island, Ward's Island and Hanlan Point) from Queen's Quay at the end of Bay Street. Schedules vary depending on the season. A round trip costs $3 for adults, $1.50 for seniors and students, and $1 for children aged under 15. The Maple Leaf ferry runs from the foot of Bathhurst Street to the Island Airport (☎ 416-392-8193 for information).

11.

MOTORING

It's almost impossible to survive in Canada without a car unless you live in the middle of one of the major cities and rarely leave it. Canada is almost 3,000mi (4,827km) from Toronto to Vancouver and around 5,000mi (8,000km) between the Atlantic and Pacific coasts. Once you travel outside the cities, towns are few and far between and, although there are buses, trains and planes, they aren't a lot of use if all you want to do is pop into the nearest town to shop. Canada has more cars per head of population than any country in the world except the USA, totalling some 13 million (plus 350,000 motorcycles), and Canadians buy nearly 1.5 million new cars per year (most made in the USA). Despite this, the average Canadian drives only some 11,000mi (18,000km) per year, with annual running costs for the typical car around $7,500.

Given the number of cars on the roads, there are surprisingly few deaths from vehicle accidents. Quebec has the highest accident rate in Canada; in Montreal in particular, local drivers have nerves of steel, excessive confidence and a devil-may-care attitude.

The first thing you notice when driving any distance in Canada is that it's a HUGE country. In some regions you can drive for miles without seeing another vehicle, and people living in remote rural areas think nothing of spending several hours behind the wheel to do the weekly shopping. Main roads and city streets are generally kept as straight as possible, and streets in most cities are designed on a grid pattern.

It's wise to avoid rush hours if possible, which vary with the city but are usually between 7 and 9.30am, and from 4 to 6.30pm (small towns usually have shorter rush hours, e.g. 7.30 to 8.30am and 4.30 to 5.30pm). In some cities there are special driving rules on major thoroughfares during rush hours, where parking is prohibited.

Unlike in most countries, responsibility for the Canadian highway system lies with provincial and municipal authorities and not with the federal government. Therefore traffic laws often vary with the province, and you should never take it for granted that the road rules in one province are the same as in another province. Nevertheless, there's general uniformity with respect to road signs and basic rules. Detailed information about road rules in all provinces and territories is provided in the *Digest of Motor Laws*, published annually by the Canadian Automobile Association (CAA – see page 233) in conjunction with the American Automobile Association and issued free to members. In general, Canadian road and automobile terms have been used throughout this chapter. Canada uses the metric system of weights and measures, and speed limits and distances are given in kilometres and fuel prices in litres; for Imperial conversion tables, see **Appendix D**.

VEHICLE IMPORTATION

If you plan to import a motor vehicle or motorcycle into Canada, either temporarily or permanently, first make sure that you're aware of the latest regulations. Taking a new or relatively new car to Canada from overseas is usually an expensive and pointless exercise: apart from the bureaucratic hassles, cars can be purchased in Canada far cheaper than in most other countries. All imported cars must meet Canadian regulations, particularly those regarding emissions, unless they're over 15 years old or are being imported temporarily.

Don't assume that motor vehicles manufactured to United States safety standards automatically meet Canadian safety standards. If you import a vehicle, you must ensure that it either complies with Canadian standards or can be modified. If in doubt, contact the Registrar of Imported Vehicles (☎ 1-800-511-7755) regarding the import of vehicles from the USA and either (☎ 1-800-333-0371 or 613-998-2570) regarding vehicles coming from Europe. If your vehicle doesn't meet the required safety standards but can be modified, the registrar's representative at your entry point into Canada charges you a fee to register it and gives you 45 days to comply with the regulations. **All petrol (gasoline) sold in Canada is unleaded and, if you're importing a car that requires leaded petrol, you must have it converted to run on unleaded fuel before you can use it in Canada.**

There are restrictions on importing vehicles that weren't manufactured in the current year from countries other than the United States. Such vehicles may be imported provided only that:

- it's for your personal use;
- you've owned it since it was new;
- you've receive it as a gift from a friend or relative abroad (you must testify in writing that no money changed hands);
- it's a replacement vehicle imported privately after a vehicle was damaged beyond repair while you were travelling abroad (you must submit a statement from the insurance company and a copy of the police report verifying this);
- you're a returning resident or a former resident of Canada, importing a used or secondhand vehicle after living in another country for at least 12 consecutive months immediately before your return to Canada;
- you've been outside Canada for a period of six consecutive months or more and owned the vehicle for at least the same period before you returned to Canada.

If you're entering Canada as a permanent resident, you can include your car in your duty-free allowance (see page 372) provided that it's for your personal use and isn't for commercial purposes. A non-resident can import a car into Canada without paying duty, although if it's sold duty must be paid. Savings can be made when importing some cars and motorcycles into Canada, although generally it isn't worth the time, trouble and expense involved.

For further information contact Transport Canada, Road Safety and Motor Vehicle Regulations Directorate, 8th floor, Place de Ville, Tower C, 330 Sparks Street, Ottawa ON K1A 0N5 (☎ 613-998-8616). Canada Customs and Revenue Agency publishes a pamphlet, *Importing a Motor Vehicle Into Canada*, available from Canada Customs and Revenue, 14th Floor, Sir Richard Scott Building, 191 Laurier Avenue West, Ottawa ON K1A 0L5 (▤ 613-998-5584).

Imported vehicles may also be subject to provincial or territorial sales tax (see **Sales Taxes** on page 358) and safety requirements, so you should check with the motor vehicle department of the province or territory to which you're moving. The underside of all vehicles taken into Canada (unless driven over the border from America) must be steam-cleaned or high-pressure washed to remove any soil or other potentially contaminating substances before they're brought into Canada (ideally this should be done immediately before shipping).

VEHICLE REGISTRATION

Vehicle registration rules and fees vary with the province. In all provinces you pay a registration fee for your number plates (equivalent to 'road tax' in other countries); in some, you also pay a fee to license the vehicle itself, which may vary according to the weight or mass of the vehicle. The registration fee may be a flat fee or may be based on a car's weight or age (or a combination). In most provinces, number plates belong to an individual and not the vehicle, and are transferred to a new car when a car is sold (there's a fee of $28 to $36 depending on the province). The exceptions are Newfoundland, where the plates remain with the vehicle, and Northwest Territories, where the old plates are scrapped and a new set issued on the sale of a vehicle. In most provinces only the buyer needs to attend the Motor Licence Office, although in Quebec both the seller and buyer must be present. Upon registration you're usually issued with two number plates (only one in Alberta and Quebec), the expiry date (month/year) of which is shown on the rear plate. In some provinces a vehicle can be registered before entry, although you may require a local address.

Registration fees are normally payable annually. The exceptions are New Brunswick (where you can choose to pay for any period from 1 to 12 months), Saskatchewan (where you choose any period from 3 to 12 months) and Ontario (where you can pay for two years at a time).

Registration is validated by a sticker affixed to the rear number plate (it's best to remove the old sticker and glue the new one directly to the plate, which makes it more difficult to steal). There are penalties for late renewal and you can be arrested for displaying an expired sticker. Duplicate plates and registration papers are available for a small fee. Most provinces don't refund a proportion of the fee if you surrender the registration before it expires. Detailed information about vehicle registration is provided by provincial motor vehicle offices and is also contained in the *Digest of Motor Laws* published annually by the Canadian Automobile Association (see page 233).

To register a car you need some or all of the following papers:

- Proof of ownership, e.g. a bill or certificate of sale showing the purchase price and date, a lease agreement or a Transfer Of Ownership Document (TOD) or, for new vehicles, a New Vehicle Information Statement (NVIS);
- Proof of identity and date of birth (such as a driving licence);
- Proof of insurance (see page 218);
- The current registration document;
- A Safety Standards Certificate (see **Safety & Emission Inspection** on page 215);
- Registration authorisation if you aren't the owner of the vehicle;
- A completed vehicle registration application form;
- The registration fee, which may include GST and provincial sales tax (see page 358).

BUYING A CAR

There are taxes on both new and used cars in Canada: GST is charged at 7.5 per cent in all provinces and PST at special rates in certain provinces as shown below. See also **Sales Taxes** on page 358.

Province	PST rate (%)
Alberta	7
British Columbia	7.5
Manitoba	7
New Brunswick	8
Newfoundland	8
Nova Scotia	8
Ontario	8
Prince Edward Island	10
Quebec	7
Saskatchewan	6

All taxes due must be paid at the time of registration.

New Cars

Most new cars sold in Canada are made in North America, with only some 100,000 per year imported from overseas. There are no Canadian makes of car, although several US and Japanese manufacturers make or assemble cars in Canada. In addition to the wide range of US models, however, most European and Japanese cars are available. US cars have reduced somewhat in size in recent years, although saloons (sedans) and estates (station wagons) are still the size of small trucks. 'Compact' (or 'economy' or 'mid-size') models are around the same size as larger European cars. 'Sub-compact' is the name given to small family cars such as the Ford Escort or VW Golf, while open sports cars are called roadsters or convertibles.

Canadian cars have traditionally had prodigious thirsts, although the 'gas-guzzlers' have largely been replaced by smaller 'economy' cars. However, many American cars still handle poorly, are too big for many people and have poor fuel consumption, so it comes as no surprise that an increasing number of Canadians have been changing from American-made cars to Japanese or European cars. As far back as 1998, sales of Japanese cars increased by over 75 per cent in nine provinces (in New Brunswick the increase was over 200 per cent!).

Many Canadian cars (or cars made for the Canadian market) are liberally adorned with 'idiot' gadgets and buzzers, e.g. those informing you that your seat belt isn't fastened, you've left your lights on or your key is in the ignition. Some Canadian cars have combination locks on the doors that can be used to lock or open them when you've locked your keys inside the car (provided you haven't forgotten the combination!).

Air-conditioning is standard on many cars and certainly isn't a luxury in the hotter months, although it decreases power and increases fuel consumption. Most Canadian cars are fitted with automatic transmission and also have power steering, both of which also increase consumption. All cars sold in Canada come with a driver's side airbag as standard and the option of passenger airbags.

Although comparisons between new car prices in different countries are often difficult (e.g. due to fluctuating exchange rates and the different levels of standard equipment), new cars are much cheaper in Canada than in most other countries, despite the high cost of meeting Canada's safety and emission regulations. The average price of a new car in spring 2003 was around $20,000.

The dealer mark-up on new cars is much lower than in most other countries and most of a dealer's profit is made on options and selling finance and insurance. The basic or 'sticker' price (e.g. in an advertisement or showroom) may, however, provide little indication of the on-the-road price, which may be thousands of dollars more. Many 'options' may be already fitted to a showroom model and you have to pay for them whether you want them or not (or look elsewhere). Some manufacturers (particularly Japanese) include many 'options' as standard equipment, while others (e.g. German) make you pay heavily for them, and usually have a list of options as long as your arm. You can save a lot of money by buying a car on which 'extras' are standard equipment. Always check that any stated options are in fact present on a car by asking the salesman to show or demonstrate them.

Note that list prices don't include GST or provincial sales tax (see above) and registration (see **Vehicle Registration** on page 210). Many dealers also include a charge, e.g. around $115, for the paperwork associated with buying a car; this is one of the many aspects you should haggle over. Dealers expect you to haggle, so don't be afraid to walk away when the price isn't right. When sales are slow, dealers may offer incentives such as free CAA membership, service discounts, options or special equipment, and a free loan car for up to five days when a repair or service is required. Many manufacturers offer optional extended warranties, which are good value if you do high mileage or intend to keep a car for a long time.

Nearly half of all new cars in Canada are purchased on lease deals, with over 80 per cent from financing companies belonging to car manufacturers. Leasing is also available from banks. Personal lease deals usually require a deposit (down payment) and monthly payments over a period of between one and five years, include a standard mileage allowance of 15,000 per year and allow you to purchase the car outright at the end of the lease period. Whether you're better off leasing or buying depends on your priorities: if you like to have a new car every two or three years, want its maintenance to be taken care of and are willing to pay a little more over the long term, leasing is preferable; if you prefer to own your car and are prepared to maintain it yourself, you should buy. If you decide to lease a car, shop around and compare a number of leasing deals, as they can vary considerably with the dealer. You may obtain a better deal towards the end of a month, when salesmen are sometimes struggling to meet their targets. All leasing offers stipulate 'qualified buyers only', which means that unless you have an excellent credit rating you won't be eligible. Toronto Dominion Bank (and others) publish a booklet entitled *Your Guide to Car Financing* (☎ 1-866-567-8888, 🖳 www.tdbank.ca/lending).

The CAA (see page 233) and *Consumer Reports* magazine (🖳 www.consumer reports.org) all provide a car 'price printout' service. This lists all standard equipment, every available option and the factory invoice cost of the vehicle. Car magazines regularly publish list and best (offer) prices and also show dealer margins, so you know exactly how much profit a dealer is making. One of the best guides is the *Complete Price Guide for 2002-2003 Models of Vehicles*, available from 390 Steelcase Road, Markham ON L3R 1G2 (☎ 905-475-9126). There are also many consumer magazines (such as *World of Wheels*) and guide books for car buyers with which you can make comparisons until your head spins. These include the annual *Car Buying Guide* (Consumer Reports) and the off-putting *So...You Wanna Buy A Car* by Bruce Fuller & Tony Whitney (Self Counsel Press Inc).

Many car dealers pay a 'bird dog' fee of $25 to $100 for referrals. Ask the salesman for his business card, write your name and phone number on the reverse, and tell your friend to give the card to the salesman when he buys a car. You get paid when the deal is finalised ('closed').

Used Cars

Used (also called secondhand, previously owned or 'pre-possessed') cars are good value in Canada, particularly low mileage cars less than a year old, where the saving on the new price can be as much as 25 per cent. The minute a new car leaves the showroom it's usually worth at least 10 per cent less than the purchase price (unless it's a limited edition model, in which case it may have appreciated). Some models depreciate much faster than others and represent excellent secondhand bargains.

Inexpensive secondhand cars can be purchased for as little as $500, although obviously you should be more circumspect when buying a 'wreck' – it must still meet the safety and emission standards. If you want a car for a short period only, an older car reduces your losses if you sell it within a short period. If you don't want a gas-guzzler, Japanese cars are generally among the cheapest and are usually both reliable and economical. Old Volkswagens are also good value and it's easy to get them repaired and find spare parts.

Obtaining spares for some imported cars is difficult or even impossible. Also the number and location of dealers for imported cars varies considerably with the province (in some provinces you may find that the nearest dealer is hundreds of miles away). Older classic European sports models can be purchased in Canada for much less than in Europe, although their condition is often poor and finding spares and expert mechanics can be difficult. When buying a secondhand car, you should check carefully for rust, as a huge amount of corrosive salt is used on Canadian roads in the winter. Make sure that the vehicle you're buying has adequate cold-weather equipment (i.e. a good heater **and** an engine-block heater).

Cars with high mileage (e.g. 20,000 per year), particularly cars sold by rental companies, can usually be purchased for substantially less than the average price and may offer excellent value, provided they've been regularly serviced, although you should be careful when buying a car with average (e.g. 11,000mi/18,000km per year) or high mileage that's over four years old, as this is the time when it may need expensive repairs. Always check that a car has been regularly serviced (check receipts and service records). You should be wary if an owner says he does his own servicing, as this may mean it has rarely been serviced. Unless you're an expert, you should take someone with you who's knowledgeable about cars or get a car's major systems checked by a dealer selling the same make. The fee is around $75, which you may be able to recoup many times over if faults are found (provided you still think the car's worth buying).

Excellent sources of information are the *Used Car Buying Guide* (Consumer Reports) and the annual *Lemon-Aid Used Cars Guide* (Stoddart). A 'lemon' is the Canadian (and American) word for anything that doesn't work properly (particularly cars) and the Lemon-Aid guide lists failure-prone models and components.

The price of a used car depends on its make, size, age, condition, the time of year and the area where it's for sale. Buying a car privately may be cheaper than buying from a dealer, although you won't get a warranty and must usually know what you're doing. You need to get up early to get a good used car in some areas, where used-car brokers (who buy cars and pass them onto dealers) do most of their deals before breakfast! You may get a better deal from a dealer who sells new cars of the make you're looking for than from a used car lot selling used cars only, although the latter may be less expensive. If possible, choose a dealer who has been recommended. You can usually check whether there has been a large number of complaints against a dealer through a local consumer protection agency or Better Business Bureau.

When purchasing a car privately, check that the seller owns it through the Personal Property Registration Office in the provincial capital, obtain a bill of sale, the proper registration and copies of all financial transactions. Check the registration month and year on the rear number plate, because if a vehicle is unregistered you could be held responsible for the past year's registration fee. **If a car is unregistered it's also uninsured and it needs temporary insurance before you can test drive it on public roads.** If you're stopped by the police, you must show proof of ownership. The fine for not having the original paperwork is around $20 – photocopies aren't acceptable.

One of the best places to buy secondhand cars (and to compare prices) is through local newspapers, e.g. the Saturday edition of the *Toronto Globe & Mail*. Free car shopper magazines and newspapers are also published in all areas. Always do your own research in your local area by comparing prices at dealers, in local papers and in the national press. Many private sellers are willing to take a considerable drop and you can haggle over the price with most dealers. The average mileage for a car in Canada is around 11,000 per year. When buying privately, used cars are usually paid for in cash or with a certified cheque.

SAFETY & EMISSION INSPECTION

An annual safety inspection is necessary in some provinces, while in others inspections are required only when vehicles change hands, e.g. within seven days of registration. Most provinces require safety inspections for commercial vehicles or buses and coaches, although few require inspections for private cars. The annual test fee is usually a nominal $10 to $20. The prescribed standards can be rather skimpy in some provinces, e.g. Ontario's rules on brake linings are much less than the thickness recommended by most manufacturers. The certification inspection includes the operation of lights, wipers, defrosters, horn, driver's seat, seat belts, driver's and passenger's side windows, bodywork, tyres, brakes, suspension, exhaust, and engine and transmission mountings. It doesn't include an evaluation of the performance of the engine or transmission. Cars that pass the inspection are issued with a Safety Standards Certificate (SSC).

Don't confuse these safety certification inspections with the 'certified' used car programmes run by manufacturers' dealerships, which are more comprehensive and provide a warranty. The CAA provides thorough inspections by approved garages at a cost of around $100 for members or $150 for non-members.

Throughout Canada, all vehicles made since 1990 must have a catalytic converter, but only British Columbia (actually Greater Vancouver and some lower mainland areas only) and Ontario require emission inspections. In British Columbia the emission inspection is called 'Air Care' (fee $26.50) and must be passed annually before you can renew your insurance and registration.

DRIVING LICENCE

The minimum age you can obtain a 'regular', full driving licence (driver's license) in Canada is 16 in all provinces except Yukon, where it's 15. For commercial vehicles (including tractor-trailers), the age limit is 18 or 19. To obtain a Canadian driving licence, you must pass a test consisting of four parts: knowledge, traffic signs, vision and roads.

Licensing in Canada is by a system called the 'graduated licensing program', run by each province. The rules vary slightly in each province, but in general new drivers are licensed to drive in stages. For example, an inexperienced driver who has passed a written test is allowed to drive during daylight hours only (but not on major roads), provided that he's accompanied by a fully licensed driver. As drivers gain experience, the restrictions are relaxed. Several provinces issue new drivers with probationary licences lasting one or two years only, after which another test must be passed to obtain a full licence. In Nova Scotia, for example, the graduated licensing programme spans 2.5 years, with two stages: a six-month learner phase, followed by a 24-month newly licensed driver phase. Since the graduated licensing scheme was introduced in the mid-1990s, crashes involving 16-year-old drivers have dropped dramatically. Nova Scotia, for example, saw a 24 per cent decrease in collisions for 16-year-olds in the first year.

The classes of driving licence issued in Canada are generally as follows, but check in the province you're moving to, as there are variations. (Licences in Ontario are classed by letters rather than numbers and are much more complex.)

Class	Licensed Vehicle(s)
1	Tractor-trailer combination
2	Bus with a seating capacity of more than 24 people (some provinces require endorsements for buses with air-brakes)
3	Vehicles with three or more axles or towing a trailer
4	Taxi, ambulance or bus seating fewer than 24 people
5	Standard passenger vehicles or light trucks
6	Motorcycles or mopeds
7	Learner's category (in some provinces you must state the stage of the graduated licensing scheme you've reached)

In Prince Edward Island, class 6 is for motorcycles only, mopeds are class 8 and farm tractors are class 9.

An application for a driving licence in Canada is usually made to the local motor licence office, although in some provinces driving licences are issued by authorised private agents or local licensing examination stations. In some provinces you can apply by post, while in others you must apply for (and renew) a licence in person at a motor licence office. You must produce the expiring licence or provide other proof of identification, pay any outstanding fines or debts owed to the motor vehicle branch, sign the renewal form, pay a fee and have your photograph taken. Most licences require a photograph (some must be in colour) and often include your social insurance number (SIN – see page 262).

You're issued with an interim licence until your new licence is sent to you in around six weeks. If you're out of your province when your licence expires, you should contact the nearest motor vehicle branch.

Licences are usually valid for five years, although in some provinces licences for those aged under 18 and over 70 are valid for a shorter period, e.g. one or two years. Most licences expire on the holder's birthday. You must pay any outstanding fines for driving offences before a new licence is issued.

Fees for licences vary considerably with the class, but a five-year licence to drive an ordinary passenger car costs around $60.

Once drivers reach a certain age, e.g. 70, they may need to take an eye test or a driving test. If your licence expires and is allowed to lapse for more than a year, a test may also be necessary.

Depending on the province, tourists and immigrants may drive in Canada for a period of 6 to 12 months with a foreign driving licence, provided that it's accompanied by an International Driving Permit (IDP). After this time you must apply for a Canadian licence and your foreign licence is taken from you. In order not to have to go through the graduated licensing program, you must bring with you a letter from the licensing office of your home country showing your driving history for at least the last 18 months, detailing any prosecutions and accidents. You should always carry your foreign licence as well as your IDP when driving in Canada, where a driving licence is the most common form of identification.

Most provinces operate a points system, where drivers receive penalty points for traffic offences. When you accumulate a certain number of points within a 12-month period, e.g. ten in Ontario, your licence is automatically suspended for a period, e.g. 30 days. When renewing your licence, you must take a written test if you accumulate more than a certain number of points. A driving licence can be suspended, cancelled or revoked.

All provinces are members of the Canadian Driver Licence Compact and exchange traffic offence conviction information. The Self Counsel Press publishes books on fighting traffic violations in some provinces, e.g. *Fight That Ticket in British Columbia* by Janice Mucalove and *Fight That Ticket in Ontario* by Allan E. Scott.

CAR INSURANCE

Car insurance (sometimes referred to as 'financial responsibility' insurance) is compulsory throughout Canada and drivers must carry proof of insurance at all times. Non-residents require a 'Non-resident Inter-Provincial Motor Vehicle Liability Insurance Card', which shows that you meet the minimum legal 'financial responsibility' requirements throughout Canada (see below).

Insurers must state the level of their financial responsibility, i.e. the maximum amount they will pay irrespective of how many people are involved in an accident or the amount of property damage caused. Each province sets a minimum financial responsibility level: in most cases, it's $500,000. It isn't difficult to calculate that this could be woefully inadequate, and experts recommend that you have minimum cover of $750,000, depending on your assets. If your liability after an accident exceeds your insurance limit, your assets are used to pay damages, if necessary until you're bankrupt. Liability limits can usually be increased significantly (e.g. to $1 million) for a modest additional premium.

Car insurance is relatively expensive in Canada and in some provinces must be purchased through the province's public insurance corporation. Usually, however, you can also buy car insurance from private corporations, independent insurance brokers and your bank's insurance division.

There are various levels of car insurance, including:

- **Collision Cover** insures you against damage caused to your own vehicle, irrespective of who was responsible for the damage. Without it, if you're totally at fault in an accident, there's no recompense for damage to your vehicle. Collision cover usually has an excess (deductible), normally of $250; the higher the excess, the lower your premium. Whether it's necessary to have collision cover (and comprehensive cover described below) usually depends on the value of your car. Both collision and comprehensive cover are always required by a lender (auto-loan) or a leasing company.

- **Comprehensive Cover** insures you against loss from fire, theft, vandalism, collisions with animals, storms, water, flood, riots, explosions, earthquakes and falling objects, and includes accidental glass breakage, e.g. from a stone thrown up by another vehicle. It doesn't cover you against accidents involving other vehicles or objects, for which you require collision cover (see above). Comprehensive cover usually has a lower excess than collision cover.

- **Miscellaneous Extra Cover** encompasses a wide range of options, including the cost of a rental car when your car is being repaired, and towing and labour costs in the event of an accident (also provided by car clubs – see page 233). If you frequently use rental cars, you may be interested in a policy that includes a collision (or loss) damage waiver (CDW/LDW) for rental cars. This may also be provided by a credit card company.

● **Extended Medical Cover** is available from some insurance companies, which offer to increase your level of medical cover beyond that provided by your province's cover as a form of protection against abnormally high medical bills. This cover is sometimes offered by employers to their staff as a perk and paid for by the employer.

Many provinces have implemented 'no-fault' schemes, whereby accident victims, irrespective of fault, may claim compensation from their insurers for injuries. These schemes range from 'pure no-fault' (in Quebec and Manitoba), where there are no restrictions on claims, to 'threshold no-fault' (in Ontario and other states), where certain limits are specified, above which lawsuits are permitted. Thresholds can be monetary (e.g. a certain value of medical expenses) or verbal (i.e. a certain type of debilitating injury, or loss or impairment of bodily functions, etc.). In Ontario, for example, seriously injured claimants (and the representatives of anyone killed in a car accident) may sue for pain and suffering (provided that the threshold is met), but not for lost income and other economic losses resulting from an injury. As with similar systems in other countries, the aim is to reduce the involvement of courts and therefore reduce insurance costs and to expedite the settlement of claims.

Canadian car insurance is valid in the USA and, if you rent a car there, some of the provisions in your Canadian car insurance may also apply to US rental cars, but check in advance. If you plan to travel in the USA with your own car, you should consult your insurance broker, as the lack of free medical care there and the generally litigious nature of Americans ('make my day – injure me and I'll be rich for life') could make an accident horrendously expensive.

Newcomers to Canada may have difficulty obtaining car insurance at a reasonable cost, particularly if they come from the UK or another country where people drive on the 'wrong' side of the road (insurance companies seem to think that this automatically makes you incapable of driving on the right!). Insurers also require a complete record of your insurance history and no-claims discount, and may not accept evidence that's satisfactory in most other countries, e.g. renewal requests and certificates of insurance for a number of years, which they claim isn't proof that you kept the policies running throughout the year. The maximum no-claims discount for foreigners may be lower than for Canadians (e.g. 40 per cent) on the basis that they're unused to Canadian road rules and roads, and particularly to driving in severe winter weather.

When completing an insurance proposal form, you should ensure that you state any previous accidents or driving offences, or your insurer can refuse to pay in the event of a claim. Drivers who have been banned for drunken or dangerous driving must usually pay at least double the standard premium for three years (even penalty points on your licence increase your premium). Your insurance company may cancel your policy if you're found guilty of drunken driving, speeding or recklessness resulting in injury or death. See also **Insurance Companies & Agents** on page 258 and **Insurance Contracts** on page 259.

A number of brochures about car insurance, including *How Cars Measure Up*, *Choosing Your Car*, and *Car Theft!*, are available from insurance companies and from the Vehicle Information Centre of Canada, 240 Duncan Mills Road, Suite 700, Don Mills ON M3B 1Z4.

SPEED LIMITS

Speed limits can vary considerably with the province or town, e.g. 62mph (100kph) on primary roads, 50mph (80kph) on non-primary roads, 31mph (50kph) or 'as posted' in urban areas, 25mph (40kph) in rural school zones, and 19mph (30kph) in urban school zones. **All speed limits are quoted in kilometres per hour.**

You're more likely to be stopped for speeding in Canada than in many other countries, particularly on major holiday weekends and in rural areas, where speeding fines often comprise a large proportion of local municipal revenue. In most provinces, non-freeway speed limits are more rigorously enforced than freeway limits and are therefore more widely observed. Speed limits are enforced by police using radar guns, fixed radar traps, marked and unmarked cars, helicopters and light aircraft. An increasing number of authorities (particularly in Alberta and Ontario) are introducing cameras that record a speeder's number plate; the first you know about it is when you receive a ticket in the post (the owner is responsible, irrespective of who was driving – unless you can prove that your car was stolen).

As in many other countries, drivers often warn oncoming drivers of radar traps by flashing their headlights, although this is illegal and can result in a fine. Some provinces permit the use of radar detector devices, while others not only ban their use but also forbid drivers from having them in a vehicle.

On roads with a 100kph limit, you may receive a warning if your speed is between 100kph and 120kph (75mph), but at 120kph you can be fined around $100 and above 140kph (87mph) around $250.

GENERAL ROAD RULES

The following list includes some of the most common road rules in Canada and some tips designed to help you adjust to driving conditions and avoid accidents. Note, however, that like many things, some rules vary according to the province.

● In Canada traffic drives on the right-hand side of the road. It saves confusion if you do likewise! If you aren't used to driving on the right, take it easy until you're accustomed to it. Be particularly alert when leaving lay-bys, T-junctions, one-way streets, gas stations and car parks, as it's easy to lapse into driving on the left. It's helpful to display a reminder (e.g. 'think right!') on your car's dashboard.

- When you want to turn left at a junction, you must pass **in front of** a car turning left coming from the opposite direction, and not behind it (as in some other countries). At major junctions in some cities there are green-arrow signals for left-hand turn lanes. Certain lanes are signposted 'RIGHT LANE MUST TURN RIGHT' or 'EXIT ONLY' and mean what they say. If you get into these lanes by mistake and leave it too late to exit from them, you **must** turn in the direction indicated.

- Use of a horn is prohibited in some cities and towns and in any case should be used only in emergencies, e.g. to avoid an accident.

- The wearing of seatbelts is compulsory for all car occupants, and adults are responsible for ensuring that anyone under 16 is wearing one. Fines are levied for violations, the amount of which varies with the province but is at least $86. In Ontario, not wearing a seatbelt also earns you two licence penalty points (see **Driving Licence** on page 216).

- There's no automatic priority to the right (or left) on any roads in Canada (as there is in many European countries), although generally a turning vehicle must give way to one going straight ahead. 'STOP' signs are red and octagonal; 'YIELD' (give way) signs are an inverted triangle (yellow with black letters). You must stop completely at a stop sign before pulling out from a junction (motorists who practise the 'rolling stop' are a favourite target of traffic cops). **Not all junctions have signs.** When approaching a main road from a secondary road, you must usually stop, even where there's no stop sign. At a 'YIELD' sign you aren't required to stop, but must give priority to other traffic.

- You must use dipped headlights (low beams) between sunset and sunrise (usually from half an hour after sunset until half an hour before sunrise) in all provinces. Dipped lights must also be used when visibility is reduced to less than 500ft (150m). Driving with dipped lights during the day is permitted in all provinces, encouraged in some and mandatory in Yukon. Full beam (high beams) must always be dipped when a car approaches within 500ft (150m) or when you're following within 500ft of another vehicle.

- Headlight flashing in Canada usually means 'after you'. As in many other countries, drivers often warn oncoming traffic of potential hazards (including police radar traps) by flashing their headlights (which may be illegal). Hazard warning lights (both indicators operating simultaneously) are usually used to warn other drivers of an accident or when your car has broken down and is causing an obstruction and should not be used when merely illegally parked.

- The sequence of Canadian traffic (stop) lights is usually red, green, yellow, red. Yellow means stop at the stop line; you may proceed only if the yellow light appears after you've crossed the stop line or when stopping may cause an accident. A green filter light may be shown in addition to the full lamp signals, which indicates you may drive in the direction shown by the arrow, irrespective of other lights showing. Stop lights are frequently set on the far side of a junction, sometimes making it difficult to judge where to stop, and are also strung across the road rather than located on posts by the roadside. In some suburban areas, there are flashing red lights to indicate a stop light ahead. Driving through (running) red lights is a major cause of accidents in Canada.

- One of the most surprising rules is that in some provinces and cities you may make a right turn at a red traffic light, unless otherwise posted. You must, however, treat a red light as a stop sign and stop before making a right turn. You must also give way to pedestrians crossing at traffic lights. Busy junctions often have signs indicating that turning on a red light isn't allowed (e.g. 'NO TURN ON RED') or is allowed at certain times only. If you've stopped and the motorist behind you is sounding his horn, it probably means that you can turn right. Although it appears to be a sensible rule, some people claim that it increases accidents. In some provinces, you can also make a left turn on a red light from a one-way street into another one-way street. **Never assume you can make a turn at a red light – if you do so when it's illegal, you can be fined heavily!**

- Always approach pedestrian crossings with caution and don't park or overtake another vehicle on the approach to a crossing. Pedestrians have the right of way once they've stepped onto a pedestrian crossing without traffic lights and you must stop; motorists who don't stop are liable to heavy penalties. In some towns, a pedestrian may indicate that he intends to cross by pointing (arm fully extended) and walking in the direction he plans to go. Where a road crosses a public footpath, e.g. at the entrance to a property or a car park bordering a road, motorists must give way to pedestrians.

- Level crossings on public roads are clearly marked, usually with a large 'X' sign (in Ontario they're white with a red border). Some crossings have automatic gates or other barriers and most have red lights that flash when a train is coming. On private roads there may be no barriers or lights, so it's wise to stop and look and listen in both directions before crossing. In heavy traffic, don't attempt to cross until your exit is clear. Never attempt to cross a railway line when the barriers are down or the lights are flashing.

- Be particularly wary of cyclists, moped riders and motorcyclists. It isn't always easy to see them, particularly when they're hidden by the blind spots of a car or are riding at night without lights. When overtaking, always give them a wide **WIDE** berth. If you knock them off their bikes, you may have a difficult time convincing the police that it wasn't your fault; far better to avoid them (and the police).

- Children on pedestrian crossings or getting on or off school buses (usually painted yellow and clearly marked 'SCHOOL BUS') have priority over all traffic. All motorists **must** stop at least 65ft (20m) from a school bus loading or unloading, indicated by flashing (usually red) lights or 'stop arms'. Vehicles must stop even when a school bus has halted on the opposite side of the road (children may run across the road) unless the road is divided by a barrier. Motorists must remain stopped until the bus moves off or the driver signals motorists to proceed. **NEVER PASS A SCHOOL BUS WITH FLASHING RED LIGHTS!** The law regarding school buses is taken very seriously and motorists convicted for the first time of passing a stopped bus are subject to a fine of at least $144, possible imprisonment or community service and six penalty points on their driving licence. If you're convicted a second time within five years, the fine could be thousands of dollars and a further six penalty points, plus a possible six-month prison sentence.

- In some cities and towns where there are trams (streetcars), you must stop well away from the rear doors when a tram stops in front of you, so that passengers can get off easily and safely – unless there are safety islands in the street at tram stops, in which case it isn't necessary to stop.

- Some provinces allow the use of radar-speed-trap detectors, while others don't and even having a detector in your car may be an offence.

- Certain provinces allow you to use studded tires during the winter months only, while others permit their use all year round. Ontario has banned their use at any time due to the damage they cause to road surfaces that aren't covered with snow.

- Road rules prohibit driving in bare feet, parking on a highway, allowing passengers to ride in the back of a pick-up truck and having an open alcoholic drink can or bottle in your car (even when it's stationary and the ignition is off).

- An unofficial but widely observed practice on Canadian highways is that, if you break down, you indicate this by opening the bonnet (hood) and boot (trunk) of your car, which a passing motorist will interpret as a call for help and contact the police. In some areas there are emergency phones, but it's usually safer to stay in the car, particularly at night and in winter. Some motorists carry a waterproof 'Please Call Police' sign.

- Most road signs in Quebec are in French only, with the exception of Montreal, where motorways (*autoroutes*) and bridges may have dual-language signs.

All provinces publish local rules of the road, e.g. *The Official Driver's Handbook* in Ontario, available from provincial ministries of transport and book shops. The Canadian Automobile Association (see page 233) publishes a *Digest of Motor Laws* containing provincial road rules and regulations relating to vehicle registration, taxes, driving licences, towing, motorcycles and mopeds, and other information. It's available from any CAA office and is free to CAA members. The CAA Traffic Safety Department also publishes a wide range of brochures and leaflets to help you improve your driving and increase your safety.

CANADIAN ROADS

Canada has over 560,000mi (900,000km) of roads and a national main road (highway) system covering around 15,000mi (24,000km), including the longest main road in the world (the Trans-Canada Highway, which stretches 4,859mi/7,820km from St Johns in Newfoundland to Victoria in British Columbia). The standard of Canadian roads varies enormously, from twelve-lane 'freeways' in urban areas to gravel or dirt tracks in remote rural areas. Generally Canadian roads have fewer road markings (e.g. reflective studs and lines) than European roads.

Streets in most cities are laid out in a grid pattern (hence the word 'gridlock' for traffic jam), all roads running either north-south or east-west, and you need to know the numbering (or lettering) system so that you can find your way around. It's also useful to know whether which part of a town or city you want when asking for directions, e.g. uptown, downtown, eastside or westside (descriptions vary with the town!).

Most major cities have multi-lane main roads, particularly Toronto, where the 401 (reputedly the busiest road in the world) has 12 lanes. Some lanes, known as 'collector' lanes, have exit warnings for towns several kilometres in advance. Main access routes are busy night and day and everybody is impatient (needless to say, it's best to avoid rush hours).

Road signs giving directions may be sparse, inconsistent and poorly placed, and are particularly difficult to read at night in urban areas. Road signs are white (reflective) on a green background and signs for attractions have a blue background.

Suburban roads and motorways are generally well surfaced and maintained, although roads can suffer frost damage in winter, which makes for 'interesting' corrugated surfaces. On gravel roads you should keep your distance from the vehicle in front to avoid flying stones and dust, and slow down and pull over to the right when someone overtakes or when a vehicle comes from the opposite direction. If you're likely to be doing a lot of driving on dirt roads, it's wise to get a mesh 'bug and gravel' screen fitted; otherwise you will be constantly replacing your windscreen (some people also fit screens to their lights and fuel tank). Driving with lights on during the day helps other drivers to see you through thick dust.

As you may have discovered already, Canada is a huge country and vast distances look small on maps (unless you've got an ENORMOUS map). When estimating journey times, carefully calculate distances and take into account the road quality and terrain. Although it's possible to make good time on major roads (e.g. an average of 60mph/100kph), your speed is greatly reduced on secondary roads, particularly in mountainous areas, where speeds may average just 20 to 30 mph (around 30 to 50kph). Most people reckon on covering between 300 and 400mi (around 500 to 650km) per day (i.e. in six to seven hours), but possibly less when travelling with children (unless you tranquillize them).

There are few toll roads in Canada, although some bridges have tolls. Some roads are referred to by their number, while others are referred to locally by a name, which can be confusing. Multi-lane roads are called freeways, except in Quebec where they're called *autoroutes*. Many freeways have just two lanes in each direction and sometimes the number of the road is changed by adding a '4' to the number, e.g. Highway 1 (the Trans-Canada Highway) changes to '401' when it becomes four lanes around Toronto. Even this major route has some poor surfaces where it goes through unpopulated areas with little traffic.

If you drive in the north or other remote areas, you should take every opportunity to top up your fuel tank (ideally never let it get below half full) and carry extra fuel in a can. You should also carry a spare tyre, some tools, a shovel, water and food (plus some insect repellent). In country areas, you should keep a lookout for wildlife on the roads. Major migration routes are marked by 'deer marker' signs (a black deer on a yellow background), although you should be prepared to encounter animals at any time of the year, particularly at night when many animals are active and visibility is poor. Keep your eyes on the edges of the road and be prepared to stop or swerve – hitting a deer or moose can do serious damage to your car (it won't do the deer or moose much good either). Animals often stop in the middle of the road at night (it's rather disconcerting to sit in your car with three or four moose staring at you, mesmerised by the lights) and you should try switching your lights off and on and using the horn to move them (although this may only provoke them into attacking). You shouldn't get out of the car, as moose and large deer can be dangerous and can move very fast when threatened. If you meet a grizzly bear, it's time to practise driving in reverse – fast!

WINTER DRIVING

With the exception of some parts of southern British Columbia, most of Canada has long, cold, snowy winters. If you need to park your car out of doors in winter (not recommended) the engine can freeze solid if you don't take precautions. It's a common sight in outdoor car parks to see cars left securely locked with their engines running, but most vehicles are fitted with engine heaters that you switch on when you turn the engine off. If you need to leave your car out overnight, you should be prepared to dig it out of a snow-drift in the morning (make sure that you have a shovel and a blanket in the car). You should also be aware that tyres acquire a flat spot after standing in the cold overnight and you need to drive slowly until the air in the tires has warmed up.

Major roads have a mixture of salt and sand spread on them to help prevent vehicles from sliding on ice. Snowploughs clear heavy falls and it isn't uncommon to see them driving two or even three abreast on major roads. In cities, the major streets are cleared first, followed by secondary streets, although it can take a couple of days before these are all cleared. You need studded or 'four-season' radial snow tyres in winter, plus snow chains and equipment such as a shovel, traction mats, a bag of sand and a tow-chain (plus a blanket and water) in case you get stuck. You can buy all the necessary equipment in an 'emergency car kit' from a hardware store. If you get stuck in deep snow and cannot get yourself out, don't sit in the car with the engine running (to operate the heater) as it may fill with carbon monoxide and kill you!

The CAA recommends that you carry matches and a candle in an open-topped tin – just one candle burning in a car keeps it reasonably warm. When travelling in country areas in winter, the CAA recommends that you carry a warm coat and other extra clothing, sleeping bags, emergency food such as fruit, chocolate or tinned soup, a torch, warning lights or road flares, jump leads, an axe, a fire extinguisher, an ice-scraper and a brush, and some methyl-hydrate for de-icing fuel lines and windows. If you think all this seems extreme, bear in mind that in January 1998 there was a severe ice-storm in south-east Canada that crippled vast areas of Ontario and Quebec and brought down power lines. In spring you should wash your car thoroughly, particularly underneath, and repair any paint chips, or salt from the roads will soon cause rust patches.

TRAFFIC POLICE

Traffic laws in Canada are taken seriously and police strictly enforce the law. The Royal Canadian Mounted Police is responsible for freeways and remote areas, provincial police (known as the *Sureté Québec* in Quebec) operate in rural areas and municipal police in towns. They're particularly hot on the wearing of seatbelts and speeding – most Canadians stick to the speed limits. Police have the right to search vehicles if they stop you for a 'valid reason' and if they arrest you they can seize anything in your possession, including your car. However, unless you're breath-tested positive you're more likely to receive a ticket than be arrested.

If a policeman wants you to stop, he usually drives along behind you flashing his overhead lights (which may be red, blue or yellow or a combination) and possibly sounding his siren. You must pull over and stop as soon as you can, if possible on the hard shoulder. Once you've stopped, stay in your car and let the officer come to you. Keep your hands in view, e.g. on the steering wheel, and don't do anything that could be misconstrued. If you're stopped by an unmarked vehicle, you should ask to see the officer's identification.

Whatever you're stopped for, the officer will ask to see your driving licence and want to see your vehicle registration document and insurance card (you **must** carry these in the car at all times). Don't antagonise an officer or joke with him (they have no sense of humour), as this may lead to a fine, whether you've done anything illegal or not. A foreign accent and an apology may get you a warning rather than a ticket. If you're stopped for speeding or another 'minor' offence such as failing to stop at a 'STOP' sign or making an illegal turn, you may get away with a caution. Although some people attempt to bribe a patrolman, e.g. by inserting a $20 note in their licence, this practice isn't recommended.

If you receive a ticket for a motoring offence, you may have the choice of paying a statutory fine or going to court. On-the-spot fines are standard for speeding, failing to carry your licence and not wearing a seatbelt (including passengers). **Fines in Quebec are higher than in other provinces** (the Quebec government is short of money and sees motorists as fair game). Note also that, if you break the law, you may be 'tagged' (spotted) by the police (but not necessarily stopped) and may receive a summons later. If you're driving a rental car, the rental company receives the summons and may debit a fine from your credit card.

Some provinces accept bail bonds from the CAA (and AAA), while others (such as New Brunswick) don't. If you're stopped for a motoring offence and are bailed to appear in court, you can (where permitted) leave your CAA membership card and a bail bond with the court and leave the province. If you appear for trial, your card and bond certificate are returned to you or the CAA. However, if you choose to forfeit your bond and don't appear for trial, the court notifies the CAA, which then arranges for payment and recovers your membership card from the court. You then reimburse the club for the amount spent on your behalf, and your membership card is returned.

MOTORCYCLES

The minimum age for riding a moped (up to 50cc) is 14. For motorcycles over 50cc, the minimum age is 16 in all provinces, although some require parental permission to issue a licence at this age.

Like cars, motorcycles are inexpensive in Canada compared with many other countries. If you want a bike for a short period only, it's probably best to buy secondhand, as you won't need to bear the initial depreciation. Most dealers sell both new and secondhand bikes. The procedure and legal requirements when buying a bike are much the same as for buying a car (see page 211). It's also possible to rent a motorcycle or moped in most areas. A useful publication is the *Motorcycle Touring International Directory* by Daniel Kennedy (White Horse Press), listing some 150 guided motorcycle tour companies, many of which provide rentals.

Insurance for motorcycles is high and similar to that for cars. The cost of insurance depends on your age (riders aged under 25 pay much more), the type and cubic capacity of your motorcycle, and the length of time you've held a licence. It's wise to have insurance well above the legal minimum (see **Car Insurance** on page 218).

In general, the road rules that apply to cars (see page 220) also apply to motorcycles; however, there are a few points that apply to motorcyclists only.

● In general, motorcycles registered for use on public roads must meet the equipment requirements in the province in which they're registered, in addition to federal safety standards.

- Carrying proof of ownership, registration and insurance of motorcycles is required in all provinces. A motorcycle driving licence is required, although this may be an authorisation on a car licence; a moped licence is required in most provinces.

- A crash helmet of an approved design is obligatory for all motorcycle and moped riders and passengers throughout Canada (unless your wear a turban or other headwear for religious reasons). Failure to wear a helmet incurs a fine of around $100.

- In many provinces, a rider is required to wear eye protection, goggles or sunglasses, if a windscreen isn't fitted to a bike.

- Motorcyclists are required to use their headlights (low beam) at all times.

- A strong lock is recommended when parking a bike in a public place.

ACCIDENTS

If you're involved in an accident, the procedure is as follows:

- Stop immediately. If possible, move your car off the road and keep your passengers and yourself off the road. If you're involved in an accident where someone is injured or there's damage costing over $300 to repair, you must remain at the scene until the police have arrived and established what happened. **It's a criminal offence to fail to stop at the scene of an accident in which you've been involved.**

- Warn other drivers of an obstruction by switching on your hazard warning lights (particularly on freeways). If necessary, e.g. when the road is partly or totally blocked, set flares, turn on your car's dipped headlamps and direct traffic around the hazard. In bad visibility, at night or in a blind spot, try to warn oncoming traffic of the danger, e.g. with a torch at night.

- If anyone is injured, immediately phone for an ambulance, the fire department (if someone is trapped or oil or chemicals are spilled) or the police, or get someone else to do it. There are telephone boxes with a direct line to the local Royal Canadian Mounted Police (RCMP) on some freeways and highways. Use them to request assistance for breakdowns and report hazards and accidents. Give first-aid only if you're qualified to do so. Don't move an injured person unless it's absolutely necessary to save him from further injury and don't leave him alone except to phone for an ambulance. Cover him with a blanket or coat to keep him warm.

- After a minor accident you must remain at the scene until personal details (names and addresses of drivers and vehicle owners, registration and insurance details, etc.) have been exchanged with other drivers or the owners of damaged property. Calling the police to the scene of an accident may result in someone being given a ticket for a driving offence. If you fail to report an accident, your driving licence may be suspended for a year. In general, it's recommended to report **all** accidents immediately to the local police, whether they're called to the scene or not, and to inquire about other reporting requirements. Make sure that you obtain a report number from the officer on duty for your insurance company (this should be given to you on a card).

- In all cases you mustn't say anything that could be interpreted as an admission of guilt. Don't agree to pay for damages or sign any papers except a traffic ticket (which you must sign) before checking with your insurance company or a lawyer. Let the police and insurance companies decide who was at fault.

- If either you or any other drivers involved decide to call the police, don't move your vehicle or allow other vehicles to be moved. If it's necessary to move vehicles to unblock the road, take photographs of the accident scene if a camera is available (it's wise to carry a disposable camera in your car) or make a drawing showing the position of all vehicles involved before moving them.

- Check immediately whether there are any witnesses to the accident and take their names and addresses, particularly noting those who support your version of events. If a motorist refuses to give his name, note his registration number. Write down the registration numbers of all vehicles involved and their drivers' and owners' names and addresses, vehicle registration certificate, licence and insurance details. You must (by law) also give these details to anyone having reasonable grounds for requiring them (e.g. anyone injured or the owner of damaged property). Don't, however, reveal how much insurance cover you have. Note also the names and badge numbers of any police present.

- If you have an accident involving a domestic animal (except a cat) and are unable to find the owner, it must also be reported to the local police. This also applies to certain wild animals, e.g. deer or moose, which are a danger on rural roads, including some freeways.

- If you're arrested by the police, you aren't required to make a statement, even if they ask for one. The best policy is not to say or sign anything until you've spoken with a lawyer or received legal advice.

- You should report all accidents to your insurance company in writing as soon as possible, even if you don't intend to make a claim (but reserve your right to make a claim later). Your insurance company will ask you to complete an accident report form, which should be returned as soon as possible. The claim procedure depends on your insurance cover and that of anyone else involved in the accident (see **Car Insurance** on page 218).

In some areas you should be extremely wary of stopping at what looks like the scene of an accident, e.g. on a deserted highway, as accidents are sometimes

staged to rob unsuspecting drivers. You may, however, be obliged to note the location of the accident and call for help from the first available phone.

DRINKING & DRIVING

Drunken driving or driving after taking drugs, known as 'impaired' driving, is taken very seriously by the police in Canada. You're considered unfit to drive when your breath contains 35 micrograms of alcohol per 100ml, or your blood contains 80mg of alcohol per 100ml. In most provinces you're considered to be driving while intoxicated (DWI) or driving under the influence (DUI) when your blood-alcohol content (BAC) is 0.1 per cent (in some cases it's lower, e.g. 0.08 per cent or even 0.05 per cent for minors). In some provinces, if your BAC is above a certain level, e.g. between 0.05 and 0.09 per cent, you may be charged with 'driving while ability impaired', although this is usually done only after an accident or in a case of reckless or dangerous driving. In some provinces, if the test shows more than 0.05 per cent, you can receive a 24-hour driving ban. In provinces with a progressive licensing system for new drivers (see **Driving Licence** on page 216), the permitted BAC is zero for drivers who haven't completed the programme.

Steep fines and other penalties for drunken driving have been imposed since the late 1980s, which has been a powerful deterrent for most people. A first conviction for drunken driving results in a fine (e.g. $250 to $500 for first offenders) and revocation of your licence for a minimum of a year. In some provinces, imprisonment for up to 60 days is mandatory after the first or second offence. In many provinces, offenders must participate in a programme of alcohol education or rehabilitation. If you have an accident while drunk, the penalties are usually more severe, particularly if you cause an injury or death. However, many people believe that the penalties are too lenient and that tougher action is required to deter habitual drinkers from driving. Ontario has taken this seriously and under its Comprehensive Road Safety Act (passed in 1998) three-time offenders face a ten-year driving ban and four-time offenders a lifetime ban. Two-time offenders receive a three-year ban and first offenders a one-year ban.

Between 1986 and 1996, the number of arrests for drunken driving dropped by almost 50 per cent and deaths of drunken drivers also fell by around 25 per cent. DUI is predominantly a male crime, but contrary to popular belief the worst offenders aren't young drivers: 60 per cent are in the 25 to 44 age bracket (although this age bracket makes up only some 20 per cent of drivers in Canada).

Random breath tests are permitted in most provinces and traffic police carry breathalysers. In many provinces police set up periodic road blocks to check drivers and they often stop drivers as they enter or leave a town. A refusal to take a test results in your driving licence being automatically suspended or revoked, e.g. for six months or a year. If you're found to be over the limit, you're arrested on the spot, your licence is taken away and you're held in jail until you appear in court (usually the next day).

Note that the rules regarding alcohol also apply when operating a boat or riding a moped, bicycle or horse, and driving under the influence of drugs carries the same penalties as those for drunken driving.

CAR THEFT

Car theft isn't such a problem in Canada as in the USA but it has doubled in the last ten years to over 170,000 in 2002 (most in the major cities). Almost half of those who are caught and charged are aged between 12 and 17. If you're driving anything other than a worthless wreck, you should have your car fitted with an alarm, immobiliser (system interrupter) or other anti-theft device, plus a visible deterrent such as a steering or transmission shift lock (many new cars are fitted with door dead locks and sophisticated alarm systems as standard equipment). An alarm system may also earn you a 5 per cent discount on your car insurance. This is particularly important if you own a car that's desirable to car thieves, which includes most new sports and executive cars, which are often stolen by professional crooks to order. A good security system won't prevent someone breaking into your car (which usually takes most crooks a matter of seconds) or even prevent your car being stolen, but it at least makes it more difficult and may persuade a thief to look for an easier target.

Radios, tape and CD players attract a lot of (the wrong) attention in most cities (e.g. Toronto), particularly in expensive foreign cars. Some drivers put a sign in their car windows proclaiming 'No Radio' (or 'No Valuables', 'Trunk is Empty' and 'Doors Open'), to deter thieves from breaking in to steal them.

When leaving your car unattended, store any valuables (including clothes) in the boot (trunks) or out of sight. This shouldn't be done immediately after parking your car in some areas, where it isn't wise to be seen putting things in the boot. In any case, boots aren't safe unless fitted with a protective steel plate (or you have a steel safe installed inside the boot).

Don't leave your car papers in your car, as this will not only help a thief to sell it fast, but also hinder its recovery (particularly if you don't have a copy of the papers).

If possible avoid parking in long-term car parks, as these are favourite hunting grounds for car thieves. When parking overnight or when it's dark, park in a well-lit area, which may help deter car thieves.

If your car is stolen (or anything is stolen from it), report it to the police in the area where it was stolen. You can report it by phone, and the police often forward the relevant paperwork to your insurance company, meaning that you don't have to visit the police station. You should also report a theft to your insurance company by phone as soon as possible, but you must usually visit their office to fill out the paperwork.

FUEL

All petrol (*gaz* in Quebec) sold is unleaded and sold by the litre. Three grades of petrol are available: regular (87 octane), special or mid-grade (89 octane) and premium (92 octane). Premium petrol is typically 20 per cent more expensive than regular, so it's wise to buy a car that runs on low-grade petrol. Diesel is also generally available, although the price difference is less than in most other western countries.

Fuel prices include a 'gas consumption tax', which varies from province to province. (Even in Alberta, where there's no general provincial sales tax, there's tax on petrol!) Fuel prices are lowest in cities and suburban areas where there's lots of competition, and highest on major roads (prices are often increased at the start of holidays and long weekends) and in rural areas (where the next petrol station may be 100 miles away). The price of petrol also varies with the region, the highest prices being in the far north (e.g. around 92¢ per litre for premium in Yellowknife) and on the east coast (e.g. around 87¢ per litre in Newfoundland). Alberta is the cheapest, at around 70¢. Diesel fuel costs between 65¢ and 75¢ per litre in most provinces. For current prices, see 💻 www.gasticker.com.

Some city service stations open 24 hours per day; on major roads, truck stops have the longest opening hours. When motoring in rural areas, however, it's recommended to keep your tank topped up (and check your oil and water), as petrol stations are few and far between and may be closed on Sundays and holidays (many petrol stations are also closed in the evenings and at weekends). It pays to keep a reserve supply in a steel can (plastic fuel containers can break when a car is travelling on uneven roads or may burst at high altitudes and petrol can ignite from a static electricity spark).

The trend is towards self-service stations, but there are some with 'full-serve' pumps, where an attendant fills your car, checks the oil and cleans your windscreen (windshield) free of charge, as well as checks your tyre pressures and radiator water level if asked (it's unnecessary to tip for these services).

When buying fuel, make sure that the pump is reset to zero, particularly if an attendant is filling your car. It's best to check your own oil level, as a garage attendant may 'short stick' the dipper so that it doesn't register. Extra services aren't available at 'self-serve' pumps, but the price of fuel may be slightly lower. At many petrol stations you must pay before filling your car, particularly at 24-hour and late night stations in cities. You pay the attendant, e.g. $20, and collect any change after filling your car.

Most petrol stations have toilets (restrooms), sometimes located outside the main building, when it may be necessary to ask an attendant for the key; cleanliness varies. Petrol stations also sell sweets (candy), hot and cold drinks (usually from machines), motoring accessories, cigarettes, newspapers, household goods and various other items.

Fuel saving and general motoring tips are available free from the Natural Resources Canada Communications Group, Ottawa ON K1A 0S9 (☎ 1-800-387-2000, 💻 http://oee.nrcan.gc.ca/vehicles).

AUTOMOBILE CLUBS

The main automobile club in Canada is the Canadian Automobile Association (CAA), which was established in 1913. The CAA acts as an advocate of road safety, is committed to the improvement of Canadian roads and lobbies federal and provincial governments to enact legislation in the interests of drivers. The CAA's most valuable service to motorists, however, is its emergency roadside assistance (☎ 1-800-222-4357) – especially during a blizzard! Another popular service is the 'triptik', a free route planning service. For example, if you want to travel from Ottawa to Charlottetown (Prince Edward Island) in two days, the CAA provides the necessary maps showing the best direct route (highlighted in yellow) and CAA-recommended motels along the way. It even books the motels for you!

CAA membership is available in the following three categories:

- **Basic membership** costs around $70 per year and includes a battery boost (when your car won't start), roadside repair, fuel delivery, lockout service, flat tyre service, triptik and travel services, and four tows up to 3mi (5km), after which you must pay by the kilometre.

- **CAA Plus** costs around $100 per year and includes all the above services plus towing to the nearest garage (or place of your choice), without a distance limit.

- **RV Plus** costs $150 and provides the same level of service as CAA Plus as well as assistance with any problems you may have with a motor home (any size), camper, pick-up truck or trailer up to a specified weight.

The headquarters of the CAA is at 1145 Hunt Club Road, Suite 200, Ottawa ON K1V 0Y3 (☎ 613-247-0117, 🖳 www.caa.ca) and it has branch offices in all provinces and territories.

There are other motor service organisations, some of which are provided by automobile manufacturers, e.g. as part of an extended warranty. Canadian Tire, Canada's oldest (75 years) motoring retail chain, is the CAA's main national competitor. However, although membership costs less than with the CAA, you must have your vehicle towed to (and repaired at) a Canadian Tire outlet (if practical).

CAR RENTAL

Car rental (Canadians don't use the term 'car hire') is common in Canada. When travelling long distances, most Canadians go by air and rent a car on arrival (air travellers represent 80 per cent of car rental business).

Airlines, charter companies, car rental companies and tour operators all offer fly-drive packages (which often include accommodation). It's usually wise to book, particularly during holiday or peak periods. Many fly-drive holiday packages (particularly when booked in Europe) include a 'free' rental car. However, fly-drive deals may not be as good value as they appear at first glance, as many contain restrictions or apply to expensive cars only. It's usually cheaper to rent a car in a city or town centre than at the airport. In some cases it's better to arrange a local deal yourself by calling local rental companies listed in the yellow pages.

The biggest national car rental companies are Avis (☎ 1-800-269-2310), Budget (☎ 1-800-268-8900), Dollar (☎ 1-800-421-6868), Hertz (☎ 1-800-263-0600), Thrifty (☎ 1-800-367-2277), and Tilden (☎ 1-800-361-5334), which is the biggest company, with 400 locations coast to coast and affiliates in the USA and throughout the world. National rental companies have offices in all major cities (open from around 8am to 10pm) and at international airports. Of the major companies, Budget and Thrifty are generally the cheapest, although all companies offer special deals, e.g. corporate rates, 24-hour rates, weekend and weekly rates, off-peak periods, holidays, extended period low rates on certain categories of car and bonus coupons for airline tickets. There are also companies that rent older cars at lower rates, such as Rent-a-Wreck (☎ 1-800-535-1391). **In recent years some of the best car rental deals have been offered by credit card companies, which have agreements with certain rental companies.**

Note that, when renting a car, it's important to ensure that you have sufficient liability insurance (see page 277). Insurance is usually included in the basic cost, although it may be restricted to the province in which you rent the car and there may be a high surcharge for inter-province travel. Check whether out-of-province insurance and collision (or loss) damage waiver (CDW/LDW) are included and, if not, how much they cost. You should also ask whether cover includes personal accident insurance (PAI), supplementary liability or extended protection insurance (SL/EPI) and personal effects cover (PEC), which are automatically included in most private policies but may be excluded from (or severely limited in) rental policies. CDW alone can cost as much as $20 per day!

Rental cars are graded into classes or sizes by body size, not engine capacity, e.g. sub-compact (the smallest), compact, mid-size and full size. Many companies also rent luxury models, convertibles (roadsters) and sports cars, four-wheel drive 'off-road' vehicles, mini-vans (seven passengers) and mini-buses (up to 11 passengers).

Car rental in Canada is more expensive than in the USA. Most companies have a standard daily rate of around $25 to $30 plus mileage, while others offer a flat 'unlimited mileage' daily rate that works out cheaper if you're travelling long distances. Many factors influence the cost of car rental, including the day of the week (it's often cheaper at weekends as most rentals are by business travellers on working days), the season (the most expensive period being July and August), the size of the town and, in the tourist season, the popularity of the local attractions. Weekend rates are usually cheaper and may include the Friday and Monday either side of the weekend. It's possible to haggle over rates with some companies, most of which also offer discounts for long-term rentals (weekly rates usually work out around 10 per cent lower per day than daily rates).

A sub-compact (e.g. Dodge Colt) costs from around $50 per day and a compact (e.g. Dodge Neon) around $60 per day, both with unlimited mileage. With limited mileage, rates are around $10 per day cheaper plus 10¢ to 20¢ per mile above 100 or 150 free miles (160 to 240km) per day.

Note that with the exception of off-road vehicles, all rental vehicles have automatic transmission.

Most rental companies insist on payment with a major credit card and won't accept cash (Budget is a rare exception). This is so that they can trace you if you steal or damage a car and also because they can deduct extra charges from credit cards without obtaining prior approval. The estimated cost of the rental is deducted or 'blocked off' your card's credit limit as soon as you drive off, so you should make sure that this doesn't leave you short of credit during a trip. When paying by credit card, check that you aren't charged for unauthorised extras or for something that you've already paid for, such as fuel.

Your own car insurance may cover you when driving a rental car, although you must usually carry collision insurance (see page 218) on your own policy or your insurer won't cover damage to a rental car if you decline CDW. If you pay for a rental with a major credit card (e.g. American Express or a Gold MasterCard/Visa card), your card company may provide CDW cover, but check the extent of cover provided, as most pay the excess (deductible) only after your insurance company pays on a claim. If you decline CDW, you're responsible for all damage to a car (however caused) and must pay a large security deposit with a credit card or travellers' cheques. See also **Car Insurance** on page 218.

Most rental companies won't rent to anyone under 21 and with some companies the age limit is 25. Those that do rent to people under 25 may levy a 'young driver' surcharge of around $25 per day. If you have a foreign licence, you usually need an International Driver's Permit (IDP), which must usually be used in conjunction with your foreign licence (it may not be accepted on its own). If a number of drivers are planning to drive a vehicle, they must all have an IDP.

You can also rent a motor home, e.g. from Cruise Canada (🖳 www.cruise canada.com), or a motorcycle, e.g. from H-C Travel (🖳 www.hctravel.com). The minimum hire period is usually seven days and daily rates for motorbike rental start at $35 for a small Suzuki to over $80 for a large BMW. The most powerful bikes may only be rented to those aged over 30.

PARKING

Parking in Canadian towns and cities can be a problem. Streets often have restricted parking, or parking is prohibited altogether and, if you park illegally, the authorities won't hesitate to tow your car away. Parking regulations may vary with the area of a city, the time of day, the day of the week and even the season. In some towns there are special parking regulations during rush-hours on major thoroughfares, where no parking is permitted on one or both sides of the street during certain times; this may also include streets with parking meters in town centres, where there's usually no parking anywhere during rush hours, i.e. between 6 and 10am and 3 to 6pm. On some streets there are parking restrictions at certain times only (shown on signs), e.g. between 9 and 11am Mondays to Thursdays.

Parking on some streets is prohibited during certain hours on some days for street cleaning; if you park during these periods, your car is impounded. If you don't see a parking meter, don't assume that parking is free, as meters tend to be set well back from the kerb so that they aren't buried by ploughed snow. In winter, some streets are designated 'snow streets', meaning you mustn't park there when snowfall exceeds a certain amount (shown on a sign), in order to leave the road free for snow ploughs. Always read all parking signs carefully. A yellow or red painted kerb also indicates that parking is forbidden.

Apart from the obvious illegal parking spots, such as across entrances and at bus stops, be careful not to park within 15 feet (5m) of a fire hydrant, often indicated by a large gap between parked cars, or your car will be towed away. Other restricted areas are in front of fire and ambulance stations and schools. Some city centre areas are also designated 'towaway' zones, where all illegally parked cars are impounded. If your car is towed away, it costs around $110 ($80 for the tow and $30 for the parking fine) to get it back. To collect your car from the pound, you must show proof of ownership, insurance card identity, registration and your driver's licence. Your car may also be clamped (called a 'tire boot' in Canada) if you park illegally in a major city. Payment of fines must be made within a certain period and there may be a reduced fine if you pay within seven days, after which it may increase dramatically. **Parking offences throughout Canada are recorded on computers and, if you have an outstanding ticket when you come to renew your annual licence fee, you must pay it on the spot.**

Parking regulations in Canadian cities are controlled by city police and private companies, who are particularly zealous, as they're paid on results and employees usually have quotas to meet. If you're in doubt about whether on-street parking is legal, don't take a chance but park in a car park.

Parking in city centres is very expensive, and on-street parking (e.g. with meters) is permitted for short periods only. For example, in central Toronto, daytime parking starts at around $4 for 30 minutes and can be as much as $20 per hour, although after 6pm it's reduced to around $6 per hour. City-owned car parks (parking lots) are indicated by a green 'P' and are slightly cheaper than privately-owned car parks. In most cities, shopping complexes and hotels have underground parking. If you live in a city and don't have private parking, it can cost anything from $100 to $500 per month, which is why many city dwellers use taxis locally and rent a car for longer trips (you also don't have to dig your car out of the snow and cold-start it in winter). Privately-owned car parks usually have security patrols, although they don't take responsibility for damage or thefts from cars.

Banks, supermarkets, large shops and other establishments often provide free parking areas for customers. However, if you remain too long (e.g. over three hours) or park after hours, you may be given a ticket or your car may even be towed away. Reserved parking spots for handicapped motorists are provided at public buildings, shopping centres and in car parks, indicated by a sign showing a wheelchair or a wheelchair symbol painted on the ground.

Parking on main roads in rural areas is forbidden and you must pull completely off the road if you wish to stop. Overnight off-road parking is usually prohibited or restricted when towing a trailer or driving a 'recreation vehicle' (RV) or motor home and you must use an official trailer or RV car park.

12.

HEALTH

Generally, Canada is a healthy place to live. Sanitation standards are extremely high, the water is safe to drink and food regulations are stringent. The average life expectancy in Canada is among the highest in the world, at an average of 76 for men and 81 for women, although it's significantly lower for the poor and underprivileged groups and varies with the region. The infant mortality rate is a low six deaths per 1,000 live births, although this also varies, with a high of around 13 per 1,000 in the Yukon. The main causes of death are heart disease and cancer.

There are no unusual health problems in Canada, although the high incidence of tuberculosis among some migrants and refugees is worrying health officials. Hay fever sufferers planning to live in southern Ontario (including the Toronto area) should note that it has one of the highest pollen counts in North America. The most common health problems for expatriates are those associated with the hustle and bustle of life in a modern society, including stress (expatriate stress is a recognised mental condition), poor diet, lack of exercise and obesity.

Of increasing concern is alcohol abuse, estimated to be directly responsible for thousands of deaths per year (most caused by motor vehicle accidents). Apart from the direct and indirect loss of life, alcohol abuse costs Canadian industry billions of dollars per year in lost production due to absenteeism. It's estimated that some 10 per cent of Canadians have a drink problem. Alcoholics Anonymous has groups in all cities and large towns in Canada, where reformed alcoholics meet to encourage each other to stay sober. If you can afford to pay for private treatment, there are a number of private clinics and hospitals that specialise in providing treatment for 'chemical dependency'. Drug abuse is also prevalent and on the increase (see **Drugs** on page 252).

Like many other western countries, Canada has an ageing population and faces an increasing burden on its health facilities. An ambitious plan to extend health care to include free prescription drugs (Pharmacare) has had to be shelved, and a plan to save money by cutting the number of hospital beds in favour of a 'home care' scheme met with public opposition. Although modern medical and surgical techniques make it safer and more comfortable to be treated at home, the public perception is that quality health care is best measured by the number of hospital beds available. An additional problem facing the authorities is the number of doctors and nurses who are moving to the US, where their skills are better rewarded and working conditions are less stressful.

If you aren't entitled to free health care (see below), you should ensure that you have adequate health insurance, generally considered to be a minimum of $500,000 per year (see **Health Insurance** on page 270). When calculating how much insurance you require, bear in mind that Canadian medical fees are comparable to those in the US (which are the highest in the world) and some prescription drugs can be even more expensive. If you're planning long-term residence, it's wise to have a thorough medical examination, including a dental and optical check before you arrive and, if you've been putting off elective medical or dental treatment, e.g. a 'nose job' or having your teeth capped, it's likely to be less expensive to have it done overseas than in Canada.

Canada is one of the world's leading countries as far as facilities for the physically disabled are concerned, particularly those who are wheelchair bound. Most public buildings are wheelchair-accessible, including tourist offices, museums and art galleries, as are many restaurants, public toilets, major hotels and motels. Canada's airlines provide special boarding and disembarkation services for the disabled and many car rental agencies provide special cars with hand controls (which must be requested in advance). Reserved parking is available for disabled drivers in the major cities and towns.

If you require general information about any health matter, you should contact the Health Promotion and Programmes Branch, Health Canada, AL 0900C2, Ottawa, Canada K1A OK9 (☎ 613-957-2991, 💻 www.hcsc.gc.ca/english/for-you/hpo/index.html) or a regional office (listed in the telephone book). Among the many books on health in Canada are the *Canadian Healthcare Sourcebook: The Direct Link to the Vital Social and Medical Support Services in Canada* (Canadian Newspaper Services) and *The Canadian Consumer's Guide to Health Care* by Sharon Lindenburger (McGraw-Hill Ryerson). Many magazines and newsletters dedicated to health matters are also published in Canada.

HEALTH SERVICE

Canada spends around 10 per cent of its gross domestic product on health care, compared with around 15 per cent in the States. Unlike the US, however, where health care is sparse or non-existent for the poor and unemployed, Canada has a government-sponsored health insurance scheme (generally known as Medicare) that provides free basic health care to Canadian citizens, permanent residents and refugees. In some provinces you must contribute, while in others it's 'free' (i.e. paid for by general taxes rather than specific payments).

Despite the free or cheap Medicare system, many people also have private health insurance (which they either pay for themselves or receive as a benefit from their employers) in order to obtain treatment that isn't covered by Medicare or to obtain faster or more specialised treatment.

Foreign students lost their right to free health care in 1994 and must now take out private health insurance before they're allowed to attend school or university.

If you qualify for free health care, you should register and apply for a health card as soon as possible after your arrival by visiting the office of the provincial ministry of health in the city or town where you're living. You're required to complete an application form and provide identification such as your birth certificate, visa and passport.

If you're unable to afford Medicare premiums, there's a 'Medical Services Plan' in Canada that provides subsidies to those in financial need, ranging from 20 to 100 per cent, based on an individual's (or a couple's) net income for the previous year, less deductions for age, family size and disability. Temporary premium assistance provides a 100 per cent subsidy to cover an unexpected financial hardship.

Although it's generally referred to as Medicare, the name of the public health scheme varies from province to province. For example, in Alberta it's the Alberta Health Care Insurance Plan (AHCIP), in British Columbia it's called the Medical Services Plan (MSP), in Ontario it's the Ontario Health Insurance Plan (OHIP), and in Quebec it's called the *Régie de l'Assurance-Maladie du Québec*.

Requirements and conditions also vary from province to province. For example, in some provinces you aren't covered for your first three months in Canada, and in others your monthly contributions increase as your family grows. Note in particular:

- In Alberta, there's no waiting period. The monthly contribution is $34 for one person and $68 for a family consisting of two or more people.
- In British Columbia, you must wait two months after the end of the month in which you apply for membership before cover commences. The monthly contribution is $36 for one person, $64 for two people and $72 for three or more people.
- In Manitoba there's no waiting period and cover is free.
- In Ontario there's a three-month waiting period, but cover is free.
- In Quebec there's no waiting period and cover is free.

Note that costs are expected to rise, either in late 2003 or 2004.

If you aren't eligible for health care straight away, temporary private health insurance is available (see page 266).

Medicare covers all medical services, including doctor's fees and hospital costs, but not the cost of all prescription drugs, except in British Columbia, where pharmacies are connected to a computerised 'Pharmanet' that tracks how much you spend in a year on 'eligible' medicines; when the total reaches $600 you must pay for further prescriptions. Further details of British Columbia's 'Pharmacare' scheme are available by phone and Internet (☎ 1-800-387-4977, 🖥 https://pharmacare.moh. hnet.ba.ca).

EMERGENCIES

Canadian emergency medical services are among the best in the world. Keep a record of the phone numbers of your doctor, dentist, local hospitals and clinics, ambulance service, poison control and other emergency services (fire, police) next to your phone. The action to take in an emergency depends on the degree of urgency and in a life-threatening emergency you should call 911. If necessary, an ambulance will be sent, usually staffed by paramedics and equipped with cardiac, oxygen and other emergency equipment. In Alberta and British Columbia, you're charged for an ambulance, while in other provinces they're free for emergencies. Each region of Canada has a poison control number, listed at the front of phone books.

If you're able, you can go to the emergency room of the nearest hospital, many of which are open 24 hours per day (check the location of your nearest hospital and the fastest route from your home in advance). It's wise to check in advance which local hospital is best equipped to deal with emergencies such as heart attacks, car accident injuries, burns and children's injuries.

If you don't need to go to hospital but are too ill to go to a doctor's surgery, you could call your doctor for advice, although most doctors don't make house calls. However, you may be able to get someone to drive you to a doctor or a walk-in clinic. If you need urgent medical advice or medicines, you can call a local doctor, hospital or pharmacy (listed in the phone book). Police stations keep a list of doctors' and pharmacists' private phone numbers in case of emergencies.

If you have an emergency dental problem, phone your own dentist. If he doesn't provide an emergency service outside normal surgery hours, phone a dentist who does (often specified in yellow pages listings). Most dentists use an answering service outside normal office hours and will return your call (or you will be called by a 'stand-in' dentist). In an emergency you may be able to obtain treatment at a university or dental hospital, where a dental surgeon is on duty. Note, however, that a dentist isn't obliged to treat anyone, even in an emergency.

DOCTORS

There are excellent doctors throughout Canada. The usual way to find one is to ask your colleagues, friends, neighbours or acquaintances if they can recommend someone (but don't rely on their recommendations alone). **The availability of medical services varies greatly with the area, and in remote areas doctors and other medical practitioners may be scarce.** Your employer may advise you about medical matters and many large companies have a company doctor. Failing a recommendation, you can contact your local city or provincial medical society, who can provide you with a list of local doctors. Some hospitals also maintain a list of doctors who accept new patients. Family doctors are listed alphabetically by specialism under 'Doctors and Surgeons' in the yellow pages. In small communities where there's insufficient business to support a dedicated practice, there may be no local doctors. If you wish to find a doctor who speaks a particular language, your local embassy or consulate should be able to help you.

It's wise to find a doctor as soon as possible after your arrival, rather than wait until you're ill, when you may have no time to choose. You may wish to choose a doctor who's part of a group practice, although some don't permit patients to choose the doctor they see. Before registering with a doctor, you may wish to know the following:

- Is he or she the right sex?
- What is the doctor's age, training and medical background?
- At which local hospitals does the doctor practise?

- Is it a group practice?
- What are the office hours?
- Does the doctor make house calls?
- Does the doctor practise preventive or complementary (alternative) medicine?

You can check a doctor's credentials in the Canadian Medical Association's directory, available at local libraries. If you're seeking a specialist, you may wish to consult a copy of the directory for the Royal College of Physicians and Surgeons of Canada.

Doctors' office hours vary but are typically from 8.30am to 6 or 7pm, Mondays to Fridays, the office sometimes closing earlier one day per week, e.g. at 5 or 5.30pm on Fridays (it may also open on a few evenings per week). Offices are usually also open on Saturday mornings, e.g. from 8.30 to 11.30am or noon, and some doctors have Sunday office hours for emergencies. Most doctors use an answering service outside office hours, which gives you the name of the doctor on call and his phone number.

All doctors operate an appointment system and you cannot just turn up during office hours and expect to be seen (unless you're going to a clinic where appointments are unnecessary or not possible). If you're an urgent case, your doctor usually sees you immediately, but you must still phone in advance. Provided that you aren't late, you generally won't need to wait to see your doctor. **If you miss an appointment without giving sufficient notice, your doctor may charge you a standard fee (although unlikely).**

If you don't have Medicare, fees are generally around $50 for a consultation and $30 for a laboratory test. If you need to see a specialist, he'll charge up to $75 for a consultation and possibly another $50 for laboratory tests. Your doctor may wish to be paid the same day you see him in order to eliminate paperwork, although many send you a bill. Doctors usually expect immediate payment in cash from temporary foreign residents, but some accept payment by credit card.

If you plan to live in Canada for a number of years, you should bring your medical and dental records with you (including test results, X-rays, laboratory reports, hospital records, etc.) or ask your overseas doctor to send them to your doctor in Canada. This is particularly important if you have an unusual health history or suffer from a long-term condition, as it can save considerable time and expense on tests or background studies. If you change doctors in Canada, ask your old doctor(s) to forward your medical records to your new doctor (your medical records are your property).

The cost of malpractice suits means that doctors usually err on the side of over-treatment rather than neglect and many prescribe medicines, tests and treatment that may be unnecessary and that probably wouldn't be required in many other countries. If you aren't comfortable with a diagnosis, you should obtain a second opinion. If you wish to complain about professional misconduct or exorbitant fees, you should contact your provincial Ministry of Health's 'Professional Medical Conduct Division'.

In addition to conventional medicine, some medical practitioners offer alternative therapies such as acupuncture and chiropractic, although these are less common than in many other countries. Note also that alternative medicine is unregulated in Canada and isn't covered by provincial health plans.

MEDICINES & PHARMACIES

Medicines can be obtained from pharmacies, drugstores and supermarkets (many of which contain pharmacies) and may be cheaper than in other western countries (although more expensive than in the US). A chain with branches throughout Canada is Shoppers Drug Mart. Pharmacies are packed with medicines for every ailment under the sun (hypochondriacs will think they've died and gone to heaven) and may stock medicines that are available in other countries on prescription only. However, there are strict controls on the licensing and sale of most medicines in Canada, where some medicines sold freely in other countries require a doctor's prescription. Many pharmacists keep a record of customers and the medicines dispensed to them, and you may be asked for certain details if you're a new customer.

Some items common in other countries are difficult to find in Canada, e.g. soluble aspirin (apart from Alka Seltzer); Canadians take tablets containing acetaminophen rather than paracetamol for headaches. Tablets containing codeine don't require a prescription but are kept behind the counter by pharmacists and must be requested. The brand names for the same medicines can vary from country to country and you should ask your doctor for the generic name of any medicines you take regularly. Any medicines you take with you to Canada should be accompanied by a doctor's letter explaining why you need them. Don't take non-prescribed medicines, and keep medicines in their original packaging (Canadian customs officials may be suspicious of anything other than aspirin).

If you're visiting Canada for a limited period, you should take sufficient medicines to cover your stay, as prescription drugs can be expensive and insurance policies don't usually cover existing medical conditions (you may also be unable to obtain your usual medicine in Canada). In some provinces, pharmacists fill prescriptions from locally-registered doctors only. If you need to refill a prescription from a doctor who's resident in another province (or abroad), you must get a local doctor to write a copy prescription. A hospital emergency room may refill a prescription from its own pharmacy or write a prescription that can be filled at a local pharmacy.

At least one pharmacy is open in most towns during the evenings and on Sundays for the emergency dispensing of medicines and drugs. A list is posted on the doors of pharmacies and published in local newspapers and guides. In most large cities there are pharmacies open 24-hours per day, seven days per week, some of which provide a free delivery service in the local area.

Most pharmacists provide free advice regarding minor ailments, suggest appropriate medicines and also sell non-prescription medicines and drugs, toiletries, cosmetics, health foods, cleaning supplies, foodstuffs, school supplies and other goods. Alternative therapies such as herbal and homeopathic medicines are popular and widely available. Health food stores sell health foods, diet foods and eternal-life-virility-youth pills and elixirs, all of which are popular in Canada.

Always use, store and dispose of unwanted drugs and medicines safely, e.g. by returning them to a pharmacist or doctor, and never leave them where children can get their hands on them.

HOSPITALS & CLINICS

Canada has many excellent hospitals and clinics, including almost 900 general public hospitals, some 225 special public hospitals and around 85 private hospitals (there are plans to build more of these).

If you're a Medicare patient, you receive free accommodation, health care and meals, but must usually share a 'ward' with two or three other patients (if you want a private room you must pay extra). You may need to wait for non-urgent treatment, although waiting lists are seldom longer than two months. A general community hospital is adequate for most medical problems and usually caters for surgery, internal medicine, obstetrics and paediatrics. For more serious illnesses or major surgery, you're usually better off at a university or teaching hospital, where specialised skills are available (or in a hospital or clinic that specialises in your illness).

If you aren't eligible for Medicare, treatment is as a private patient, when every test, doctor's visit, pill, meal or fluff of your pillows is likely to be added to your bill. The cost of a hospital room alone is likely to exceed the cost of the most expensive hotel room and even a stay of a few days is likely to result in a bill for thousands of dollars. If you have insufficient insurance, you may be discharged from hospital earlier than would otherwise be the case (but not if your condition is critical). You should ensure that you have adequate hospital insurance before an emergency arises, as without it hospitalisation can be an economic disaster. If your condition is critical (life-threatening), you're usually taken to the nearest hospital, even if you have no medical insurance and are unable to pay. If you're uninsured and need non-emergency hospital treatment, you can go to the emergency room of a public hospital where, although you may have to wait, you will be treated without advance payment.

In many areas there are private walk-in medical clinics or urgent care centres (known as 'doc-in-a-box' centres). Typical services include treating a sprained ankle, earache or perhaps a broken arm. No appointment is necessary at a walk-in clinic, many of which are open 365 days per year. They're often located in shopping malls, so you can drop in for a check-up while you're buying the groceries. Walk-in clinics usually have a minimum charge of $30 to $55, to which must be added the cost of any special treatments or diagnostic tests. Most require immediate payment and usually accept major credit cards, although some will wait for payment from an insurance company. Public hospitals also have walk-in clinics and medical centres.

The admission procedure for a private hospital varies but is similar everywhere. You must report to the admitting office on arrival, where the first question you're likely to be asked is about your medical insurance or how you intend to pay for treatment. You're asked to complete a set of admission application forms, including a 'consent for treatment' form and a consent to release information to the provincial medical department. If you have insurance, you should take your certificate or proof with you. If you don't have insurance, you must pay a large deposit, which could run to thousands of dollars, or complete a financial agreement. A deposit can usually be paid in cash or by personal cheque and sometimes by credit card. It's wise to check the admission procedure in advance and ask how the deposit (if applicable) should be paid. Hospital bills may need to be paid in full before you leave a hospital.

CHILDBIRTH

The traditional place to give birth in Canada is in the maternity ward of a hospital, where a stay of around three days is normal. If you wish to have your child at home, you must find a doctor and/or midwife (see below) who's willing to attend you. Some doctors are opposed to home births, particularly in cases where there could be complications, when specialists and special hospital facilities may be required. Failing this you can hire through an agency a private midwife (a qualified nurse with special training), who'll attend you at home throughout your pregnancy and after the birth. Another option is to attend a maternity or birth centre staffed by experienced midwives, where mother and baby usually go home around 12 hours after the birth.

For hospital births, you can usually decide (with the help of your doctor or midwife) the hospital where you wish to have your baby. You aren't required to use the hospital suggested by your doctor but should book a bed as early as possible. Your doctor may refer you to an obstetrician or you can find your own. Find out as much as possible about local hospital methods and policies on childbirth, either directly or from friends or neighbours, before booking a bed. 'Natural childbirth', which involves giving birth in a crouching position (possibly in water) with minimum use of artificial aids such as an epidural, is common in Canada and many hospitals expect mothers to attend natural childbirth lessons (they may also request the participation of the father). The policy regarding a father's attendance at a birth may vary from hospital to hospital. If the presence of your husband or another person is important to you, check that it's permitted at the hospital where you plan to have your baby, plus any other rules that may be in force. Birth centres usually allow family members to be present.

In Canada, midwives are responsible for educating and supporting women and their families during the childbearing period. They can advise women before they become pregnant, in addition to providing moral, physical and emotional support throughout a pregnancy and after the birth. Your midwife may also advise you about parental education and ante-natal classes for mothers. All cities and towns have pre-natal registries (listed in the yellow pages). Information about contraception, pregnancy and abortion is also available from your family doctor.

In Canada it's usual for children to be vaccinated against diphtheria, whooping cough, tetanus, tuberculosis, polio and measles.

Abortion is legal in Canada when carried out by a qualified doctor, and some 115,000 abortions are performed annually. They can be performed in hospitals by referral from your doctor or in private clinics without referral (which may charge less than hospitals if you don't have Medicare). As in many countries, abortion is a highly contentious subject and Canadians are fairly evenly divided on whether it should be permitted. For information about abortion and counselling contact the Abortion Hotline Canada (☎ 1-800-424-2280) and for information about the alternatives contact the Campaign for Life Coalition (☎ 416-368-8479).

Note that private health insurance policies won't pay the medical costs associated with childbirth if you were pregnant before you took out health insurance. If you have health insurance, don't forget to inform your insurance company about your new arrival.

It isn't compulsory to register a birth in Canada and there are many people whose existence has never been registered (thus depriving them of various benefits, including the right to pay taxes!). When babies are born in hospital (as most are) the parents are given a 'statement of birth' form, which should be signed by both parents and sent with a registration form to the divisional registrar at the local municipal office (forms are available from municipal offices, city halls and land registry offices). There's a fee of $27 if a birth is registered within 12 months, after which period there's an additional $22 late registration fee. Without registration, a Social Insurance Number (SIN) cannot be obtained for a child and the various tax breaks for education cannot be claimed.

Births of foreigners may have to be reported to an embassy or consulate in order to obtain a national birth certificate and passport. If a citizen of another country has a baby with a Canadian citizen (either in their native country or in Canada), Canada recognises that child as a Canadian citizen because one of the parents is Canadian (see **Citizenship** on page 378).

DENTISTS

Canadian dentists use the most up-to-date equipment and techniques and provide excellent dental treatment. The best way to find a dentist is to ask your colleagues, friends or neighbours (particularly those with beautiful teeth) if they can recommend someone. Your local city, county or provincial dental society can give you the names of local dentists, although it won't recommend one. Dentists are listed alphabetically in the yellow pages with their specialisms, e.g.

general (or family) dentistry, paediatric dentistry, oral and maxillofacial surgery, endodontics, orthodontics and periodontics. Check whether a dentist provides a 24-hour emergency service, dental hygienist and evening or Saturday business hours (many dentists have evening office hours on one day per week or open on Saturday mornings).

Most dentists send you a postcard to remind you of a check-up every six months and may even call the day before to remind you of an appointment. **If you miss a dental appointment without giving 24 hours' notice, your dentist may charge you a standard fee.**

If you plan to live in Canada for a number of years, it's recommended to take a copy of your dental records with you. This is particularly important if you have an unusual dental history, when it may save you both time and money. It may pay you to have your teeth checked and (if necessary) fixed before arriving in Canada, as dental treatment, particularly cosmetic treatment, is very expensive and can run to many thousands of dollars.

Medicare doesn't cover non-hospital dental treatment (although children and the elderly receive subsidised treatment in some provinces) and most Canadians take out private dental insurance or are covered by schemes through their employers. Dentists may expect payment on the spot (credit cards are usually accepted), although some provide payment plans when major (i.e. expensive) treatment is necessary. In many areas there are walk-in dental clinics in health centres, department stores and shopping malls.

You should obtain a written detailed quotation before starting a course of treatment (a 'rough estimate' may be just a fraction of a final bill) and an itemised bill when work is complete. If you have regular check-ups and usually have little or no treatment, you should be suspicious if a new dentist suggests that you need a lot of treatment. If this happens, obtain a second opinion before going ahead, but bear in mind that two dentists rarely agree exactly. If you're concerned about unnecessary treatment, you should contact Health Canada, Public Inquiries (☎ 613-957-2991, 🖳 www.hc-sc.gc.ca). If you have a complaint that you're unable to resolve with your dentist, contact your local city or provincial dental association or the Canadian Dental Association, 1815 Alta Vista Drive, Ottawa ON K1G 3Y6 (☎ 613-523-1770, 🖳 www.cda-adc.ca), which is the national professional association of Canada's 17,000 dentists.

OPTICIANS

There are three kinds of professionals providing eye care in Canada. The most highly qualified is an ophthalmologist, who's a specialist doctor trained in diagnosing and treating disorders of the eye; in addition to performing eye surgery and prescribing drugs, he may perform sight tests and prescribe glasses (spectacles) and contact lenses. You may be referred to an ophthalmologist by an optometrist or your family doctor. Optometrists are licensed to examine eyes, prescribe corrective lenses, and dispense glasses and contact lenses. They're also trained to detect eye diseases and may prescribe drugs and treatment. A

Canadian optician isn't the same as an optometrist (as in some other countries) and may not examine eyes or prescribe lenses. Opticians are licensed in many provinces to fill prescriptions written by optometrists and ophthalmologists, and to fit and adjust glasses.

As with dentists, there's no need to register with an optometrist or optician. You simply make an appointment with anyone you wish, although it's wise to ask your colleagues, friends or neighbours if they can recommend someone. Opticians and optometrists are listed in the yellow pages, where they may advertise their services.

The optometrist business is very competitive and, unless someone is highly recommended, you should shop around for the best deal. Prices for both glasses and contact lenses vary considerably, so it's wise to compare costs (although make sure you're comparing similar services and products). The prices charged for most services (glasses, lenses, contact lenses) are among the lowest in the world. For example, glasses (frames and lenses) can be purchased in Canada for $100 or less (usually inclusive of an eye examination). Note, however, that these and other special deals (e.g. 'buy one get one free') aren't necessarily good value. Always ask about extra charges for eye examinations, fittings, adjustments, lens-care kit, follow-up visits and the cost of replacement lenses (if they're expensive, it may be worthwhile taking out insurance). Many opticians and retailers provide insurance against the accidental damage of glasses for a nominal fee.

There are many optical retail chain stores in Canada where you can have a pair of glasses made within an hour.

Around one in nine Canadians wears contact lenses, two-thirds of them women. Extended-wear soft contact lenses are widely available, although medical experts warn that they should be used with caution, as they greatly increase the risk of potentially blinding eye infections. Obtain advice from your doctor or ophthalmologist before buying them.

The cost of a sight test is usually between $50 and $70. You aren't required to buy your glasses or contact lenses from the optometrist who tests your sight, who must give you your prescription at no extra charge. However, this doesn't apply to a lens-fitting prescription for contact lenses.

It's wise to have your eyes tested before your arrival in Canada and to bring a spare pair of glasses or contact lenses with you. It's also recommended that you bring a copy of your prescription, in case you need to obtain replacement glasses or contact lenses in a hurry.

You can donate your old glasses to charity by giving them to an optician or optometrist. They're sent either to Canadian charities who give them to needy people or overseas to developing countries.

COUNSELLING

Counselling and assistance for health and social problems is available from a variety of local community groups, volunteer organisations, national associations and self-help groups. In most provinces there are toll-free helplines for a wide range of problems, and counselling may also be available by phone. Many colleges and educational establishments provide a counselling service for students. Look in the yellow pages under 'Social Service Organizations'. If you or a member of your family are the victims of a violent crime, the police can put you in touch with a local victim support scheme.

Problems for which help is available are numerous and include general health complaints, substance abuse (see **Drugs** below), alcoholism (e.g. Alcoholics Anonymous) and alcohol-related problems, gambling, dieting (e.g. Weight Watchers), smoking, teenage pregnancy, poison control, attempted suicide and psychiatric problems, homosexual and lesbian-related problems, youth problems, parent-child problems, child abuse, family violence (e.g. battered wives), runaways, marriage and relationship problems, and rape. Many communities also provide a range of free health services for the homeless.

In times of need there's nearly always someone to turn to and all services are strictly confidential. In major cities, counselling may be available in your own language if you don't speak English. If you need help desperately, someone who speaks your language can usually be found. See also **Sexually Transmitted Diseases** on page 253.

SMOKING

Smokers are public health enemy number one in Canada, where they're a persecuted minority threatened with extinction. Around 22 per cent of Canadians smoke, although the figure is dropping every year; most of them are below the age of 44, the 20 to 24 age group being the most addicted. It's long been known that smoking causes lung and other types of cancer, as well as heart disease, bronchial complaints and a variety of other life-threatening illnesses. Health warnings on cigarette packets predict dire consequences for those who smoke, particularly pregnant women ('smoking during pregnancy can result in foetal injury, premature birth and low birth weight'). There's a ban on advertising tobacco products on radio and TV, and in magazines (many people believe cigarette advertisements directly target children) and, as in many countries with a strong anti-smoking lobby, sponsorship by tobacco companies (e.g. for arts and sporting events) has been banned.

In recent years the effects of passive smoking or 'secondhand smoke', i.e. inhaling the smoke from smokers' cigarettes, cigars and pipes, has become a heated issue in Canada. You can still smoke in your own home, but public places where you can smoke are becoming rare. Most provinces have passed laws banning smoking in restaurants, public toilets (restrooms), shops, banks, cinemas and theatres, shopping malls and other public places. Most hotels have non-smoking rooms and car rental companies also have non-smoking cars. Smoking is also banned in federal buildings, in lifts, on most public transport (including taxis, buses, undergrounds, trains and aircraft) and in most schools, although in 1998 some school boards decided that it was better for pupils to smoke on school grounds than outside the gates, where they could fall prey to drug dealers.

Before you light up in a public place, it's therefore wise to check whether smoking is permitted. A 'Thank You For Not Smoking' sign is a polite way of saying 'try smoking here and you're in trouble, buster!' Even in places where it's legal to smoke, people may ask or tell you to put out your cigarette or fall about in a paroxysm of coughing if you light a cigar or pipe.

Most businesses and government offices restrict or ban smoking in the workplace, and many run programmes to encourage employees to quit. In fact smoking is fast becoming a career hazard, as employers may refuse to employ smokers on the grounds that their habit may lead to costlier health insurance and lost working days due to sickness (smoking is responsible for millions of sick days per year).

Canadian health and life insurance companies often offer discounts to non-smokers. Homeowner or tenant insurance costs less for non-smokers and in some cities you may find it difficult to rent an apartment if you smoke (unless you lie!).

You must be aged 18 to purchase tobacco products, and shopkeepers face fines of at least $2,000 for selling tobacco products to minors.

DRUGS

It's estimated that between 12 and 18 per cent of Canadians use illicit drugs and almost 1,000 deaths per year are attributed to their use, almost 90 per cent of them men (over 50 per cent of murders are also attributed to drug use). Drug importation and abuse is a major problem in Canada, where officials estimate it costs each Canadian around $50 per year (a total of some $1.4 billion) for health care, prevention, law enforcement and lost productivity due to illness and premature death. Canada has also become a drug exporter thanks to a booming marijuana business. Officials believe marijuana now ranks as British Columbia's most lucrative agricultural product, illegal revenues being variously estimated at between $500 million and $3.5 billion per year.

Although violent crime is falling in Canada (see page 381), overall crime in the last 30 years has been increasing as a direct result of drug trafficking. In the 1960s, the drug trade in Canada consisted of not much more than a few hippies smoking joints. Today, it's a mega-business, and the use of cocaine, crack cocaine, heroin and various chemical cocktails has exploded in the last couple of decades. At the street level the drug trade is controlled by gangs who are armed to the teeth and don't take kindly to others trying to muscle in on their territory. Drug addicts frequently turn to crime to finance their expensive habit, which explains the increase in thefts from homes and cars.

Canada has a more lenient jail policy than the US, which many believe has helped to attract drug dealers, who smuggle drugs into the US, where demand and prices are higher. The Royal Canadian Mounted Police (RCMP) has launched campaigns to stem the tide and in some areas they're effective, particularly where Canadian and US customs officers have combined forces. Except in British Columbia, which has a 'soft' attitude to the use of marijuana, the possession or use of marijuana incurs a fine and trial. For small quantities, you will probably receive a suspended sentence and no criminal record. However, for large quantities of marijuana (when it's assumed that you're a dealer) or any quantity of harder drugs (e.g. heroin, cocaine or their derivatives) you can expect a five-year jail sentence.

There are drug help organizations in most cities (many with toll-free lines). Look in the yellow pages under 'Drug Abuse & Addiction' or 'Social Service Organizations' or call information for the phone numbers. For example, in Toronto there's Cocaine Anonymous, the Drug Abuse Information Line, Drugs Anonymous and Narcotics Anonymous, to name but a few.

SEXUALLY TRANSMITTED DISEASES

Like most western countries, Canada has its share of sexually transmitted diseases (STDs), particularly in the major cities. Most common are syphilis and gonorrhoea, along with genital herpes and AIDS. In the ten years to 1996, a total of 12,434 cases of syphilis were reported, steadily reducing from a high of 2,376 in 1987 to fewer than 800 in 1996; in the same ten-year period, the number of AIDS cases reported totalled 10,494, cases steadily reducing from a high of 1,249 in 1992 to 919 in 1996. For both syphilis and AIDS, the majority of cases are males (around 60 per cent and 90 per cent respectively). Unfortunately, the 21st century has seen these declines halt and there are signs that the figures released in the ten years to 2006 will show increased rates of infection for all STDs.

Most AIDS victims are homosexuals, needle-sharing drug addicts or promiscuous visitors to some African and Asian countries where the disease is endemic. Male homosexuals continue to be most at risk from AIDS, with two-thirds of all reported cases in this group. AIDS cases due to needle sharing increased from 2 per cent in 1991 to around 16 per cent in 1996.

Slogans in advertisements encourage Canadian women to say 'No glove, no love', but despite this only 25 per cent of Canadians always use a condom with a casual partner. Condoms are on sale at pharmacies, drugstores, some supermarkets, men's hairdressers, and vending machines in toilets in bars and other public places.

If you would like to talk to someone in confidence about AIDS or other sexually transmitted diseases, there are organisations and self-help groups in all cities providing information, advice and help, including local and provincial health departments. For further information, contact the Canadian AIDS Society (☎ 613-230-3580, 🖳 www.cdnaids.ca).

DEATH

Dying can be expensive in Canada, although a simple cremation without any ceremony costs as little as $165. In stark contrast, the average 'traditional' funeral costs around $4,000 and if you opt for a pricey coffin at around $10,000, plus embalming, limousines and an elaborate headstone, you won't see much change out of $25,000. If you pay for your funeral in advance, under the Funeral Directors and Establishments Act your money is placed in a trust fund until your death or until you request its return.

In the event of the death of a resident of Canada, all interested parties must be notified (see **Chapter 20**). You will need a number of copies of the 'Proof of Death' certificate, e.g. for probate for a will, pension claims, insurance companies and financial institutions. If you need to obtain a copy of a birth, marriage or death certificate, the cheapest way is to apply to the registrar in the area where it was registered. See also **Wills** on page 307.

Deaths of foreigners may have to be reported to an embassy or consulate in order to for them to be registered in the deceased's country of birth.

13.

INSURANCE

Canadians spend over $18 billion per year on insurance, including cover for their homes, cars, health and lives. However, there are a few occasions in Canada where insurance for individuals is compulsory: these include third party liability car insurance (required by law throughout Canada) and title, fire and mortgage life insurance (always required by lenders) for homeowners. If you rent a car or buy one on credit, your lender will also insist that you have collision and comprehensive car insurance. Canada's social insurance (social security) system includes benefits for the unemployed, the aged, the disabled and those on very low incomes. Voluntary insurance includes private pensions, disability, health, homeowner's (casualty and liability), legal, dental, travel, automobile breakdown and life insurance.

It's unnecessary to spend half your income insuring yourself against every eventuality, from the common cold to being sued for your last nickel, but it's important to be covered against any event that could precipitate a major financial disaster (such as a long illness or redundancy). As with anything connected with finance, it's important to shop around when buying insurance. Just picking up a few brochures from insurance agents, or making a few phone calls could save you a lot of money. Regrettably, you cannot insure yourself against being uninsured or sue your insurance agent for giving you bad advice.

If you wish to make an insurance claim against a third party or if someone is claiming against you, you should seek legal advice, as Canadian law is likely to be different from that in your previous country of residence. **Never assume that it's the same**. For information about car insurance, see page 218.

INSURANCE COMPANIES & AGENTS

Canadian insurance companies offer a wide variety of insurance and many also provide other financial services. However, under federal law, financial services companies that own insurance companies aren't permitted to sell insurance themselves (except in British Columbia). While some companies are privately owned, most are owned by the shareholders of stock companies, the policyholders of mutual companies or by the government. There are over 450 Canadian insurance companies and almost 200 foreign companies (which have some 60 per cent of the market) licensed to operate on a branch basis.

There are numerous insurance companies to choose from, many of which provide a wide range of insurance services, while others operate in certain fields only. The major insurance companies have offices or agents in most large towns throughout Canada and include Manufacturers Life Insurance Co., Sun Life Assurance Co. of Canada, Great-West Life Assurance Co. of Canada and the London Life Insurance Group, Inc.. Major 'property and casualty' insurers ('property and casualty insurance includes all types of insurance except health and life insurance) include the Co-operators Financial Service Ltd., Zurich Canada, Royal Insurance Co. of Canada and National Nederlanden P&C Group.

The majority of Canadians buy their insurance through insurance brokers and agents. You're usually better off buying insurance through an independent agent who deals with a number of insurance companies than through an agent who sells the policies of one insurance company only (a so-called 'captive'). Most agents provide a free analysis of your family's insurance needs, but make sure this isn't influenced by their commission earnings. Agents or companies who charge a flat fee for their advice, rather than earn commission for selling policies, are usually the most objective. According to independent experts, most agents offer terrible advice, particularly regarding life insurance, and are interested only in selling policies (**any** policy). Always get recommendations from at least three agents, but bear in mind that this will almost certainly result in wildly different recommendations. When you've found a reliable agent, it's often wise to buy all your insurance through him, although you should still obtain quotations for new insurance from other agents or companies. Never allow yourself to be rushed into buying insurance (experts recommend that you 'shop till you drop' when buying insurance).

When comparing policies, bear in mind that the cheaper policies may offer poorer value than more expensive policies and the cheaper companies may be slow to pay claims. Ask a broker how long particular companies take to settle claims; although all insurance companies are pleased to take your money, many aren't nearly so happy to pay up. Some companies use any available loophole to avoid settling claims, particularly if they think they can prove negligence, and you may need to threaten them with litigation before they pay. If you need to make a claim, don't send original bills or documents to your insurance company **unless absolutely necessary** (you can always send a certified copy). Keep a copy of all bills, documents and correspondence, and send letters by registered post. If you receive a cheque in settlement of a claim, don't bank it if you think it's insufficient to cover your claim, as you may be deemed to have accepted it as full and final settlement.

Make sure that the insurance company you select is one with an AAA credit rating. Before making a final decision check with consumer groups, Better Business Bureaux and insurance associations such as the Consumers Association of Canada, 404-267 O'Connor Street, Ottawa ON K2P 1V3 (☎ 613-238-2533, ▢ www.con sumer.ca) or the Consumers Council of Canada, 35 Madison Avenue, Suite 100, Toronto ON M5R 2S2 (☎ 416-961-3487, ▢ www.consumerscouncil.com). It's wise to select an agent who's a member of the Insurance Bureau of Canada, 151 Yonge Street, Suite 1800, Toronto ON M5C 2W7 (☎ 416-362-2031, ▢ www.ibc.ca), which sets ethical and professional standards for its members.

INSURANCE CONTRACTS

Read all insurance contracts carefully before signing them. If you don't understand everything, ask a friend or colleague to 'translate' it or take legal advice. If a policy has pages of legal jargon and 'gobbledegook' in very small print, you have a right to be suspicious, particularly as it's common practice nowadays to be as brief as possible and write clearly and concisely in simple language. Some provinces have laws requiring all agreements and contracts between commercial institutions and consumers to be written in plain language.

Be particularly wary of policy exclusions, which may demolish the very protection that you think you're paying for, and be careful how you answer questions in an insurance proposal form. Even if you unwittingly provide false information, an insurance company can refuse to pay out when you make a claim.

Before signing any insurance contract, you should shop around and take a few days to think it over – never sign on the spot as you may regret it later. Note in particular that:

- a medical report may be required for certain insurance policies, e.g. health insurance, a pension plan or life insurance;

- most insurance policies run for a calendar year from a specified date, so make sure that this date meets your requirements;

- all premiums should be paid punctually, as late payments could result in cancellation and denial of a claim.

The Office of the Superintendent of Financial Institutions oversees and regulates the insurance industry and there's a regional office in each province. Provinces may also have their own laws and regulations governing insurance. If you require information about local provincial insurance laws or wish to make a complaint (almost 50 per cent of complaints to local Better Business Bureaux concern insurance), contact the provincial financial services government listing, which can be found in the blue pages of your local telephone directory. For general insurance information contact the Office of the Superintendent of Financial Institutions, 255 Albert Street, Ottawa ON K1A 0H2 (☎ 1-800-385-8647, 💻 www.osfi-bsif.gc.ca).

In addition to federal and provincial governments overseeing the industry, there are several consumer protection groups set up by insurance companies. The life and health insurance industry has a policyholder protection group, The Canadian Life and Health Insurance Association (💻 www.clhia.ca), which provides free advice to consumers in English (☎ 1-800-268-8099) and French (☎ 1-800-361-8070). The property and casualty insurance industry has a consumer protection group, the Insurance Bureau of Canada, 151 Yonge Street, Suite 1800, Toronto ON M5C 2W7, (☎ 416-362-2031, 💻 www.ibc.ca).

SOCIAL INSURANCE

Federal and provincial governments share the responsibility for social insurance (the name for social security in Canada), which includes benefits for the unemployed, the aged, the disabled and those with very low incomes. Social insurance contributions are compulsory for most Canadian residents and are deducted from salaries by employers. You pay 4.7 per cent of your gross salary up to a maximum contribution of $1,673.20 (in 2003 – figures adjusted annually for inflation.

Canada's federally regulated income security programmes are administered by Human Resources Development Canada (HRDC). HRDC administers the Canada Pension Plan (CPP), which replaces part of the earnings that are lost when a Canadian retires or becomes seriously disabled, in addition to providing benefits for a surviving spouse and dependent children in the event of the death of a contributor. HRDC is also responsible for the 'seniors benefit' (see below) and 'spouse's allowance', which ensure a basic income to all eligible residents. HRDC is also responsible for the Employment Insurance programme (through the Canada Employment Insurance Commission) and negotiates and administers international social security agreements that assist immigrants to Canada (and emigrants from Canada) to qualify for state pensions paid by Canada and other countries.

Other federal agencies involved in income security include Canada Customs and Revenue Agency, which collects Canada Pension Plan contributions and pays child tax benefit, and the Department of Veterans Affairs, which is responsible for pensions and allowances for veterans and their dependants.

Provincial governments are responsible for social assistance programmes that ensure minimum levels of income for those in need. The provincial and territorial authorities determine both eligibility and benefits for these programmes and have jurisdiction over workers' compensation plans, which provide benefits for injury or death at work. Several provinces also provide income support to the elderly by supplementing benefits from the seniors benefit.

As in most countries, social insurance fraud is widespread and there are periodic crackdowns. For example, in the late 1990s fraud investigations in Ontario saved the province over $100 million and made over 1,000 convictions.

International Agreements & Eligibility

International social security agreements provide for those who have lived or worked in both Canada and another country and who qualify for old age, retirement, disability or survivor pensions from one or more countries. Through these agreements, continuity of cover is assured during periods spent working abroad and the possibility of making double payments (having to contribute to two countries' schemes for the same work) is eliminated. Such protection is granted only for a limited period abroad, e.g. up to five years.

Visitors and migrants must be resident in Canada for a minimum number of years before they become eligible for benefits. However, periods of residence or contributions in Canada and other countries (with international agreements) can be added together to meet these requirements. For example, there's a 10-year residence requirement before a person living in Canada becomes eligible for seniors benefit or spouse's allowance, and a 20-year residence requirement before a person can receive seniors benefit outside Canada for an indefinite period. Once eligibility has been established, the amount of benefit payable is based on your contributions to the Canada Pension Plan.

To obtain more information about Canada's international social security agreements, contact International Operations, Income Security Programmes, Human Resources Development Canada, Ottawa ON K1A 0L4 (☎ 613-957-1954, 🖳 www. hrdc-drhc.gc.ca).

Registration & Benefits

In order to work, pay taxes and receive social benefits and free medical care in Canada, you require a Social Insurance Number (SIN), which is a nine-digit number used as identification on all official documents. On arrival in Canada you must register at your nearest HRDC office at a Canada Employment Centre and apply for an SIN by producing your birth certificate, passport and record of landing. You receive your SIN by post in the form of an identity card (without a photo) around four to six weeks after your application. You can also apply for an SIN by post, when you must send your completed application form and identity documents to Social Insurance Registration, PO Box 7000, Bathurst NB E2A 4T1. The card is issued free, although a replacement costs $10. If you change your name, you must apply for a replacement card in your new name (which is provided free of charge).

Social security benefits (see 🖳 www.hrdc-drhc.gc.ca) include the following:

Seniors Benefit: From 2001, the income-tested 'seniors benefit' replaced the 'old age security pension' (OAS) and the 'guaranteed income supplement' (GIS), the latter being a form of supplementary pension. It's estimated that around 75 per cent of recipients (individuals and couples) receive the same or higher benefits than under the previous system.

Seniors benefit is tax-free (and doesn't have to be declared on your income tax return) and incorporates existing and pension income tax credits. CPP and QPP benefit payments (see page 263) aren't affected by this benefit.

In general, all those aged 65 or over and their spouses (irrespective of the spouse's age) are entitled to seniors benefit. However, single people with an income of over $52,000 and couples with a combined income of over $78,000 aren't entitled to benefit.

In 2002, seniors benefit was around $11,420 for single people and $18,440 for couples; these figures are adjusted annually for inflation. Seniors benefit is paid monthly by cheque to individuals and payments to couples are split into two separate cheques for equal amounts.

Spouse's Allowance: A 'spouse's allowance' (SPA) may be paid to the spouse of a seniors benefit pensioner or to a widow or widower. To qualify, you must be between the ages of 60 and 64 and have lived in Canada for at least ten years after the age of 18. You must be a Canadian citizen or a legal resident of Canada on the day preceding the approval of your application. SPA is paid monthly for one year, at the end of which you must re-apply. Benefits aren't regarded as income for income tax purposes. SPA isn't payable outside Canada for more than six months, irrespective of how long you've lived in Canada.

Payment of SPA stops when you become eligible for seniors benefit at the age of 65, if you leave Canada for more than six months or when you die. Your eligibility is reviewed by the government if your spouse dies or you separate from your spouse. In 2002 the maximum SPA was $804.31 per month (for those on an income of less than $24,114) and $887.98 for a widowed person (with an income of less than $17,736).

Retirement Benefits: There are two levels to the Canadian state pension system, as follows:

- **Elderly benefits** include seniors benefit and the spouse's allowance for low-income widowed and married people aged between 60 and 64 (see above). In addition, five provinces and two territories provide income supplements for their elderly poor. The income tax system provides a non-refundable tax credit for low-income and middle-income elderly taxpayers and a non-refundable pension income credit for all taxpayers with private pension income.

- **The Canada Pension Plan (CPP)** and the parallel Quebec Pension Plan (QPP) are retirement income programmes covering the entire labour force and financed by contributions from employees, employers and the self-employed as well as by interest from the Canada Pension Plan Fund. The two plans provide similar cover and benefits.

Retirement benefits are calculated according to the age at which you retire and how much and for how long you've contributed to the CPP (or to both the CPP and the QPP if you're a 'dual' contributor). The minimum period is six years, during which you must have been making contributions that were deducted from your pay at source. The CPP adjusts your lifetime earnings, taking into account the growth in wage levels over your whole career, before calculating your pension.

A pension is normally paid from the month following the month in which you turn 65, but it isn't paid automatically and you must make an application (☎ 1-800-277-9914). You can choose to start drawing your pension at any time between the ages of 60 and 70, but must start drawing it at the age of 70. If you choose to take it before the age of 65, it's a smaller amount than the standard payment; if you choose to take it later, it's larger. The amount payable is adjusted by 0.5 per cent for each month that a pension is started before or after your 65th birthday and is permanent, i.e. it isn't recalculated when you reach the age of 65. For example, if you start to draw your pension at the age of 60, your monthly payments are 30 per cent lower than if you'd waited until the age of 65 (although by starting it sooner you receive the pension for a longer period). If you choose to wait for your pension until the age of 70, your monthly payment is 30 per cent higher than if it was taken at the age of 65.

In 2003 the maximum CPP benefit was $801.25 for retirement at age 65 and $971.26 for disability.

As a regular contributor to the CPP, you should receive a 'statement of contribution' every few years, which you should check for inaccuracies. If any are found or you have any questions about your pension, you can call the Canadian Pension Plan (☎ 1-800-277-9914).

Canada has the same problems with a falling birth rate and ageing population as other western countries, and the federal government is keen to reduce expenditure on pensions. The average age of Canadians is expected to continue rising and within 40 years it's estimated that some 25 per cent of the population will be 65 or older, placing an increasing burden on the already creaking pension system. To offset rising costs, workers under 65 and employers have been paying more into the CPP since 1997, and contributions will continue to rise over the next few years until they reach a ceiling of 9.9 per cent of contributed earnings. One suggestion, which has so far been rejected, is to raise the usual retirement age (there isn't an official one) from 65 to 70, which would save the CPP some $2 billion per year.

Survivor Benefits: Survivor benefits are paid on the death of a CPP contributor, his surviving spouse and dependent children. To be eligible for survivor benefits, contributions must have been made to the CPP for at least three years.

There are three types of benefit:

- **Death benefit** is a one-time lump sum payment to the estate of the deceased. The amount paid depends on how long and how much was contributed to the CPP by the deceased. HRDC calculates what the retirement pension would have been had the contributor survived until the age of 65. The lump sum death benefit is then calculated as six months' pension payments up to a maximum of $2,500.

- A **surviving spouse's pension** is a monthly pension paid to the legal or common law spouse of the deceased at the time of death. When there's no cohabiting common law spouse, a separated legal spouse may also qualify for the benefit. The amount payable depends on how much and for how long contributions have been made to the plan, the spouse's age when the contributor died and whether the spouse is also receiving a CPP, disability or retirement pension. In 2002, the maximum survivor's pension paid to those aged under 65 was $428.70 per month and for those aged 65 or over $465.

- **Children's benefits** are monthly payments for the natural or adopted children of the deceased or a child who was in the care and control of the deceased at the time of his death, and are usually paid to the person who now has custody of the children, e.g. another parent or a legal guardian. The monthly children's benefit is a flat rate adjusted annually and in 2002 was $178.42 per month. A child may receive up to two benefits when both parents paid into the CPP and each parent is either disabled or deceased.

If you have children who are under 18 years of age, you may be eligible for monthly child tax benefit payments and, in certain provinces, provincial payments (see page 302).

Disability Benefits: Disability benefits are paid to those who have contributed to the CPP for a minimum number of years, who are disabled according to CPP legislation and who are aged between 18 and 65. The disabling condition can be physical or mental, but must be sufficiently severe and prolonged to prevent the disabled person from working regularly at any job long-term, or which may result in death. The disabled person must have contributed to the CPP for four of the last six years and during this period must have earned 10 per cent of each 'year's maximum pensionable earnings' (YMPE). In 2002 the YMPE was $39,100; it changes annually.

Disability benefits consists of two parts: a flat-rate amount and a supplementary amount based on how much and for how long you've contributed to the CPP. There's a maximum sum that can be paid, adjusted annually in January in line with cost of living increases. In 2002, maximum disability benefits were $935.12 per month.

CPP officials periodically check that a disability continues and work with the disabled to help him to return to work. School may be attended or volunteer work carried out without losing benefits, provided that the capacity to work full time hasn't been regained. Benefits continue to be paid for three months after returning to work and, if the same disability prevents you from working again, a new application is given priority.

An application for a disability pension must be made in writing. For information or to apply for a disability pension, call ☎ 1-800-277-9914. Those with a hearing or speech impairment can call the TDD/TTY phone service (☎1-800-255-4786). You must provide application forms for yourself and your dependent children, a completed questionnaire containing details of your work history and medical condition, a medical report completed by your doctor, a consent form that the CPP may use to obtain additional information, and a form to be completed if you've reduced your working hours or stopped working to look after your children under the age of seven.

Many provinces have a compulsory disability insurance scheme, usually financed by workers through payroll deductions. Benefits normally begin after a seven-day waiting period or the first day of hospitalisation, and are based on wages paid during a specific 12-month base period. See also **Disability Insurance** on page 271.

EMPLOYMENT INSURANCE

What used to be known as unemployment insurance is now officially (and optimistically) called employment insurance (EI). The federal employment insurance system is financed by premiums paid by employers and employees and contributions from the federal government. To qualify for employment insurance benefits (unemployment benefit to the man in the street), applicants must show that they were employed for between 420 and 700 hours in the previous year, depending on the provincial unemployment rate. To receive benefits you must file a claim stating that you're unemployed and willing to work, and must be registered at a Human Resource Centre.

After a waiting period of two weeks (new claims only) you're eligible to receive 55 per cent of your average weekly insured earnings up to a maximum of $413 per week. The number of weeks for which benefits are paid varies with the length of your previous employment, your previous employment insurance claims, and the national and regional unemployment rate.

Further information is available on the HRDC website (🖥 www.hrdcdrhc. gc.ca/ae-ei/employment_insurance.shtml).

MEDICARE

Canada has a national health care system (widely known as Medicare) that's administered by federal and provincial governments. The Canadian government used to pay half of Medicare's operating costs, but this has been reduced to a third, the remainder being paid by the provinces. Medical services are paid for by various taxes and in some provinces direct contributions are also made by individuals.

Medicare is available to all permanent residents of Canada who are registered under the national health insurance programme. To qualify for Medicare, you must obtain an official health card from the province where you live.

Medicare pays for most necessary medical services, although what's covered varies from province to province. In all provinces, basic hospital charges and doctors' fees are covered, but not services that aren't medically necessary (such as cosmetic surgery). Some provinces provide cover for non-medical services such as prescription drugs and medical apparatus. **It's important that you know exactly what's covered in your province of residence and to take out private health insurance to cover any additional services required.** See also **Health Service** on page 241.

PRIVATE HEALTH INSURANCE

It's important to check whether your family will be eligible for Medicare before you arrive in Canada, as holiday or travel health policies won't cover you if you come to Canada to live or work. If possible, it's usually wise to extend your present health insurance policy rather than take out a new policy.

If you're living or working in Canada and aren't covered by Medicare or a company policy, it's extremely risky not to have private health insurance for your family, as you could be faced with some **very** high medical bills. When deciding on the kind and extent of health insurance, make sure that it covers **all** your family's present and possible future health needs before you receive a large bill.

When changing employers or leaving Canada, you should ensure that you have continuous health insurance. If you and your family are covered by a company health plan, your insurance may cease after your last official day of employment. If you're planning to change your health insurance plan, ensure that no important benefits are lost, e.g. existing medical conditions usually won't be covered. When changing health insurance companies, it's wise to inform your old company if you have any outstanding bills for which they're liable.

It's best to arrange cover before you arrive in Canada, although if you arrive without health insurance you can still obtain temporary cover from a number of Canadian companies. Major Canadian health insurance companies include Blue Cross/Blue Shield, Aetna and the Industrial-Alliance Life Insurance Company.

As the cost of Medicare continues to rise and federal and provincial governments reduce the cover, an increasing number of Canadians are turning to private insurance (called extended health cover) to cover them for non-insured hospital and medical expenses. Over a third of Canadians have extended health cover. Canadians spend over $7 billion per year on private health insurance, which typically covers the cost of private hospital rooms, special duty nursing, paramedic services and eye treatment.

Some employers provide free or low-cost group insurance for employees to supplement procedures and costs that aren't covered by Medicare. It's voluntary, however, and few companies pay 100 per cent of premiums; there may also be a qualification period (e.g. six months). Some companies offer 'no-frills' insurance for basic medical expenses, while others offer comprehensive plans (although few cover all medical expenses). Most plans offer a range of medical 'packages' (see below), plus optional or supplementary packages such as dental, optical, maternity and disability insurance.

Never assume that your employer is taking care of your all health insurance requirements in Canada, but check with them; if you need to pay your own premiums, it will make a big hole in your salary.

Major Medical: A standard health insurance policy is called 'major medical' and includes doctors', surgeons' and anaesthetists' fees, outpatient prescription drugs, consultations with specialists, hospital accommodation and meals, operations or other treatment (e.g. physiotherapy, radiotherapy, chemotherapy), X-rays and diagnostic tests, maternity care (after a 12-month qualification period), medicines, X-rays and dressings while in hospital, physical and mental health treatment, substance abuse treatment, and home nursing and extended care facilities.

Options: All health plans offer options or supplements that vary from policy to policy. Options that aren't usually included in a standard health plan (particularly a direct-pay one) include dental care, maternity and baby care, routine physical examinations, eye and ear examinations, hospice care for the terminally ill, intensive care, disability, and organ transplants.

A basic plan also usually excludes extras for hospital in-patients such as a phone, TV or visitors' meals.

Pre-Existing Conditions: Treatment of any medical condition for which you've already received medical attention or which existed before the start of the policy are called 'pre-existing' and may not be covered. This includes childbirth if you were pregnant when you took out health insurance (however, comprehensive medical insurance usually covers complications associated with childbirth, such as a Caesarean section). Check that regular maternity charges are covered as 'any illness'. Some policies don't cover childbirth in a hospital, but do cover the cost of a birth centre (see **Childbirth** on page 247).

Families: Insurance provided by an employer often offers different levels of cover for families and single people. Children over 18 may not be included in a family policy. Few employers offer free comprehensive cover (i.e. pay all medical bills) for employees and their families, although there are a few exceptions such as companies who transfer employees to Canada. If you're offered a job in Canada, check the extent of the health insurance cover provided.

Travellers: If you do a lot of overseas travelling, ensure that your health plan covers you outside Canada (most do). All bills, particularly those received for treatment outside Canada, must include precise details of all treatment and prescriptions received. Terms such as 'Dental Treatment' or 'Consultation' are insufficient. It's also helpful if bills are written in English or French, although this obviously isn't possible in all countries.

Premiums & Payment

Private health insurance can be expensive, depending on the policy or cover you select. A typical personal health option, covering two or more people in one family, can cost from $60 to $200 per month, increasing as options and family members are added. Premiums for men are usually lower than for women, although the highest premiums are usually for babies under two years old.

Most policies have an annual excess (deductible), typically $100 to $500 for an individual and $500 to $1,000 for a family. This is the amount you must pay towards your total medical bills in any year before your insurance company starts paying. Consider taking a higher excess if you're young and/or in good health, e.g. $1,000, rather than paying higher premiums, and avoid buying excess cover, i.e. more than you need or something you don't need. Some policies also levy an excess on a variety of services, e.g. $10 for each routine visit to a doctor, 20 per cent of ambulance costs, and 20 per cent or $1,000 per hospital admission (in-patient). There may be a maximum limit on the amount an insurer will pay in any one year, e.g. $50,000, and a lifetime maximum such as $1 million. Many insurers require a second opinion or a pre-admission review on non-emergency surgery and may penalise you (e.g. up to $1,000) if you don't follow the rules.

With some plans, premiums increase if you make frequent claims. If you have a long-term illness or a poor medical history, you may be unable to obtain health insurance at any price (although some provinces operate a provincial insurance scheme for those who have been rejected for cover by at least two insurance companies). If you or a member of your family contracts a serious, expensive or chronic disease you may find that your health insurance is cancelled or that your premiums rocket. Some insurance companies settle bills directly with doctors or hospitals and send you a bill for your contribution, while others require you to pay medical bills and apply for reimbursement. File all claims promptly, as some insurers reject claims that aren't filed within six months of treatment.

You may qualify for low-cost group insurance through a professional association or other organisation. However, never assume that group rates are lower than a direct-pay plan, as some organisations levy huge commissions.

Retirees can obtain a low-cost policy from the Canadian Association of Retired Persons (CARP), 27 Queen Street East, Suite 300, Toronto ON M5C 2M6 (🖥 www.50plus.com).

Students

Full-time students in Canadian colleges or universities may be eligible for Medicare depending on the province, so check with your provincial Medicare office. If you aren't eligible, you may be able to pay a college infirmary fee entitling you to receive infirmary treatment. Students' families aren't covered by a student's college infirmary fee and must be covered privately. You can also buy low cost accident insurance, which is recommended and may be compulsory. All Canadian colleges and universities provide foreign students with information about compulsory and recommended health insurance before their arrival in Canada.

DENTAL INSURANCE

Only certain groups, such as children and the elderly, are eligible for subsidised dental expenses in some provinces. For example, Nova Scotia and Newfoundland provide free dental care for children, while Alberta provides cover for those aged over 65. Approximately 20 per cent of the population (ranging from less than 5 per cent in the Maritime provinces to over 40 per cent in British Columbia) therefore has some form of dental care provided through private insurers.

Dental insurance is often provided by employer health insurance plans and may be part of a comprehensive medical and dental plan or a separate dental plan offered in addition to medical cover. Often employers offer separate dental cover that can be linked to a choice of medical plans. Some two-thirds of workers in medium and large companies participate in an employer dental plan, around half of them being required to contribute towards their own dental treatment costs and two-thirds towards those of their families. Dental benefits may be available under foreign health insurance policies or international health schemes (although they're usually optional).

Dental plans usually cover both preventive and restorative treatment and most also cover orthodontic expenses, particularly for children. Preventive care typically includes examinations, cleaning and X-rays, while restorative treatment includes fillings, periodontal and endodontic care, prosthetics and crowns. Preventive care is usually covered at between 80 and 100 per cent; fillings, surgery endodontics and periodontics are covered at 60 to 80 per cent; expensive inlays, crowns, prosthetics and orthodontia at 50 per cent. Under some plans, members are offered a reimbursement based on a schedule of cash allowances for restorative services, such as fillings and crowns. The percentage of dental expenses paid by a plan may be increased annually, provided that you're examined regularly by a dentist.

Some plans require members to pay a fixed contribution, e.g. $15 for preventive care, or an annual excess, e.g. $75 per year. Most plans have an annual maximum benefit, e.g. $1,000 per year, and orthodontic services usually also have a lifetime maximum of around $5,000. Expensive treatment, e.g. over $100 or $200, usually needs pre-authorisation.

LONG-TERM HEALTH CARE INSURANCE

Private nursing homes can cost over $3,000 per month, although government nursing homes are less expensive (but usually have long waiting lists). Home care providers, who may include private registered nurses, charge a rate of around $40 per hour, while less skilled care such as assistance with eating or light housework costs around $20 per hour.

Very few health insurance policies cover the cost of long-term health care, which usually includes nursing care, 'custodial care' (i.e. care in a nursing home or hospice) and home health care. Many Canadians therefore take out long-term health care (or nursing-home) insurance policies, although some employers offer long-term care policies as an employee benefit. By the year 2020, it's estimated that one in five Canadians will be aged over 65 and, with an expected shortage of federal nursing homes, long-term insurance may be a good option.

Always check exactly what's covered and under what circumstances benefits apply. The majority of long-term care plans have severe restrictions covering hospital admissions, level of care, length of cover, custodial care, cancellation provisions and exclusions such as Alzheimer's and AIDS. Many people discover that they aren't covered for nursing home care when it's too late, and policies with these restrictions should be avoided. Some policies claim to cover you for everything at any age without a medical examination or an exhaustive questionnaire about your medical history; this allows the insurance company to claim that virtually any ailment you contract was pre-existing and therefore not covered! Choose a policy where you're evaluated first and complete a medical questionnaire before agree to a policy (called 'front-end underwriting').

As with disability insurance, the longer the waiting period before you collect on a policy, the lower your premiums are. For example, if you pay for the first 20 or 30 days (or longer) in a nursing home, your premiums are reduced.

DISABILITY INSURANCE

Disability or 'income protection' insurance provides you with a weekly or monthly income when you're unable to work. Federal disability benefits (see page 265) are unlikely to be sufficient to meet your financial commitments, so you may need to top these up with a private disability insurance policy that guarantees you a fixed income each week or month, or a percentage of your salary when you're ill for a long period or permanently disabled. The chance of being disabled between the ages of 35 and 60 is much greater than the chance of dying.

There are two types of disability insurance: short-term and long-term. Short-term disability policies pay benefits for a limited period only, e.g. up to two years, while long-term cover may continue payments until you return to work or reach retirement age (e.g. 65) or longer. Some employers provide long-term disability insurance (where payments usually begin after six months of disability and continue until retirement age or for a specified number of years) and/or short-term disability insurance, which pays your salary for a limited number of weeks, depending on your length of service.

When shopping for disability insurance, make sure that the policy cannot be cancelled, that it has a guaranteed renewal to ensure that you can retain cover after an injury or illness without an increase in premiums and that the benefits are index-linked. It's also wise to obtain a clause guaranteeing benefits if you return to work part-time while recovering from a disability. You should carefully consider the definition of disability used by the insurer. While every contract has its own definition, 'total disability' pays you only if you're unable to work at all, while 'own (or regular) occupation' considers you disabled if you're unable to work at your usual job (far preferable). Even within that definition, beware of policies that won't pay for mental or nervous disorders, or disabilities arising from alcohol abuse or smoking. Like all forms of insurance, disability insurance must be reviewed and updated regularly to reflect your changing requirements.

All disability policies specify a qualifying period before benefit payments begin, e.g. three to six months. The longer you can wait for your disability insurance to pay out, the lower your monthly premiums are. Usually you can choose when the payments start, e.g. 30, 60 or 90 days, or even one year after the disability or onset of an illness. Your employer may, for example, pay your salary for a period, in which case you can choose to defer payments from your disability insurance for this period.

The longer the period for which you require cover and the higher the monthly income you require, the higher your monthly premiums. So by reducing the amount of monthly income or terminating payments after you reach retirement age, you can lower your premiums. Needless to say, the younger you are, the lower your premiums are. Non-smokers may also pay lower premiums.

Many professional organisations offer low-cost policies, a typical policy costing around $12 to $15 per month for benefits of $3,000 per month. The maximum amount that can be insured is usually calculated as a percentage (e.g. 60 to 75 per cent) of your net monthly earnings, as you need to replace your after-tax income only (benefits from a disability policy aren't taxed). Depending on your age and type of job, some insurance companies may require you to have a medical examination or obtain a report from your family doctor.

PRIVATE PENSION PLANS

Canadians can save privately for their retirement through two types of authorised tax-assisted plans: the Registered Pension Plan (RPP) and the Registered Retirement Savings Plan (RRSP). Both plans permit limited tax-free deductions from gross income. Note, however, that payments received from these plans are included in your income, unless they're transferred to another plan within certain time limits.

There are essentially two kinds of RPP: defined benefit plans and money purchase plans. In a defined benefit plan the employer or sponsor pays a fixed sum or percentage of your income for each year of service. A money purchase plan provides whatever pension income the accumulated contributions and return on investment in the plan will buy.

Most plans require contributions from both the employer and the employee. An individual is allowed to contribute 18 per cent of his earned income or the RRSP limit for the year, whichever is lower. The maximum annual RRSP contribution was set at $14,500 in 1995, increasing to $15,500 by 2005, after which it will be tied to the average industrial wage.

There are many useful books on how to save for your retirement, including *RRSPs and Other Retirement Strategies* by Steven G. Kelman (Globe and Mail Personal Finance Library series) and *Make The Most Of What You've Got: The Canadian Guide to Managing Retirement Income* by Sandra E. Foster (John Wiley & Sons). You may also be interested in *Benefits Canada* magazine, which is dedicated to pension investment and employee benefits (🖳 www.benefits canada.com).

HOUSEHOLD INSURANCE

If you buy a home in Canada, you must take out household insurance, which covers the building and its contents (contents only for condominium owners and tenants of rented property) for 'direct loss' or damage caused by insured perils, which may be stated individually or described as 'all risks'. (Theft insurance applies only when a building is ready for occupation, and vacant buildings aren't normally insured for longer than 30 days.)

Homeowner's insurance cover on your home should begin as soon as you become the legal owner or tenant, even if the property is still under construction. A homeowner's policy can even cover building materials on or adjacent to your property. Insurance covers outbuildings on your land such as a garage, barn, pool house or workshop, which are automatically covered for 20 per cent of the insured value of your home: for example. if you home is insured for $100,000, any outbuildings are insured for a total of $20,000.

Contents insurance is limited to between 70 and 80 per cent of your home's insurance value: for example, if your home is insured for $100,000, your contents are insured for $70,000 to $80,000. Homeowner's policies usually limit third party liability to around $25,000. If any of these amounts is too low, you can buy additional insurance (see **Liability Insurance** on page 277). There's usually an excess of $500 for each claim, although this may be as low as $200 with some companies. By paying an extra premium of around $30, you can have a lower excess.

If you own or rent a second home (e.g. a summer or winter holiday home), you can add it to the homeowner's policy for your principal home or buy a separate policy, but your liability cover doesn't extend to your second home.

It's important to ensure that you're comparing like with like when evaluating different policies. All policies contain maximum dollar limits, which may vary between insurance companies. The amount you should insure your home for isn't the current market value, but its replacement value, i.e. the cost of rebuilding the property should it be totally destroyed (this is less than the market value of your home, as it excludes the value of the land). It's wise for a home to be insured on a guaranteed replacement cost basis, whereby if it costs more to rebuild than provided for in the policy, the insurance company pays for it. Guaranteed replacement cost covers such contingencies as increases in the cost of materials and labour, but not additional costs to conform to new building codes, e.g. if a frame dwelling has to be replaced with a brick one.

Many insurers insist that you insure your home for at least 80 per cent of the replacement cost. If you insure for less than 80 per cent, you receive a pro rata settlement of any claim, however small. For example, if you insure for 50 per cent of the replacement cost, you receive only 50 per cent of the value of a claim.

If you're buying your home with a mortgage, your lender will insist that it's covered by a homeowner's insurance policy. When the mortgage is paid off, it's wise to continue the insurance cover, as many people lose their homes each year in Canada as a result of fires or natural disasters such as landslips, fires and floods.

All agents and insurance companies provide information and free advice, and usually inspect your home to assess your insurance needs if requested to do so (if they won't, go elsewhere). Note, however, that an assessment should be performed by a professional appraiser and the cost varies considerably.

The following types of homeowner's insurance policy are offered by most companies, although some companies don't use the standard 'HO' categories:

Basic Policy (HO-1): The basic homeowner's policy insures your home and possessions against losses caused by the 11 'common perils' (fire or lightning, windstorm or hail, explosion, riot or civil commotion, aircraft, vehicles, smoke, vandalism or malicious mischief, theft, glass breakage, and volcanic eruption). The basic policy is inadequate for most homeowners.

Broad Policy (HO-2): The 'broad' homeowner's policy insures your home and possessions against losses caused by the 11 'common perils' listed above and a further six perils (falling objects; weight of ice, snow or sleet; failure of, overflow from or freezing of a steam or hot water heating system, air-conditioning or automatic fire protective sprinkler system; accidental discharge or overflow of water or steam from a plumbing, heating, air-conditioning or automatic fire protective sprinkler system; freezing of plumbing or household appliances; and sudden and accidental damage from an 'artificially generated electrical current' created by appliances, devices, fixtures and wiring).

All-Risk Policy (HO-3): An all-risk policy protects your home against all the perils included in an HO-2 policy, plus any other perils not specifically excluded by the policy. Your possessions, however, have the same cover as with an HO-2 policy. This is the most popular form of policy and provides the most extensive protection, including everything except flood, earthquake, war, nuclear accident and certain other specified risks. (You can usually insure against extra risks such as floods or earthquakes for an extra – very large – premium, although this can be done only with special insurance companies.) An HO-3 policy also provides protection for loss of use, i.e. when your home becomes uninhabitable and you're required to find alternative accommodation and incur additional living expenses.

Renter's Policy (HO-4): A renter's policy (tenant's insurance) provides the same protection as an HO-2 policy for your possessions and, most importantly, damage caused by you to the property you're renting. It doesn't cover the building itself, which must be insured by the landlord.

Comprehensive Policy (HO-5): A comprehensive policy covers everything, including your possessions, on an all-risk basis, with the exception of any specific exclusions listed in the policy. The best policies include insurance against damage to glass (windows, patio doors, etc.), although you may have to pay extra for accidental damage, e.g. when your son blasts a ball through a window, and should expect your premium to rise the following year. It's the best type of policy and the most expensive.

Condominium & Co-Op Policy (HO-6): This policy is for owners of a condominium or co-op dwelling. It covers possessions and improvements but excludes the building itself, which is separately insured by the condominium or co-op association.

Premiums & Claims

The cost of homeowner's insurance varies widely according to the value of your home and its location (i.e. the province and neighbourhood). Owners of houses vulnerable to subsidence (e.g. those built on clay) and those living in areas liable to flooding are likely to have to pay much higher homeowner's insurance premiums (if you live in a flood plain, you should have a sump pump and call the fire department if there's a flood). Premiums may also depend on other considerations, such as whether your home is constructed of bricks/concrete or wood (wood-frame homes cost more to insure) and how far it is from a fire hydrant. If you have extra security, such as high security door and window locks, a monitored intruder alarm system, fire extinguishers, sprinklers or smoke alarms, you usually receive a discount. You may also receive a discount if you're over 55, work for a particular organisation, qualify for an 'affinity' discount through an organisation such as a credit union or alumni association, or if your family are all non-smokers. You can also reduce your premium by accepting a higher deductible (see above).

Another way to save money is to carry some of the financial risk yourself with a 'named perils' policy that covers only specified risks (such as fire). If you find a comprehensive policy too expensive and a 'named perils' policy too risky, a compromise is a so-called 'broad' policy (not to be confused with an HO-2, known as a Broad Policy – see above) that provides comprehensive cover on buildings and 'named perils' cover on contents.

Rates for the same level of cover from different companies can vary by as much as 100 per cent, so shop around and obtain at least three estimates, but make sure that all quotes are for the same level of cover. Always ask your insurer what isn't covered and what it costs to include it.

Homeowner's insurance must usually be renewed annually, and insurance companies are continually updating their policies, so you must ensure that a policy still provides the cover you require when you receive the renewal notice. **It's your responsibility to ensure that your level of cover is adequate, particularly if you carry out expensive home improvements that substantially increase the value of your home.** If you're about to move to a new home, ask your insurer if your current policy covers your contents at both locations and while they're in transit.

Many insurance companies allow you to pay your insurance premium in monthly instalments.

If you've suffered a loss for which you're insured, inform your insurance agent or broker about it as soon as possible. If there has been a burglary or theft, the police must also be informed. You're required to provide information about the circumstances of the claim as well as reasonable evidence to justify the amount claimed. Your insurer will want to know exactly what was stolen or damaged, when you acquired it and what you paid for it. A claims adjuster may be appointed to investigate a claim. You should take reasonable steps to protect against further damage: for example, if a pipe has burst, you should shut off the water supply. Don't dispose of damaged goods without first obtaining your insurer's approval. In some cases your insurer may arrange assistance for temporary repairs, such as covering a damaged roof or boarding over a broken window. If you have replacement cost cover, some insurers provide an immediate cash advance, which is adjusted when you provide proof of replacement purchase.

Bear in mind that, if you make a claim, you may have to wait months for it to be settled. Generally the larger the claim, the longer you must wait for your money, although in an emergency a company may make an interim payment. If you're dissatisfied with the amount offered, don't accept it and try to negotiate a higher figure or take legal advice.

In the event of an insurer going bust, the Property and Casualty Insurance Compensation Corporation (PACICC, ☎ 416-364-8677, 💻 www.pacicc.com) will consider claims under most policies issued by homeowner's insurance companies. The maximum recovery from PACICC is $250,000 for losses arising from a single occurrence. PACICC will also refund 70 per cent of the unused premium (maximum $700) from the date of an insurer's collapse until the policy's expiry date.

CONTENTS INSURANCE

Contents insurance is usually offered as part of a homeowner's insurance policy (see above), which includes insurance for your furniture, clothing, electrical and electronic equipment and household appliances. However, owners of condominiums and tenants of rented property aren't required to insure the building and may take out insurance for contents only.

In Canada, possessions aren't usually insured for their replacement value (new for old) but for their 'actual cash value' (cost minus depreciation). You can, however, buy replacement-cost insurance, although policies often include limits and are obviously more expensive. When contents insurance is included in your homeowner's insurance policy, you usually have no choice between replacement value and actual cash value insurance.

Note also that a basic contents policy may not include such items as credit cards (and their fraudulent use), cash, musical instruments, jewellery, valuables, sports equipment and bicycles, for which you may need to take out extra cover. A basic policy **doesn't** usually include accidental damage caused by you or members of your family to your own property or your home freezer contents (in the event of a breakdown or power failure).

When insuring your possessions, don't buy more insurance than you need; unless you have valuable possessions, insurance may cost more than replacing your possessions. You may be better off insuring just a few valuable items, rather than everything. To calculate the amount of insurance you require, make an inventory of your possessions containing descriptions, purchase prices and dates, and their location in your home. Keep the list and all receipts in a safe place (such as a safety deposit box) and add new purchases to your list and make adjustments to your insurance cover when necessary. There are maximum limits on cover for individual items in a standard homeowner's policy (listed in contracts).

High-value possessions (called 'scheduled property') such as works of art, furs and jewellery, aren't fully covered by a standard policy and should be insured separately for their full value or through a basic policy clause (rider). For these items you must purchase extra insurance and have them appraised and listed as 'scheduled' items on your policy. You're charged a premium per $100 of coverage for the replacement cost. You're recommended to take photographs of such items, which can help with identification if they're stolen. The cost of insuring high-value items varies with the area and the local crime rate.

A policy may also insure your possessions if they're stolen from somewhere other than your home, e.g. a car or hotel room.

LIABILITY INSURANCE

Liability insurance is the homeowner's version of third party insurance for car owners. It covers you for damage caused either at your home or elsewhere to other people such as visitors or employees, or to your neighbours (e.g. by your son hitting a baseball through a neighbour's window and smashing his collection of rare porcelain). Cover doesn't apply to injuries sustained by you or by members of your immediate household nor, if you operate a business at home, to injuries sustained by employees or people visiting you for work purposes. If you operate a business from home you must inform your insurance company, or a claim will be denied.

Liability insurance is usually included in a homeowner's policy (see page 277), but can be purchased separately if you don't require homeowner's insurance or consider the liability insurance provided by your homeowner's policy inadequate. Homeowner's policies usually limit liability claims to around $25,000, although most companies offer optional extra cover. Considering the low cost of liability insurance and the high cost of law suits, most experts recommend $250,000 to be the **minimum** cover necessary, and most Canadians purchase cover of between $500,000 and $1 million.

Many people take out a personal liability 'umbrella' policy to extend the cover of their homeowner's and car insurance policies, and usually include protection against claims arising from business activities and other 'injuries', such as slander. An umbrella policy provides cover **in addition to** the amount covered by a basic policy and isn't a replacement for these policies.

If you own or rent a second home (e.g. a summer or winter holiday home), you can add it to the homeowner's policy for your principal home or buy a separate policy, but your liability cover doesn't extend to your second home.

HOLIDAY & TRAVEL INSURANCE

Holiday and travel insurance is recommended for anyone who doesn't wish to risk having his holiday or travel spoiled by financial problems. The following information applies to Canadian residents travelling within Canada and abroad and to those visiting Canada on holiday. **Nobody should go abroad (and certainly not over the border into the US) without travel and health insurance!**

Travel insurance is available from many sources, including travel agents, insurance brokers, banks, automobile clubs and transport companies (airline, rail and bus). Package holiday companies and tour operators also offer insurance policies. You can also buy 24-hour accident insurance and flight insurance at major airports, although it's expensive and doesn't offer the best cover. Before taking out travel insurance, carefully consider the range and level of cover you require and compare policies.

Short-term holiday and travel insurance policies may include insurance against holiday cancellation or interruption, missing your flight, departure delay at both the start and end of a holiday (a common occurrence), delayed, lost or damaged baggage, lost or stolen personal effects and money, medical expenses and accidents (including evacuation home), flight cancellation, personal liability and legal expenses, and default or bankruptcy (e.g. the tour operator or airline goes bust).

The cost of travel insurance varies considerably according to your destination. Many companies have different rates for different areas, e.g. North America, Europe and worldwide. Premiums may also be increased for those aged over 65 or 70. Generally the longer the period covered, the cheaper the daily cost, although the maximum period is usually limited, e.g. six months or a year. With some policies an excess of around $50 or $100 must be paid for each claim. For those who travel abroad frequently, whether on business or pleasure, an annual travel policy provides better value but may have restrictions on the length of trips, e.g. 90 days.

Make sure that your travel insurance includes personal liability (e.g. $1 or $2 million) and repatriation expenses. If your travel insurance expires while you're visiting Canada, you can buy further insurance from an insurance agent, although this won't include repatriation expenses. Flight insurance and comprehensive travel insurance is available from insurance desks at most airports, including travel accident, personal accident, world-wide medical expenses and in-transit baggage.

If you need to make a claim, you should provide as much documentary evidence as possible. Although travel insurance companies eagerly take your money, they aren't always so keen to settle claims, and you may need to persevere before they pay up. Always be persistent and make a claim **irrespective** of any small print, as this may be unreasonable and therefore invalid in law.

14.

FINANCE

Canada is one of the richest countries in the world, with a GDP of over a trillion dollars ($1,000,000,000,000) and GDP per capita of around $30,000. In terms of gross national product (GNP), Canada ranks around eighth in the world and has a similar standard of living to the US and the wealthiest European countries. Basic bank rate and consumer loan rates have fallen steadily from highs of around 13 per cent and 17 per cent respectively in 1990 to 3.5 per cent and 8.5 per cent in early 2003, encouraging Canadian businesses and employers to expand. In the late 20th century, Canada was one of the few countries in the world with a balanced budget, and in 2003 inflation was running at just 1 per cent. The country has entered the new millennium with high levels of job creation and economic growth, and the government plans to reduce income tax, starting with those on lower incomes.

The Canadian financial services system has undergone many changes in the last 15 years, which have enhanced domestic competition and efficiency and increased foreign participation. These changes included the Canada-US Free Trade Agreement (CFTA) in 1989, a comprehensive reform of federal financial services legislation in 1992, and the North American Free Trade Agreement (NAFTA) between Canada, the USA and Mexico in 1994. The 1992 federal reforms expanded competition within Canada's banking, loan/trust, securities and insurance industries. With the formation of CFTA and NAFTA, Canadian banks and foreign financial institutions have been allowed to operate or expand in sectors where they were previously barred.

Despite the widespread use of credit and charge cards (the average Canadian has three), which account for around half of all payments, almost the same number are made in cash, with just 5 per cent by cheque. In some circles your financial status may be calculated by the number of credit cards you carry, although newcomers will find it difficult to obtain even one. If you have an international credit card issued by a foreign bank, it's wise to retain it until you've replaced it in Canada. Surprisingly, over 20 per cent of Canada's economy is estimated to be 'underground', with transactions made in cash in order to evade the attentions of the tax authorities.

When you arrive to take up residence or employment in Canada, make sure you have sufficient funds to last you until your first pay day. **Don't, however, carry a lot of cash.** During the first few weeks you will probably find a major credit card (e.g. MasterCard or Visa) invaluable; without one you will be expected to prepay many bills, including hotel and car rental bills (when you pay these by credit card, the estimated amount is 'blocked off' your credit limit,although it isn't debited until you check out or return the car and the final bill is calculated).

Personal finance is one of Canada's favourite subjects and there are numerous books on the subject, including *The MacLean's Money Companion – Financial Lingo for the Uninitiated* by Ted M. Ohasi (Raincoast Books), *The Money Adviser* by Bruce Cohen & Alyssa Diamond Stoddart and the *Money Guide For Modern Families* by Ellen Roseman, plus many personal finance magazines such as the *Financial Post* and *Your Money*. See also **Social Insurance** on page 260 and **Private Pension Plans** on page 272.

For details of goods and services and provincial sales taxes, see **Sales Taxes** on page 358.

CANADIAN CURRENCY

The unit of currency is the Canadian dollar, which is divided into 100 cents (¢). Canadian coins are minted in values of 1¢ (penny), 5¢ (nickel), 10¢ (dime), 25¢ (quarter) and 50¢ (half-dollar, which is rarely seen nowadays), one dollar and two-dollars. The penny is copper, the 5, 10, 25 and 50 cent coins are silver-coloured (an amalgam of silver and copper), the $1 coin is 11-sided and gold-coloured, and the $2 has a nickel outer rim and an aluminium-bronze centre. There are also silver dollars and a $1 pure gold coin, the Maple Leaf, the price (and value) of which fluctuate with the price of gold and silver. All coins have an image of Queen Elizabeth II on one side. The $1 coin has a bird (the loon) on the reverse and is called a 'loonie', while the two-dollar coin (which has a polar bear on the reverse) is called a 'twonie' (pronounced 'toonie'). The quarter is the most useful coin and you should carry some with you for parking meters, bus and underground fares, road tolls, payphones, baggage lockers, vending machines, tips, etc..

Banknotes (bills) are printed in denominations of $5 (blue), $10 (purple), $20 (green), $50 (red), $100 (brown) and $1,000 (purple). Canada no longer has a $1 bill; the $2 bill (red), although still legal tender, is no longer produced and is rapidly disappearing. All Canadian notes are the same size but depict different Canadian luminaries, as follows: $5 (Sir Wilfred Laurier, Canada's second prime minister), $10 (Sir John A. MacDonald, Canada's father of confederation and first prime minister), $20 (Queen Elizabeth II), $50 (William Lyon MacKenzie, Canada's third prime minister), $100 (Sir Robert Borden, Canada's eighth prime minister). If you're unfamiliar with Canadian bills, you should stick to low denominations ($5 to $20) and check them carefully to avoid errors, both when receiving bills in change and when spending them. Bills above $20 are often regarded with suspicion (they're a favourite target of counterfeiters) and may not be accepted.

In most places in Canada you can use US dollars, although Canadian dollars aren't accepted in America (Americans refer to them as Monopoly money). The Canadian/US dollar conversion rate is usually around C$1 = US70¢ and shops often have a sign by the cash register saying 'US currency 30 per cent' or something similar, meaning that, if you pay in US$, you will in effect be given an exchange of C$1.30 = US$1 (or C$1 = US77¢), which is around 10 per cent below the normal rate. The US$ is Canada's 'intervention currency' (a currency that's bought or bought by central banks when it's thought to be beneficial), and the value of the Canadian dollar is closely linked to that of the US dollar.

It's wise to obtain some Canadian notes before arriving in Canada and to familiarise yourself and your family with them. You should have some Canadian dollars in cash (e.g. $50 to $100 in small notes), but take the rest of your 'pocket' money in travellers' cheques.

IMPORTING & EXPORTING MONEY

Canada has no constraints on the movement of funds into or out of the country, and banks, corporations and individuals can deal in foreign funds or arrange payments in any currency they choose. Gold may be freely purchased by Canadian residents, who may also hold and sell it in any form. However, gold originating in the US requires a permit when re-exported to any country other than the States. Importing gold articles such as watches or jewellery is unrestricted and doesn't require a licence, but gold coins or ingots must be declared on arrival. If you're planning to transfer a large amount of money to Canada (e.g. to buy a home or business), you can fix the exchange rate in advance on payment of a deposit in order to take advantage of (what you hope is) a favourable exchange rate.

With the exception of US dollars, most shops and businesses in Canada don't accept foreign currency (including foreign currency travellers' cheques), and it's best to avoid bringing them to Canada. It can even be difficult to find a bank or other financial institution that will exchange foreign currency or foreign currency travellers' cheques, particularly in small towns. You usually receive an unfavourable exchange rate or pay a high commission when changing money at a hotel or a *bureau de change*. If you change foreign money or foreign currency travellers' cheques, try to do so in large cities, where increased competition usually ensures a better exchange rate (although still worse than you would obtain abroad). You may be asked for identification (ID) when changing foreign notes at a bank.

Apart from travellers' cheques issued by major Canadian banks, the most widely recognised and accepted travellers' cheques are American Express, followed closely by Visa and Thomas Cook cheques. The normal fee when buying travellers' cheques worldwide is 1 per cent of their value, although this may be waived when travel arrangements are made with the company issuing the cheques (e.g. American Express or Thomas Cook). The commission on American Express cheques may be higher when they aren't purchased directly from an American Express office. Canadian dollar travellers' cheques can be cashed at most banks, although most levy a fee of around $3 if you don't have an account with them.

Almost all businesses and retailers (exceptions include taxi drivers and some small businesses) in Canada readily accept Canadian dollar travellers' cheques and give you change as if you had paid in cash. Small value cheques such as $10 or $20 are accepted almost everywhere, while larger denominations may be accepted only for expensive purchases (so don't try to pay for a coffee with a $50 cheque). You may be asked for identification, e.g. a driving licence or credit card, when cashing in travellers' cheques. The sign 'No cheques' applies only to personal cheques and not to travellers' cheques. Many hotels change travellers' cheques for residents, although they usually give a poor exchange rate.

Always keep a separate record of cheque numbers and note where and when they were cashed. American Express provides a free one-day replacement service for lost or stolen travellers' cheques at any of their offices worldwide, provided that you know the serial numbers of the lost cheques. Without the serial numbers, replacement can take up to three days. Most companies provide toll-free numbers for reporting lost or stolen travellers' cheques in Canada, including American Express (☎ 1-800-221-7282), MasterCard (☎ 1-800-307-7309), Thomas Cook (☎ 1-800-223-7322) and Visa (☎ 1-800-336-8472).

If you have money transferred to Canada by banker's draft or a letter of credit, bear in mind that it may take up to two weeks to be cleared. You can also have money sent to you by telegraphic transfer, e.g. via Western Union Canada (the fastest and safest method, but also the most expensive). A telegraphic or cable transfer to Canada from overseas takes 24 to 48 hours and costs around $35. Within Canada a cash wire transfer via Western Union costs a minimum of $17 (for up to $100), and an extra $7 for each additional $100 or part thereof, and takes as little as 15 minutes. It costs $4.50 to collect transferred funds from any of Western Union's 1,000 Canadian offices and for an additional $4.50 they notify you by phone when they arrive. Up to $3,000 can be sent from a MasterCard or Visa account via Western Union (☎ 1-800-235-0000, 🖥 www.westernunion.com). American Express cardholders can transfer up to $15,000 (depending on your credit limit) by 'Moneygram', both within Canada and internationally.

A less expensive way to transfer funds to Canada from some countries is by purchasing an international money order from a post office or bank, for which there's a standard charge. A money order can be made payable to yourself at a receiving Canadian bank at face value. Transfers can also be made by airmail letter, which takes longer, e.g. around eight days from Europe, but is much cheaper, or by bank draft (see **Banks** below). You can send money within Canada via a post office money order, which can be purchased or cashed at any Canadian post office (American Express also provide money orders).

You need your passport or other identification to collect money transferred from abroad or to cash a bank draft (or other credit note). If you're sending money abroad, it's best to send it in local currency so that the recipient doesn't have to pay conversion charges. You can send money direct from your bank to another bank via an inter-bank transfer. Most banks have a minimum service charge for international transfers, which generally makes it very expensive for small sums. Receiving banks may also take a cut, e.g. 1 or 2 per cent of the amount transferred.

CREDIT RATING

It's difficult for new arrivals in Canada to establish a credit rating (or 'line of credit') or obtain credit without excellent references from an employer, who may need to secure any borrowing, or from a foreign bank. Newcomers must establish a new credit rating in Canada, as a foreign credit rating (however good) isn't taken into account. Usually you must have been employed by the same company for at least a year and earn more than a specified salary, although it can still take a number of years to establish a **good** credit rating. Many foreigners find that they must 'build up' their credit rating by obtaining credit from local businesses and shops. It's usually even more difficult for self-employed people to obtain credit, as most credit applications are geared towards employees. It may, however, be possible to convince your bank by presenting your income tax returns.

You should pay all your bills promptly and never bounce cheques, as it can wreck your credit rating. Once you've established a good credit rating, you can usually obtain far more credit than is good for you (paradoxically, the more you buy on credit, the more credit-worthy you become), and banks, finance companies, credit card companies and other financial institutions constantly tempt you with credit offers.

In Canada, everyone's credit history is maintained by private companies which are called credit-reporting agencies or credit bureaux (e.g. Equifax, Creditel and Associated Credit Bureaux of Canada). They collect information reported to them by banks, mortgage companies, shops and other businesses. Your credit record contains information such as judgments or liens against you or your property, bankruptcies or foreclosures, as well as the failure to pay your debts, e.g. payments on revolving charge accounts. Credit bureaux can legally report negative credit information for seven years and bankruptcy information for 14 years. The only information that can be changed in your credit report is incorrect items and items which are outside the 7 or 14-year reporting periods.

If a company denies your request for credit because of your credit report, it must (under the Credit Reporting Agencies Act) tell you so and identify the bureau that supplied the report. All credit bureaux are required by law to share with you any information they have on file about you. This must be provided free if you've been denied credit within the past 30 days; otherwise you can be charged a fee, e.g. between $5 and $20.

In some provinces credit-reporting agencies are required by law to make an investigation into complaints within 30 days, erase non-verifiable items, provide free reports once per year, and provide consumers with the credit-rating scores it gives to lenders. Employers may obtain a credit report on prospective employees, particularly when they will be in a position of trust or will be handling cash.

BANKS

Canada's banking system is dominated by the 'big five' chartered banks (Canadian Imperial Bank of Commerce, Bank of Montreal, Bank of Nova Scotia, Royal Bank of Canada and TD/Canada Trust), which between them control 90 per cent of all banking assets (in excess of $7.5 trillion). The big five have a network of over 8,000 branches and also offer telephone and Internet banking. There are also many smaller domestic banks, including credit unions (which are increasingly popular because of their range of services, lower charges and friendly service) and *caisses populaires* in Quebec, and over 40 foreign banks operating in Canada. The chartered banks dominate the market for consumer credit (excluding mortgages) and make around 70 per cent of all consumer loans. The rest are made by credit unions, trust and mortgage loan companies, and life insurance companies.

Canada's banking system is regulated by the Bank of Canada, the federal government institution that's directly responsible for the country's monetary policy. Canadian banks are prohibited from direct participation in the insurance industry and cannot offer insurance products through their branches (except in British Columbia), although they're permitted to own, develop and manage land through property corporations and may own property (real estate) companies.

Canadians usually do their banking with one of the chartered or foreign banks, a credit union or a trust company. To bank with a credit union you must become a member and are then eligible for loans at lower interest rates than those charged by banks and you also receive a share of the profits. Trust companies operate in much the same way as banks, except that their service is more personal. If in doubt about which to choose, ask your Canadian colleagues and acquaintances for advice – most are less than happy with their bank, so if someone does recommend a particular institution it's worth heeding his advice.

A wide range of accounts and services is available and it's worth shopping around. Some pay you interest when you're in credit, while others simply desist from charging you (although you must usually have a balance of at least $1,000), and some either charge for each service (e.g. cashing a cheque or clearing a payment into the account) or charge you a blanket monthly 'maintenance' fee for the privilege of banking with them. See **Bank Accounts** below.

Like the rest of the world, Canadian banks have embraced electronic banking and you can pay bills, transfer money between accounts, arrange a loan or mortgage, apply for a credit card and print account statements (thus saving the fee charged by banks) 24 hours per day from the comfort of your home or office.

Banks also offer a range of other services including:

- **Money Orders And Drafts** – instructions to your bank to pay a specified amount to a named person or company. You must pay for a money order or draft at the time of purchase.

- **Certified Cheques** – designed for recipients who need to cash a cheque immediately or who want a guarantee that the funds are available;
- **Standing Orders And Direct Debits** – called 'pre-authorised payments', e.g. for utility bill payments;
- **Overdraft Protection** – whereby a bank allows you to overdraw your account up to an agreed amount. There's a service fee of around $1 per month for this 'service', plus interest on the amount overdrawn. The overdraft limit is determined when you sign up and may be linked to a credit card or savings account, where the amount overdrawn is debited to the card or account.

Banks also offer a range of financial products and services, including mortgages, term deposits, Canada Savings Bonds, treasury bills, retirement savings and income plans, guaranteed investment certificates (GICs) and mutual funds.

When choosing a bank, it's wise to pick one that's covered by the Canadian Deposit Insurance Corporation (CDIC), 50 O'Connor Street, 17th Floor, PO Box 2340, Station D, Ottawa ON K1P 5W5 (☎ 1-800-461-2342, ⌨ www.cdic.ca). In the event of a bank failure, the CDIC guarantees 'eligible deposits' up to a maximum of $60,000 per person (principal and interest). Eligible deposits consist of savings and cheque (chequing) accounts, term deposits such as GICs, bonds (debentures) issued by loan companies, money orders, drafts, and travellers' cheques issued by member institutions. The CDIC doesn't cover foreign currency deposits, term deposits that mature over five years after the date of deposit, bonds issued by banks, bonds issued by governments and corporations, treasury bills, mutual funds, stocks, and investments in mortgages. Always ensure that each bank you bank with holds no more than $60,000 and that deposits are covered by the CDIC guarantee. If you wish to check a bank's financial standing before opening an account, you can contact the Bank of Canada, Public Information, 234 Wellington, Ottawa ON K1A 0G9 (☎ 1-800-303-1282, ⌨ www.bank-banque-canada.ca).

Drive-in (or 'drive-up') banks, where people who live in their cars can obtain cash without forsaking the comfort and security of their vehicles, were invented in the US and Canadians have embraced the concept. Some banks have automatic tellers (ATMs) at car-window height, while others have a complicated system of vacuum pipes, microphones and loudspeakers connecting you with an invisible teller. If you're unfamiliar with this method of doing business, take time to read the instructions before attempting it (or leave your car and walk!).

Banking Hours

Usual bank opening hours are from 9am to 5pm, Mondays to Fridays (some open until 6pm on Fridays), and from 10am to 3pm on Saturdays. All banks are closed on federal and provincial holidays (see page 49). Trust companies generally have much longer business hours than chartered banks, e.g. from

8.30am until 8pm. There are full service banks at major airports (usually with standard banking hours), and ATMs are provided in most terminals. Most Canadian banks have 24-hour ATMs (see page 292) at all branches for cash withdrawals and deposits or separate ATM centres. Some banks have also introduced 24-hour telephone banking in recent years and most banks offer Internet banking.

Bank Accounts

There are three types of bank account in Canada: current or cheque (chequing) accounts, savings (deposit) accounts and a combination of the two known as 'cheque-savings' accounts. Few Canadians are without at least one bank account and most have a number of accounts.

Before opening an account, you should shop around among local banks and compare accounts, interest rates, services and fees. You may also like to check the queues (lines) at the times when you wish to use the bank – some have huge queues, particularly on Friday afternoons and Saturdays. You should take particular note of a bank's charges (see above), which have increased considerably in recent years. To avoid charges, you should never overdraw your account or accept cheques from unreliable sources, keep a minimum balance in a cheque account, use your own bank's ATMs rather than other banks', obtain overdraft protection (see below) and read your bank's 'fee-disclosure' literature.

Most Canadians are paid by cheque, either bi-weekly or monthly, which they then cash or deposit in a bank account. You can also have your salary paid directly into your bank account by direct deposit and an increasing number of people choose this option (just give your account details to your employer). If you want to cash a cheque, you must take it to the branch where it was drawn or a branch of the same bank.

Cheque Accounts

The best kind of account to open initially is a cheque account, which is the usual account for day-to-day financial transactions in Canada. To open an account, simply go to the bank of your choice and tell them you wish to open an account. You usually need a permanent address and you're asked to provide a range of personal information, including your date of birth, details of your employer, a contact number for a relative in case they cannot reach you, and at least two forms of identification (ID) which have your signature and photograph on them, such as a driving licence and a passport. If you choose an account that pays interest, you must produce your social insurance number (SIN). You may also be asked for a reference or 'co-signer', although many banks waive this requirement in the never-ending quest for new customers. If you want to deposit a large amount of cash to open the account, you may need to sign a declaration attesting to the source of the funds.

The standard cheque account is called a 'flat fee account', of which there are various kinds. For example, Canada Trust offers the following accounts: a 'value account' with a service fee of $3.95 per month or free if you maintain a minimum balance of $1,000; a 'self-service account' (via ATMs) for $6.95 per month (free with a balance of $1,500); a 'full service account' for $9.95 per month (free with a balance of $2,000); an 'infinity account' for $12.95 per month (free with a balance of $3,000); and a 'CT select service account' (unlimited transactions) for $24.95 per month (free with a balance of $5,000). All these accounts include an Internet service, phone service, branch service, monthly statements, bill-paying, standing orders/direct debits (pre-authorised payments), transfers between accounts and cheque books.

All banks also offer special accounts for students at universities and colleges. These offer a guaranteed overdraft for around four years, e.g. $5,500 per year or a total of $22,000, and provide a full range of banking services, including cheques, credit or debit cards, and telephone and ATM banking. While at college (and for the first year after graduating) only the interest on the loan is paid, after which there's a 20-year repayment plan. Most banks and other financial institutions are keen to add students to their customer base (not surprisingly, as many students remain in debt for decades) and generous offers are made to new students to encourage them to open accounts.

Cheques aren't provided free by Canadian banks and typically cost $7.95 for a box containing five pads of 20 to 25 cheques. It may be cheaper to buy your cheques from a cheque printing company (see the yellow pages). New customers can order 200 cheques for around $10 in a wide variety of designs and typefaces. Most banks offer customers the option of having their cancelled cheques returned for a fee of around $2 per month. All cheques must be printed with your name; it's also wise to have your address printed on them to avoid suspicion.

Canadian banks don't issue cheque guarantee cards, and cheques are therefore subject to far more scrutiny than in many other countries, and may be accepted only when drawn on a local or in-province bank or by a business where you're known personally. (The lack of guarantee cards also means that cheque theft is common.) Most retailers have strict rules regarding the acceptance of cheques and some businesses won't accept cheques at all; petrol stations and restaurants often have signs proclaiming firmly 'NO CHEQUES'. When paying by cheque in some shops and supermarkets, you must go to a special desk and have your cheque approved before going to the check-out. You must present identification (usually a driving licence and another form of identification such as a credit card, social insurance card, passport or employer or college identity card). Some shops insist that customers are issued with a store identity card before being allowed to use personal cheques. On the other hand, in shops where you're known, you may be allowed to write a cheque for more than the amount of your bill and receive the difference in cash.

When writing cheques, Canadians write cents as a percentage; see the example below:

> $107.42 is written **one hundred and seven and** 42
>   100
>
> The date is written month/day/year and not day/month/year; for example, 12th October 2003 is written **10/12/03** and not 12/10/03.

When you deposit a cheque in a bank, most banks require you to endorse it with your signature or an endorsement stamp. They prefer you to write on the reverse sideways at the left (perforated) end of the cheque and not lengthwise (so that there's room for the bank's stamp). If you want to endorse a cheque payable to you so that it can be paid into another account, you must write on the back 'Pay to the order of _____ (name)' and sign it (using the same form of your name entered under payee). This is called a 'third party cheque' and some banks won't accept them.

Cheque bouncing, i.e. writing a cheque for more than the balance of your account, is taken seriously in Canada, where you can be prosecuted. Banks charge various fees for bouncing cheques (usually $15 to $20) which, more importantly, may damage your credit rating (see page 286). If the payee is a company, they may also charge you a fee of $25 or $30 plus the amount of the cheque. All banks offer customers overdraft protection on certain accounts, thus protecting customers from 'inadvertently' bouncing cheques (see above).

Savings Accounts

All banks, credit unions and trust companies and various other financial institutions offer a wide range of savings (or deposit) accounts, most of which are intended for short or medium term saving, rather than long-term growth. Trusts generally offer a higher rate of interest than commercial banks, and brokerage houses may offer even higher rates of interest (but don't guarantee that your money is safe). It doesn't pay to keep long-term savings in a savings account when interest rates are low (Canadian savings bonds, treasury securities and money market mutual funds pay higher interest).

Savings accounts pay interest on your balance and allow a few free transactions (e.g. two debit transactions or automatic transactions per month) and charge you for the rest. Expect to be charged 40¢ to 60¢ per transaction, and around $1 for monthly statements. Most of these accounts pay higher rates of interest for larger balances. You can also open these accounts for children under 18 ('no withdrawals allowed' is an option) and senior citizens (over 60, at preferential rates) and in US$.

When opening an account, the most important considerations are how much money you wish to save (which may be a lump sum or a monthly amount) and how quickly you need access to it in an emergency. It's often wise to have your cheque and savings accounts at the same bank, so that, for example, the bank may automatically transfer surplus money from your cheque to your savings account (or money from your savings account to cover an overdraft on your cheque account), or will provide a free cheque account if you maintain a savings account with a minimum balance, e.g. $500 to $1,500. Most banks provide a range of combined cheque and savings accounts, where interest is paid on deposits, usually on a sliding scale depending on the balance.

There are two main types of savings account: statement savings accounts and passbook savings accounts. With a statement savings account, you have access to funds via ATMs and receive regular monthly or quarterly statements. With a passbook savings account, all transactions are recorded in a passbook, which must be presented to the teller each time you deposit or withdraw funds.

Tax must be paid on the interest earned on a savings account, although there are tax-free savings accounts for long-term savings, such as a Registered Retirement Savings Plan (RRSP – see **Private Pension Plans** on page 272).

Bank Cards

A bank (or cash or debit or ATM) card allows bank account holders to withdraw money from their accounts, 24 hours per day, seven days per week (some ATMs are situated so you can do so without even getting out of your car). The freedom from queuing, banking hours and bank tellers (who, let it be said, are usually agreeable people) provided by bank cards is convenient, and you should think twice before opening an account not offering (lots of) local ATMs. Canadians have wholeheartedly embraced this method of banking and the country ranks second in the world for the availability of ATM machines, with around six machines per 10,000 people (Japan leads with ten per 10,000). ATMs are located in the lobbies of most banks and can also be found in shopping malls, supermarkets, department stores, airports and railway stations. When a bank is closed, you must usually insert your card in a slot at the door to gain entry to the lobby. Your bank provides you with a personal identification number (PIN) to access the machines.

You can usually withdraw a maximum of $600 daily (provided that you have the money in your account) and make deposits, transfer funds between accounts, check balances and make payments. There's no charge for using a bank card when you use an ATM at a branch of your own bank, but there's normally a charge (e.g. $1 or $2) each time you use an ATM at an affiliated bank. Purchases using a bank card are always free.

ATMs are linked together by computers into networks, allowing customers of different banks to draw cash from machines in major cities across the world. All banks have their own network of ATMs and most are linked with others in Canada and abroad (Cirrus or Plus). Cirrus (owned by MasterCard) is the largest North American network, with over 35,000 ATMs in Canada and America and 65,000 worldwide; Plus, affiliated with Visa, is the second-largest. If you do a lot of travelling, you may wish to have cheque or savings accounts with different banks with different ATM networks, thus allowing you to use a wider range of ATMs both in Canada and abroad.

When using ATMs to withdraw cash abroad, you receive the wholesale bank rate, which is a better rate than you can get over the counter anywhere. If possible, you should use a bank card that allows you to tap into a cheque or savings account, rather than a credit card, which incurs interest on cash advances and a hefty fee. However, never rely solely on ATMs to obtain cash, as they can be fickle things and may not accept your card or may even 'swallow' it. Sometimes your card may be rejected by a machine at one bank and be accepted by a machine at another bank.

It's sensible to not keep a lot of money in an account for which you have a bank card and **never** have a bank card for a savings account with a large balance. Don't use ATMs in 'high risk' areas at night, as muggings occasionally occur. If you lose your bank card, you must notify the issuing bank immediately so that they can cancel it.

Credit & Charge Cards

Over 600 institutions in Canada issue credit and charge cards, including American Express (Amex), Diners Club, Discover, MasterCard and Visa. There are over 31 million such cards in circulation with a combined debt of over $20 billion. Before issuing a credit card, companies require an assurance that you won't disappear owing them a fortune, and they check your bank, employer and credit bureaux to ensure that you're credit worthy (see **Credit Rating** on page 286).

It's difficult for newcomers to obtain credit cards, even when they have excellent references or have previously held credit cards in another country. New arrivals should present a letter of introduction from their bank manager in their home country regarding their banking status. A credit card company may offer you only a pre-paid card, whereby you deposit money with the credit card company and use the card to spend it! Even with a pre-paid card you may have a paltry 'credit' limit. It may also be possible to obtain a card from an offshore bank that can be paid in Canadian dollars.

If your application is approved, you usually receive your card within two to four weeks. You can apply for a MasterCard or Visa card from your bank, but American Express and Diners Club applications must be made direct to the card companies.

You can obtain as many credit cards as you wish, although you should bear in mind the monthly or annual fees, e.g. $50 to $100 for charge cards. The annual fees for MasterCards and Visa cards vary considerably, e.g. from zero to $55, the average being around $25. Cards with annual fees often charge lower interest rates than those without. The only two things that matter when obtaining credit cards are the card's annual fee and its interest rate, so shop around for the best deal you can find. If you know that you will always be able to pay off the balance each month, you should choose a card with no annual fee and other benefits.

Interest on any balance owed is charged at a high annual rate set by the issuing bank, which is usually three or four times the current savings rate.

However, as a response to the demand for lower interest rates, many banks have lowered their rates, although the average is still around 15 percentage points above what banks pay to borrow. Most cards have a grace period of 20 to 30 days for repayment, and charge fees (or increase interest rates) for late payments and exceeding credit limits . **Many banks charge interest on credit cards from the purchase date, not from the first billing date.** So even if you pay off the total owed each month, you will still incur interest charges.

When using a credit card in Canada, you may be subject to a more rigorous check than in other countries. For example, you may be asked for further identification (e.g. a driving licence). On the other hand, many people are extremely lax about checking signatures, which makes it easy for crooks to use stolen cards. Keep all receipts and check them against your credit card statements, as dishonest sales clerks may add a digit or two to their copy of the sales receipt.

You can use MasterCard and Visa cards to obtain cash from ATMs and banks displaying the MasterCard or Visa symbol, and can also obtain cash advances at ATMs and participating banks world-wide. However, take care when relying on ATMs, as they can gobble up your card leaving you plastic-less (and possibly short of funds), and banks make high charges for cash withdrawals.

American Express and Diners Club cards allow you to cash personal cheques, buy travellers' cheques for limited sums, and provide free travel, car rental collision damage waiver (CDW) insurance and baggage insurance. Many Visa cards and MasterCards also provide free travel accident insurance and some cards provide a free 90-day insurance against accidental damage to purchases, extended warranties and price protection schemes. In addition to standard bank cards, most banks issue 'gold' and 'platinum' cards (they've even turned to jewel names such as 'emerald') offering additional services and extra 'status', although there's usually a fee of $75 to $125 per year and the cards are seldom worth the extra cost.

Some card companies participate in bonus schemes such as a 'frequent flyer' scheme, where cardholders earn air miles each time they use their cards, or a 'bonus' system such as Visa's 'rewards' scheme, where customers receive points each time they use their cards that are exchangeable for credits on travel, goods and discounts at department stores. Often a number of air miles or points are awarded just for signing up with a card company. The General Motors card offers holders a 5 per cent rebate on purchases to spend on GM vehicles.

If you lose a credit card or it's stolen, report it immediately to the police and the issuing office (e.g. a bank or store) or phone the 24-hour, toll-free number provided by the card company, e.g. American Express (☎ 1-800-268-9805), Carte Blanche/Diners Club (☎ 1-800-525-9135), Discover (☎ 1-800-347-2683), MasterCard (☎ 1-800-263-2263) and Visa (☎ 1-800-847-2911). Note the name of the person to whom you reported the loss and the date and time of the call, and confirm the loss as soon as possible in writing. If you report the loss before the card is used, the card company cannot hold you responsible for any subsequent charges. If a thief uses your card before you report it, your liability is limited to

$50. You can register all your credit cards with a credit card security club. In the event that your cards are stolen, a phone call to the club ensures that all your cards are cancelled and that new cards are issued. It's wise to keep a list of the numbers of all your credit cards.

MORTGAGES

Mortgages (home loans) in Canada are available from a number of sources, including commercial banks, mortgage bankers, insurance companies, builders and developers, and government agencies. By law, Canadian financial institutions cannot lend more than 75 per cent of the market value of a property, which means that if you want to buy a $100,000 home, you must find a deposit of at least $25,000. Lenders evaluate a property and check your credit rating (see page 286), employment history, income, assets, residence and liabilities. It's recommended to check your own credit rating before applying for a mortgage, in case it could adversely affect your application. Your credit history must usually be perfect to qualify for a mortgage. New immigrants can obtain mortgages but may have to pay a deposit (down payment) of at least 35 per cent and make the first year's mortgage payments in advance. It's often difficult or more expensive to raise finance for a Canadian property from lenders in other countries.

For those who cannot afford the 25 per cent deposit required by most lenders in Canada, the federal government provides mortgages insured by the Central Mortgage and Housing Corporation (CMHC). The CMHC was established in 1945 as a Crown Corporation to administer federal participation in housing as prescribed under the National Housing Act. The mortgage insurance provided by the CMHC allows lenders to borrow up to 90 or 95 per cent of a home's value.

The maximum amount a lender will lend you depends on your income. Most lenders insist that a mortgage is no more than three times your annual salary or that monthly repayments are no more than 30 per cent of your gross monthly income. When calculating how large a mortgage you can afford, take into account the purchase (closing) costs, which average 3 to 5 per cent of the price of a property and depend on location, cost and other factors. 'Non-income status' mortgages of 65 to 70 per cent with no proof of income or tax returns are also available, although borrowers usually require large cash reserves.

The traditional Canadian mortgage period is 25 or 30 years, although lenders also offer 10 to 20-year fixed-rate mortgages, requiring a higher deposit and/or higher monthly repayments than a 25-year mortgage. If you can afford the repayments, a 10 or 15-year mortgage can save you a considerable amount in interest compared with a 30-year mortgage. A 15-year mortgage is usually offered at a slightly lower interest rate (e.g. a 0.25 to 0.75 percentage point reduction) than a 30-year mortgage, meaning you make even greater savings.

It can take up to 90 days to arrange a mortgage, depending on its complexity.

Types Of Mortgage

There are essentially two types of mortgage: open mortgages that allow you to pay off your mortgage at any time without an early repayment penalty, and closed mortgages where there's a penalty payment for early repayment.

Mortgages can have a fixed or variable rate of interest. With fixed-rate mortgages the monthly repayments and the interest rate are fixed for an agreed period. Even when you fix your interest rates for 1, 2, 3 or 5 years, lending institutions allow you to make some additional payments, e.g. up to an additional 20 per cent per annum, without incurring any penalties, these payments being deducted from the principal, thus saving a lot of interest. A fixed-rate mortgage offers stability, although interest rates are initially higher than with a variable-rate mortgage and you run the risk that they will remain higher. A fixed-rate mortgage isn't assumable, e.g. a buyer cannot take over the seller's original below-market rate mortgage. If your income is fixed or rises slowly, you're generally better off with a fixed-rate mortgage, although some people don't qualify because their income is too low.

With a variable-rate mortgage the interest rate is adjusted over the life of the mortgage, although the monthly repayments usually remain the same. If there are large fluctuations in interest rates, the amount of monthly repayments may change each year. Because it involves greater risk, a variable-rate mortgage is usually available at a lower interest rate than a fixed-rate mortgage. You should choose a mortgage with a ceiling or cap on the rate of interest that can be charged (irrespective of how high the index goes), which can be an annual or 'lifetime' (i.e. over the full period of the mortgage) limit. Wide fluctuations in interest rates can cause 'negative amortisation' (where the balance on the loan increases instead of reduces, despite the fact that you're making maximum monthly payments). Variable-rate mortgages are a good choice for someone who expects his future income to rise sufficiently to offset the possible higher repayments.

When comparing the cost of variable with fixed-rate mortgages, bear in mind that an increase of just 1 per cent in the interest rate increases your repayments and overall debt considerably.

Interest rates vary slightly with the region, but on a typical 30-year fixed-rate mortgage the rate was around 7.35 per cent in 2003. Rates are expected to rise slightly during the rest of the year and then to return to a similar level.

Whatever kind of mortgage you choose, it's sensible to take time to investigate all the options available, taking into account your present and probable future income. Generally the more money you can put down as a deposit, the more choice you have.

When interest rates plunge, as happened in the early 1990s, many borrowers want to refinance their mortgage. This is generally worthwhile only when the interest rate on your mortgage is at least 2 per cent higher than the prevailing market rate, although it also depends on the size of your mortgage. Bear in mind that it can take months to refinance a loan and you must take into account changing interest rates and all associated costs and other payments. Refinancing costs usually range from 4.5 to 5 per cent of your mortgage value.

Getting The Best Deal

The sort of mortgage deal you're able to negotiate depends on a number of factors, not least the state of the housing and money markets. Lenders usually charge a fee for granting a mortgage, expressed as a number of points, each of which is equal to 1 per cent of the loan amount. You can sometimes get a mortgage with no points. Or you can purchase points and lower your interest rates. Points can increase the up-front cost of your mortgage considerably but can lower your long-term costs if you stay in your house for ten years or more.

To attract new customers, lenders may offer inducements such as below-market interest rates (or no interest for the first year), loans of over 30 years, discounts, rebates and gifts ('giveaways'), most of which don't provide real savings or long-term advantages. Always shop around for the best deal you can find (including all costs).

If you're buying a property in Alberta, you may be able to take over (assume) the existing mortgage from the owner without having to go through the usual qualification process. You take on the mortgage payments and pay the vendor the difference between the balance of the mortgage and the sale price, thus saving yourself a great deal of hassle and delay.

You can employ a local mortgage search company, which uses a computerised network to find the best mortgage deal. A similar service is provided by *Canada Mortgage* magazine (available at ▣ www.canmortgage.com) and includes a weekly-updated list of local lenders, with loan rates, points, fees, indexes, margins, caps, commitment periods, 'rate locks' (whereby the interest rate can be fixed for a period) and other vital information to enable you to find the best mortgage deal. Using the services of an independent mortgage broker is another way to find a good mortgage deal.

A number of books are published about mortgages in Canada, including *Canadian Mortgage Payments* by Stephen Solomon, *The Perfect Mortgage* by Alan Silverstein (Stoddart Publishing), *Mortgages and Foreclosure* by David M. Golderberg (Self Counsel Press Inc) and *Home Ownership* published by the CMHC (☎ 1-800-668-2642 or 613-748-2003).

INCOME TAX

If you're resident in Canada (see **Tax Residence** below), you must pay both federal and provincial income tax (see below). Non-residents are taxed at a standard rate of 25 per cent on their Canadian source gross income, e.g. from employment or a business. If there's a double-taxation treaty between Canada and the country where you're resident, this usually prevents you having to pay tax twice on the same income. When you arrive in Canada (or depart from the country) during the tax year, which is the same as the calendar year, you may be taxed as a part-time resident and can claim a pro-rata portion of any tax credits to which you're normally entitled. Treaties also cover short-stay visitors, teachers and professors, employees of foreign governments, trainees, students and apprentices, and also apply to capital gains tax. Information about income tax for non-residents is contained in information circular 77-16, *Non-Resident Income Tax*.

Federal income tax is levied on the world-wide income of Canadian citizens and resident expatriates (known as 'aliens'), and on certain kinds of Canadian income (including deferred profit-sharing plan payments and death benefits) earned by non-resident expatriates.

In addition to Canadian taxes, you may also be liable for taxes in your home country, although citizens of most countries are exempt from paying taxes in their home country when they spend a minimum period abroad, e.g. a year. If you're in doubt about your tax liability in your home country or country of domicile, check with your country's embassy in Canada (see **Appendix A**).

The agency responsible for the administration of federal tax laws and the collection of taxes is the Canada Customs and Revenue Agency (CCRA). Federal income tax was introduced in 1917 as a temporary measure under the Income War Tax Act to finance Canada's participation in World War I. Not surprisingly, the tax wasn't repealed after the war and in 1949 the federal government officially removed 'war' from the act's title and it became the Income Tax Act. The act has been amended many times, most notably in 1972, when the tax base was broadened and a capital gains tax was introduced (see page 306).

All provinces except Quebec levy a provincial income tax (see page 301) through the federal tax programme, which means that you aren't required to file a separate return for provincial income tax. Quebec residents must file separate federal and Quebec income tax returns.

The calculation of an individual's tax is a two-step process. First, your income liable to federal income tax is calculated. You may deduct from this amount whatever personal tax credits are available and a tax credit for dividend income. The result is your 'basic federal tax payable', to which federal surtax is applied (if applicable – see page 300). Provincial income tax (except for Quebec) is then calculated by applying the appropriate provincial rate to the 'basic federal tax payable' for the tax year.

In Canada, your employer usually deducts income tax from your pay, while those with business or property income usually pay their income taxes by instalments throughout the year. The Canadian tax system is based on self-assessment, which requires a less bureaucracy than in many other countries but puts the onus on individuals to declare their income. The Declaration of Taxpayer Rights (printed on the back of the *General Income Tax Guide*) outlines your rights when dealing with The CCRA.

Although The CCRA are usually helpful, they have sweeping powers at their disposal and aren't slow to use them if they suspect somebody of fraud. Tax fraud is a major crime in Canada, where it's estimated to cost as much as $20 billion per year. The CCRA carries out random checks and can demand a full-scale inspection or audit of any taxpayer at any time. The CCRA processes returns, looking for obvious errors and discrepancies, and also runs them through a computer programme to select some for auditing. The selection criteria are a secret, but generally the wealthier you are, the greater your chance of being audited. The 'field audit' is the main tool in the department's audit programme and can take from a few hours to several weeks, depending on the nature of the examination and/or the size and complexity of the taxpayer's income (the process is described in publication IC71-14R3, *The Tax Audit*). If you're selected for an audit, you can have professional representation at an interview or have someone represent you in your absence.

If you're found to owe additional tax, you must pay interest from the date payment was due, although when a CCRA error was responsible for a delay you may be entitled to a reduction in the interest. The CCRA attempts to resolve tax disputes through an administrative appeals system. If you disagree with your tax bill after an audit of your tax return, you're entitled to an independent review of your case, although you should start the process with the appeals officer at your local tax office. The CCRA recommends that you keep all tax documents for at least six years after filing a return.

Reducing your tax burden is both a national sport and an obsession in Canada, where a wealth of tax books, magazines and free advice in financial magazines and newspapers is published, particularly during the few months before April 30th (tax filing day). The best-selling tax guides include *Price Waterhouse Personal Tax Strategy, Keys to Saving Money on Income Taxes* by Warren Boroson (Barron's Educational Series), *Complete Canadian Home Business Guide To Taxes* by Evelyn Jacks (McGraw-Hill Ryerson) and *Grant Thorton Tax Tips.* Cheaper magazine-style guides include *How to Reduce the Tax You Pay* and *Preparing Your Income Tax Returns.* All tax guides (and computer programmes) are updated annually (the cost **isn't** tax deductible!).

The CCRA publishes numerous free publications on a range of subjects, including a *General Income Tax Guide, Newcomers To Canada, Taxpayer Rights, Telefile – Filing Your Return by Telephone, General Income Tax and Benefits* and *Non-Residents and Temporary Residents of Canada.* You can order CCRA publications and tax forms direct from the CCRA (☎ 1-800-959-2221, 🖳 www.ccra.adrc.gc.ca).

During the last two decades there have been several sharp increases in income taxes, most notably by almost 30 per cent in 1988, when all personal exemptions and many deductions were changed to 'non-refundable tax credits' (see **Credits & Deductions** on page 301).

Tax Residence

The Canadian Income Taxes Act doesn't define income tax residence, but anyone who resides in Canada for 183 days or more in a year is considered a resident and is taxed on their world-wide income for the full year. Tax residence isn't dependent on your status as a citizen or immigrant or on your domicile, but may be determined on 'residential ties'. For example, you're considered to be tax resident if any of the following applies:

- Your spouse and children live in Canada and you habitually visit them;
- You maintain a purchased or rented property which is used by you and your family when you visit Canada;
- You have other property such as a car or furniture that remain in Canada;
- You have 'social ties' such as a Canadian driving licence, bank account, credit cards or health insurance with a Canadian province.

If you're in doubt about your residence status, you should complete tax form NR74, *Determination of Residency Status (Entering Canada)*, or contact the international tax office (☎ 1-800-267-5177 or 613-952-3741). Information is also contained in a *Newcomers to Canada* pamphlet available from local tax offices or the international tax office. Additional information about tax residence is contained in bulletin IT-221, *Determination of an Individual's Residence Status*, available from the Canada Customs and Revenue Agency, Client Services Directorate, 400 Cumberland Street, Ottawa ON K1A 0L8.

Federal Income Tax

Canada has four rates of federal income tax: 16, 22, 26 and 29 per cent. Although these may seem low compared with other industrial nations, provincial income tax of between around 40 and 70 per cent of these rates must be added (see below), bringing the top rate of income tax to almost 50 per cent of income in some provinces. Federal tax rates in spring 2003 were as follows:

Income Band	Tax Rate (%)
Up to $31,677	16
$31,678 – $63,354	22
$63,355 – $103,000	26
Over $103,000	29

Since 1986, a 3 per cent 'general surtax' (a 'tax on tax') has been applied to federal taxes when necessary to help reduce budget deficits. However, as there's currently little or no deficit, the surtax has recently been waived for individuals with incomes below $50,000 and reduced to 2 per cent for those in the $50,000 to $65,000 income bracket.

Quebec residents receive a federal tax reduction of 16.5 per cent.

Provincial Income Tax

Provincial income tax rates are calculated as percentages of your basic federal tax payable and not of your income, and they vary considerably from province to province: from around 43 per cent in Ontario to around 69 per cent in Newfoundland. With the exception of Quebec, where federal and provincial taxes are collected separately, these two taxes are collected together by The CCRA. Residents of other provinces who spend part of the year working in Quebec must file a separate Quebec tax return to cover that period. In Quebec, provincial tax is quoted as a percentage of income (e.g. 16 to 23 per cent).

Provincial income tax is calculated using the forms provided. If you live in British Columbia, Manitoba, Nova Scotia or Ontario, you must use form T1C-TC; in all other provinces (except Quebec) you use form T1C.

Where the federal government provides tax credits for items such as tuition fees, Quebec allows these expenses to be deducted from provincial tax. Quebec also levies a provincial surtax of 5 per cent on the amount of provincial tax that exceeds $5,000 and a further 5 per cent surtax on the amount of provincial tax that exceeds $10,000.

Limited provincial foreign tax credit relief is also provided.

Credits & Deductions

Deductions are used to reduce taxable income, while non-refundable credits are used to reduce the amount of tax payable. This means that, although you can use credits to reduce or eliminate federal tax, any unused portion isn't refunded. Credits are calculated by multiplying eligible amounts by 16 per cent (the same as the lowest personal tax rate).

There are a few deductions allowed when calculating your employment income. These include employee contributions to a registered pension plan (up to a certain maximum), travelling and certain other expenses of commissioned salesmen, certain travelling expenses of other employees, and union or professional fees. Interest may be claimed as a deduction in the year that it's paid provided that the money was borrowed for the purpose of earning income. Other carrying costs such as investment counselling fees and accounting costs are deductible. Personal interest such as the interest on mortgages or charge accounts isn't deductible.

Other deductions include contributions to RRSPs, certain child care expenses, moving expenses for relocation within Canada and maintenance (alimony) payments. Capital gains (see page 306) are generally included in gross income at a rate of 75 per cent (this applies to individuals, estates and trusts, but not to corporations).

If you move home within Canada to start a job or business or as a student, you may be able to deduct your moving expenses. However, students can only deduct the expenses incurred to move to Canada from abroad if they're attending a full-time course at a college, university or other institution providing post-secondary education and have received a scholarship, bursary, fellowship or research grant to attend that institution. Information is provided in *Claim for Moving Expenses* (form T1-M).

If you make maintenance or other support payments, you may be able to deduct the amount paid, even if your former spouse doesn't live in Canada. Details are provided in an *Alimony or Maintenance* pamphlet available from tax offices. **You must withhold tax on maintenance paid or credited to a non-resident of Canada, unless stated otherwise in a tax treaty.**

An individual is allowed to deduct a number of 'personal tax credits'. These include a 'basic personal credit' of $7,634, a 'spousal credit' (depending on your spouse's income), a disabled dependant's credit, an age credit, a disability credit, education and tuition fee credits, and child care credits. There are no joint allowances or married couples' allowances. However, for some tax deductions and credits, a family's income is combined to determine their entitlement.

Canada/Quebec Pension Plan contributions and employment insurance contributions are also eligible as credits. Charitable donations (up to 75 per cent of net income) are eligible for a tax credit of 17 per cent on the first $200 and 29 per cent above this amount. The unused portion of the donation credit can be carried forward for up to five years. Similarly, medical expenses in excess of the lesser of $1,728 or 3 per cent of net income are eligible for a tax credit of 17 per cent. An individual is also eligible for a tax credit of up to $160 on the first $1,000 of qualifying pension income.

If you have children under 18 years of age, you may be eligible for monthly child tax benefit payments and, if you live in British Columbia, Alberta or New Brunswick, you may be entitled to provincial payments. For information, obtain a copy of the pamphlet, *Your Child Tax Benefit*, from your local tax office. To apply for the child tax benefit you must complete a *Canada Child Tax Benefit Application* (form RC66) as soon as possible after you arrive in Canada or when a child is born or begins to live with you.

Income from a self-employed business or property is similar to that for a corporation, business income generally being computed on the accrual basis of accounting (whereby income is reported when earned and expenses when incurred) as opposed to the cash basis (which reports income when received and expenses when paid). Interest and other charges that were incurred to acquire business assets or investment property can usually be deducted, although there are limitations on the deduction of vehicle and home office expenses. Deductions for business meals and entertainment expenses are limited to 50 per cent of expenditure.

Tax Return

Individuals resident in Canada (unless exempt) must file a tax return for the previous tax year (January 1st to December 31st) by April 30th, when main post offices remain open until midnight to date stamp tax returns (if you owe tax and are a day late filing, you're charged interest). Individuals aren't permitted to establish a different tax year end, although corporations are. Corporations must file annual tax returns, although individuals need to file only if they owe taxes or if they're eligible to claim tax credits such as the child tax credit or a sales tax credit (see **Sales Taxes** on page 358). There are no joint tax returns for married couples and families.

If the CCRA doesn't send you the necessary forms and information automatically, they're available from tax service offices, Government of Canada Infocenters and post offices throughout the country. The standard set of forms is called a 'general income tax package'. There's a 'simplified tax package' for those who don't require the full package, such as pensioners, employees (see below) and others with straightforward tax situations, and people who have no income to declare or tax to pay but want to claim child tax benefit or other entitlements. You must use the tax package for the province or territory where you resided on December 31st of the relevant tax year.

If you were a non-resident and earned income from employment in a particular province or territory in Canada, you should use the package for that province or territory.

Employees with no income other than their wages have their income tax withheld (deducted) from their salary by their employer, who pays it to the CCRA. Employers must provide employees with a T4 form by the end of February, which details their total salary in the previous year and the amount of tax withheld (plus other withheld items such as Canada Pension Plan or employment insurance contributions). You must copy these figures onto your tax return. Self-employed people or those who receive over 25 per cent of their income from sources other than a wage or salary (e.g. investments or rents) must complete an additional 'business and professional income statement' and pay tax on their income every three months, on 15th March, June, September and December.

The CCRA identifies you by your Social Insurance Number (SIN), which you must enter on your tax return and use in any correspondence. It's important that you quote this number correctly, as the CCRA uses it to update your record of earnings for your contributions to the Canada Pension Plan (CPP) or the Quebec Pension Plan (QPP). Your SIN is also used to determine your eligibility for child tax benefit and goods and services tax (GST) credit. Even if you have no income to report or tax to pay, you may be eligible for a GST credit or other provincial or territorial tax credits, but you must file an income tax return to apply for these credits. You also need to give your SIN to anyone who prepares a tax information slip (such as a T3, T4, T5 or T600 slip) for you. If you fail to provide your SIN, your return is sent back to you with the omission highlighted.

However you choose to file your return, you should start by gathering all the documents required to complete it correctly. You can also employ an accountant or another professional to complete your tax return, in which case you should make sure that you provide him with all the relevant documents. The best way to find a qualified professional is through a recommendation from a friend, relative or business associate (they're also listed in yellow pages). As with all professional services, the size of the fee is determined by the complexity of your return and the number of forms prepared, but the average person with an uncomplicated tax situation usually pays between $50 and $100. The most appropriate professional isn't necessarily the least expensive one but the one who best meets your tax requirements. You should be wary of using anyone other than a reputable company or professional to complete your return, as anyone can set themselves up as a tax 'expert' in Canada. **Whoever you choose, most tax consultants are incapable of completing totally error-free returns.** You can authorise a representative to obtain information on your tax matters by completing an individual consent form (T1013).

Some accountants and tax advisers (preparers) offer a facility called Efile that allows you to file your tax return electronically. The CCRA is in favour of this, as it improves accuracy, reduces costs and facilitates the processing of returns and payments (including refunds). Even if you prepare your own return, you can take it to an Efile service provider to submit it electronically. For more information see the Efile Association of Canada's website (🖳 www.efile.ca). If you have a home or office computer, you may prefer to complete your own tax return using a programme (the cost of which isn't tax deductible) such as Timeworks' *Easy Tax* or *Turbotax* (the top seller), Intuit Canada's *QuickTax*, Softkey's *HomeTax*, CanTax's *CanTax T1* or *GriffTax* from Colin Griffiths & Associates. Tax programmes are designed for people who already know something about taxes or who are willing to learn.

The CCRA operates a system of volunteers during the tax filing season to assist taxpayers with preparing federal and provincial tax returns. Some 15,000 volunteers across the country attend training sessions at local tax offices and assist over 270,000 people with their returns. Income tax returns, schedules, guides, supplementary guides, pamphlets and other common documents are available in large print, Braille, and on audio cassette and computer disks that can be used with voice synthesisers. Other publications can be provided on cassette or disk on request (☎ 1-800-267-1267). For clients who are deaf or hard of hearing or who have a speech impairment, a 'teletypewriter' (TTY) service is available (☎ 1-800-665-0354). The CCRA also maintains an automated telephone system called TIPS, which provides general and personal tax information (instructions for using TIPS are contained in your income tax package). TIPS is accessed by calling ☎ 1-800-267-6999 and is available in English and French.

If you're filing a paper return, you must submit all original documents, receipts and T4 slips, but make sure that you keep a copy. Your return, guide explanations and the forms and schedules themselves tell you when to attach other supporting documents such as certificates, forms, schedules or official receipts. If you're using Efile, you must include your Efile service provider on all your supporting documents. It's important to ensure that all your paperwork and supporting documentation is in order when filing your return; if you make a claim without the required documentation, it may be disallowed or could delay the processing of your return. Even if you don't need to attach certain supporting documents to your return, or you're using Efile, you must retain them in case your return is reviewed.

Make sure that you file the return on time even if slips or receipts are missing. If you know that you won't be able to get a slip by the due date, attach a note stating which slips are missing, the payer's name and address and what you're doing to obtain the slips.

Generally, you should keep your supporting documents and a copy of your return, the related notice of assessment and any notice of reassessment for six years. These also help you complete your return for the following year.

No extensions beyond the filing date of 30th April are given and you must file your tax return on time or pay a penalty. Penalties start at a minimum of 5 per cent of the tax due, plus another 1 per cent for each month you're late. If you cannot pay the full amount due by April 30th, send in as much as you can and file your tax form on time anyway (the CCRA will contact you to arrange a payment schedule). However, the penalty may be waived if you file your return late due to circumstances beyond your control (if this is the case, include a letter with your return stating why it has been filed late).

Failure to report an amount on your return may also result in a penalty and if you do this more than once within a four-year period, you may have to pay another penalty. Information is provided in *Guidelines for the Cancellation and Waiver of Interest and Penalties* (Circular 92-2).

If you discover that you've made a mistake after filing your return (particularly one which will result in a refund!) or a mistake on a return made in the previous three years, you can file an *Amended Income Tax Return* (form T1-ADJ) for each year you're changing.

PROPERTY TAX

Property tax is levied annually on property owners in all provinces to help pay for local services such as health care, primary and secondary education, police and fire services, libraries, public transport, waste disposal, highways and road safety, maintaining trading standards, and social services. Tax rates are fixed by communities and are expressed as an amount per $100 or $1,000 (the 'millage' rate) of the assessed value of a property. For example, if your home is valued at $100,000 and your local tax rate is $15 per $1,000 value, your annual property tax bill will be $1,500.

The rating method varies considerably with the province, county and municipality and there may be hundreds of different rates within a single province (e.g. in 2003 British Columbia had 1,400 tax rates in its 70 jurisdictions). Property taxes on a house of average value vary from zero in areas where houses valued below a certain amount are exempt to over $5,000 per year in high value communities. In a recent survey, taxes were highest in Winnipeg, Regina and Montreal, averaging over 2 per cent of a home's market value, and lowest in Saint John (New Brunswick) and Vancouver at less than 1 per cent.

Middle-income families have been particularly hard hit by increases in property taxes in recent years. In some provinces, a portion of property tax is reimbursed to senior citizens and blind and disabled people with low incomes.

One way to reduce your property tax is to appeal against your property value assessment, which may cut your local tax bill by as much as 10 per cent. Check your property record card at your local assessor's office. If you find that your assessment is based on incorrect or incomplete information, ask the assessor for a review. Tax appeal deadlines vary with the province or city. If you appeal against your property value, be prepared to back it up with some convincing evidence, e.g. lower assessments on many similar properties and incorrect details, particularly wrong property and land dimensions. If necessary, hire a professional appraiser. **The assessor and tax board are permitted a margin for error, which may be as much as 15 per cent!**

There are many books designed to help you reduce your property taxes, including *Challenge Your Taxes: Homeowners Guide to Reducing Property Taxes* by Jim Lumley (John Wiley & Sons Canada Ltd.) and *How To Reduce Your Property Tax: A Comprehensive Guide to Property Taxes in the US and Canada* by Frank J Adler (Harper Collins Canada).

Taxes are usually assessed annually on January 1st, but in many provinces you receive the bill at the end of June, requiring you to pay six months in arrears and six months in advance. However, many provinces are converting to a monthly payment system.

CAPITAL GAINS TAX

Capital gains tax (CGT) in Canada is applicable whenever you sell or otherwise dispose of (e.g. lease, exchange or lose) an asset, i.e. when:

- you give assets other than cash as a gift;
- shares or other securities in your name are converted or cancelled;
- you settle or cancel a debt owed to you;
- you transfer certain assets to a trust;
- your assets are stolen, destroyed or expropriated;
- an option that you hold to buy or sell goods expires;
- you change all or part of an asset's use;
- you leave Canada.

Changes to the Tax Act (1971) excluded a principal residence from capital gains tax and there's a general capital gains tax exemption, which is currently under review but may be up to a lifetime limit of $500,000 for certain assets. As there was no CGT before 1972, special rules apply if you dispose of an asset owned since before that year.

The maximum capital gains tax rate is 39 per cent. There are exceptions for certain types of property received by a surviving spouse. The taxable portion of capital gains and the deductible portion of capital losses are each 50 per cent. Net capital losses may be carried back three years and carried forward indefinitely but may be applied only against taxable capital gains.

Subject to tax treaty statutes, non-residents must pay CGT on capital gains arising on the disposition of taxable Canadian property. This includes land situated in Canada, shares in Canadian private corporations, shares in Canadian public corporations in certain circumstances, property used in a business carried on by a non-resident in Canada, an interest in a partnership in which over 50 per cent of the assets consist of taxable Canadian property, and interests in certain trusts resident in Canada. For dispositions occurring after April 26th 1995, taxable Canadian property has included the shares of a non-resident corporation or an interest in a non-resident trust, if more than 50 per cent of the value of the corporation or trust is derived from Canadian property.

For more information on CGT, consult Canada Customs and Revenue's website (🖥 www.ccra-adrc.gc.ca).

INHERITANCE & GIFT TAX

Canada has no estate, inheritance, gift or succession taxes. On death there's a deemed disposition of assets (see **Wills** below) and tax must be paid by the estate on capital gains that arise as a result of those dispositions (see **Capital Gains Tax** above).

WILLS

It's an unfortunate fact of life, but you're unable to take your worldly goods with you when you take your final bow (even if you plan to come back in a later life). Therefore it's preferable to leave them to someone or something you love than leave them to the CCRA or leave a mess which everyone will fight over (unless that's your intention!). A surprising number of people in Canada die intestate, i.e. without making a will, meaning that their estates are distributed according to local provincial law rather than as they may have wished. The biggest problem with leaving no will is often the delay in the winding up of an estate (while perhaps searching for a will), which can cause considerable hardship and distress at an already stressful time.

If you don't have a will, most provinces in Canada divide your estate according to an established formula. Typically, two-thirds of your estate goes to your spouse and the remainder is divided between your children. When someone dies, the estate's assets cannot be touched until probate (the official proving of a will) has been granted. Couples who aren't married are considered in most provinces to be married if they've cohabited for a certain period, which can be as little as six months.

With a little forethought, you can sidestep probate for some assets. If, for example, you name a beneficiary for your life insurance, RRSPs and RRIFs, they can be paid out in the event of your death without a will. Other assets, such as bank accounts, stocks and property, may be owned jointly with right of survivorship, which means that they pass to the surviving partner automatically. In the case of a surviving spouse, the transfer won't be taxed (see **Inheritance & Gift Tax** above); in all other cases it will be treated by the CCRA as a sale of assets and there may be income tax or capital gains tax to pay.

You may wish to calculate the approximate tax liability in advance and buy sufficient 'first-to-die' term life insurance to cover it (although specific bequests of personal property should be detailed in a will). If you own a business, estate planning becomes more complicated and may require the creation of a trust or a separate will. Consult your lawyer and accountant. You can also minimize taxes by transferring property to your heirs, particularly if you haven't used up your capital gains tax exemption (see **Capital Gains Tax** on page 306). If you intend to make gifts to grandchildren, you should be aware that interest and dividends earned on financial gifts made to children under 18 who are close relatives are attributed to the donor and taxed accordingly. However, any capital gains tax is payable by the beneficiary.

All adults should make a will, irrespective of the value of their assets. If your circumstances change dramatically, e.g. you get married, you must make a new will, as marriage automatically revokes any existing wills. Husbands and wives should make separate wills. Similarly, if you separate or are divorced, you should consider making a new will, but make sure that you have only one valid will. You should check your will every few years to make sure that it still fits your wishes and circumstances. **A change of province may necessitate changing your will to comply with (or take advantage of) local law.**

Once you've accepted that you're mortal, you will find that making a will isn't a complicated or lengthy process. You can draw up your own will (which is better than none), although it's recommended to obtain legal advice from an experienced estate planning and probate lawyer. The fee for a straightforward will is around $200 for an individual and $300 for a couple.

Many provinces provide fill-in-the-blanks will forms costing around $5 that are designed for parents or married couples with modest estates. They help you to leave your estate to your children or spouse, allow you to give money to one other person or charity, and usually allow you to name a guardian and an executor. You normally need two witnesses (to your signature, not the contents of the will) who cannot be either a beneficiary or your spouse, although some provinces allow 'self-proved' handwritten wills. There are a number of books about wills and probate available, including *The Complete Idiots Guide to Wills and Estates for Canadians* by Edward Olkovich and Steve Maple (Prentice Hall) and more detailed guides for various provinces published by Self Counsel Press Inc.

If you're a foreign national and don't want your estate to be subject to Canadian law, you may be eligible to have your will interpreted under the law of another country. In this case, you should employ a lawyer who's conversant with the law of both countries. If you don't specify in your will that the law of another country applies to your estate, Canadian law applies.

Your bank or lawyer usually acts as the executor of your will, but you should ideally visit a few banks and lawyers and compare fees. These may vary considerably according to the size of your estate but all tend to include a percentage of your total estate plus hourly charges. **It's best to make your beneficiaries the executors, who can then instruct a lawyer after your death if they require legal assistance.** Note that wills become part of the public record after probate.

Keep a copy of your will in a safe place (e.g. a bank) and another copy with your solicitor or the executors of your estate. You should keep information regarding bank accounts and insurance policies with your will(s), but don't forget to tell someone where they are!

COST OF LIVING

No doubt you would like to know how far your Canadian dollars will stretch and how much money (if any) you will have left after paying your bills. Canadians enjoy one of the highest standards of living in the world, although it has been fairly stagnant for many people in the last decade or so and inflation is currently running at around 1 per cent. However, there are some 6 million Canadians (around 20 per cent of the population) who live below the official 'poverty' level (which, in the interest of political correctness, is now called the Low Income Cutoff). This varies considerably between provinces and cities; for example, in Vancouver in 2003 the Cutoff was $30,411 for a family of four.

The cost of living in Canada varies considerably according to where and how you live. It's difficult to calculate an average cost of living, even for those living in the same city, as it depends very much on each individual's circumstances and lifestyle. Your food bill will generally be less than in most European countries: around $300 should be sufficient to feed two adults for a month in most areas (excluding alcohol, fillet steak and caviar). Apart from the cost of accommodation, goods and services, you should also take into account the level of local taxes (income, property and sales taxes) and the cost of education.

The most expensive item for most people is their rent or mortgage payments, which can be astronomical in some cities. For example, in major cities such as Toronto and Vancouver the rent for a small one or two-bedroom apartment may be $750 or more per month, while in most rural areas you can rent a three-bedroom house for around $750 to $800 per month (a mortgage on the same property is likely to cost around $1,000 per month). However, even in the most expensive areas the cost of living needn't be astronomical (apart from rents). If you shop wisely, compare prices and services before buying, and don't live too extravagantly, you may be pleasantly surprised at how little you can live on.

15.

LEISURE

Canada is a vast country (the second-largest in the world), stretching some 5,000mi (almost 8,000km) from the Atlantic to the Pacific, and is famous for its immense natural beauty. It encompasses some of the most dramatic landscapes in the world, from the majesty of the Rockies to the frozen splendour of the Arctic, interspersed with a profusion of huge lakes, raging rivers, dense forests and endless plains and prairies. It's a nature and sports lovers' paradise, offering some of the best skiing, fishing, boating, hunting, flying, hiking and climbing (to name but a few activities) in the world. Getting away from it all isn't difficult in Canada, which has areas of wilderness bigger than most countries!

Canada also has some of North America's great cities, boasting the dramatic setting of Vancouver, the grandeur of Toronto, the French-Canadian chic of Montreal and Quebec City, and the tranquillity of the capital Ottawa. Canada provides something for everyone and, not surprisingly, is one of the top ten tourist destinations in the world, attracting millions of visitors per year.

Canadians believe in working and playing hard and make the most of their free time, spending around 10 per cent of their disposable income on recreation. Although admission to major attractions can be expensive, free entertainment is provided in many cities during the summer and winter, including theatrical performances, classical, military and popular music, opera, dance, puppet shows, mime, jugglers and comedians.

Although mass culture, such as films, TV and popular music, reaps the bulk of receipts, so-called 'high culture' such as classical music, ballet, opera, museums and art also flourishes. Most Canadians live within a reasonable distance of one of the major cities, where there are numerous theatres, art galleries, museums and other cultural centres. Annual spending on entertainment and performances is around $500 per household, with almost 10 million theatre tickets sold annually, over 1 million for the opera, 1.5 million for dance performances and 3.5 million for concert performances. The Canada Council for the Arts spends millions of dollars per year supporting the arts, although in the last decade there has been a gradual shift from the literary arts of book and poetry writing to the performing arts, which now receive some two-thirds of funds. Nevertheless, tickets for the theatre, opera, orchestral concerts and even comedy shows in Canada aren't cheap (often between $60 and $110). Montreal is generally the most expensive, while Calgary and Edmonton are the least expensive. Canada is populated by peoples from a multitude of cultures, backgrounds and heritages, which is reflected in the diversity and boundless energy displayed in the arts.

Canadians don't let the long, harsh winters put a stop to their fun, and most cities stage winter festivals that may include dog-sled races, events celebrating the fur-trappers and early explorers, ice-skating, ice-sculpture and almost anything else you can think of connected with snow and ice (plus of course a wide range of winter sports). The Winter Carnival in Quebec City has been described as 'New Orleans' Mardi Gras on ice', with sculptures, parades, a canoe race across the frozen St Lawrence river, an ice hotel (see 🖥 www.icehotel.canada.com for further details) and copious quantities of a local drink called Caribou (a mixture of whiskey and red wine). Other major events include a Winterlude festival in Ottawa held over several weekends in February, a Festival of Lights in Niagara, Montreal and Vancouver, a First Nations Storytelling Festival in mid-January in Saskatchewan, and events celebrating the return of the sun in January in the Northwest Territories after a month of total darkness.

Open-air events at other times of year include a Tulip Festival held in May in Quebec, including concerts, parades and a flotilla on the canal, with floral sculptures, floral tapestries and garden displays. Vancouver hosts a four-day (or rather night) firework festival called the Symphony of Fire at the end of July, and there's a similar event in Toronto in August.

Tickets for virtually every important event (theatre, music, sport, etc.) can be purchased through national chains of ticket agencies such as Ticketmaster. Reduced price tickets are often available for local events on the day of performances. The 'Arts and Leisure' section of local newspapers and local arts and entertainment newspapers and magazines (often free) carry information about current and forthcoming shows, ticket prices and availability. Information about local events and entertainment is also available from tourist offices, libraries and town halls. Entertainment newspapers and magazines are published in all major cities, including *Toronto Life* magazine, *Taxi Vancouver* and *The Georgia Strait* (Vancouver), *AfterHour* (Montreal) *Jam!*, *Cameo*, and *IT Magazine*. All major newspapers provide entertainment news and many have weekly guides on Fridays, e.g. the *Globe & Mail* 'Weekend' sections.

Montreal, Toronto and Vancouver have large gay and lesbian communities with clubs, bars, support groups, specialised bookshops, newspapers and magazines, including *Xtra* (Toronto), *Fugues* (Montreal), *Wayves* (Halifax), *Xtra West* (Vancouver) and *Capital Xtra* (Ottawa). Toronto and Vancouver have Gay Pride days with parades and other celebrations that attract large crowds. In the major cities the traditional Halloween fancy-dress parties have been adopted by the gay community, who hold famously wild parties at their night-clubs.

The main purpose of this chapter (and indeed the whole book) is to provide information that **isn't** usually found in other books. General tourist information is available in dozens of Canadian travel books that cover the whole country or concentrate on a particular city or region. Among the best general travel guides are *Let's Go: Canada*, *Lonely Planet Canada*, *Rough Guide Canada* and *Fodor's Canada* (see **Appendix B** for a list). For information about sports facilities see **Chapter 16**.

TOURIST INFORMATION

Tourist information is generally handled at provincial or territorial level, although the Canadian Tourism Commission (CTC), 55 Metcalfe Street, Suite 600, Ottawa, Ontario K1P 6L5 promotes Canada internationally and provides general information. Contact CTC for a *Rediscover Canada Guide* (☎ 1-877-822-6232) containing general information about travel, accommodation, festivals, special events, etc. and to obtain general information on any tourism-related subject (☎ 613-946-1000, 🖳 www.canadatourism.com).

There's at least one provincial tourist office in each province, usually in the capital city, and others at major tourist attractions. Offices have toll-free phone numbers, listed in the blue section of the local yellow pages under 'Tourism' or 'Travel' (with the exception of Alberta and Northwest Territories, where numbers are listed under 'Economic development and tourism').

Tourist offices provide a wealth of free information, including maps, campsite and accommodation guides, and information about local attractions and special events scheduled for the coming year. Most provincial offices provide specialised information relating to particular events or sports, but they don't generally keep much information about any given area, for which you need to contact the nearest city tourist office.

City and town tourist and information offices have a plethora of local information on every conceivable subject, both within their borders and in the surrounding area, all of which they will post to you on request. Brochures for many attractions are also distributed via hotels, campsites and other accommodation centres, public offices, libraries and many other outlets. Travel agents, both within Canada and abroad, can also provide details about many attractions, events and tours, as can offices of Air Canada.

PARKS

Canada has 39 national parks and is in the process of creating more in the far north after agreements with the indigenous peoples. It has been suggested that national parks be franchised to private businesses, but to date they're run by the federal Canadian Heritage Ministry. Most national parks provide a range of facilities including campsites (campground), canoe and boat hire, and hiking trails. Some parks charge for entry (some offer multi-entry permits), while others are free for day use but charge for camping. Where applicable, you can expect to pay a fee of around $5 per person or $10 per car. Canada also has hundreds of provincial parks (over 300 in British Columbia alone).

The high season is July and August, when parking queues (lines) are interminable. The most popular parks are overcrowded from May to October, when bookings for campsites and other accommodation are essential. It's best to avoid the most popular parks in summer and to visit them in spring or autumn (fall), when many are also at their most beautiful. Many parks provide educational talks, guided tours and hikes, and other organised activities. Park superintendents and staff can tell you anything you wish to know about a park, including its history, flora and fauna, ecology and geology. Many parks have a visitor centre providing free information and often staging exhibitions, films and slide presentations, and many guide books are available covering the whole park system or individual parks.

For information about national parks contact Parks Canada, Publications Unit, 25 Eddy Street, Hull, Quebec K1A 0M5 (☎ 888-773-8888, ▭ www.parks canada.gc.ca). Parks Canada also maintains many historic parks featuring historic sites and buildings, many of which have special programmes of events in summer. There are also a number of excellent books available, including *National Parks of Canada* by Kevin P. McNamee and *National Parks of North America: Canada, United States, Mexico* (National Geographic Society).

Most cities have extensive park areas that are welcome retreats from the surrounding noise; the most famous is Stanley Park (1,000 acres/400ha) in Vancouver. Most major cities also have botanical gardens, where entrance is often free, and many have zoos or bird sanctuaries. Entrance fees and opening times vary with the time of year, so check in advance.

Wildlife

Canada has a rich wildlife that includes various species of bear, beaver, buffalo (bison), over 500 species of bird, a plethora of fish, including the famous Atlantic and Pacific salmon, whales, wolves, coyote, deer, moose, elk, caribou, rocky mountain goats, lynx, cougars, skunks, porcupines, raccoons and chipmunks. Many of Canada's animals are dangerous, including the seemingly-cute raccoon, which sometimes carries rabies, the normally placid moose, which charges at humans if scared, and, of course, bears.

Although there are relatively few bear attacks in Canada, they're widely reported and, if you're a victim, you're likely to be seriously injured and may even be killed. Canada has four types of bear: black, brown, grizzly and polar. All are very large and dangerous when provoked. They aren't, as many people think, slow and lumbering, although they're slow to get up speed, and are expert (and fast) tree climbers (apart from grizzlies). Bears don't just inhabit remote regions (one recent fatal attack took place in a car park in Banff) and, if you're likely to be visiting an area inhabited by bears, you should take precautions and heed the warnings! When camping, you should keep your food in an air-tight container and store it a good distance from your camp (preferably up a tree to deter other animals such as raccoons). Some campsites have bear-proof wooden cupboards where campers can store their food.

There are a number of books designed to help you survive a 'walk on the wild side', including *Wilderness Survival* by Gregory J. Davenport and *Planning a Wilderness Trip in Canada and Alaska* by Keith Morton.

The biggest and most dangerous of all bears are the majestic polar bears, which may look cuddly in a zoo but are the mightiest predators on earth (the largest males weigh up to 1,500kg/3,300lb). They live in the Arctic and sub-Arctic regions and, if you want to see them in the wild, one of the best places is Churchill (Manitoba) on the edge of Hudson Bay. Here bear-watching from huge tundra buggies is a popular pastime and the bears come right up to the buggies to inspect their occupants. The bears migrate past Churchill in October and November and earlier in the year (from June to August) white beluga whales feed in the Bay (they're also a favourite prey of polar bears).

You can join a whale-watching boat trip from many places along the Canadian coast, where the sights off the Atlantic coast include blue, finback, humpback, beluga and sometimes minke and right whales. In the Pacific,

Californian grey whales reach Vancouver Island on their annual migration north in March and April, returning south in September and October. Orcas (or 'killer whales') can be seen in the Inside Passage between Vancouver Island and the mainland. The cheapest way to see them (and other whales) is to take the regular ferry from Vancouver to South Alaska (a 15-hour trip), which costs around $100 instead of the thousands of dollars charged for a whale-watching cruise.

CAMPING & CARAVANNING

Canada has over 4,000 caravan (trailer) and chalet parks and campsites (campgrounds), both public and private. Camping in Canada encompasses everything from backpackers sleeping rough or with a 'pup' tent to those touring in a luxury mobile home or 'recreational vehicle' (RV). Facilities at privately-owned campsites range from non-existent (sometimes not even water) to luxury cabins and cottages. All provinces with a shoreline provide seafront campsites, ranging from bare stretches of beach to luxury developments with all modern conveniences. Campsites have strict rules regarding noise (e.g. none between 11pm and 7am), alcohol (only on your site) and dogs (which must be on leads and mustn't foul the site).

A campsite usually has a fireplace (with free wood), picnic table and parking space, with toilets and running water available nearby. Higher-priced sites have caravan and RV 'hook-ups' for electricity, water and cable TV. Campsites usually have 'dumping stations' (for waste), flush or dry toilets, a children's area, a recreation room, restaurants and snack bars and laundry facilities and they sometimes also have hot showers and camp shops, although you shouldn't rely on these being provided. Campsites often provide sports facilities, which may include tennis, shuffleboard, volleyball, swimming, fishing, canoeing and boating. Many national and provincial parks have sporting campsites for hunters and fishermen, lodgings consisting of cabins or a central lodge with sleeping cabins (meals may be included). A float-plane (sea-plane) is necessary to reach some areas and a guide service is usually available.

For many Canadians, camping means using an RV or motor home or a caravan, rather than a tent. RVs equipped for a family of four can be rented throughout Canada from $600 to $900 per week. You're usually prohibited from parking a motor home or caravan overnight on a public road. Tent campers are advised to avoid RV-oriented campsites, which may offer superior facilities but are plagued by noise and vehicle fumes. To RV 'campers', getting back to nature means taking all the modern conveniences of home with you, and few stray further than a few hundred feet from their vehicles.

Most national and provincial parks permit camping. You should try to arrive by 5pm or earlier (at the most popular parks queuing all night for a space isn't unheard of). Many parks close their gates to visitors at 11pm and don't reopen them until 6am. Some sites display a 'No Vacancy' sign all summer, so ask about vacancies. The peak season runs from mid-May to the end of September at the most popular parks, many of which have a one or two-week limit on stays during the summer. You should book as far in advance as possible, particularly for holiday weekends. In addition to camping facilities, many parks maintain a number of cabins and lodges that can be rented year-round and reserved six months to a year in advance. Many national parks provide wilderness camping in designated areas and have special facilities for RVs. All campsites have minimum age limits and many won't issue permits to anyone under 18.

Campsites vary considerably, as do their fees, which usually range from $15 to $20 per night in national parks to $40 per night in privately-owned sites, depending on the popularity, season, facilities, location, tent size and the number sharing (group rates are usually available). A new trend in Canada's campsites is to charge according to the classification (size) of your RV and not by the person.

The American and Canadian Automobile Associations (AAA and CAA) provide an abundance of camping information for their members and produce *Kampgrounds of America (KOA)*, a guide to the KOA network of private campsites(over 60 in Canada). These offer hook-ups for RVs at around $25 per night and 'kamping kabins' (log cabins for four to six people) for around $35 per night. Although more expensive than many others, KOA campsites generally provide the best facilities, including showers, electricity, flush toilets and phones, and often have swimming pools, launderettes and shops. A KOA directory (USA and Canada) is available for US$3 from KOA, PO Box 30558, Billings, Montana 59114-0558, USA (☎ 406-248-7444, 💻 www.koakamp grounds.com).

An excellent review of camping in Canada and useful information is available on the Internet (💻 www.myvacationguide.com), while camping enthusiasts may also be interested in *Camping Life* magazine, Magazania.com, 3700 S Westport Avenue, 1290 Sioux Falls, SD 57106 USA, published four times per year, in February, April, June and August. One of the best Canadian camping guides is *Woodall's Camping Guide Canada*.

AMUSEMENT PARKS

Canada is a great country for the young (and young at heart) and many leisure facilities are geared to children. Among the most popular amusement parks are the roller-coaster parks, which have a cult following among Canadians. There's even an organisation called Coaster Enthusiasts of Canada (💻 http://cec.che butco.org). One of the country's biggest amusement parks is Paramount's Canada's Wonderland (💻 www.canadas-wonderland.com), owned by the film company Paramount, which is a 30-minute drive from the centre of Toronto on Highway 400. In addition to the obligatory roller-coaster that lands in a pool of water, it has a climbing wall (harness mandatory!), a James Bond simulator and over 180 other attractions. At most amusement parks daily tickets (allowing unlimited rides) cost around $40 per day for adults, $20 for children over three (usually free for under threes) and adults over 60. You can buy a season ticket for around $80 for an individual or $250 for a family of four, and there are special rates for groups of 25 or more, offering a discount of up to 60 per cent.

MUSEUMS & ART GALLERIES

Canadian cities and towns have a wide variety of museums and art galleries, including works by a number of excellent Canadian artists. The so-called 'group of seven' artists led by Tom Thompson (the others are Franklin Carmichael, A. J. Casson, Lawren Harris, A. Y. Jackson, Arthur Lismer, J. E. H. Macdonald and Frederick Varley) are famous for their paintings of the eastern Canadian lakelands. Over 2,000 of their works, as well as many by Inuit and north-west coast native artists, can be seen at the McMichael Canadian Collection at Kleinburg near Toronto. Other famous Canadian artists include Emily Carr, who painted the west coast (particularly the villages of the Haida Indians with their totems and the surrounding forest) and Paul Kane.

Native Indian art includes some paintings and prints, but the majority, and the best, consists of carvings of animals, birds, fish, and native figures. Inuit carvers use bone, ivory (often from walruses), antlers and soapstone. A group of soapstone musk oxen standing in a defensive circle with the calves in the middle, displayed at Calgary airport is in the 'once seen, never forgotten' category. The Winnipeg Art Gallery houses the world's largest collection of Inuit art, although there's also an extensive collection at the Inuit Gallery of Eskimo Art in Toronto.

There are also many bizarre museums, including a shoes museum, a theatre museum of 'the unusual, the absurd and the ridiculous' and the History of Contraception Museum, which houses such fascinating exhibits as a recipe for an oral contraceptive consisting of dried beaver's testicle brewed in strong alcohol.

Many Canadian museums are refreshingly modern and stimulating, particularly those offering hands-on exhibits, such as the Science Centres in major cities. These bear little resemblance to the traditional image of rows of glass cases full of stuffed animals and dusty static exhibits. Most museums are well designed and sometimes the buildings housing museums and galleries are as artistically or historically important as the collections themselves.

In many cities (and shopping malls) there are also commercial (contemporary) galleries, which are often well worth a visit even if you have no intention of buying. Many rural museums are operated by local historical societies and private interests, and they often preserve local history or long-defunct local industries.

The opening hours of museums and galleries vary considerably. Many close on Mondays and open in the early evening one day per week, e.g. until 9pm, when admission may be free or fees reduced. Entrance to some galleries and museums is free at all times. Admission fees, when charged, can vary from $2 to $15 for adults, with discounts for children and senior citizens. There may be an extra fee for special exhibitions. Some museums offer free entry to students on certain days or evenings and most have student discounts. Many museums and galleries provide reductions for the disabled and some have special access or provide wheelchairs.

CINEMA

Although cinemas (movie theaters) face increasing competition from TV, videos and DVDs, the movie industry is thriving in Canada, particularly in the major cities, where millions of tickets are sold each year. Vancouver is often referred to as 'Hollywood North', as many major films and TV series are filmed there, and Toronto hosts an annual film festival in September that some claim is better than Cannes. Each year, over 250 films from over 50 countries are screened in around 20 cinemas, and tickets are available from Bell Infoline (☎ 416-968-3456).

Among the many world-famous Canadian film stars (past and present) are Dan Ackroyd, John Candy, Jim Carrey, Michael J. Fox, Lorne Greene, Mike Myers (Austin Powers), Mary Pickford, Christopher Plummer, William Shatner and Donald Sutherland.

Nevertheless, Canadian-made films account for just 5 per cent of the fare in Canadian cinemas, most of which show the latest American blockbusters. Every large city, however, has a 'review' theatre, where 'classic' films, foreign (subtitled) and the really obscure releases are screened. In Ottawa, the Bytown and Mayfair theatres publish a monthly newsletter available from newsstands. In cities such as Toronto and Vancouver, where there are large ethnic populations, some cinemas specialise in Chinese and Indian films. Outside the major cities, however, it's difficult to find cinemas showing 'serious', classic, art (avant-garde), experimental or foreign-language films.

Surprisingly, films made by Canadians about Canada are easier to find outside the country than inside it, despite the best efforts of the National Film Board of Canada (NFBC), which releases a set of dramatic, animated or documentary films each year. The NFBC has offices in most major Canadian cities, where films are shown regularly and videos can be purchased. Outside the major cities it's difficult to find anything other than the latest blockbusters, and many cinemas are under threat of closure.

There are large multi-screen (e.g. 12 to 18) cinemas in most Canadian cities. Cineplex Odeon has spawned an entity known as the 'Collosus' (sic), which is housed in a round building containing shops, fast food outlets and video arcades as well as cinema screens. Cineplex's main competitor is Famous Players, whose box-shaped buildings are enormous and whose high-priced concession foods may tempt you to bring your own refreshments.

Drive-in cinemas, once popular throughout southern Canada, are rapidly disappearing; in the late 1960s there were over 250 but there are now fewer than 80. At a drive-in cinema you pay at the entrance and drive to a parking place, where you clip a small loudspeaker to your car window and watch the action on a gigantic screen. Obviously, drive-in cinemas operate only when it's dark and often in the summer only (they aren't popular when it's raining or snowing, except with couples who don't plan to watch the movie). One of the advantages is that you can smoke at drive-in movies!

A seat for a typical 'first-run' movie costs $8.50, with discounts for children and senior citizens. Cinemas occasionally have cross-promotional (sponsorship) days with a charity, when, if you bring a donation of non-perishable foods, admission is either reduced or free. Cinemas also frequently run promotional features in conjunction with local radio stations and, if you listen carefully you're almost assured of a free pass.

All films on general release in Canada are given a rating under the Motion Picture Code of Self-Regulation, as follows:

Classification	Restrictions
G (general)	None
PG (parental guidance)	Some material may be inappropriate for children
PG-13	Some material may be inappropriate for children under 13
R (restricted)	Children under 18 require an accompanying parent or adult guardian

Children (or adults) who look younger than their years may be asked for proof of their age, e.g. a school or student card, social insurance card or driving licence, for admittance to showings of restricted films.

THEATRE

Theatre in Canada is alive and well with thriving professional and amateur theatre companies in the cities and also in many smaller towns. Stratford Ontario is home to a world-renowned Shakespearean company and hosts a summer festival each year (most of which consists of works by Shakespeare). Amateur dramatic companies also thrive throughout the country. Much of the theatre in Quebec, particularly in Montreal, is in French. Toronto is the world's third-largest centre for English-language theatre (after New York and London); over 6 million people have seen Phantom of the Opera there since it opened in 1989!

However, tickets for the theatre aren't cheap (often between $60 and $110). Toronto's restored period theatre, Pantages, in the heart of the theatre district (Yonge Street) charges $115 per ticket or even more for popular shows such as Phantom of the Opera. In Ottawa, the National Arts Centre is partly subsidised and consequently less expensive, e.g. it costs from around $25 to see a ballet. In Canadian theatres (as in older cinemas) the 'orchestra' refers to the front seats, while the upper stalls (dress circle) are called the balcony or mezzanine.

Tickets can be purchased through Ticketmaster ticket agencies or direct from box offices, either by phone or in person. Most people book tickets by phone and pay by credit card through 24-hour phone/charge card agencies, which usually add $2.50 per ticket for their services. Tickets ordered by credit card can be collected from the theatre box office on production of your card. Tickets can also be purchased by writing directly to theatres, when you should apply well in advance and give at least two possible dates. Often certain dates are reserved for charity or other special evenings. Discounted tickets are also available through various clubs and organisations.

Check performance times with the box office or in a newspaper or entertainment magazine. If you're late for a performance, you may need to wait until the interval before being permitted to take your seat, although it may be possible to watch the show on a monitor. There are usually daily evening performances from Mondays to Saturdays and matinee performances (2 or 3pm) on Wednesdays, Saturdays and Sundays. Matinee (and preview) tickets are usually slightly cheaper than evening tickets. Like cinemas, theatres occasionally have cross-promotional (sponsorship) days with a charity, when, if you bring a donation of non-perishable foods, admission is either reduced or free.

Most theatres have a number of spaces for wheelchairs, induction loops for the hard of hearing and toilets (restrooms) for wheelchair users (mention when booking). Some theatres produce Braille programmes and brochures and most allow entry to guide dogs (seeing-eye dogs) for the blind. Most theatres, both city and regional, have restaurants and bars, and some have their own car parks.

There's also an abundance of free street theatre in the major cities, including a ten-day International Busker Festival in Halifax (Nova Scotia) in August that attracts street performers from all over the world. 'Fringe' theatre festivals are new to Canada and are typically held in smaller communities (suburbs or smaller towns) where 'new' performers try to attract attention from show-business bosses. These are often run alongside a town's annual commemorative events.

Many communities boast their own amateur theatre groups, known as 'community theatre', which perform classic plays, ballet and even opera. Community theatre is usually of a high standard. In fact some Canadian amateur theatre companies, whether drama, comedy or musical, would put professional repertory companies to shame in some countries. However, if you're a budding Brad Pitt or Julia Roberts, don't let the high standards deter you. Community theatre companies are usually on the lookout for new talent and people to assist in other areas such as costumes, lighting and stage scenery.

MUSIC & BALLET

Canada has a dynamic and varied music scene. Although they're often assumed to be American, Bryan Adams, Céline Dion, K. D. Lang, Gordon Lightfoot, Sarah Mclachlan, Leonard Cohen, Joni Mitchell and Anne Murray are just a few Canadian singers who have enjoyed world-wide fame. Contemporary popular music artists include Rush, Tragically Hip, Bare Naked Ladies, Shania Twain and Alannis Morissette. In the Atlantic provinces there's a tradition of Celtic-based music, top bands including the Barra MacNeils, the Rankin Family and the Irish Descendants. There's also a record label called First Nations that specialises in native Canadian music.

Canadians are particularly fond of jazz and Montreal hosts a world-famous jazz festival in summer, when many musicians perform in the streets and plazas for free. In fact some of the best musical entertainment in Canada is provided free by street musicians (buskers) and free concerts are staged in the major cities. Street music caters for all tastes, including jazz, rock, folk, blues, country and classical. The club and bar music scene thrives in Canadian cities, where most clubs have a cover charge but few are restricted to members only.

Tickets for rock concerts are available from agencies such as Ticketmaster and from local music shops. The best sources of information about forthcoming concerts are music newspapers and magazines such as the *Georgia Strait* (Vancouver) and *Now* (Toronto). Local newspapers also list forthcoming concerts and music festivals, and free music newspapers and magazines are published in some cities. There are also several Internet music magazines such as *ACCESS Online*, *Chart Magazine* and *RhiG Magazine*. Information about local concerts is also available from tourist offices.

Classical music concerts and opera and ballet performances are major social events in Canada and are regularly staged by the cream of Canadian and international musicians. Concerts generally have a strong following in most cities and performances are of a high (often international) standard. The main Canadian orchestras are the internationally-renowned Montreal Symphony Orchestra, the National Arts Centre Orchestra, based in Ottawa, and the Symphony Orchestras of Ottawa, Toronto and Vancouver. Many smaller towns and cities also have orchestras, including Kanata and Nepean. The leading opera companies are the Canadian Opera Company (based at the O'Keefe Centre in Toronto), the Vancouver Opera Association and *L'Opéra de Montréal*. Canada has three internationally-renowned ballet companies: the Royal Winnipeg Ballet, *Les Grand Ballets Canadiens* and the National Ballet of Canada (also based at the O'Keefe Centre in Toronto), plus the *Ballet Classique de Montréal*. Major international ballet companies perform regularly in Canada, including Moscow's Bolshoi and Kirov companies, London's Royal Ballet and the Paris Opera Ballet.

Tickets for classical music, opera and ballet performances in most cities cost from $60 to $110, although when international stars are performing you can expect to pay much more. Major Canadian orchestras may hold a winter season at their local concert hall and, when not touring, an open-air summer season. All orchestras (and ballet and opera companies) offer season or series tickets, which for many music lovers is the only way to obtain tickets. Enquire early about tickets for the coming season. Forthcoming concerts are listed in music and entertainment magazines, and local newspapers contain performance details and reviews. Information can also be obtained from tourist offices.

SOCIAL CLUBS

There are numerous 'social' clubs in Canada (as used here, the term refers to any group of people who get together to share an interest), and all Canadian cities and towns have a wide range of clubs. Joining a club is an excellent way to meet new people, make social and business contacts and be accepted into the local community. In smaller towns, social life revolves around the church and social clubs, and if you aren't a member your life can be dull. In the major cities, there are exclusive private clubs where the 'old boy' network thrives, such as the Chelsea club in Ottawa. There are also posh country clubs, although these are usually golf or tennis clubs rather than strictly social clubs.

Popular and widespread clubs and organisations include the Royal Canadian Legion, Masons, Shriners, YWCA/YMCA, Kiwanis (who hold an annual charity fund-raising 'duck' race on Ottawa's Rideau Canal), Lion and Lioness, Toastmasters, Oddfellows, the Canadian Federation of University Women and Big Brothers/Sisters (a charitable organisation that pairs adults with young children whose parents have died or divorced). There are also a number of fraternal associations and professional organisations, many of which are ethnic, political or labour-oriented groups with a large membership and extensive facilities available to their members.

Canada also has a range of children's groups and clubs such as the Girl Guides (including the Sparks, Brownies and Pathfinders) and the Boy Scouts (including the Beavers and Cubs).

NIGHT-LIFE

The best night-life in Canada is, not surprisingly, found in the major cities and embraces everything from ritzy clubs with expensive floor shows to sleazy back street bars and strip joints. The most popular forms of night-life include music bars, discos and dance clubs. The most popular discos, with amazing sound and light systems, charge an entrance fee of around $8 and as much as they can get away with for drinks ($4 for a soft drink isn't uncommon and for cocktails the sky's the limit). Most night clubs have bouncers on the door, whose job is to 'approve' guests and remove anyone who causes trouble from the premises.

Dress codes vary considerably with the venue. If you're unsure, smart casual is best (black is safest). Jeans, leather, T-shirts and trainers are usually **excluded**, although in some establishments may be the perfect gear (fashion dictates). If you don't look the part, you may be excluded or may feel uncomfortable when everyone else is wearing something different, so it's best to check in advance. An up-to-date guide giving a run-down of local hot-spots is a must if you want to be seen in the best places and avoid the dives. Always check who's playing, show times and cover charges, as they often change at short notice. Consult local newspapers and entertainment guides for the latest information.

GAMBLING

The old 'kill-joy' attitude introduced to Canada by Presbyterian Scottish immigrants has taken a long time to die out, and it's only since the early 1990s that gambling of any sort has become accepted (which isn't to say that it didn't exist before then). Now Canadians and visitors can (legally) visit casinos without having to cross the border to the US, but some of the old attitudes still linger, particularly when it comes to dress codes. Some casinos merely suggest that appropriate dress is 'smart casual', while others produce a list stating 'no blue jeans, jogging outfits, cut-offs, shorts or beachwear' and one even proclaims 'no bustiers or clothing associated with organisations known to be violent' (whatever that means!). Many casinos don't allow alcohol in gambling areas and all exclude anyone under the age of 18.

The most popular forms of gambling are the games red dog, roulette, stud poker, baccarat and blackjack, and the ubiquitous slot machines. If you wish to leave with your shirt, books such as *The Everything Casino Book* by George Mandos (Media Corp. Publications), *The Idiot's Guide to Gambling like a Pro* by Stanford Wong & Susan Spector (Alpha Books), and the *Unofficial Guide to Casino Gambling* by Basil Neston (Macmillian USA) may help (as will a large slice of luck).

All of Canada's provinces and territories run their own lotteries (there's no national lottery) each week called 'Lotto 649' – so called because you need to select six numbers out of 49 – and Lotto Super 7 (Fridays). To participate you simply complete an entry form at a lottery kiosk in a shopping mall or convenience store. Tickets are $1 each and must be purchased by 5pm on the day of the draw (which is at 6.49pm on Wednesdays and Saturdays in each province). You can also choose a 'quick pick' option whereby a computer selects the numbers for you. Prizes vary according to the number of tickets sold, but jackpots of $5 to $20 million aren't uncommon. Instant lotteries are also popular, where you buy a 'scratch' card for $1, $2 or $5 and can win prizes of $10,000 to $50,000.

Another popular form of gambling is the Video Lottery Terminal (VLT), a machine similar to a 'one-armed bandit' but more lucrative (usually not for the player), as it's possible to pump as much as five to ten thousand dollars into a VLT in just half an hour! They're located at racetracks, in public halls, bars, Legion clubs and convenience stores (making losing your money more convenient). The proceeds of VLT machines go directly to the provincial government (otherwise they would be banned).

Canada has both ordinary horse racing and trotting (saddle and harness horse racing) and most cities have at least one track, although very few are open in winter. All legal horse race betting is based on the totaliser (tote) system, where the total amount bet on a race is divided among the winners (after the organisers and Canada Customs and Revenue Agency have taken their cuts). Bets of between $1 and $1,000 can be made. The different kinds of bets are explained in the official programme, as is the form of the horses and riders. Generally bets are the same as in other countries, although the terminology may be different. Bets can be made for a win (or 'on the nose'), a place (to come second) and to show (to come third). An 'across the board' bet is a bet on a horse to win or be placed second or third. In the major cities, illegal bookies who take bets on horses and many other things (particularly professional sports) are widespread.

BARS

Social drinking in Canada is usually done in bars, which include cocktail bars, singles bars, music bars, piano bars, hotel lounge bars, 'artistic' bars, business bars, ethnic bars, gay bars, neighbourhood bars, working men's bars and endless other varieties. At the bottom end of the scale are dingy, mainly men's bars, with a noisy, beer-drinking, working-class clientele, while at the other extreme are expensive cocktail bars inhabited by executives and professionals having a quiet drink after a day at the office. There are also British and Irish-style pubs with a variety of imported British and Irish beers and traditional pub games such as darts or pool, and their interpretation of 'traditional pub grub' such as shepherd's pie or Irish stew. Many bars serve excellent lunches and snacks, and most serve some kind of food (expect to pay between $5 and $10 for a platter-sized serving). A new trend in cities is 'sports' bars, with numerous TVs showing an array of live sporting events.

Those who want a quiet chat over a drink, perhaps at lunch time or after work, are likely to go to a cocktail lounge. Similar to European wine bars in decor and clientele, they're the main venue for middle-class social drinkers, particularly in large cities. Singles bars are cocktail bars where customers pay high prices (e.g. $5 for a beer) for the privilege of chatting up the opposite (or same) sex. At their best they can be good fun, although many are simply 'meat markets' where casual pick-ups are common. Many bars are noisy places (often with live music) where people go for an expensive night out to drink, listen to music or dance. Bars with live music usually have a cover charge of around $3 to $12. There are topless bars in some areas (these **aren't** bars without roofs).

Other bars cater particularly to homosexuals and lesbians, so check in advance if this isn't your scene (some 'straight' bars also have gay evenings on certain days of the week). To find a gay club or bar, look for 'alternative lifestyle' advertisements in local newspapers and in the yellow pages. In Ottawa, there's a weekly newspaper called *X-Press* that contains the most comprehensive listings of what's on for people of all persuasions. Toronto's Queen Street (that's its real name!) is an acknowledged area for transvestites and gays to assemble. Like Americans, Canadians aren't usually homophobic (at least in the major cities), and Ottawa, Toronto and Vancouver all stage a Gay Pride week sanctioned by the local city councils, including a parade and exhibitions of artwork by the local gay community.

Although better than American beer, Canadian beer is fairly weak (around 5 per cent by volume) unless you ask for an 'ice' beer (with a higher alcohol level) or an extra-strong beer such as Molson's XXX, which packs 7.3 per cent alcohol by volume (Canadians say the XXX means "three beers and you're outta here!"). All beer (not just 'ice' beer) is usually served ice cold – much colder than most foreigners (except Americans and Australians) are used to. The best-known Canadian brewers are Molson, Labatt's and Carling-O'Keefe, although the tastiest beers often come from small local breweries ('microbreweries') and 'brewpubs' (where beer is brewed on the premises). Among the most popular beers are Molson's Canadian, Golden, Oktoberfest, Export, Dry and Ice, and Labatt's Blue, Extra and Dry. In Quebec and the Atlantic provinces, locals drink non-alcoholic spruce beer, although the taste takes some getting used to. Draught beer (or beer 'on tap') is sold by the glass in bars and restaurants for $2 to $2.25 for a 340ml glass (just over half a pint). When in groups, Canadians tend to buy their own drinks rather than rounds.

Like many laws in Canada, licensing hours vary with the province, but most bars, pubs and lounges open at noon and close at 1 or 2am. Laws in Quebec are more liberal, allowing bars to stay open until 3 or 4am. Large cities usually have after-hours bars that stay open for music and dancing but stop serving alcohol.

The minimum age for drinking alcohol in Alberta, Manitoba and Quebec is 18, while in the rest of Canada it's 19. The barkeeper is supposed to ask your age and may ask for identification (ID), but in practice this rarely happens if you look old enough. Acceptable identification usually consists of a driving licence or a provincial 'identification card', which you can obtain from your local motor licence office. Some city bars run 'designated driver schemes', whereby the designated driver of a group of people gets free non-alcoholic drinks all night (drinking and driving is a serious offence throughout Canada – see page 230).

Generally, there's a much stricter attitude towards drunkenness in Canada than in many other countries and, if you look as if you've had one too many, you're likely to be refused service and may even be 'asked to leave'. Business drinking is modest and disciplined and drunken behaviour is socially unacceptable and regarded with contempt (and can also get you arrested or mugged if you aren't careful).

RESTAURANTS

While the backwoods areas of Canada tend to be served only by 'family' diners (where you may be lucky to get steak and chips and little else), pizza parlours and other fast-food chains, the major cities contain a wealth of restaurants and other eating places. In fact, the ethnic potpourri that is Canada is most evident in the range and variety of its eating establishments, the most common of which include Chinese (most regional styles), Italian (plus pizza parlours), Japanese (particularly sushi bars), Jewish, Korean, Mexican (or Tex-Mex), Thai and Vietnamese. For example, Vancouver and Toronto have many Chinese and other Asian restaurants, and Quebec has many excellent 'French' restaurants and bistros. In Vancouver and Victoria, the trend (as well as reflecting the tastes of the many recent Asian immigrants) is to follow the current fads from California, whether Italian, Korean or 'fusion' cooking (a bit of everything mixed together). Canada's ethnic restaurants are one of the joys of eating out and they do more to promote international goodwill and cross-cultural exchange in a day than the United Nations does in a year.

The most 'interesting' dining experiences are most likely to be found in the Atlantic provinces, where Newfoundland prides itself on such bizarre dishes as cod cheeks, capelin (tiny fish which have been pickled and smoked before being pinned to fences to dry), brewis (soaked hard-tack biscuit boiled with cod), seal flipper pie, seal soup, and moose and rabbit pie. However, the Atlantic provinces also offer some of the best seafood in North America, including superb lobster in New Brunswick, scallops in Nova Scotia and mussels on Prince Edward Island. British Columbia is famous for its salmon, where the annual barbecues of Pacific sockeye salmon hot-smoked over alder wood mustn't be missed.

Other eating places include cafeterias, diners, truck-stops, cafes, delicatessens ('delis'), snack bars, lunch counters, take-outs, coffee shops and street vendors. Canadian eating places are listed in the yellow pages by specialty or national cuisine and often also by area. Whatever your preference or price range, you will find something to your taste and pocket in Canadian cities.

Local restaurant guides are available in most cities, and most travel guides provide recommendations at all price levels. Local free newspapers and entertainment guides in cities and towns are packed with advertisements for local eating places and bars, many providing coupons and other discounts. Your Canadian friends, colleagues, neighbours and acquaintances will usually also be glad to recommend their favourite places (and tell you what to avoid).

LIBRARIES

Canada is proud of its excellent public library service and there are libraries in all cities and most towns. In cities, most libraries open from 10am to 9pm during the week and 10am to 8pm on Saturdays and many also open on Sunday afternoons (e.g. 1 to 5pm), although they may shut on Mondays. In addition to books, newspapers and magazines, libraries usually offer books on tape, videos, large print books and books in Braille.

Membership is free for local residents. The standard loan period is three weeks and there are fines for overdue items (usually around 30¢ per day). Books in the 'reference' section may be used on-site only, although some encyclopaedias can be borrowed (but usually for one day only). University libraries are also open to the public, although non-students allowed to take books home. Inter-library loans are a common practice, although you may have to pay a small surcharge depending upon the distance involved.

All libraries have various sections, including children's, juvenile, fiction, paperbacks (soft covers) and foreign books. Public libraries in major cities have business sections and sometimes there are separate business libraries.

Local libraries are also one of the best sources of free information about local community services and information (e.g. housing, consumer rights, money problems, voluntary work and job search skills), public transport, clubs and organisations. Many libraries have children's centres and activities such as story-telling, films, workshops and exhibitions; some publish a monthly schedule of events for children. Most reference libraries provide coin-operated photocopiers (some central libraries have colour laser copiers) and many provide telephones and fax facilities (or machines that accept credit cards) and free Internet access.

16.

SPORTS

Sport is very popular in Canada, where people take their sport seriously, both as participants and as spectators. Over half of all Canadians participate regularly in some form of physical activity and those who don't play are usually keen spectators – if only on TV. The top spectator sports (including TV audiences) are ice hockey, baseball, football and basketball, while the most popular participant sports include swimming, hiking, cycling and running. Other popular sports are lacrosse, skiing, aerial sports, boxing, golf, fishing, motor racing, softball, tennis, bowling, athletics, and watersports such as sailing and boating. Working out is popular in Canada, where many people go to gyms or have equipment at home.

The cost of using private sports facilities is high in major cities such as Toronto and Vancouver, but generally inexpensive in smaller towns. Most communities have recreational parks (ball parks) with tennis courts, a running track and a swimming pool, which may be free to local residents. Many towns also have an inexpensive YMCA sports centre with a swimming pool, gymnasium, training centre, tennis and squash/racquetball courts, basketball and volleyball. Courses and coaching are provided in a wide range of sports. Many community schools and municipal recreation departments organise a variety of sports classes and most large corporations have indoor gymnasiums and sports teams. For those who can afford the high membership fees, there are exclusive country clubs and health and fitness centres in all areas, catering mainly for basketball, golf, handball, racquetball, squash, swimming, tennis and volleyball. Most clubs provide professional coaching and training programmes.

Canada is proud of its athletes and the federal government Sports Canada scheme supports around 1,000 top athletes through the Athlete Assistance Programme. Sports Canada also spends over $20m per year supporting around 40 national sports organisations, from athletics to yachting. Many professional athletes are paid huge amounts, particularly in top sports such as ice hockey, baseball and football, where star players earn astronomical salaries. Most of the country's highest paid athletes are US-born, however, and there are some professional teams with only one or two Canadians.

The big games of the year are the Grey Cup for the Canadian Football League (CFL) at around the same time as Canadian Thanksgiving, the Stanley Cup for the National Hockey League (NHL) at the end of May or early in June, and baseball's World Series, which Canadians are proud to tell you was won in 1992 and 1993 by the Toronto Blue Jays. The NHL Super Bowl is also huge in Canada, being celebrated there with as much fervour as in the US. The major TV networks compete vigorously for the TV rights to top sporting events and professional sport is dominated by TV, although the frequency of commercial breaks makes watching most TV sport a frustrating experience.

Tickets for top events in many cities can be purchased through ticket agencies such as Ticketmaster but are generally best purchased at the venue. Ticket prices for a hockey game are usually around $35, although you can pay around $120 for a seat in a box, which comes with wider seating and waiters to bring you refreshments. In recent years a number of new vast stadiums have opened, including the Air Canada Centre in Toronto, which replaced the Maple Leaf Gardens, and Ottawa's Corel Centre. You can obtain the latest sports results by phone from the 'talking yellow pages' (the number is listed on the inside cover of yellow pages).

Gymnasiums & Health Clubs

There are gymnasiums (gyms) and health and fitness clubs in most towns in Canada that are often combined with sports or racquet clubs (e.g. tennis and squash). In addition to fully-equipped gymnasiums, health clubs may also offer swimming pools, jogging tracks, and aerobics and keep-fit classes. Most health clubs are mixed, with a variety of membership levels depending on the facilities you wish to use, e.g. gym and exercise rooms only or gym plus squash or tennis. Most health and fitness clubs have facilities such as saunas, solariums, Jacuzzis, steam baths, whirlpools and massage, and many have a childcare service.

Some health and sports clubs operate a number of centres, e.g. city-wide or in a number of cities, and members can usually use the facilities at any centre. The cost of membership at a private club varies considerably with the area, the facilities provided and the local competition (some offer reduced rates for couples or family membership).

Clubs are usually open seven days a week from around 6am until 9 or 10pm Mondays to Fridays and usually have shorter opening hours on Saturdays and Sundays (when some clubs are closed). All clubs provide a free trial and assessment and produce personal training programmes.

Many top class hotels have health clubs and swimming pools that may be open to the public (although access may be restricted to residents at certain times). Fitness classes are organised by local community schools, and some municipal swimming pools have gymnasiums and exercise facilities that can be used free of charge by local residents.

AERIAL SPORTS

Aerial ('sky') sports aren't as popular in Canada as they are in the US, although there are clubs for flying light aircraft, gliding, microlighting, hang-gliding, paragliding, para-sailing and ballooning in all the major cities and also in many smaller towns. Parachute jumping and sky diving are also popular, as is hot-air ballooning, although a one-hour ride in a two-man balloon costs around $250. Balloons are launched either early in the morning or just before sundown, when the winds are at their lightest. One of the largest annual balloon events in Canada is held in September in the Gatineau Hills north of Ottawa. This is a three-day festival and attracts balloonists from around the world, who come to show off their paces and their amazing balloons, which may include a 150ft rabbit in a magician's hat, a bunch of carrots, a brown bear, an eagle, tropical fish, the yellow pages directory, a castle, pink elephants, a T-Rex, the Statue of Liberty and a Mountie on a horse!

BASEBALL

Although predominantly a US sport, baseball is also played in Canada, which has two teams in the US major leagues: the Montréal Expos (National League) and the Toronto Blue Jays (American League), who won the World Series Championship in 1992 and 1993. The season runs from April to early October, games often being played under floodlights. In October the top two teams in the American and National leagues compete against each other in the 'play-offs' to decide who will contest the World Series (established in 1903), played over seven games. Both 'big' Canadian teams have their own enormous stadiums, the Olympic Stadium in Montreal and the Skydome in Toronto, although the Expos are experiencing financial difficulties and are looking for another stadium. It's easier to get tickets for the Expos (☎ 1-800-GO-EXPOS) than for the Blue Jays (☎ 416-341-1234).

There are also minor league teams throughout Canada, including the Calgary Cannons (☎ 403-284-1111), the Edmonton Trappers (☎ 780-451-8000) and the Vancouver Canadiens (☎ 604-872-5232), who play in the Pacific Coast League.

A baseball field is laid out as a diamond, with a base at each corner. Each team of nine players takes it in turn to bat while the other team fields. One player bats, striking at the ball with a hard wooden bat, then scores runs by dashing from base to base while the fielders try to get him out by catching the ball before it touches the ground or by throwing the ball to a base before the batter reaches it. The man who throws the ball (from a raised 'pitcher's mound' in the centre of the diamond) is called the pitcher, and the man who stands behind the batter in the hope of catching the ball if he misses it (wearing a vast leather mitt and protective clothing) is called the catcher.

Obviously the game is much more complicated than outlined above, with a scoring system that builds during the season with batting and run averages leading to much discussion among fans. It usually takes foreigners some time to understand baseball (about ten years). It has a language all of its own, with many terms that have found their way into everyday Canadian (and American) speech, the most common of which is to 'strike out', i.e. to fail. Other terms include walk, bull pen, curve ball, shut-out, no-hitter, perfect game, chopper, foul out, and many more. For those seeking more information, there are numerous baseball books in libraries and bookstores. However, watching a baseball game is an interesting day out, even if you haven't a clue what's going on. Crowds are vastly entertaining and fans are usually friendly and sociable.

Games usually last two to three hours and are normally played in the evening. Ticket prices have risen in recent years and now start at around $25, with some tickets available on the day of the game; 'bleacher' seats (in the sun and farthest away from the field) are the cheapest. When you buy a ticket for a baseball game that's 'called' (postponed), e.g. due to a 'rainout', you're entitled to a free ticket for another game (the origin of the term 'rain cheque').

As with ice hockey (see page 339), there are also many 'farm' teams. College, high school and little league baseball (played by children from the age of seven to their teens) are also hugely popular. Like professional teams, minor league teams are sponsored by companies who pay to have their name emblazoned on the players' jerseys. It costs around $100 to equip a child to play baseball, most of it going on a baseball glove (from around $50).

CANADIAN FOOTBALL

Canadian football is virtually the same as American football, the main differences being that the field is slightly larger (328 by 153ft/100 by 46.6m as opposed to 300 by 120ft/91.4 by 36.6m) and there are 12 instead of 11 players. There are only three 'downs' instead of the American four and there are other differences in the permitted movements of players and the times allowed between plays, all of which help to produce a faster and higher-scoring game, with ties often decided by last-minute efforts or even in overtime. In recent years American football has gained popularity in Europe, where TV has brought the game to a wider international audience, while Canadian football has been struggling for media and spectator support. Although Canadian football is played in America, it hasn't expanded as hoped. If anything, its popularity is falling due to several franchise failures, and in 1997 one of the most popular Canadian teams, the Ottawa Rough Riders, was forced to close its doors.

The Canadian Football League (CFL) is divided into two divisions, the West (BC Lions, Calgary Stampeders, Edmonton Eskimos, Saskatchewan Roughriders and Winnipeg Blue Bombers) and the East (Hamilton Tiger-Cats, Montréal Alouettes, Ottawa Renegades and Toronto Argonauts). Some teams are owned by communities and others privately. The culmination of the football season is the Grey Cup, which is televised nationally and attracts one of the biggest TV audiences of the year. The student equivalent is the Vanier Cup, administered by the Canadian Intercollegiate Athletic Union and contested by student teams organised into four leagues across the country.

Foreigners brought up on a diet of soccer or rugby may initially find Canadian football complicated, slow and boring. However, once you learn the rules and strategy (like chess, with feints to throw your opponents off guard), you will probably find it a fascinating and exciting sport. Despite the heavy protective clothing, serious injuries are common, most caused by the widespread use of artificial turf, which has replaced safer natural grass in many stadiums. The heavy physical exchanges rarely dissolve into violence and the behaviour of players is usually exemplary. Tickets for games cost between $25 and $65.

For more information contact the Canadian Football League, 50 Wellington Street East, Third Floor, Toronto ON M5E 1C8 (☎ 416-322-9650, 🖥 www.cfl.ca). If you don't know the difference between a touchdown and a field goal you may wish to read *The Complete Idiot's Guide to Understanding Football like a Pro* by Joe Theismann with Brian Tracy (Alpha Books).

CLIMBING

Those who find hiking a bit tame may like to try abseiling (rappelling), rock-climbing, mountaineering or caving (spelunking). Although experienced high-altitude mountaineers may not find Canada's mountains sufficiently demanding, they offer plenty of challenges for less experienced climbers. If you're a novice, it's wise to attend a course at a mountaineering or mountain school before heading for the hills. There are climbing schools in all the main climbing areas, providing basic to advanced ice, snow and rock climbing courses lasting from a day to several weeks. Most clubs have indoor training apparatus (e.g. a climbing wall) for aspiring mountaineers. They allow you to climb in bad weather, practise existing skills and learn new techniques.

Many climbers are killed each year in Canada, Mount Robson in British Columbia claiming the most deaths. Most victims are inexperienced and reckless and many more climbers owe their survival to rescuers who risk their own lives to rescue them. **It's extremely foolish, not to mention highly dangerous, to venture off into the hills (or caves) without an experienced guide, proper preparation, excellent physical condition, sufficient training and the appropriate equipment.** See also **Hiking** on page 337.

CYCLING

Cycling has enjoyed a surge in popularity in recent years due to the interest in health and exercise and the opening of cycle tracks (bike paths) in the major cities. Canadian bicycling is seasonal and the length of the cycling season varies with the location. Many Canadian cyclists use mudguards (fenders) to get through rain showers but the first snowfall shuts down the cycling season. Only some 2 per cent of Canadian adults use bicycles for transport and most cycling is done for enjoyment, exercise and competition, rather than as a means of getting from A to B. Competitive cycling includes road and track racing, cycle speedway, time-trials, cross-country racing, touring, bicycle polo, mountain bike racing, downhill racing and bicycle moto-cross (BMX) for children. The Tour du Canada is an annual ride across the country, as well as the name of Canada's premier cycling club (see below), which is supposedly restricted to those who have taken part in or intend to take part in the Tour. Bicycle touring is popular, and many couples take to the road on tandems.

Most of the large Canadian cities aren't particularly bicycle-friendly, as the road network is dedicated to the automobile as in the US, although federal and provincial governments are trying to encourage cycling and there are programmes similar to the US 'bike path' and 'bike lane' programmes. However, most cities have a network of outlying bicycle paths where you can enjoy cycling without risking your life. Outside the cities, there's plenty of good cross-country cycling with lots of open roads, although when cycling on narrow roads you should beware of lorries and particularly motor homes, which are often driven by older and less skilled drivers.

Around 40 per cent of Canadians own a bicycle and some 1.5 million are purchased every year. Mountain bikes are the sales leader, followed by 'hybrid' and city bikes and racing (road) bikes. There are three Canadian bicycle manufacturers: Raleigh, Victoria Precision and Procycle (made under licence from Peugeot); high-priced bicycles such as Trek and Cannondale are imported from the USA. The cheapest bikes are imported from China or Taiwan (Rocky Mountain and Norco are the major importers). Ten-speed touring bikes (e.g. Bridgestone or Schwinn) are the most common and cost from around $250 new, while a reasonable quality mountain or hybrid bike costs around $300.

Advertisements in *Pedal Magazine* will tell you where to find the lowest prices. Buying by mail order is common but you won't receive the same service as from a neighbourhood bicycle shop. Before buying a bicycle, you should obtain expert advice (e.g. from a specialist cycle store) and ensure that you buy a bike with the correct frame size. It's best to avoid the cheapest bikes that are sold by the mass market stores (known as 'gas-pipe' bikes on account of the low quality steel tubing used to construct the frames). If you're on a tight budget and are comfortable doing your own repairs, you may wish to consider a secondhand bike. Check the classified ads in the local newspapers.

Bicycle brakes are sometimes the reverse of what's found in other countries, e.g. right-hand brake for the rear wheel and left-hand for the front wheel, and some operate on the rear wheel by pedalling backwards. Most Canadian cyclists wear approved cycling helmets to protect them from accidents, which are mandatory in some provinces, both on and off-road.

The Canadian Cycling Association, 702-2197 Riverside Drive, Ottawa, ON K1H 7X3 (☎ 613-248-1353, 🖳 www.canadian-cycling.com) publishes *Pedal Magazine* and the *Complete Guide to Cycling in Canada*, and provides a wealth of information on touring, recreational and competitive cycling. *Pedal Magazine* includes in-depth product and bicycle reviews and an annual buyer's guide. The major Canadian bicycle clubs include the Elbow Valley Cycle Club, 1111 Memorial Drive NW, Calgary AB T2N 3E4 (🖳 www.elbowvalleycc.org), Tour du Canada, 145 King Street West, Suite 1000, Toronto, Ontario M58 1J8 (☎ 800-214-7798, 🖳 www.tourducanada.com) and the Vancouver Bicycle Club, PO Box 2235, Vancouver BC V6B 3W2 (🖳 http://vbc.bc.ca).

There are many books about cycling in Canada, including *Freewheeling: The Story of Bicycling in Canada* (The Boston Mills Press), *Cycling Canada: Bike Touring Adventures in Canada* (Bicycle Books Inc., 729 Prospect Avenue, Osceola, WI 54020, USA) and the *Tour du Canada Cycling Guide,* 145 King Street West, Suite 1000, Toronto Ontario M58 1J8, the price of which includes membership of Tour du Canada (see above). Cycle magazines include *Velo Mag*, Geo Plein Air, Les Editions Tricycle, 1251 East Rachel, Montreal, QU H2J 2J9 (🖳 www.velo mag.com), which is devoted to touring, mountain biking and racing, and includes guides to day-long and multi-day rides in Quebec. Touring maps are available from the Canadian Cycling Association (see above) or from the Adventure Cycling Association, PO Box 8308, 150 East Pine Street, Missoula, MT 59807, USA (⌨ www.adv-cycling.org).

FISHING

Canada's inland waterways and lakes are an angler's paradise, particularly the thousands of lakes in the north, where trout, walleye and northern pike grow to a great size (the latter up to six feet). In the vast rivers that run north into the Arctic ocean, the Arctic char (a cousin of the salmon) is a popular quarry. In contrast, in certain rivers and waters along the Atlantic and Pacific coasts, some salmon species are becoming rare and there are strict catch limits or even fishing bans. However, not all salmon species or all rivers are threatened and the rules governing catch limits change frequently, so you must check locally to find out the current situation.

In general the fishing season extends from the thaw in mid-April until October. Angling for some fish is regulated by season and in some areas 'catch-and-release' fishing is enforced. All regulations are precisely formulated to preserve stocks and there are strictly enforced seasons and limits for all freshwater and some saltwater fish (although fishing for some saltwater species is unrestricted and permitted all year).

Ice fishing is also popular in many provinces and consists of fishing through a hole in the ice from inside a 'fish-house' (a wooden hut on the ice), which isn't quite as cold as it sounds, as wood-burning stoves keep both you and your lunch warm. Essential equipment includes a giant 'corkscrew' to make the fishing hole in the ice, thermal underwear, a balaclava, several sweaters, gloves and a fleecy 'overall'. The most popular ice-fishing lakes turn into little villages in winter, with anything up to 2,000 fish-houses.

There are fishing charter companies in all areas, many of which fly clients to private lakes to seek out their favourite catch. Most operate in northern Ontario and Quebec, but enthusiasts with several days to spare can go further afield.

Fishing in Canada is regulated either by local government or by local tribes and you must have the appropriate licence, which costs around $30 (much less than the **minimum** $100 fine for being caught fishing without one).

Information about local fishing spots and fishing contests is provided in local newspapers and available from local fish and game authorities, marinas, and bait and tackle stores. There are many books on fishing, including *First Cast* by Phil Genova, *Fly Fishing for Dummies* by Peter Kaminsky and *Lake Fishing: Best of BC* by Karl Bruhn (Whitecap Books).

GOLF

Golf is a popular sport in Canada, where you don't need to be a millionaire to play (unless you plan to spend all day at the '19th hole'). In addition to the many expensive private golf courses and complexes (usually restricted to members or residents only), there are many public courses, ranging from 3 to 18 holes. Membership isn't required to play on a public golf course, although it's wise to book in advance (sometimes it's mandatory). In some areas, private clubs are open to non-members ('green fee' golfers), although you usually need a handicap card and access may be restricted or barred at weekends, on federal holidays and during tournaments.

Annual membership of a Canadian 'country' or golf club costs at least $2,000 per year. You must also find several current members to sponsor you as a new member and club privileges may need to be earned by a points system or by doing duty on a committee planning an event. You can expect to pay around $40 per round at a public course, which is invariably never as well groomed as a private course, electric buggies (carts) costing around $35 per day. Lessons are available at most clubs from around $35 for half an hour. Many clubs have driving ranges, practice greens, bunkers (sand traps), and a pro shop.

For more information consult the relevant *Tee Off Guide* (there are separate guides for Alberta, British Columbia, Manitoba and Saskatchewan, 🖳 www.tee-off.ca) or *The Great Golf Courses of Canada* by John Gordon.

HIKING

Hiking is popular in Canada, not least because it has some of the most dramatic and unspoiled hiking country in the world. This includes millions of acres of national and provincial parks, all with marked hiking trails, ranging from easy nature hikes to long-distance trails into the back-country. Every province boasts vast areas of outstanding natural beauty. The most popular region is the Rockies, although the wooded areas of Quebec and the Atlantic provinces are also exceptionally attractive. Newfoundland's Gros Morne (French for 'Big Gloomy') National Park is a fascinating 500-million-year-old tableland of mountains with superb coastal trails, scenic waterfalls and landlocked fjords, but there are few plants on account of the high magnesium levels in the rocks. Summer and early autumn are the best times to hike, as spring comes late and trails in mountainous areas are often snowbound until June or July.

If you're hiking in national or provincial parks and camping or sleeping rough, you may require a permit and should obtain information about weather conditions and general information about your intended route. In some parks and forests there's a system of hosted 'huts' for hikers, usually located around one day's hiking distance apart. Inexpensive accommodation is also available in many hiking areas in lodges and camps. There are numerous hiking and mountain clubs in all areas, many of which maintain their own mountain lodges, publish guidebooks and produce books about local wildlife and other topics. Most parks provide free hiking and trail information and details about accessible trails for those with mobility problems.

If you're taking a long trip, you should evaluate your fitness and equipment before you leave; once in the back-country there's no way out except on foot, so make sure that your boots fit and that you understand the risks you're taking. Take a beacon (which sends out a homing signal) so you can be found even if you fall unconscious or become buried under snow. You can also 'heli-hike', although not in the National Parks, as it isn't permitted. Like heli-skiing, you're taken into the wilderness by a helicopter and collected at the end of your hike (you hope!). You should leave a detailed itinerary of a hike with someone and give them an estimated time by which you will contact them to confirm that you're okay. If you fail to contact them within a specified period, they should alert the authorities to start looking for you.

Mountain or hill-walking shouldn't be confused with 'ordinary' hiking, as it's generally done at much higher altitudes and in more difficult terrain, and should be attempted only with an experienced leader. It can be dangerous for the untrained or inexperienced and should be approached with much the same caution and preparation as mountain climbing (see page 334).

There's currently a project to create a multi-use (walking, cycling, horseback riding, cross-country skiing and snowmobiling) trail right across Canada, paid for by donations from private citizens and organisations. For a (tax deductible) donation of $36, your name goes on the roll of honour as having paid for a metre of the trail. The total length of the trail will be around 11,234mi (18,078km), with 62 per cent of it already completed (6,965mi/11,208km). For more information or to make a donation contact the Trans Canada Trail Foundation, 43 Westminster Avenue North, Montreal, Quebec H4X 1Y8 (☎ 1-800-465-3636, 💻 www.tctrail.ca).

The Sierra Club of Canada, 421-1 Nicholas Street, Ottawa ON K1N 7B7 (☎ 613-241-4611, 💻 www.sierraclub.ca), which is associated with the American Sierra Club, is Canada's premier hiking and environmental organisation. It offers three levels of membership: individual ($40 per year), joint ($50) and seniors/students ($20). As a member you receive the monthly US magazine *Sierra* and the quarterly Canadian magazine *Scan*, in addition to a newsletter from your local chapter.

Orienteering, which is a combination of hiking and a treasure hunt (or competitive navigation on foot), is also popular in Canada. It's unnecessary to be super fit and is fun for the whole family. The only equipment that's required (in addition to suitable walking attire) is a detailed map and a compass. If you're an inexperienced hiker, you may wish to attend a course in backpacking and learn how to handle yourself in the wilderness. Orienteering is taught in high schools as part of gym lessons, so that students know how to use a compass and to find their way should they become lost in the wilderness. Orienteering maps can be purchased from A1 Maps in Toronto (☎ 1-800-853-6277) and courses are run by a number of organisations, including Outward Bound Canada, 996 Chetwynd Rd, RR#2, Burk's Falls, Ontario P0A 1C0 (☎ 1-888-688-9273, 💻 www.outwardbound.ca).

There are dozens of books about hiking in Canada, including *The Complete Idiot's Guide to Hiking, Camping and Outdoors, 103 Hikes in Southwestern BC* by David and Mary Macaree, *The Complete Guide to Walking in Canada* by Elliot Katz,

A Hiker's Guide to New Brunswick by H. Eiselt, *A Hiker's Guide to the National Parks and Historic Sites of Newfoundland* by Barbara Maryniak and *Classic Hikes in the Canadian Rockies* by Graeme Pole. Books on orienteering include *Orienteering* by Tom Renfrew and *The Complete Orienteering Manual* by Peter Palmer.

HUNTING

Hunting is extremely popular in Canada, where it isn't the preserve of the wealthy or upper classes as in some countries. Hunting is prohibited in Canada's national and provincial parks, game reserves and adjacent areas, and guns are strictly forbidden in these areas. The game available includes bear, caribou, moose, elk, deer, wild hog, bighorn sheep, rabbit, raccoon, opossum, coyote, nutria, skunk, beaver, squirrel and game birds (e.g. partridge, pheasant, grouse, wild turkey, waterfowl, quail, goose and duck). **Some animals and birds, such as Canada Geese, are protected, and there are huge fines for killing them.**

You can hunt big game only during certain seasons (which may limited to a month for moose). You must generally be aged 16 or over to hunt big game, although younger people are often permitted to hunt small game. You must pass a three-day hunter's safety course costing around $100 and obtain a hunting licence from the authorities in the province or territory where you plan to hunt. Fees usually vary with the location and the prey. You should expect to pay around $40 for a licence to hunt moose, $33 for a bear/deer licence, and $17.50 for small game and birds. You receive a tag with your licence that must be attached to the carcass, and there are very large fines (up to $250,000) and jail sentences (up to two years) for killing an animal for which you don't have a licence. You're usually restricted to one deer or moose only.

For further information, check with a gun dealer or the Ministry of Natural Resources (☎ 613-258-8204).

ICE HOCKEY

Ice hockey (called simply 'hockey' in Canada, where hockey played on grass is called field hockey and isn't a major sport), which was invented in Canada in 1879, is the world's fastest game and **the** major sporting passion for Canadians. It's so popular and the gear such a common sight that you could get on a bus wearing a goalie's pads and helmet and hardly anyone would give you a second look (but don't go into a bank with a face mask on, as they may think you're planning to rob it). Canada produces around 65 per cent of North America's ice hockey players, most of the rest coming from Europe.

The National Hockey League or NHL (🖥 www.nhl.com) was formed in 1917 and in 2003 consisted of 30 teams, only six of which were Canadian: the Calgary Flames, Edmonton Oilers, Montréal Canadiens, Ottawa Senators, Toronto Maple Leafs (*sic*) and Vancouver Canucks. Teams are divided into two 'conferences', western and eastern, each of which has two divisions. For example, the Montréal Canadiens and the Ottawa senators play American teams from Buffalo, Boston, Carolina and Pittsburgh, while the Toronto Maple Leafs play Chicago, Dallas, Detroit, St Louis and Phoenix.

The NHL season starts in October and finishes in May, during which teams play over 90 games, culminating in the play-offs for the Stanley Cup (played over a seven game series). The Stanley Cup was an all-Canadian affair from 1893 to 1917, when it was strictly an amateur competition. In 1917 the NHA disbanded and the NHL was born, thus creating the 'modern' era of the Stanley Cup. Over the 85 years from 1918 to 2002, Canadian teams have won the cup 50 times.

Six players from each side are permitted on the ice at any time, but substitutions are allowed throughout the game, so players are constantly changing. There's a centre, free to roam all over the ice and the team's most important player and goal scorer, two wingmen, two defence men and a goalie (who's well padded to protect him from injury, the puck being struck at up to 130mph/210kph). The referees (there are two) call the two centres to 'centre ice' where the puck is dropped and the game begins.

Although games are meant to consist of three 20-minute periods, the clock is stopped every time there's a pause in play and games therefore usually last around three hours. Hockey is often a violent sport, with body-checking and players striking each other with their sticks almost as often as they hit the puck (hence the joke "I went to a fight and a hockey game broke out"). Punch-ups are an integral part of the 'game' although there can be severe penalties for the guilty parties.

Tickets for NHL hockey games are expensive, starting at around $35 for ordinary games and rising to $2,000 for the Stanley Cup final (if you can get one). The numbers to call for tickets are Calgary Flames (☎ 403-777-0000), Edmonton Oilers (☎ 780-414-GOAL), Montréal Canadiens (☎ 514-790-1245), Ottawa Senators (☎ 1-800-444-SENS), Toronto Maple Leafs (☎ 416-872-5000) and Vancouver Canucks (☎ 604-280-4400).

Every school or small town has a junior team, which take part in local leagues. Minor league or college teams are often referred to as 'farm' teams because they provide the talent for the NHL teams. There are even women's teams who play in their own amateur leagues. The first women's world championship was held in 1990 and there was a women's hockey tournament in the 1998 winter Olympics. Canada won the gold medals for men's and women's hockey at the 2002 Winter Olympics in Salt Lake City, the cause of much patriotic pride.

Enthusiasts may like to visit the Hockey Hall of Fame in Toronto, 30 Yonge Street, Toronto ON M5E 1X8 (☎ 416-360-7765). There's a wealth of books about hockey, including *Hockey for Dummies* for the uninitiated, the *Hockey Annual* by Murray Townsend (Warwick Publishers), which chronicles the events of the last season and speculates on forthcoming trends and player profiles, and *A day in the life of the NHL* (Harper Collins Press).

JOGGING & RUNNING

Competitive running has a strong following in Canada and jogging is extremely popular in the summer (jogging on snow and ice isn't popular). In towns and cities there are usually marked jogging trails (many with exercise stations en route), although you may have to compete for space with roller-bladers, skateboarders and cyclists. Races are organised throughout the year in all areas, from fun runs (and walks) of a few miles up to half and full marathons, most to raise money for charity (many are sponsored by the Dairy Bureau of Canada). It costs between $10 and $25 to enter fun runs, for which you receive a commemorative T-shirt (and aching feet!). At some events participants are asked to obtain sponsors. Ottawa hosts the National Capital Marathon each May and Toronto stages a marathon in September. There are running clubs in all major cities, most of which organise an extensive calendar of races, clinics and running classes.

LACROSSE

Lacrosse is Canada's official national sport, but it doesn't compare with hockey in popularity. North America's oldest organised sport, lacrosse was invented by the Algonquin Indians of the St Lawrence valley, who called it *baggataway* or *tewaarathon* and played it as part of a ceremonial religious rite, starting each game with rituals and dances. Lacrosse is more popular on the west coast, although there are some enthusiasts in parts of Ontario. It's played with a stick like a broom handle with a long thin net made from woven leather at one end in which the hard rubber ball is carried and passed between players (the original sticks were thought to look like a bishop's crozier, hence the French name 'la crosse').

A lacrosse field has boundaries set 13ft (4m) inside any obstacles, such as trees, bushes or stands, the ideal playing area being 361 by 210ft (110 by 64m). Goal lines are marked at each end of the field, 302ft (92m) apart and there's at least 30ft (9m) of playing space behind each goal line. As no physical contact is permitted, players wear no protective headgear, facemasks or padded gloves, with the exception of the goalie. As in ice-hockey, the object is to get the ball into the opposing team's net.

A men's lacrosse team consists of ten players: three attack (offence), three mid-field, three defence and a goalkeeper. Substitutions are permitted and are essential, particularly for the mid-fielders, who must cover a huge area. The defence and the attacking players normally restrict their play to half the field, while the goalie operates mainly in the area around the goal. Men's games consist of four, 25-minute periods known as 'quarters' and the winning team is the one that has scored the most goals at the end of the game. Tied games are decided by two five-minute overtime periods, followed by 'sudden death' periods of four minutes, during which the first team to score wins the game.

Women's lacrosse teams have 12 players, including the goalkeeper; the others can play anywhere on the field. The playing time is 25 minutes per half, with a 10-minute break between halves. There's also an indoor version of lacrosse, played by a seven-person team in the same space as is occupied by an indoor (field) hockey arena.

MOTOR SPORTS

Motor sports have a large following in Canada and attract more spectators than any other sport. Events embrace everything from single-seat 'formula' racing to stock car and drag racing. Most major events are held from spring to autumn on purpose-built tracks and occasionally on (closed) public roads. Among the most important races are the Indy races in Toronto (June) and Vancouver (September), which are part of the CART IndyCar World Series of races for single-seat cars, the North American equivalent of the international Formula One Grand Prix series.

However, the most popular form of motor racing is stock car racing, which is a professional sport and attracts many of Canada's and America's best drivers. Unlike those in most other countries, Canadian stock cars aren't old wrecks but highly modified production line models capable of 200mph (321kph), and races are held at specially built tracks. Stock car racing in Canada is run under the auspices of North American Stock Car Auto Racing (NASCAR).

Other popular motor sports include demolition derbies (where the aim is simply to outlast the other cars), drag racing, where cars reach 100mph (161kph) in two or three seconds and approach a top speed of 300mph (482kph), and off-road driving, for which you can buy special (expensive) off-road vehicles.

The dates and locations of all Canadian motor sport events and racing calendars are published in various magazines, including *Motorsports News International*, *Performance Racing News*, *Sportscar World* and *Stock Car Racing*.

RACQUET SPORTS

There are excellent facilities in Canada for most racquet sports, particularly tennis, squash and racquetball, although badminton is generally played only at high school level. Most outdoor tennis courts are clay or hard (i.e. asphalt or cement), while indoor courts may be synthetic (e.g. AstroTurf) or hard. There are many public tennis courts in parks in cities, and many communities have municipal courts that can be used for a small fee by local residents. However, courts are often available on a first-come, first-served basis and it may be impossible to book. Annual or season tickets are required in some towns and are inexpensive, e.g. from $65 per year for adults, with reductions of up to 50 per cent for senior citizens, students and juniors. Non-permit holders can play on some public courts at an hourly or daily rate.

There are numerous private tennis clubs in both cities and rural areas, and some top-class hotels also have tennis courts that can be rented by non-residents. The cost of hiring a court at a private club is much higher than for a public court. Some private tennis clubs also incorporate health and fitness clubs, where tennis membership entitles members to use all the club's facilities. Most private clubs have resident professionals, and some tennis centres and clubs specialise in tennis packages and coaching by top pros. Tennis instruction is also provided at local clubs by certified trainers.

Tennis camps are held in many cities during the summer months, costing from $150 per week. Most tennis camps and clinics are intended for reasonably fit and serious beginners or 'improvers' and aren't for those who play just a few social games of doubles per year. Whatever course of lessons you sign up for, make sure that they're designed to match your ability and fitness (this applies to all sports instruction).

SKIING & OTHER SNOW SPORTS

Skiing is one of the biggest participant sports in Canada, which has the most reliable skiing conditions in the world and is one of the top destinations for experienced skiers. The Rockies are considered best for downhill skiing, while eastern Canada, with its drier, heavier snow, is good for cross-country skiing (see below). The Canadian ski season lasts from October or mid-November until May or even June in some areas and most resorts are extremely busy over Christmas, New Year and Easter. During these periods it's usually necessary to book well in advance (or better still, avoid them altogether). Queues (lines), although practically unknown in some resorts, are orderly, and staff everywhere are usually friendly and helpful (a pleasant change from many European resorts).

Most resorts provide a variety of sports and leisure facilities, including cross-country skiing, snow-cat skiing, bob-sledding, snowmobiling (see below), ice-skating, swimming (heated indoor and outdoor pools), racquet sports, horse-riding, rock and ice climbing, and hot-air ballooning. Other diversions may include sleigh rides, dog-sledding, snowshoe tours, natural hot springs and snowmobile tours. Most resort hotels and inns have saunas, Jacuzzis, steam baths and hot tubs, and many have their own health clubs, fitness rooms, gymnasiums, and aerobics and games rooms, all of which are usually free to residents. In most resorts there's a lack of good mountain restaurants, although there's usually no shortage of self-service cafeterias.

Skiing is less expensive in Canada than in the US, and even with rented equipment and lift passes, you should be able to have a day's skiing for no more than around $80 (unless you go to Whistler, Canada's answer to Aspen, Colorado, where the beautiful people go to ski and be seen. Whistler is currently bidding to host the 2010 Winter Olympics – see 🖳 www.winter 2010.com for more details).

Lift passes cost from around $20 (to $50 in Whistler and Lake Louise) per day for 'adults' (12 and over) and $15 to $30 for children aged 5 to 11 (passes for those under five are usually free). Costs vary with the size of the skiing area and the number of lifts and are usually lower on weekdays than at weekends and with multi-day passes. Package deals including transport, lodging and lift tickets for a period of several days or weeks reduce the overall cost considerably. For example, Lake Louise offers a season-long family pass for around $800 (if you buy it before the end of September), which provides unlimited skiing until the end of May. Skis, boots and poles can be rented from $15 to $30 per day for adults, slightly less for children under 12.

In many resorts there are special deals to attract skiers at the beginning and end of the season, sometimes including free skiing for women. Most resorts offer discounted passes (up to two-thirds reduction) for senior citizens (usually those aged between 65 and 70) and free passes for those aged 70 or over. Information on special offers can also be found on resort websites (e.g. 🖥 www.ski louise.com or 🖥 www.skibanff.com).

Accommodation and amenities in the major resorts are superb, and comfort, service and attention to detail are second to none. Most resorts have a huge range of accommodation, including hotels and inns, self-catering 'aparthotels', studios, apartments and condominiums.

If you're taking your family, you may find it best to choose a resort with a centralised lift system on one mountain, making it easier to get together for lunch or at the end of the day. Most resorts have excellent facilities for children, including a wide range of non-skiing entertainment. All major resorts have ski schools, many of which teach the Graduated Length Method (GLM), the North American equivalent of the French *ski évolutif* (which starts beginners on skis around three feet long). Most nursery and children's ski schools provide all-day supervision, although some require parents to pick up their children for lunch. Many resorts provide a nursery for children aged from two months to three years, costing from around $40 per day ($20 to $30 per half-day). Children's ski school (usually ages 3 to 12) costs around $25 per day and may include lunch and lunchtime supervision. Babysitters are also available in most resorts.

If you're an advanced skier, it's best to choose a multi-centre area of two or three resorts, as even the largest Canadian ski areas are small compared with the many linked areas in Europe. Even many intermediate skiers find that they can ski most of the runs (trails) in the majority of Canadian resorts within around five days. Most resorts have a variety of graded runs for all standards, from beginner to expert. Black runs may be graded as single diamond (steep) or double diamond (help!). Many resorts also have illuminated runs for night skiing.

Skiing varies from immaculately groomed 'freeway' runs to challenging off-piste (back-country) skiing. Off-piste skiing is strictly controlled and areas are usually clearly marked. If you're an experienced off-piste skier (and rich), you can go heli-skiing in some areas, which entails renting a helicopter to reach virgin areas. You can expect to pay $3,000 or more for the helicopter, a guide and four nights' accommodation. **Off-piste skiing is dangerous due to the risk of** avalanches (particularly in the west) and all off-piste skiers should wear avalanche beacons and attend survival seminars. Among the companies offering heli-skiing are Last Frontier Heli-Skiing, PO Box 1118, Vernon BC V1T 6N4 (☎ 250-558-5379, 💻 www.tlhheliskiing.com) and Selkirk Tangiers Helicopter Skiing, Box 130, Revelstoke BC V0E 2S0 (☎ 250-837-5378, 💻 www. selkirk-tangiers.com).

Skiing in Canadian resorts is generally much more regulated than in Europe and to avoid crowding some resorts restrict the number of passes sold. Stewards armed with walkie-talkies are posted everywhere and, if you ski recklessly you're given a warning; repeat offenders lose their ski lift passes. Not surprisingly, resort owners are keen to avoid accidents and all skiers should have personal liability insurance (in addition to accident and health insurance). Almost all lifts are chair-lifts (double, triple and quadruple), as most mountains aren't high enough to need cable cars.

The best skiing in the east is in Newfoundland (e.g. Marble Mountain, which has the highest snowfall in eastern North America at over 200ft/60m annually) and Quebec (e.g. Mont Tremblant, Mont Sainte Anne and Mont Saint Saveur). There's a wealth of resorts to choose from in the west, including Jasper, Banff and Lake Louise (Alberta), and Blackcomb/Whistler, Big White, Sun Peaks, Cypress Mountain and Grouse Mountain (British Columbia). The combined resort of Blackcomb and Whistler is reckoned by many to be the best in North America, although its steep gradients and long runs aren't suitable for beginners. There's also good skiing in dozens of smaller resorts and superb skiing over the border in the States.

Snowboarding has become a fashionable sport in recent years, particularly among the young, trendy set (nicknamed the 'teenage death dwarfs' by one commentator because of the danger to skiers as they hurtle down the slopes and try tricks like 'the flip'). Snowboarding is much like surfing and is said to be easier to learn than skiing; experts reckon it shouldn't take more than three days to become competent. Snowboards aren't permitted on all ski runs, although many resorts (in recognition of the potential of this market) offer special 'parks' for snowboarders. If you want to get off the beaten track, some heli-ski operators offer snowboarding packages.

Although *après-ski* entertainment in Canada isn't always up to European standards, facilities in the best resorts are excellent and most have a wide choice of restaurants and bars (particularly in Quebec, where they have a distinctly French flavour).

There are many books about skiing in North America, among the best of which are *Ski Canada – Where to Ski and Snowboard* by Patrick Twomey, *The Skiers Book of Trail Maps, USA and Canada* by Cynthia Blair & Mike Bell, and *The Complete Guide to Cross-Country Skiing in Canada* by John Peaker. A number of ski magazines are published in Canada, including *Ski Canada* (💻 www.skicanadamag.com), which provides subscribers with a discount card for equipment, passes, etc.. The Ski Council of Canada also has a website (💻 www.skicanada.org).

Cross-Country Skiing

Cross-country skiing is popular throughout Canada and is an inexpensive alternative to downhill skiing, a set of skis, poles and boots costing as little as $125. You can enjoy cross-country skiing in Alberta, British Columbia and Ontario (where Thunder Bay on Lake Superior has hosted the World Nordic Ski Championships), although the best cross-country skiing is to be found in the eastern provinces. New Brunswick has more than 900km (560mi) of marked trails in national and provincial parks, as well as many others maintained by hotels and small communities. Quebec also has an extensive network of trails.

Although you can enjoy cross-country skiing wherever there's sufficient snow, cross-country skiing centres are becoming increasingly popular and offer lessons, ski hire and man-made trails (a lot easier, although less adventurous, than making your own). Trail maps are provided and are a necessity when you're faced with miles of trails running in all directions. Costs (including parking) are between $5 and $12 per day, although in some areas (such as the National Capital region near Ottawa) skiing is free. (However, donation boxes are provided for those who would like to contribute to the upkeep of the trails, which most people happily do.) Many trails have cabins where you can have a rest or a drink or snack. For information about cross-country skiing, visit the website of Cross Country Canada (🖳 http://canada.x-c.com).

Snowmobiling

Invented in Canada in 1922, snowmobiles are motorbikes without wheels, driven across the snow by a spinning rubber track and steered by metal skis connected to handlebars. Modern snowmobiles are capable of speeds of up to 100mph (160kph), but if you're planning to do that sort of speed, it's wise to stick to the marked tracks (it isn't unknown for landowners to 'discourage' trespassers by stringing wires across their land at neck height!) and to avoid frozen lakes (fatal accidents occasionally occur when snowmobiles crash through the ice). Even at lower speeds you need to wrap up well to protect yourself from the constant high-speed blast of icy air.

Snowmobiles are a standard way of getting around in winter for people who live in the 'great white north' and many Canadians also own them just for fun. There are snowmobile clubs that stage various competitions and other events throughout the winter, such as the North American Snowmobile Festival in Thetford Mines or the Provincial Snowmobile Festival in Saint-Gabriel (both in Quebec, which has a vast linked network of snowmobile trails). There's even a snowmobile Grand Prix in Valcourt and a snowmobile museum at 1001, J-A-Bombardier Ave, Valcourt, Quebec JOE 2LO (☎ 450-532-5300). New Brunswick has over 3,728mi (6,000km) of 'groomed' trails and Newfoundland has an annual snowmobile endurance race, the Viking 1,000, covering over 777mi (1,250km) of untracked wilderness and lasting four days!

The Canadian Council of Snowmobile Organizations has established a set of standard hand signals (turning, slowing, snowmobile approaching, etc.) rather like those used for motorcycles. There's a wide range of snowmobile models (starting at around $10,000) from a number of manufacturers (e.g. Ski-Doo, Arctic Cat, Polaris and Yamaha), plus a huge range of accessories for enthusiasts, such as saddlebags. You can also hire snowmobiles, although most rental agencies prefer to take you on one of their guided tours first, to see how you get on – not only are the machines expensive, but if you go off into the wilderness on your own and get into trouble you're liable to die, and they don't want to take the responsibility for that!

Guided tours cost around $200 per day for a standard 500cc machine; a week (with accommodation and meals) costs from $1,450 (during the first two weeks in December) to $2,000 (during high season in February and March). If you want to try a more powerful machine, it costs an additional $180 for a 600cc machine or $270 for a 700cc machine. Protective clothing is provided, but it's recommended that you also wear a T-shirt and turtle-neck pullover, 'long-john' underwear, a neck warmer or balaclava, woollen socks, sunglasses and sunscreen. If you want to go up into the mountains, you should also rent an avalanche kit, consisting of avalanche beacon/transceiver, avalanche probe, shovel and Global Position System (GPS) for around $30 per day. Among the many snowmobile tour companies are the Great Canadian Motor Corp (☎ 1-800-667-8865, ▭ www.gcmc.com) and Great Canadian Snowmobile Tours, Box 9242, RPO #3, Revelstoke BC VOE 3KO (☎ 250-837-6500, ▭ www.snow-mobilerevelstoke.com).

Dog-Sledding

Dog-sledding has become a major sport in North America, where races attract contestants from all over the world. As well as the Iditerarod race in Alaska (famous in dog-sledding circles), there's the 1,000-mile Yukon Quest race through the Yukon and Alaska (you can read about it in *Yukon Quest* by John Firth, published by Lost Moose Publishing). However, it isn't necessary to go quite so far to try dog-sledding and in winter it's possible in most areas to take anything from a half-day trip to a seven-day tour. You should expect to pay around $80 (adult) or $30 (child) for a half-day trip, or up to $2,750 for a seven-day trip including accommodation.

SWIMMING

Swimming is the most popular sport (or pastime) in Canada. Private pools are quite common, particularly in the warmer areas, where they're often a standard feature of family houses and condominium complexes. There are public heated indoor and outdoor swimming pools in most towns, and numerous beaches along Canada's thousands of miles of ocean and lake shores. Many of Canada's

National Parks have supervised beaches with professional and bilingual staff. However, there are often dangerous tides, so always heed the warning signs (a red flag means danger!). **Lakes and rivers are generally colder than sea waters and often have dangerous rapids and whirlpools.**

Many hotels and motels have indoor or outdoor pools, but these are rarely if ever supervised by a professional, indicated by 'Use at your own risk' or 'The management assumes no liability' notices.

A visit to a public pool costs from around $3. Many municipalities offer introductory swimming lessons for children and youths. The aim of many swimmers is to earn a bronze medallion, which means not only that you're a proficient swimmer, but also that you're trained in life-saving. Lessons are taught under the auspices and supervision of qualified Red Cross instructors.

Joining a swimming club costs around $250 per person per year, which entitles you to exclusive use of the pool during certain times of the day/week, with appointed times for everyone from toddlers to senior citizens, with public admission at least once a week.

WATERSPORTS

Watersports are hugely popular in Canada and include sailing, windsurfing (also called sailboarding), waterskiing, rowing, power boating, canoeing, surfing and sub-aqua. This is hardly surprising when you consider that Canada has thousands of lakes and rivers and a vast coastline. Boats and equipment can be hired at coastal resorts, lakes and rivers, and instruction is available for most watersports in towns and holiday areas. Sailing and powerboats, canoes and rowing boats are generally available for hire in coastal towns and on inland waterways. Jet skis or wet bikes can also be hired at many resorts (although they should be avoided by the inexperienced, as they can be fatal in the wrong hands). Wetsuits are often required for surfing, windsurfing, waterskiing and sub-aqua, even in summer, and they're essential during the winter months, when the water is freezing.

Useful books for watersports enthusiasts include *Water-skiing – Getting Off the Ground* by Mark & Gary Solomon and *Canoeing, the Complete Guide to Equipment and Techniques* by Dave Harrison.

Surfing

There are several types of surfing, including traditional board surfing, body surfing and 'boogie boarding' (body surfing with a short foam board). Windsurfers (or sailboards), surfboards, bodyboards and wetsuits can be hired at most locations. Windsurfing is popular on both coasts and on the St Lawrence river near Montreal, but isn't permitted everywhere. Waterskiing is popular on lakes and in calm coastal areas. You can hire a tow-boat and skis for a reasonable fee in many areas.

Canoeing & Kayaking

Canoeing and kayaking are popular on Canada's lakes, rivers and in Pacific coastal waters (the most famous venue is Algonquin Park, two hours north-west of Ottawa). Canoes are popular as a way of exploring the calmer lakes and the back-country waterways in summer and early autumn. If you lack experience (and the longer the trip, the more experience you should have of wilderness expeditions, which can involve bad weather, unfriendly wildlife and injury) it makes sense to go with an organised, supervised group. Organisations called outfitters arrange expeditions for small groups, although you must make sure that you choose one that's licensed by the local province, which means that they're experienced and carry insurance. Provincial tourist authorities can provide a list of licensed outfitters.

If you want to use a kayak (a one or two-man enclosed boat), you need some previous experience or training. Handling a kayak isn't as easy as it looks, even on a river, and for sea kayaking you need instruction in a sheltered cove before heading out into the surf (in addition to knowing the tide times, weather forecast and information about the coastal rock formations). Most coastal towns in British Columbia offer kayak hire, instruction and guided trips.

Sailing

Sailing is a very popular summer sport and there are sailing clubs all along Canada's vast coastline. There are also exclusive yacht clubs which social-climbers often join for the prestige and social contacts rather than for the sailing (membership fees can be astronomical). You can hire anything from a modest sailing dinghy to an ocean-going yacht in most areas, although you need experience to hire some craft. All craft must be registered and licensed. Canada's Department of Fisheries and Oceans and the Royal Canadian Mounted Police (RCMP) are adept at ensuring that owners and users have the correct documentation and there are large fines for offenders. Always check with the coastguard before setting sail, as frequent and sudden fierce storms are common in some areas, and make sure that you have the proper navigation charts.

Sub-Aqua

Scuba diving is popular in Canada, and you can receive instruction by certified diving instructors at indoor pools, courses costing from around $60 to $125 depending on the location. Due to the fact that everyone is equally buoyant under water, there's great interest from organisations caring for disabled people to allow them to enjoy this sport. Most dealers selling scuba apparatus provide on-site maintenance and support for equipment, and many offer a 'try it for free the first time' deal.

Whitewater Rafting

Whitewater river rafting (or river running) is hugely popular throughout Canada, particularly on the fast rivers of British Columbia and the Rockies, e.g. the Fraser River, and is an unforgettable experience (better than the hairiest of roller-coasters). The best (or worst, if you're terrified) time to go is in April or May, when waters are at their most turbulent due to melting snow. Experience is usually unnecessary, as the inflatable rubber pontoon-type boats are virtually unsinkable (although **you** won't be if you fall out). However, not all trips are suitable for families or novices. Expect to get wet and don't be surprised if you're thrown out of the raft. It isn't recommended for poor swimmers, although life jackets are provided. If you're inexperienced you should be accompanied by a professional guide, who will (hopefully) reduce the danger but not the thrills.

Trips cost from $60 for half a day up to hundreds of dollars for a week-long excursion with meals. Dozens of companies organise whitewater rafting expeditions throughout Canada and in most cases all you have to do is turn up at the riverside, find the organiser's trailer and book on the spot for the next trip.

There are a number of books for whitewater fans, including the *Whitewater Rafting Manual: Tactics and Techniques for Great River Adventures* by Jimmie Johnson, *Whitewater Rafting in North America* by Lloyd D. Armstead (Pequot Press) and *Whitewater Rafting: An Introductory Guide* by Cecil Kuhne. You can also locate rafting companies and other water sports outfitters on the Internet (e.g. 🖳 www.travelsource.com/rafting.html).

OTHER SPORTS

Outlined below is a selection of other popular sports and activities in Canada.

Athletics: Most towns and villages have local athletics (track) clubs, which hold local competitions and sports days. For information about local clubs and facilities contact Athletics Canada, Suite 606-1185, Eglinton Avenue East, Toronto ON M3C 3C6 (☎ 416-426-7181, 🖳 www.athleticscanada.com).

Basketball: Although basketball was invented in Canada (in 1891 by Dr James A. Naismith, a Canadian whose name can be found adorning many streets in Canadian cities), it's principally played in the US, where the professional basketball league, the National Basketball Association (NBA) was formed in 1949. It took until 1995 for Canada to gain entry with two teams, but now there's only one, the Toronto Raptors (☎ 416-872-5000), the other team – the Vancouver Grizzlies – having moved to Memphis in the US. The Raptors have a new stadium in the Air Canada Centre in Toronto. The NBA consists of 29 teams, divided into the Eastern and Western Conference, each of which has two divisions. Teams play a total of around 82 games during the regular season, running from November to April.

Curling: Curling is a winter sport which involves sliding a lump of granite (a 'rock') across a patch of ice. Each team consists of four players, known as skip (the captain), third (second in charge, who 'throws' third), second (who throws second) and lead (who throws first). The teams throw alternately, until eight rocks have been thrown, each aiming at a series of marked spots called 'buttons'. Other team members have a brush with which they sweep the ice to smooth the progress of the rock, which has an attached handle, of a different colour for each team. The skill is in throwing the rock so that it veers and swerves over the lumpy ice, although as a spectator sport it's rather like watching paint dry. The main body governing curling, which is now an Olympic sport, is the Canadian Curling Association, 1660 Vimont Court, Cumberland, Ontario K4A 4J4 (☎ 800-550-2875, 🖥 www.curling.ca).

Horse Riding: Horse riding and equestrian sports have a large following throughout Canada, in both urban and rural areas. There are three types of saddle: Western or 'stock seat', the most common (and the type you're most likely to be offered if you want to ride in the National Parks), 'hunt seat' (basically the way most Europeans ride) and 'saddle seat' (like hunt seat, but used for specialist riding). There are also dressage and show-jumping events. Horse riding costs around $100 per hour, including an experienced guide. Lessons cost from around $20 per hour, depending on the level of teaching and on whether you sign up for a series or a single lesson. Most national and provincial parks have a network of bridle paths and riding trails, and horses can be hired in many parks, where horse riding is an excellent way to get off the beaten track. Organised riding holidays are arranged at ranches throughout Canada.

Ice Skating: Ice skating is a popular indoor and outdoor sport, and major cities have numerous skating rinks open throughout the year, although the ice is often occupied by hockey players. All rinks have skate hire and a skate sharpening service and offer lessons for individuals and groups. It's an inexpensive activity and may even be free in many smaller towns (outdoor rinks, which are mostly just frozen lakes, ponds or rivers, are also usually free). Some rinks hold ice-dancing evenings costing less than $10 (including skate hire). Ottawa boasts that its Rideau Canal (4.8mi/7.7km) is the longest 'skating rink' in the world. Books about ice-skating include the *Skater's Edge Sourcebook: Ice Skating Resource Guide* by Alice Berman (Skaters Edge).

Roller-Skating: Roller-skating is a popular pastime, although traditional roller-skates have been largely replaced by 'in-line' skates or rollerblades. In-line roller hockey is played by Canadian youths on the streets and many people even skate to work during the snow-free months. The cost of skates varies according to the manufacturer (and current fashion), but you can buy used skates at 'Play it Again' shops throughout Canada (see **Clothing** on page 364).

Skateboarding & BMX Biking: Rinks and specially designed circuits are provided in many towns for skateboarding and BMX cycles. Children can start at around seven years old; participants of all ages should be protected against falls with crash helmets and elbow and knee pads. It's difficult to hire skateboards, as they're too easily stolen, although BMX bikes can usually be hired.

17.

SHOPPING

As it shares a border with the ultimate consumer nation (the US), it's hardly surprising that Canada is also a major consumer society. Newspaper, magazine and TV advertisements all exhort Canadians to spend liberally, and most do, leading to annual consumer spending of over $500 billion. Shopping facilities in the major cities are the equivalent of those in the States or Europe, with most top brands and designer names available. Toronto's Yonge Street and Montreal's 'underground city' are considered to be Canada's best shopping areas, although all the major cities offer plenty of opportunity to part with money. But be warned: like most of the rest of the world, Canada's cities are home to bag-snatchers and pickpockets who will empty your wallet before you even get to the shops if you don't keep a tight hold on it (wearing a money belt is recommended in some places).

Many Canadians work long hours, which leaves little time for shopping. Therefore they prefer one-stop shopping in supermarkets, department stores or suburban malls. Canada's shops (stores) and shopping centres (malls) offer a vast choice of goods in every shape, colour and size you could desire (plus many that you couldn't imagine anyone wanting!). Prices are competitive, particularly when compared with those in Europe; computer hardware and software, stereo systems, CDs, videos, cameras and sports equipment are particularly good value. Clothes are also good value (unless you want designer label clothes, which are as exorbitantly priced in Canada as they are everywhere else), the best bargains being in casual and winter clothing. Low prices and value aren't always the same thing, but many stores offer a 'price guarantee', which means that they 'meet or beat' any advertised price for goods, so it pays to comparison-shop.

In the major cities, you may find some shop assistants (store clerks) who are brusque and rude, but in general they're friendly and helpful. With few exceptions, you're refused entry if you're carrying open food or drink containers, are smoking, or have bare feet or no shirt.

Most shops accept major credit cards, although American Express is becoming unpopular with smaller shops and many won't accept it. Most stores also accept Canadian or American dollar travellers' cheques and some give change. Unlike American shops, where the offer of cash causes panic, Canadian shops are usually happy to accept cash and some may even insist on it. Cash machines (ATMs) are located in most malls, large stores and supermarkets.

Many shops provide free catalogues at various times of year (often delivered to homes), and free shopping guides are published in most areas. If you're looking for a particular item or want to save time, check the yellow pages.

You don't need to worry about returning faulty goods, as the customer is 'always right' and most shops exchange goods or give refunds without question. On the rare occasions when there's a problem, a complaint to the local consumer protection agency or Better Business Bureau usually resolves the matter. See also **Consumer Associations** on page 375.

Canadian shops use Imperial measures; those who are used to metric measures may find **Appendix D** useful.

Bargain Shopping

One lesson Canadians learned from the recession in the early 1990s is that only the foolish or wealthy pay the full price and, although most goods have price labels, you stand a good chance of getting a discount if you're prepared to haggle. Seasonal sales offer good bargains and many people delay making major purchases until the sales. Most stores hold sales at various times of the year, the largest of which are in January, July and October. Top department stores usually have pre-season clothing sales, e.g. autumn/winter clothes are on sale for a limited period in August or September. Sales are also common on statutory holidays such as Labour Day and Canada Day weekends, although the biggest sales traditionally start on Boxing Day (26th December).

Often 'end-of-line' reductions can be found outside the sale season and there are some items where the last of a shop's stock of a particular item (such as the end of a roll of carpet) can go for as little as 25 per cent of its normal price. The secret of buying at low prices is to comparison shop till you drop, checking prices at many locations. However, make sure that you're comparing like with like, as it's easy to save money by buying inferior goods, and beware of bargains that seem too good to be true, as they usually are!

The best bargains can be found at discount malls and centres, factory outlets and warehouse clubs. Discount stores and factory outlets are able to offer lower prices on branded goods because profit margins and overheads are cut to the bone and the middleman is excluded. Factory outlet malls usually have rules stating that tenants must discount merchandise at least 10 per cent below any local discount store or offer at least one-third off regular retail prices. Many discount stores operate on the 'pile 'em high and sell 'em low' principle, with no fancy displays or customer areas, no demonstrations and little customer or after-sales service – just rock-bottom prices. You should know exactly what you want when shopping at discount stores as staff don't waste time discussing products and are likely to employ the hard sell or ignore you if you're undecided. Discount malls may offer entertainment as well as unbeatable prices.

There are also chains of discount stores in ordinary shopping malls, such as Loonie Stores (after the colloquial name for a dollar coin), where everything in the store is under $5.

Factory outlets are common in Canada. Most are owned and operated by manufacturers, although there are also special malls dedicated to them. What is claimed to be Canada's largest factory outlet mall, The Factory Outlet Shopper, opened in 1999 at Niagara Falls. Although they may sell obsolete or overstocked items, most factory outlets don't sell poor quality goods or 'seconds' (flawed or damaged goods) but quality products at bargain prices. Ask your friends and neighbours if there are any factory outlets in your area and look out for them on your travels. Designer clothes can also be purchased from factory outlets in cities. **Some factory outlets accept cash only.**

In most cities there are also huge warehouse stores specialising in selling remainders, leftover stock, overruns and cancelled orders at reduced prices, which can be as little as 10 per cent of the normal retail price.

Since the mid-1980s, 'warehouse clubs' such as Costco have become the fastest-growing retail sector in Canada. They charge an annual membership fee of between $60 and $80 (which can often be recouped in one visit) and offer huge discounts on branded goods (particularly food, with prices for bulk quantities typically 20 per cent below supermarket prices). The hackneyed slogan 'the more you spend, the more you save' is true, although discerning shoppers profit most.

Supermarkets also offer discount coupons (e.g. 20¢ or 50¢ off branded items), which are either printed in newspapers and magazines or issued as books of coupons that are delivered to local homes and available at stores. Cutting out (clipping) coupons is a way of life for many Canadian shoppers, who can save up to $20 per week by using them. In fact, prices are set in the expectation that you will use coupons, so you're paying too much if you **don't** use them. Canadian Tire (a chain selling automotive accessories and hardware) offers discounts in the form of Canadian Tire coupons to customers. The coupons look like currency and can be spent at Canadian Tire just like cash (there's even a Canadian Tire Coupon Collectors' Club!). Some stores accept coupons issued by their rivals. Local newspapers, yellow pages and flyers delivered to homes contain literally hundreds of coupons from local businesses such as restaurants, fast food outlets, cinemas, hotels, car rental companies, dry cleaners and numerous others. Note that most coupons have an expiry date. When shopping with a coupon or special offer voucher, it isn't recommended to tell the assistant (clerk) until you've verified that the goods are in stock. If he knows that you have a discount voucher, you may find that the shop is suddenly 'out of stock', as your discount usually comes out of his commission.

There's a number of books dedicated to helping you to save money. *Smart Shopping Montréal* is a typical saver's 'bible'; its author, Sandra Phillips, reckons to be able to save up to 30 per cent on furniture and $40 per week on feeding her family of four. (One of her tips is to team up with other families and buy frozen meals in bulk for around half price from Delta Dailyfood, a Montreal supplier of airline food, although one airline meal per year is enough for most people.) Ian Nicholson, author of the best-selling book *The Miser's Guide to Wealth*, also publishes a monthly newsletter called *Misers Gazette*, PO Box 13344, Kanata, Ontario, Canada (🖥 www.misersgazette.com) costing $30 per year.

Secondhand Goods

There's a huge market in Canada for secondhand goods, which can be purchased from special bargain shops and charity shops, at auction rooms and garage sales, and through classified ads in newspapers and magazines..

There's a large market in used (often called 'antique' or 'vintage') clothes in major cities, sold by consignment stores with names such as 'Second Chance' or 'Second Fiddle', which sell secondhand clothes on commission. Some of these have never been worn, having been purchased by shopping addicts who buy everything in sight and then never wear it. The new craze among working women is to hold 'swap meets', where they take unwanted clothes and swap them, and donate any left over to women's shelters

Charity shops (thrift stores) are a good place to pick up inexpensive and fashionable new and secondhand clothing, donated by shops and individuals. Many charity shops also sell inexpensive good qualilty secondhand clothing.

Another place to pick up a bargain is at a public auction, although it's usually necessary to have specialist knowledge about whatever it is that you're planning to buy (particularly antiques), as you will probably be competing with experts. Auctions are held throughout the year for everything from antiques to houses, while car auctions, which were originally open to the trade only, have now opened their doors to the public. Estate and bankruptcy auction sales are frequent and a source of good bargains. Charity-run antique and craft fairs and flea markets are also decent hunting grounds. These are typically organized as fund raisers and held in local schools, churches, women's clubs, town squares and on college campuses. Local auctions and fairs are widely advertised in local newspapers and through leaflets. For information about local markets enquire at your local tourist office, chamber of commerce or library.

One of the best places to obtain secondhand bargains in Canada is at private 'yard' and 'tag' sales (garage sales), an American invention. Families moving house or periodically emptying their attics, store rooms and wardrobes often sell unwanted clothes, furniture, records, books and assorted oddments in their garage or driveway or on their front lawn. Sometimes people moving abroad or across the country sell practically the entire contents of their homes. Most garage sales take place on spring or summer Saturdays and are advertised in local newspapers and via posters, flyers, supermarket bulletin boards, home-made street signs and word of mouth. They can be found simply by driving around neighbourhoods on a Saturday. They're often a good place to find interesting 'Canadiana', considered junk by Canadians but collectible by foreigners. Prices are negotiable and items can often be bought for next-to nothing, as Canadians don't ask or expect to get much for secondhand goods. At the end of the day, anything left is practically given away. It's possible to furnish an entire apartment with items purchased at garage and estate sales. The best bargains are found in high and middle-class areas (where some people sell their designer clothes after wearing them only once or twice).

When seeking specific items, such as cameras or sports equipment, it's wise to check the classified ads in specialist magazines. Specialist shops often have a bulletin board where private ads are placed by customers, with detachable slips containing the vendor's phone number at the bottom. Many shopping malls and office buildings also have public bulletin boards that attract ads, and most local newspapers contain dedicated classified sections for cars, boats, household goods and miscellaneous items. A good source of furniture and household items

Special newspapers and magazines for bargain hunters, such as *Bargain Finder* (🖳 www.buysell.com), are published in most areas, some of which have separate editions for automotive and general merchandise. Publications may be distributed free (when the advertiser pays) or ads may be free to private advertisers, in which case publications usually cost a couple of dollars. Advertisers are normally required to indicate their status (private or dealer) so that prospective buyers know who they're dealing with. is expatriate club newsletters, particularly when members are returning home.

SALES TAXES

The prices of goods and services are usually shown and quoted **exclusive** of sales taxes (although tax is sometimes included as a sales ploy to make you feel as if you're getting away without paying it). This means that, if you have only $10 in your pocket, you won't usually be able to buy something priced at $10, which will cost at least $10.75 and as much as $11.75 (in Prince Edward Island).

There are two types of sales tax: federal goods and services tax (GST – some Canadians maintain stands for the 'gouge and screw tax'), which was introduced on 1st January 1991 and is 7.5 per cent throughout Canada, and provincial or territorial sales tax (PST), which is levied in most provinces and territories at various rates (see below). In Quebec, GST is known as *taux produits et services (TPS)*.

Sales taxes are calculated on the amount paid for an item (usually less any trade-in, if applicable) and is paid by the buyer. It applies to almost all goods and services that are sold, leased, transferred or otherwise provided through the production and distribution process. **Sales tax not only applies to new goods and goods sold by businesses, but also to the sale of certain used products such as cars, motor homes, boats and aircraft.**

Certain goods and services are sales tax exempt (i.e. aren't subject to GST or HST). These include basic food stuffs, most health, medical and dental services that are performed for medical reasons by licensed doctors or dentists, bridge, road and ferry tolls, most educational services such as university courses leading to certificates or diplomas and tutoring provided for a credit course (but not courses provided by profit-making companies), and most financial services. Some goods or services that are exempt from sales taxes in other countries aren't exempt in Canada, including newspapers and magazines, professional services and mail order catalogue purchases.

A number of goods and services are zero-rated, which means that they've been declared taxable, but the rate has been set at zero for the time being (i.e. until the government gets desperate for money!). Examples include agricultural products (e.g. wheat, grain, raw wool and unprocessed tobacco), farm livestock (with some exceptions, such as horses) and most fishery products (e.g. fish for human consumption), prescription medicines, most medical devices (e.g. hearing aids and false teeth), international passenger air travel except to the continental United States and St Pierre and Miquelon, and inbound and international freight transport subject to certain conditions.

In addition to GST, most provinces and territories levy a provincial or territorial sales tax (PST). In Quebec, PST is known as *taux des ventes et services Québec* (*TVQ*). The tax is levied at the following rates on most goods (for rates on cars, see page 211):

Province/Territory	Rate
Alberta	zero, except on hotel rooms, when it's 5 per cent
British Columbia	7.5 per cent, except on hotel rooms, when it's between 8 and 10 per cent
Manitoba	7 per cent
New Brunswick	7.5 per cent*
Newfoundland	7.5 per cent*
Northwest Territories	zero
Nova Scotia	7.5 per cent*
Nunavut	zero
Ontario	8 per cent, except on hotel rooms, when it's 5 per cent
Prince Edward Island	10 per cent
Quebec	7.5 per cent, except on hotel rooms, when it's 6.5 per cent
Saskatchewan	6 per cent
Yukon	zero

* In New Brunswick, Newfoundland and Nova Scotia, GST and PST are combined into a single harmonised sales tax (HST) of 15 per cent.

PST may apply to different goods and services depending on the province, although there's no PST on clothes for children under the age of 15 in Canada.

GST only applies to residents in Canada and visitors can reclaim it (PST can also be reclaimed in Manitoba, Newfoundland, Nova Scotia and Quebec) on purchases of $50 or above that are exported from the country and on short-term accommodation (other than motor-home rental). Refunds (up to a maximum of $500) are made at duty-free shops at the border as you leave or by post during the 60 days after departure. You need to obtain a copy of the *Tax Refund Application for Visitors* (RC4031E) leaflet available from travel agents, duty-free shops, customs officials or Canada Customs and Revenue Agency, complete the form and attach your receipts for accommodation and other non-consumable purchases. If you forget the form or need help completing it, you can phone ☎ 1-800-668-4748 within Canada or ☎ 1-902-432-5608 from outside Canada.

Residents are also entitled to GST and PST refunds in certain cases. Both taxes can be reclaimed when goods are sent abroad, and PST can be reclaimed when goods are purchased in another province. You can apply for a refund when you complete your annual tax return (see **Tax Return** on page 302); refunds are paid quarterly.

Some provinces also levy a refundable 'environment tax' on recyclable items such as drink and food cans and bottles and plastic fruit cartons. These can be returned to the shop where you purchased them for a tax refund, which incidentally is one of the few chores children are happy to do!

SHOPPING HOURS

Canada's cities and large towns have long shopping hours. Many drugstores, petrol stations and convenience stores are open 24 hours a day, seven days a week in most areas (you can even shop at 3am if you want!). On major roads, 24-hour service stations also sell food. Other stores, particularly supermarkets and drugstores, are generally open from 7.30am to 9pm. In almost all major cities, at least one pharmacy is open until midnight or even 24 hours (see yellow pages for a list). In town centre (downtown) shopping areas, major stores may open from 9.30am to 6pm from Mondays to Wednesdays, 9.30am to 9pm on Thursdays and Fridays and from 9.30am to 7pm on Saturdays. Most malls open at around 10am and close at 9pm. In smaller towns, shops usually open between 9 and 10am and close at 6pm, Mondays to Saturdays. Whenever possible, avoid shopping at lunchtimes and on Saturdays, when shops are usually packed.

Sunday opening is subject to provincial and/or municipal laws. It's rare in New Brunswick, Newfoundland, Nova Scotia and Prince Edward Island, although most other provinces have shops that are open from noon until 5pm on Sundays. Business hours on statutory holidays are usually at the discretion of individual shopkeepers, although you rarely find a shop open on Christmas Day. Shops usually post their holiday business hours a week or so before a holiday.

SHOPPING CENTRES

All Canadian cities and suburbs have vast indoor shopping centres, called malls (pronounced 'mawls'). The mall concept was invented in Canada and has spread throughout North America and most of the rest of the world. Many malls boast that you're under cover from the time you drive into the car park (parking lot) – a considerable advantage in a country which can be under snow for six (or more) months per year. Discount or outlet malls, comprising cheap and factory outlet shops, are also common throughout Canada (see **Bargain Shopping** on page 355). The success of the mall concept has led to a change in the facilities in most town centres, which retailers have largely abandoned.

Malls vary from enormous luxury shopping centres such as Toronto's Eaton Centre and Vancouver's Pacific Centre to smaller centres in country towns. The average mall contains 50 to 100 stores, including many department and chain stores as well as supermarkets, clothing shops, furniture and furnishing outlets, film processing shops, jewellers, music shops, book shops, banks, launderettes, hairdressers, opticians, restaurants, fast food outlets, and a wide selection of boutiques and specialist shops. In some malls there are car hire offices, airline booking desks and even clinics, and many contain leisure and entertainment facilities such as a skating rink, ten-pin bowling alley, cinemas, amusement arcades and art galleries. Alberta's West Edmonton Mall (the second-largest in the world) boasts its own indoor amusement park (with a roller coaster), the world's largest indoor water park with a wave pool and water slides, mini golf (a replica of the American Pebble Beach course), submarine ride, aquarium, 120 restaurants, 20 bars/nightclubs, recreation centre with bowling alleys and arcades, cinemas, casino, chapel, hotels complete with several different 'theme rooms', plus over 800 shops and services (for those who actually come to shop!).

MARKETS

In many cities there are farmers' or 'green' markets, where local farmers sell fresh and reasonably priced produce most days of the week, although Canadian street markets generally don't compare with those in Europe. Local fishermen also set up stalls in fishing towns. As in most countries, markets are usually the best place to shop for really fresh food and are a good place to buy an assortment of bread and a wider variety of cheeses than you find in most supermarkets. Most stall-holders offer tastings and some shoppers get their breakfast by 'grazing' from stall to stall. Flea (i.e. junk) markets are common in major cities and specialise in clothing, jewellery, antiques and miscellaneous bric-a-brac.

In provinces with severe winters, markets may be held between spring and autumn only or may be held indoors. There are often small impromptu markets in many cities, although it's illegal to sell goods in the street without a vendor's licence. Secondhand markets are common in cities and towns across Canada and are generally held in vacant buildings, in malls or (in the summer) on church lawns or in car parks. Ask at your local tourist office, library or town hall for information about local markets.

DEPARTMENT & CHAIN STORES

There are excellent department and chain stores throughout Canada, many of which specialise in clothing. Department stores, as their name implies, consist of separate departments selling everything from clothes to perfume, electrical apparatus to furniture. Each floor may be dedicated to a particular kind of goods, such as ladies' or men's clothes (which are often sold through franchised boutiques) or furniture and furnishings, and they usually include restaurants, cafeterias, phones and toilets (restrooms).

In a department store, the floor at street level is designated the first floor (not the ground floor), the floor below the ground floor is usually called the basement and the floor above may be called the mezzanine. The basement or lower basement is usually occupied by a bargain department where reduced price or inexpensive goods are sold. Some stores, such as BiWay and the Army & Navy, operate basement stores famous for their cut-price branded clothes and unbeatable prices.

The best Canadian department stores include The Bay (run by the Hudson's Bay Company) and Sears (which used to be known as Sears Roebuck and which invented the shopping catalogue in the 19th century). The largest nationwide discount department stores, sometimes called mass merchandisers, include Wal-Mart and Zellers, which have branches in a number of cities, along with Fields, Holt Renfrew and Saan. Most department stores have mail order catalogues and operate a home delivery service; many will deliver goods anywhere in the world.

Chain stores, which are also often franchised, are stores with two or more branches, often located in different towns, e.g. Canadian Tire and Home Hardware. Many department stores are also chain stores. Saan is typical: having started business in 1947 in Winnipeg, it now has some 350 outlets throughout Canada. There are dozens of chain stores in Canada, selling everything from electrical items to food, books and clothes. Some are to be found country-wide while others are regional; for example, Canadian Superstore, IGA, Safeway and Save-on-Foods and are dominant in the west, while in Ontario you're more likely to find Independent Grocers, Loblaws and Loeb.

Some department and chain stores accept all major credit cards, although some issue their own cards (with high interest rates). If you have a store credit card, you're inundated with pre-sale post, special offers and seasonal catalogues.

FOOD SHOPS & SUPERMARKETS

Most Canadians buy their food in supermarkets, and the average family of four spends around $600 per month on groceries – less than in many other countries. Food is cheapest overall in western Canada and most expensive in the Northwest Territories, Nunavut and the Yukon, where most food must be imported. Like department stores, supermarkets are losing business to warehouse clubs (see above), although the latter cannot compete with supermarkets for variety and typically stock around 4,000 lines (many non-food) compared to a supermarket's 20,000.

The quality, variety and size of produce (fruit and vegetables) in Canadian supermarkets is excellent and often overwhelming to the newcomer. Stores are huge and packed year-round with the most exotic produce, mountains of meat and dairy products (although fresh fish isn't so easy to find away from coastal areas), and convenience foods by the truckload. Canadian supermarkets invariably carry larger stocks and offer a wider variety of merchandise than their counterparts in Europe. The choice is mind-boggling, e.g. 40 or 50 flavours of coffee, including mint and orange (although why anyone would want mint-flavoured coffee is a mystery), and countless brands of breakfast cereal, sold in boxes of different sizes.

Produce departments are self-service and fruit and vegetables aren't usually pre-packed, so you can buy as little or as much as you like. Organically-grown produce is becoming increasingly widely available.

Compared with Europe, meat is inexpensive in Canada, chicken breast costing less than $2.70 per pound, pork loin around $4.90 per pound, lean minced (ground) beef around $3 per pound and sirloin steak less than $4.50 per pound. Canadians eat a lot of beef. Most cattle are 'finished' (fattened before slaughter) in vast feed-lots in order to produce large animals in the shortest possible time (a process that may include feeding them steroids and antibiotics). Meat from naturally reared livestock is also available but may cost a little more.

Many foreign foods and ingredients are available in supermarkets and there are also ethnic food stores and supermarkets in many neighbourhoods. Food shops in areas with a large Jewish population often have a kosher section.

Most Canadian supermarkets sell own brand (private label) foods and also have a 'generic' section, where tins and packets bear only the name of the product, statutory information (e.g. weight, contents) and a bar code. These may sell for as little as half (average three-quarters) the price of their name-brand counterparts (it's estimated that a family of four can save almost $2,000 per year by buying own brand items) and in some cases the product is virtually identical to the branded item and may even be produced in the same factory. When comparing different brands, ensure that the quality (grade) and quantity are the same.

All supermarkets have bargain offers on certain items to attract customers, when goods are often sold at below cost ('loss leaders') and displayed at the end of aisles. Many supermarkets have regular discount days, offering such items as a two-litre bottle of soft drink for less than a dollar instead of the usual $1.50. ($1.49 has become a fashionable price and large chain stores such as the Co-op have a monthly 'Dollar 49' day, offering many items at this price on the first Monday of the month.) Other stores (e.g. Safeway and Save-on-Foods) offer a 10 per cent discount to senior citizens on a certain day of the week.

Canadian supermarket check-out assistants use scanners to scan bar codes, and purchases and prices are displayed on screens as they're scanned. Always check screens and your bill, as mistakes are sometimes made (on as many as one in ten products, according to 'thrifty shopping' expert Ian Nicholson). It's rarely necessary to take a shopping bag, as most stores provide free or inexpensive bags at the checkout, where an assistant often packs your bags for you and may even carry them to your car.

In some suburban areas there are few specialist food shops, so you may have little choice but to shop at a supermarket. In neighbourhoods without local supermarkets, corner stores may be open for up to 20 hours per day. It's possible to buy inexpensive naturally-grown fruit and vegetables from local farmers or co-operatives in rural areas (including 'pick your own' farms). Many have roadside stalls or signs advertising their produce. See also **Markets** on page 361.

There are numerous specialist food shops, gourmet food stores, markets and delicatessens in all major cities, selling every luxury food imaginable, although they're generally too expensive to use for buying basic foodstuffs. Larger food shops may provide catering services for anything from a small dinner party or picnic to a 100-person banquet or wedding reception, complete with crockery, furniture, flowers and staff.

CLOTHING

Most Canadians are quite conservative in their dress, eschewing the loud checked trousers and garish Bermuda shorts of their American neighbours, although they do tend to follow American fashion trends (except in Quebec, where they follow European/French fashion). The eastern provinces are generally more conservative than the central and western provinces, where people dress more casually. Whatever the style of dress, the rule followed by most people is to dress in layers that you can take off or put on as you go from centrally heated home to the cold outdoors to an overheated shop or a car that takes a while to warm up.

If you arrive in winter from a country that doesn't have cold winters, you need to buy warm clothing as soon as you arrive. For any sort of outdoor winter activity you need thermal underwear (ideally made of fabric such as polypropylene which draws perspiration away from the body), woollen or thermal socks, mittens and hats, and a pair of waterproof winter boots. Most Canadians in the north wear jackets and under-vests filled with duck or goose-down that keep out the wind as well as the cold.

Apart from the Puffa down-filled jacket, Canada's favourite garment is the humble 'blue jean' – good value at around $40 to $50 for top brands such as Levi's and Wrangler (although you can pay a fortune for 'designer' jeans such as Calvin Klein and Ralph Lauren). T-shirts, often with original designs and slogans, are fashionable and sold everywhere. Shops selling designs from the world's top fashion houses flourish in Canada's largest (and richest) cities; labels include Boss, Calvin Klein, Cambridge, Chanel, Giorgio Armani, Gucci, Hardy Amies, Konen, Polo (Ralph Lauren), Manzoni, Samuelsohn and Tommy Hilfiger.

As in many countries, large department stores are the showcases for new fashions and stage fashion shows to which they invite favoured clients (i.e. those who spend lots of money). Trendy boutiques, where the emphasis is on designer clothes and chic accessories, are found everywhere. Among the most famous Canadian men's stores is Henry Singer, which has a reputation for selling high quality, classic men's clothing. The most popular mainstream clothes stores are Banana Republic, Benetton, Gap (and GapKids) and Roots Canada. The best value specialist clothing chains include Below the Belt, Bootlegger, Stitches and Thrifty's. A popular chain of around 70 sports shops (and some 630 in the US) is Play It Again, which offers secondhand as well as new clothing and equipment.

One of the most surprising things about shopping for quality clothes in Canada is the number of shops selling quality branded clothes at much lower prices than in other countries. However, in smaller towns the reverse may be true. Some successful clothing companies, particularly those which supply clothing for outdoor activities, sell almost entirely by mail-order. Some of the best outlets for bargain-priced designer clothes are chains such as Winners and Hangers, which buy factory overruns and clothes that department stores cannot sell (although there may be no refunds or exchanges). Department stores also have their own outlet stores such as Sears Clearance Centre and The Bay Clearance Centre.

Although many clothes shops also sell shoes, there's a wide variety of specialist shoe shops in Canada. Most Canadian shoes are imported from the US and include Alden, Bass, Docksides, Florsheim, Hush Puppies, Mephisto, Rockport, Sebago, Selby, Sioux, Sperry and Timberland (famous for their boots). European brands are also widely available, such as Bally and Clarks. When buying winter boots, choose those with non-slip soles as well as waterproof outers, which won't discolour from slushy ice and snow. Good children's shoes are produced by Bass, Capezio and Striderite.

Shoe repairers can be found in all towns and in department stores, where repairs may be done while you wait. In most cities and towns, there are sports shoe shops selling specialist sports shoes, leisure shoes and trainers (sneakers). Sports shoes are good value in Canada.

The average North American (male and female) is larger than the average person in most other countries and therefore Canadian and American clothes are often cut larger. Men's shirts sometimes come in different sleeve lengths (as well as collar sizes), which is fine as long as you know the size you need. (See **Appendix D** for comparison tables between Canadian, British and continental European sizes.) Whenever possible, try clothes on before buying and don't be afraid to return them if they don't fit. Most Canadian shops exchange clothes or give a refund (if you're unsure, ask when buying) unless they were purchased during a sale, although the exchange and refund periods can vary considerably.

FURNITURE & FURNISHINGS

Canada has millions of trees and thus has a thriving furniture manufacturing industry. Home-manufactured furniture is good value, and top quality furniture is often cheaper in Canada than in many other countries. There's a huge choice of both traditional and contemporary designs in every price range, although as with most things the quality is usually reflected in the price. A number of manufacturers and wholesalers sell directly to the public, offering savings of up to 30 per cent on shop prices, although you should compare quality before buying. There are stores specialising in beds, leather furniture and reproduction and antique furniture, and companies that both manufacture and install fitted bedrooms, bathrooms and kitchens.

If you want reasonably priced, good quality, modern furniture, there are a number of companies (e.g. Ikea, Leons and The Brick) selling furniture for home assembly.

All large furniture retailers publish catalogues or flyers that may be distributed to local homes. Furniture and home furnishings is a competitive business in Canada, where you may be able to haggle over prices, particularly when you're spending a large amount or are paying cash (credit card companies charge shops a minimum of 3 per cent). Many shops offer 'rooms-to-go' or even 'homes-to-go', where you can buy everything you need at the same time at a discounted price. Another way to save money is to wait for the sales, when prices may be reduced by as much as 50 per cent or more (see **Bargain Shopping** on page 361). If you cannot wait and don't want to pay cash, look for an interest-free credit deal, but don't expect to get a bargain price as well. Check the advertisements in local newspapers (particularly 'home' or 'habitat' sections) and home and design magazines.

Secondhand furniture can be purchased from charity shops, through ads in local newspapers and garage sales (see **Secondhand Goods** on page 356). Furniture for both home and office can also be rented in Canada, although it isn't cost-effective in the long term.

HOUSEHOLD GOODS

The electricity supply in Canada is 110/120 volts AC with a frequency of 60 Hertz (cycles) and therefore imported electrical apparatus made for a 220/240V 50 cycle supply won't work unless it has a 'dual voltage' switch or is used with a transformer (see page 123). It usually isn't worthwhile bringing electrical equipment to Canada, as a wide range of Canadian and American-made items are available at reasonable prices. Also don't bring a TV or VCR made for a different market (e.g. Europe) to Canada, as it won't work (see page 158). Most new homes come complete with major appliances such as a stove and dishwasher and may also include a microwave, refrigerator and washer. Large household appliances such as cookers (stoves or ranges) and refrigerators are usually provided in rented accommodation. Dishwashers are common in Canada, although they aren't usually found in rented accommodation. Practically nobody brings large household appliances to Canada, particularly as the standard width in Canada isn't the same as in other countries, except the US.

Canadian refrigerators are huge and usually have the capacity to store a year's supply of food for a family of 14. Small appliances, such as vacuum cleaners, grills, toasters and electric irons, are inexpensive in Canada and of good quality. Always shop around when buying large appliances and be prepared to haggle over prices, even when goods are on offer. Look for interest-free deals but also make sure that the price is competitive. Bear in mind that some inexpensive deals don't include delivery and installation, so compare inclusive prices.

Canadian beds and bed linen such as sheets, pillowcases and quilts (comforters) aren't the same size or shape as in many other countries.

NEWSPAPERS, MAGAZINES & BOOKS

Canada has daily and weekly newspapers with morning, evening and Sunday editions, plus many free and foreign-language newspapers in the major cities. Quebec's newspapers are printed in French and some other newspapers are printed in both French and English editions. In addition to newspapers, a large number of periodicals are published in weekly, monthly, bi-monthly, quarterly or bi-annual editions. GST (see page 358) is levied on all newspapers, magazines and books, and although most provinces don't levy PST on newspapers or magazines, most do tax books. Canada doesn't have a genuine national press as is common in many European countries, and most newspapers are regional (city or province) or local. Local entertainment magazines and newspapers are published in all major cities, and free newspapers (some of which are surprisingly good) containing local community news are published in all regions and delivered to homes.

The closest Canada has to a national newspaper is the influential and respected *Globe & Mail*, a Toronto newspaper that prints stories of interest to Canadians from coast to coast, although it does have a habit of printing condescending statements such as 'out in Vancouver...'. The only other 'national' paper is the *National Post*, which incorporates the old *Financial Post*. Quality regional newspapers include the *Edmonton Journal*, the *Ottawa Citizen* and the *Vancouver Sun*; less serious 'tabloids' such as the *Edmonton Sun*, *Calgary Sun*, *Toronto Sun* and *The Province* (Vancouver) feature pictures of attractive young ladies (but not topless, which is illegal) and men, known as 'Sunshine Girls' and 'Sunshine Boys'. As in many western countries, the serious newspapers are usually broadsheets, while the tabloids are more interested in scandal, sex and sport (not necessarily in that order).

Most Canadians read newspapers for the comics, sport, fashion, crime reports and local news, and rely on TV for 'serious' news. Major Canadian newspapers contain comprehensive sport and entertainment sections, as well as international news and foreign sports cover. Many newspapers have magazine-format 'lifestyle' and 'home living' sections in order to compete with magazines.

Large city newspapers print two editions per day (a city and rural edition) and some dailies (although not the *Globe & Mail*) also publish Sunday editions. Friday and Saturday editions are often huge and contain ten or more sections on world news, local news, sport, entertainment, finance, home and lifestyle, TV and radio programmes, comic strips, and car and property information (these sections are full of advertisements and are known as 'cat-box liners'). However, Friday and Saturday editions usually cost three times as much as other editions so it may be cheaper to buy a bag of cat litter.

Weekly news magazines such as *MacLean's* (known cynically as Maclone's by those who think it's a copy of *Time*) are hugely popular and are a good way to catch up on the most important Canadian and international news. Other popular Canadian magazines include *Canadian Geographic*, *Today's Parent*, *Saturday Night*,

Harrowsmith, Now and *Chatelaine*. If you have a taste for anarchical reportage, try *Frank Magazine*, which contains hot gossip and smutty stories.

Around a third of Canadians (i.e. those living in the major cities) have newspapers delivered to their homes. Newspapers are sold in towns from 'honour' vending machines located on street corners, in shopping malls, and at railway and bus stations. You insert the exact price (usually 50¢ to 75¢) in a slot and pull down a handle to open the door (you're trusted to take one copy only, hence 'honour'). These machines are the only place you can buy a newspaper without paying sales tax, as the machine manufacturers haven't yet figured out an easy way to cope with the few extra cents. In major cities, newspapers and magazines are sold from newsstands.

Some foreign newspapers and periodicals are available from specialist newsstands in major cities, although they're expensive and newspapers are usually a few days old (with the exception of *The New York Times* and *The Wall Street Journal*, which are available on the day of publication). Some public and university libraries keep a selection of foreign daily newspapers in their reading rooms, although they're usually old copies.

Most Canadian and foreign newspapers and magazines can be purchased on subscription at huge savings over newsstand prices, and many Canadian magazines offer gifts to new subscribers (a list of Canadian newspapers and magazines is available via the Internet at 🖥 www-2.cs.edu/Unofficial/Canadiana). You can buy the most popular foreign magazines through subscription services such as International Subscriptions Inc., 1 Meadowlands Plaza, Suite 900, East Rutherford, NJ 07073, USA (☎ 800-544-6748).

Don't throw your old magazines away when you've finished with them, as some secondhand book shops will buy them from you for around a quarter of their original price.

Despite the imposition of sales tax, Canada is still one of the cheapest countries in the world in which to buy books, particularly paperbacks. There are cut-price and remainder bookstores in major cities, and most general bookstores have a bargain basement, where discount books are sold. Some stores, e.g. Wal-Mart or K-Mart, discount all books – typically a 25 per cent reduction. The biggest nationwide chains include Coles & Smith Books, which have huge outlets called Chapters.

In major cities there are secondhand and exchange book shops for collectors and bargain hunters, often located near university campuses. Specialist book shops are common, including some selling foreign-language books. Except in Quebec and New Brunswick, French-language books are available only at specialised shops in the major cities. In major cities, many book shops are open until late evening (some until midnight) and some are also open on Sundays. Many offer comfortable places to sit and read and some even serve coffee.

Credit card orders are generally accepted by phone and fax, and orders are shipped overnight, e.g. via UPS, FedEx, DHL and Purolator. The easiest way to buy books is via the Internet, through booksellers such as Amazon

(💻 www.amazon.com) or the Canadian Booksellers Association (💻 www.cba
book.org/default.asp).

There are also mail-order book clubs in Canada, most of which have
introductory offers at hugely discounted prices. Some book clubs offer a wide
range of general books, while others specialise in a particular subject, e.g.
photography or computers (clubs advertise in newspapers and magazines).
Many organisations and clubs run their own libraries or book exchanges, and
public libraries in all towns usually have a wide selection of books (see page 327).

ALCOHOL & TOBACCO

The sale of alcohol (liquor) in Canada is strictly controlled in most areas and
licensing laws are set by provinces and municipalities. You can buy spirits only
at shops operated by the provincial Liquor Control Board (LCB), but wines and
beers are sold in supermarkets and at privately-owned beer and wine shops.
Shops selling alcohol cannot open before 10am and must close no later than local
bars. Government 'liquor stores' close any time between 6pm and 11pm on
weekdays and Saturdays, while beer and wine shops usually close at 11pm. All
shops selling alcohol are closed on Sundays. When shops are closed, you can buy
beer or wine from some local bars (called off-sales, for drinking off the premises).

Prices vary little (if at all) in LCB stores, although in some cities prices are
lower and people may travel from out of town to stock up. Sales tax (PST) on
alcohol varies from province to province, so people who live near the border of
a province with lower PST often drive over the border to buy it. It's illegal to
import large quantities of alcohol from the US (where it's cheaper), which is
classed as smuggling.

An 'open container' law forbids the consumption of any alcoholic drink in
public and it's illegal to have an open container in a vehicle, even in the boot.
The minimum legal age for buying alcohol is 18 in Alberta, Quebec and
Saskatchewan, and 19 in the rest of Canada. These age limits also represent the
minimum drinking age in bars. A retailer is supposed to ask your age and may
ask for identification. In practice, however, this rarely happens if you look old
enough. Acceptable identification usually consists of a driving licence or a
Provincial Identification Card issued by the provincial Liquor Control Board
(where there is one).

Canada produces excellent wine (there are import duties on foreign wine to
protect the Canadian wine industry, although you can still find reasonably
priced French and Californian wines). When buying Canadian wine, look for the
Vintner's Quality Assurance (VQA) sign on the labels (the Canadian equivalent
of the French *appellation contrôlée* system), which indicates better quality wines.

Beer is sold in 341ml and 355ml sizes, usually in packs of six (a 'six-pack' or
'half-sack') or cases of 12 ('twelve-pack') or 24 (a 'two-four'); 'supercans' are also
available in 473ml or 950ml sizes. Canadian beer usually has an alcohol content
of 5 or 6 per cent. In Quebec and the Atlantic provinces a non-alcoholic spruce

'beer' is made (from the sap of spruce trees) and in the fruit-growing areas of British Columbia, Ontario and Quebec you can find apple or cherry 'ciders' with varying alcohol content.

The price of rye whisky (such as Canadian Club and Seagrams) and other spirits is around $22 for a 26oz bottle.

Like alcohol, the purchase and use of tobacco and tobacco products is restricted to those over the age of 18 in Alberta, Quebec and Saskatchewan and 19 elsewhere. Canadian cigarettes are generally milder than American, the major brands including Player's, Craven A, DuMaurier, Matinee and Export A (you can also buy Cuban cigars, which are banned in the US).

LAUNDRY & DRY CLEANING

There are self-service launderettes (laundromats) in most towns, open from around 9am until 10pm, seven days a week. A wash usually costs around $1.75 and a dry around $1.25 for 40 minutes. In some areas, launderettes offer free coffee and special offers to attract customers. Usually, for an extra dollar or two per load, launderette staff will wash and dry your clothes for you. Soap powder is sold from machines but it's expensive (e.g. $1.50 to $1.75 per load) and it's best to bring your own.

There are also laundries in most cities that take from one to four days to clean items such as sheets and shirts.

Most Canadian towns have at least one dry cleaner, where you can also usually have minor clothes repairs, invisible mending, alterations and dyeing done. Some dry cleaners offer an emergency one-hour service and a same day alterations service and remove stains within a day or two. In the major cities, many provide a free local delivery and collection service (e.g. within a ten block radius) and most outlets issue coupons and accept coupons issued by their competitors. For some inexplicable reason it can cost around twice as much to have women's clothes dry-cleaned as men's, e.g. $10 for a woman's blouse but $5 for a man's shirt. Other prices include $12 for a suit, $16.50 for an overcoat and $25 for a quilt. Some launderettes have self-service dry-cleaning machines.

Most hotels provide an expensive laundry and dry cleaning service, although a few have coin-operated machines in the basement for residents' use.

MAIL-ORDER SHOPPING

Mail order shopping is widespread in Canada, where busy lifestyles have caused many Canadians to favour the convenience of shopping by catalogue, telephone and Internet. Over 50 per cent of Canadians shop by phone or post and almost anything can be purchased by post and delivered overnight (although you pay extra for this service). Mail-order has a long tradition in Canada, where the mail-order catalogue was invented and those living in remote areas have purchased the latest fashions and consumer goods by post since the late 19th century. Despite increased competition from shops, mail-order remains big business. Canadian mail-order firms don't use agents but deal directly with customers, thus reducing overheads and keeping down prices. Many Canadian manufacturers sell their products by mail-order only, to both corporate and private customers. Some shops, such as The Bay, publish catalogues and will send goods anywhere in the world, and specialist companies such as Pennies and Canadian Tire also produce elaborate catalogues. Orders can usually be placed by phone (toll-free) at local retail outlets and delivery can be made to your home or office. Catalogues are free or cost up to around $5 and often come with gifts and/or discount coupons. Once you've purchased by mail-order, your name goes on a list which is traded by list 'brokers' and you receive countless other catalogues through the post. To prevent this you can contact the Canadian Marketing Association (CDMA), 1 Concorde Gate, Suite 607, Don Mills ON M3C 3N6 (☎ 416-391-2362, 🖳 www.the-cma.org) and ask to be registered on their 'don't post, don't call' service.

There's generally little risk when buying goods by mail-order in Canada, as consumer-protection laws and Canada Post's rules governing mail-order sales are strict. If you have any doubts about a company's reputation, you should check with your provincial or local consumer protection agency, CDMA or a Better Business Bureau before ordering. Keep a copy of the advertisement or offer and a record of your order, including the company's name, address and phone number, the price of items ordered, any handling or other charges, the date you posted or telephoned your order, and your method of payment. Also keep copies of all cancelled cheques and statements. Before committing yourself to buying anything by post, make sure you know what you're signing and don't send cash through the post or pay for anything in advance unless necessary. It's foolish to send advance payment by post in response to an ad (or to anyone) unless you're sure that the company is reputable and provides a money-back guarantee.

A number of companies operate mail-order clubs for books, CDs and cassettes, computer software and DVDs and video cassettes. New members are offered a number of items at a nominal introductory price (e.g. CDs for 10¢ and videos for 49¢ each) in return for an agreement to purchase a further number of items at full price during the following one or two years. There's no catch, although the choice may be restricted and if you want to resign before you've fulfilled your side of the bargain, you must repay the savings made on the introductory offer. You also need to be sure to return the form each month when you don't want to buy anything, as many clubs operate on the premise that, if you don't indicate otherwise, you want the 'selection of the month' and you're then committed to paying for it.

Shopping by phone has increased dramatically in recent years, particularly with the proliferation of charge, credit and debit cards. One of the most popular methods of telephone shopping is via TV through companies such as the Shopping Channel. Cable TV shopping shows offer goods at seemingly bargain prices, some even providing a 24-hour service for insomniac shoppers. Orders are placed by phone and goods are posted to you. Payment can be made by credit card, cheque or money order. However, before placing an order, check that an item isn't available cheaper in local discount stores and set a spending limit before switching on the box.

Be extremely wary of unsolicited telemarketing sales, which have increased dramatically in recent years. A caller will try to sell direct or arrange an appointment to visit you and may offer a variety of gifts and inducements to tempt you. If you aren't interested, just say 'No thank you' and put the phone down. If you're tempted, ask for written information by post and check out the company or organisation, e.g. with a Better Business Bureau. **Never give credit card or bank account details over the phone.** As a general rule, it's wise to ignore all unsolicited phone calls, as you never know whether the caller is a confidence trickster or some other type of crook. Although many reputable companies sell their products or services by phone, they rarely resort to unsolicited phone calls to obtain business.

Using international credit cards, you can buy goods from America and other foreign countries. Commercial shipments under $20 and non-commercial gifts valued at under $60 sent from outside Canada can be received free of duty and tax in Canada, although they must bear a complete description of the contents and their value. For further information about international post imports, contact the Automated Customs Information Service of Canada Customs and Revenue Agency (☎ 1-800-461-9999, 🖥 www.ccra-adrc.gc.ca).

Shopping via the Internet is the fastest-growing form of retailing and, although it's still in its infancy, sales are already worth billions of dollars per year. Shopping on the Internet is secure (secure servers, with addresses beginning https:// rather than http://, are almost impossible to crack) and in most cases safer than shopping by phone or post. There are literally thousands of shopping sites on the Internet and you can compare the price of goods via websites such as Webcentric (🖥 www.bottomdollar.com) and Buy Sell (🖥 www. buysell.com), which combine Internet shopping services with information services. With Internet shopping the world is literally your oyster and savings can be made on a wide range of goods, including CDs, clothes, sports equipment, electronic gadgets, jewellery, books, wine, computer software and services such as insurance, pensions and mortgages. Huge savings can also be made on holidays and travel.

DUTY-FREE ALLOWANCES

Duty-free allowances depend on whether you're a resident or a non-resident (see below). Generally speaking, if you leave Canada to travel, work or study abroad and return to resume residence in Canada, you're classified as a resident by customs. Canadian residents living abroad temporarily are classified as non-residents, provided that they re-export any goods acquired abroad when they leave the country. Children of Canadian citizens who were born abroad and have never resided in Canada are entitled to the customs exemptions granted to non-residents and, with the exception of alcoholic beverages and tobacco, are entitled to the same exemptions as adults.

You may verbally declare any articles acquired abroad if they're accompanying you and you haven't exceeded your duty-free exemption. The head of a family may make a joint declaration for all members residing in the same household and entering Canada together. Family members may combine their personal exemptions, even if the articles acquired by one family member exceed his personal exemption.

After your allowances have been deducted, a flat rate duty of 10 per cent is applied to the next $1,000 value of dutiable goods. The value of imported goods is based on the fair retail value of each item in the country where it was acquired and not necessarily the price paid. **If you underestimate the value of an article or misrepresent an article in your declaration, you may have to pay a penalty in addition to duty.** If you're in doubt about the value of an article, declare it at the price paid. If you fail to declare an article acquired abroad, you're liable to a penalty equivalent to the value of the article in Canada. In addition, the article is subject to seizure and forfeiture and you may be liable to criminal prosecution. **If you're in doubt about whether an article should be declared, always declare it and let the customs official decide.**

Articles exempt from duty must have been acquired for your personal or household use, must be brought with you when you enter Canada and must be properly declared to customs. For further information contact Canada Customs and Revenue Agency's Automated Customs Information Service (☎ 1-800-461-9999 – call between 8am and 4pm Mondays to Fridays if you wish to speak to a customs officer).

When travelling abroad (including to the US), you should take receipts for cameras and video cameras (etc.) with you and declare them to customs before leaving Canada, so that you aren't charged duty on them when you return.

Whether or not you're a resident, you may not bring certain goods into Canada or you may need a permit (see **Restricted Goods** on page 93).

Residents: If you live close to the border with America, you may want to cross it for shopping trips. What you may bring into Canada duty-free depends on how long you've been away, as follows:

Duration of Absence	Allowance
24 hours	Goods (**excluding** tobacco and alcohol products) worth up to $50
48 hours	Goods (**including** tobacco and alcohol products – see below) worth up to $200
7 days	Goods (**including** tobacco and alcohol products – see below) worth up to $500

After an absence of 24 or 48 hours, you may need to make a written declaration; after an absence of seven days, you **must** make a written declaration. You may claim these allowances an unlimited number of times per year.

Non-Residents: Non-residents are allowed to import the following items duty-free provided that the gifts accompany you, you're planning to stay 72 hours or more and haven't claimed this exemption within the previous six months:

- 200 cigarettes **and** 50 cigars **and** 7oz (200g) of loose tobacco for each person who's allowed to smoke (18 years of age when entering Alberta, Manitoba or Quebec and 19 for all other provinces and territories);

- 1 bottle (0.75l) of wine **or** spirits **and** 24 x 355ml (12oz) tins or bottles (total 8.5 litres) of beer or ale **or** 1.5 litres of wine for each person who's allowed to drink (18 years of age when entering Alberta, Manitoba or Quebec and 19 years for all other provinces and territories). You may also bring in alcohol in addition to your duty-free allowance, provided that you pay the duty and that the total amount doesn't exceed the limits set by the province or territory you're entering.

- A 'reasonable amount' of perfume for personal use;

- Gifts (excluding alcohol and tobacco products) to the value of $60 each.

There's no restriction on the number of cameras you may import, although you're permitted only a 'reasonable amount' of film!

Non-residents can reclaim GST on many goods and short-term accommodation in Canada, and PST can also be reclaimed in Manitoba, Newfoundland, Nova Scotia and Quebec (see **Sales Taxes** on page 358).

RECEIPTS & WARRANTIES

When shopping in Canada you should insist on a receipt as proof of payment (this is particularly useful when an automatic alarm is activated as you're leaving a shop!). It may also be impossible to return or exchange goods without a receipt and you may need one to return an item for repair or replacement under a warranty. You should check receipts immediately on paying (particularly in supermarkets); if you're overcharged, you cannot usually obtain redress later.

Although it isn't required by law, most shops give a cash refund or credit on a charge account or credit card within a certain period, e.g. one to two weeks (although you may be offered only a shop credit or exchange on discounted goods). Some discount and outlet stores don't allow any returns. Shops usually display their refund policy on a sign or it's stated on your receipt.

All goods sold in Canada carry an implied warranty of 'merchantability', meaning that they must perform the function for which they were designed. If they don't, you can return them to the store where you purchased them and demand a replacement or your money back. In addition to the implied warranty, some goods carry written warranties. Although written warranties are voluntary, when provided they must (by law) be written in clear, everyday language, and the precise terms and duration must be specified at the top of the warranty document.

The period of a warranty varies considerably, e.g. from one to five years, and may be an important consideration when making a purchase. Warranties can also be full or limited, a full warranty providing you with maximum protection, although usually for a limited period. You may be offered the chance to purchase an extension warranty when you buy certain goods. These cost from $60 to $100 and aren't usually worth the money, as they rarely extend beyond the natural working life of a product. Warranties may be transferable when goods are sold or given away during the warranty period. You're often asked to complete and post a warranty card confirming the date of purchase, although under a full warranty this isn't necessary. Most warranties are with the manufacturer or importer, to whom goods must usually be returned.

A local or provincial consumer protection agency, Better Business Bureau or consumer association can usually advise you of your rights.

When travelling abroad, you should take your receipts for cameras and video cameras (etc.) with you (see **Duty-Free Allowances** above).

CONSUMER ASSOCIATIONS

There's a number of consumers' organisations in Canada, including the Consumers Association of Canada, 404-267 O'Connor Street, Ottawa ON K2P 1V3 (☎ 613-238-2533, ☐ www.consumer.ca), which promotes and explains consumer rights and helps individuals to resolve disputes with retailers, and the Canadian Council of Better Business Bureaus, 44 Byward Market Square, Suite 220, Ottawa, Ontario K1N 7A2, Canada (☎ 613-7898-5151, ☐ www.canadian councilbbb.ca), which claims to promote high ethical standards of business practice and provide a 'platform' for the discussion of retailer-consumer relations as well as helping to resolve disputes.

18.

ODDS & ENDS

378 Odds & Ends

This chapter contains miscellaneous information. Although not all topics included are of vital importance, most are of general interest to anyone living or working in Canada, including such weighty matters as tipping and toilets.

CANADIAN CITIZENSHIP

In general, those who are born in Canada automatically become Canadian citizens. You may also be a Canadian citizen if you were born abroad and one of your parents was Canadian at the time of your birth. If you think you may come under this category, check with your local Canadian High Commission, embassy or consulate. All others can become a Canada citizen only through a process called naturalisation. To be eligible for naturalisation you must be aged 18 or over, be in Canada legally as a 'permanent resident', have lived in Canada for three of the past four years (except for children) and be able to understand, speak, read and write English or French. You must undergo a written 'citizenship test' of around 20 questions to demonstrate that you know about the rights and responsibilities of a citizen, and have a reasonable knowledge of Canada's geography, history and political system.

The test is in two parts: general questions about Canada and questions about the region where you live. Typical questions cover native Americans, the early explorers, railway building, when Canada became a country, who has the right to apply for a Canadian passport, what the names of the provinces are, when European settlers first came to your region, the capital city, mineral and natural resources in the region, and which political party is in power. You're given a study guide of typical questions when you apply for citizenship, with some recommended books to read to prepare for the test. The questions you may be asked and other information about naturalisation are listed in a free booklet, *How To become a Canadian Citizen*, available from citizenship offices or the Registrar of Canada Citizenship, PO Box 10000, Sydney NS B1P 7C1. You can also attend citizenship classes and information is available on the Internet too (🖳 www.cic.gc.ca).

Children don't need to have lived in Canada for three years before applying for citizenship. Parents can apply for citizenship for their children as soon as they receive permanent resident status, provided that the parents are already Canadian citizens themselves or are in the process of applying for citizenship (which means that you can submit the papers for the whole family at the same time). A separate application form is required for each child. Children (under 18) don't have to sit a written test, but if they're over 14 they must take the oath of citizenship. The fee for processing citizenship applications is $200 for adults and $100 for children. If an application is refused, adults receive a refund of $100 but children don't receive a refund. You cannot become a Canadian citizen if you're under a deportation order and shouldn't be in Canada, if you've been charged with an indictable offence or have been convicted of one in the past three years, or if you've been in prison, on parole or on probation within the last four years.

Naturalisation is a legal status and therefore Canadian citizenship is conferred by a judge in a 'naturalisation ceremony', when an 'oath of citizenship' is taken. The oath is normally sworn on the bible, but if you wish to use your own holy book, you may do so (take it with you as they may not have one available). Canadian law permits dual nationality for naturalised citizens, who have virtually the same rights as native-born Canadians, but your previous country of citizenship may not allow you to retain it after you've taken Canadian nationality. There's no compulsion for immigrants to become Canadian citizens and they're free to live in Canada for as long as they wish, provided that they abide by the laws of the land.

Passports

Once you become a Canadian citizen you can apply for a Canadian passport. Children under 16 years of age can be included in a parent's passport, but can then travel only with that parent, or be issued with their own passport. Application forms (available from your local passport office) must be accompanied by two photographs, one of which must be signed on the reverse (along with the form) by an eligible guarantor (as listed on the form). You must also provide evidence of Canadian citizenship, any previous Canadian passport, a certificate of identity or a refugee travel document issued in the last five years, and pay a fee of $60 ($20 for children under the age of three and $35 for those between three and 15) plus a supplementary 'consular' fee of $25 (which is to support Canadian consulates abroad). The fee can be paid in cash in person at a passport office, by money order (postal or bank), certified cheque or bank draft payable to the Receiver General for Canada. If you live in an area where there's a passport office, you can submit your application in person, which takes around five days compared with ten or more for postal applications (passport offices are listed in the yellow pages or you can phone ☎ 1-800-567-6868 for information). Alternatively you can post your application to the Passport Office, Place du Centre, 200 Promenade du Portage, Commercial Level 2, Quebec (🖳 www.ppt.gc.ca).

CLIMATE

Due to its vast size and varied topography, ranging from temperate rainforest to tundra and permafrost, Canada's climate varies enormously. Temperatures in the southern region of the prairie provinces of Alberta, Manitoba and Saskatchewan vary from 100°F (38°C) in summer to -12°F (-24°C) in winter. In Yellowknife (Northwest Territories) the winter temperature drops to -28°F (-33°C), although the Yukon holds the record for the coldest temperature ever recorded in Canada which was -81°F (-61°C). Fortunately not too many people live in these inhospitable areas. Not surprisingly the northern region of some provinces and the northern territories are referred to as the Great White North, where summer (the frost-free period) lasts barely two months. Vancouver and Victoria on the Pacific coast have the smallest annual temperature swings, while the largest variations are experienced in Ontario and Quebec, which have harsh winters and hot, humid summers. In the Atlantic provinces of New Brunswick, Prince Edward Island, Nova Scotia and Newfoundland, spring and summer are warm and pleasant, but winter can be very cold and windy.

In winter it's cold or freezing everywhere except on the southern coast of British Columbia (e.g. Vancouver), which has the most temperate climate thanks to warm, moist Pacific Ocean airstreams. Everywhere else experiences a lot of snow, plus chilling winds and occasionally ice storms, when 'snow' instantly freezes forming a thick coat of ice on everything. During a particularly severe ice-storm in southern Ontario and Quebec in early 1998, power lines were brought crashing down by the weight of the ice and the region was without electricity for several days. If you're a keen skier you will welcome some snow, but won't perhaps be so enthusiastic when snowdrifts make the roads impassable, engulf your home and cut you off from the outside world for days on end.

Temperatures are often reduced considerably by the wind speed. This creates what's known as the wind chill factor, where a temperature of 10°F (-12°C) combined with a wind speed of 25mph (40kph) results in a wind chill factor of -29°F (-34°C). The wind chill factor can cause temperatures to drop as low as -60°F (-51°C), when people (not surprisingly) are warned to stay at home. However, in southern Alberta there's often a warm, dry winter wind called a chinook, which can raise temperatures by more than 25°C in less than an hour (**but don't be fooled by this as it soon turns cold again!**). Canadian meteorologists are constantly on the alert for severe weather patterns, and warnings are issued if a heavy snowfall or ice storm is expected and storm watches are broadcast on TV and radio (some radios have a special national weather service band).

Spring and autumn (fall) are quite short in some regions and the most pleasant seasons in Canada, although temperatures can vary considerably from week to week. Spring and autumn are warm and sunny with low humidity in most regions, although it can be very wet in some areas (particularly on the Atlantic and Pacific coasts). The Atlantic provinces are a blaze of colour in the autumn from their maple trees and many tourists flock to see the display. At the end of winter (on February 2nd) Canadians celebrate 'Groundhog Day', when Wiarton Willie the groundhog is supposed to come out of his hole to check the weather. The story goes that if it's a bright sunny day and Willie sees his shadow on the ground at midday, he will dash back down because winter is going to stay for another six weeks. There was a major fuss in 1999 when Willie died and someone started a 'Who Whacked Willie' website, which is now defunct. However, the good people of Wiarton appointed a new groundhog, known as Wee Willie Junior, in good time for the next year's tourist season (see 🖳 www.wiarton-willie.org/).

Canadians usually overreact to extremes of climate, with freezing air-conditioning in summer and sweltering heating in winter. Because most buildings are too hot or too cold, it's often a problem knowing what to wear and many people dress in layers that they take off or put on, depending on the indoor or outdoor temperature. The average maximum temperatures for selected cities are shown below:

	Average Temperature			
City	Winter (Jan)	Spring (Apr)	Summer (Jul)	Autumn (Oct)
Calgary	-6 C (21 F)	8 C (46 F)	22 C (72 F)	10 C (50 F)
Halifax	-1 C (30 F)	9 C (48 F)	23 C (73 F)	14 C (57 F)
Montreal	-6 C (21 F)	11 C (52 F)	26 C (79 F)	13 C (55 F)
Ottawa	-6 C (21 F)	11 C (52 F)	26 C (79 F)	13 C (55 F)
St John's	0 C (32 F)	5 C (41 F)	21 C (70 F)	11 C (52 F)
Toronto	-7 C (19 F)	6 C (43 F)	21 C (70 F)	9 C (48 F)
Vancouver	5 C (41 F)	13 C (55 F)	22 C (72 F)	14 C (57 F)
Whitehorse	-16 C (3 F)	6 C (43 F)	20 C (68 F)	4 C (39 F)
Winnipeg	-14 C (7 F)	9 C (48 F)	26 C (79 F)	12 C (54 F)
Yellowknife	-25 C (-13 F)	-1 C (30 F)	21 C (70 F)	1 C (34 F)

Weather forecasts are given in daily newspapers and broadcast by radio and TV stations, including the 24-hour Weather Channel.

CRIME

Unlike its neighbour to the south, Canada experiences relatively little crime. In fact it's low crime rate is cited as one of the reasons why Canada is one of the most desirable places in the world to live. That's not to say that you should leave your valuables in an unlocked car or walk the inner city streets on your own late at night! Crime is naturally more common in the major cities and popular tourist areas, where petty thieves haunt bus and train stations, car parks and camping areas.

Prevention & Safety

Staying safe in a large city is mostly a matter of common sense. Most areas are safe most of the time, particularly when there are a lot of people about, although at night you should keep to brightly lit main streets and avoid secluded areas (best of all, take a taxi). Walk in the opposite direction to the traffic so nobody can drive alongside (curb-crawl) you at night, and walk on the outside of the pavement (sidewalk), so you're less likely to be mugged from a doorway. Avoid parks at night and keep to a park's main paths or where there are other people during the day. When you're in an unfamiliar city, ask a policeman, taxi driver or local person if there are any unsafe neighbourhoods – and avoid them!

Most city apartments are fitted with a security system, so you can speak to visitors before allowing them access to your building, and doors have a peephole and security chain so that you can check a caller's identity before opening the door. **Be careful who you let into your home and always check the identity of anyone claiming to be an official or an employee of a utility company (check by phone with their office if you aren't expecting anybody).** Store anything of value in a home safe or a bank safety deposit box and ensure that you have adequate insurance (see page 276). Never make it obvious that nobody is at home by leaving tell-tale signs such as a pile of newspapers or post. Many people leave lights, a radio or a TV on (activated by random timers) when they aren't at home and ask their neighbours to keep an eye on their homes when they're on holiday (vacation). Many towns have 'crime watch' areas, where residents keep an eye open for suspicious characters and report them to the local police. If you have something stolen and need to claim on your insurance, you must report the theft to the police and make a note of the crime report number for the claim form.

Guns & Other Weapons

Canada has very strict laws on guns (firearms) and a new Firearms Act in 1998 tightened gun ownership further. Since 1st January 2001, all guns have had to be licensed, with the licence valid for five years, and since 31st December 2002, all firearms have also had to be registered. You must register a gun in order to inform the government who owns the weapon and where it's to be kept, and then the licence allows you to own it. The minimum age to register and own a gun is 18, in Spring 2003, it was estimated that around 35 per cent of guns presently owned are unregistered. There's a long list of prohibited weapons that you may not own or import, including various automatic shotguns, automatic and semi-automatic rifles and carbines, submachine guns and assault pistols (not to mention a long list of other prohibited weapons, including tear gas, stun guns, spiked wristbands and brass knuckles). Even sporting guns must be registered, licensed and declared when taking them into Canada, and you cannot import anything except a regular sporting rifle or shotgun with a barrel at least 18.5in (470mm) long and an overall length of 26in (660mm) manufactured for sporting, hunting or competition use only. For full details contact Canada Firearms Centre, 284 Wellington St., Ottawa, Ontario K1A 0H8 (☎ 1-800-731-4000).

GEOGRAPHY

Even larger than its southern neighbour the US, Canada covers an area of 3.85 million mi² (9.97 million km²) and is, since the disintegration of the USSR, the second-largest country in the world, after China. Canada is a federation made up of ten provinces and three territories: Alberta, British Columbia, Manitoba, New Brunswick, Newfoundland, Nova Scotia, Ontario, Prince Edward Island, Quebec and Saskatchewan, and the Northwest Territories, Nunavut and the Yukon Territory. Canada stretches around 4,800mi (7,700km) from east to west, from the Atlantic Ocean to the Pacific Ocean. The country extends around 3,000mi (4,800km) from north to south, from Pelee Island in Lake Erie to Ellesmere Island in the Arctic Ocean, and the southern border with the US is 5,525mi (8,892km) in length. The country is divided into seven main geographical regions.

The Arctic Or Great White North

The Arctic region contains the Northwest Territories, Nunavut and the Yukon, comprising around 40 per cent of Canada's land area. North of the tree-line, the Arctic is a land of harsh beauty with long, dark and freezing cold winters. North of the mainland is a maze of islands separated by convoluted straits and sounds, the most famous of which form the fabled Northwest Passage (the route to the Orient sought by many early explorers). The harsh climate of this remote area means that relatively few people live there and those that do usually scratch a living from the fur trade or work in mining. Dawson City (in the Yukon) was the scene of the Klondyke Gold Rush in 1898, which for a brief period was the richest gold field of all time. Apart from the indigenous First Nations people, most inhabitants are transients such as miners, hunters and government employees on a short tour of duty. The total population of this vast region is barely 100,000, with around half of those in the two major towns of Whitehorse and Yellowknife. After much lobbying, the eastern part of the Northwest Territories became Nunavut ('our land') on April 1st 1999, with its capital at Iqaluit (population 4,400) on the southern tip of Baffin Island.

The Atlantic Provinces-Appalachian Region

This region was the first to be settled by Europeans and takes in Canada's smallest provinces of New Brunswick, Newfoundland, Nova Scotia and Prince Edward Island. These provinces, which are an extension of the Appalachians (an ancient mountain range), consist mainly of forested hills, low mountains and rocky coastlines, with the population mostly comprised of scattered small communities. The Grand Banks, extending 250mi (around 400km) off the coast, is one of the world's richest fishing grounds, although it has been ravaged by over-fishing in recent years. Some 10 per cent of the Canadian population lives here, mostly relying on forestry and fishing for a living.

The Canadian Shield

The Canadian (or Laurentian) Shield is Canada's largest geographical feature (covering half the mainland) and is billions of years old. It extends from the region around Hudson Bay in the north stretching east to Labrador, south to Kingston on Lake Ontario and north-west as far as the Arctic Ocean. The region is rich in minerals, although it has only a thin layer of soil on a solid granite base, so not much grows (apart from trees) and the population is sparse.

The Cordillera

This region encompasses all of the Yukon and most of British Columbia, and is part of the 9,000mi (14,500km) chain of mountains stretching from Tierra del Fuego (Chile) to Alaska. The region includes the highest point in Canada, Mount Logan (6,050m/19,849ft) in the St Elias Mountains in the south-west corner of the Yukon. It's home to around 13 per cent of the population, most of whom live within 150mi (240km) of the US border. Apart from some farming and fruit production, the main industries are forestry and tourism.

The Great Lakes And St Lawrence Lowlands

The southern areas of Ontario and Quebec, the industrial heartland of Canada, contain Canada's two largest cities, Toronto and Montreal. The region has some prime agricultural land and the large expanses of Lakes Erie and Ontario moderate the climate and extend the number of frost-free days, permitting the cultivation of grapes, pears, peaches and other fruit. The Great Lakes and St Lawrence region is also sugar maple country. With rich soil, easy access to the sea via the St Lawrence Seaway and a long border with the US, this region is home to over half of Canada's population.

The Pacific Coast

The British Columbia coast in the west is indented with deep fjords, shielded from Pacific storms and bathed by warm, moist Pacific air currents. These help provide the most moderate climate in Canada, although Vancouver Island's west coast receives an exceptional amount of rain, hence it's temperate rain forest climate. The region encompasses three major mountain ranges: The Rocky Mountains, the Columbia Mountains and the Coast Mountains, and is home to Canada's oldest (Western Canadian cedars up to 1,300 years old) and tallest (Douglas firs) trees.

The Prairies

The southern areas of Alberta, Manitoba and Saskatchewan (also known as the Interior Plains or Heartland) are Canada's 'breadbasket' (and one of the richest grain-producing regions in the world), consisting largely of cereal fields. Around a quarter of its population is descended from migrants from Germany, Russia, the Ukraine and other eastern European countries (most of whose ancestors arrived in the early 20th century). Manitoba and Saskatchewan are home to around 8 per cent of the population, while Alberta has around 10 per cent, which has risen rapidly with the oil boom. Alberta also has the distinction of being the source of more dinosaur bones than anywhere else in the world and boasts a world-class fossil museum at the main site, Drumheller.

GOVERNMENT

Canada is a confederation of provinces and was officially created as a country on 1st July 1867 from the provinces now known as Ontario, Quebec, New Brunswick and Nova Scotia. The other provinces and territories joined the confederation between then and 1949, when Newfoundland was the last to join (apart from Nunavut, which was created on 1st April 1999). July 1st is celebrated annually as the federal holiday, Canada Day. Canada is a constitutional monarchy, with Queen Elizabeth II as the constitutional head of state. Except when in Canada, she delegates her (mainly ceremonial) duties to her Canadian representatives, the Governor General (GG) and the provincial representatives called Lieutenant Governors. In theory, the Prime Minister (PM) and the cabinet advise the Queen, but in practical terms the country is run by the elected federal and provincial governments.

The GG, who's always a Canadian citizen, is appointed by the Queen on the advice of the PM and acts on the cabinet's advice, giving royal assent to bills passed in parliament, summoning, opening and closing parliament, and dissolving it before an election. In 1982 a new Constitution Act was passed which included the 'Canada Charter of Rights and Freedoms', that defines and protects the personal rights and basic freedoms of Canadian citizens and residents (prior to this date, changes to the Canadian Constitution had to be approved by the British government).

Canada is a democracy with three levels of government, federal, provincial and municipal, each elected by popular vote. The Canadian system of government is based on the British constitution and has a House of Commons and a Senate (roughly equivalent to the British House of Lords). The House of Commons has around 300 members, from which the Cabinet is mostly drawn (ministers may also be appointed from the Senate). Federal elections must be held every five years (or sooner), when the Prime Minister (and head of government) is chosen by the members of the political party with the most members of the House of Commons. The Senate consists of 105 senators appointed by the Prime Minister and the Governor General. Senators must retire at age 75 and aren't allowed to introduce financial bills or defeat constitutional amendments (although they can delay them from becoming law).

Each house has specific duties. For example, the Senate's duties include confirming laws initiated by the House of Commons, but it cannot initiate bills to spend public money or raise taxes. It has three basic functions: to review government bills, investigate (via committees) major social and economic issues, and to provide a national forum for debating public issues and regional concerns. The House of Commons mainly exists to introduce and discuss legislation (bills) that may eventually become law. Each bill has several readings, the first of which is just a simple reading with no debate. Then it's printed and distributed to Members before having a second reading and moving to committee stage. After this it goes back to the house, with or without amendments, for a vote on whether to make it law. The federal government is responsible for national defence, foreign policy, trade and commerce, currency, banking, criminal law, fisheries, shipping, postal services, some social benefits and taxation.

There's no system of proportional representation in Canada, and Canada has many political parties, both large and small. The major parties are the Liberals (or Grits), Progressive Conservatives (PC or Tories), the New Democratic Party (NDP) and the Reform Party. Parties promoting Quebec independence are the *Bloc Québécois* (federally) and the *Parti Québécois* (provincially). On a scale from right wing to left wing, the national parties line up as follows: Reform, PC, Liberal and NDP. There are also fringe parties such as the Green Party and the Natural Law Party.

Provincial & Territorial

Each province has its own government, organised in the same way as the federal parliament. The territories have seats in the federal House of Commons, but are administered by the federal government. Those elected to the legislature are called Members of the Legislative Assembly (MLA), Members of the National Assembly (MNA), Members of Provincial Parliament (MPP) or Members of the House of Assembly (MHA), depending on the province or territory. The provinces have a large degree of autonomy that includes raising their own provincial taxes and drafting provincial laws with regard to trade and commerce, education, provincial highways and driving, marriage, divorce, licensing, firearms, social services (e.g. health and welfare), wages and criminal justice. Provincial governments are also responsible for civil and some criminal law, property rights, vehicle and marriage licensing, municipal institutions and working conditions. The responsibility for immigration and agriculture is shared between the federal and provincial governments.

Local

Each province is made up of a number of municipalities, each with its own separate local government (council) that passes local by-laws in its community. Its responsibilities include primary and secondary education, police, fire and ambulance services, courts and jails, libraries, health and welfare, public transport subsidies, parks and recreation, waste disposal, highways and road safety (including snow removal), and trading standards. The council is headed by a mayor and other elected representatives, usually called councillors. Around 4,700 municipal governments report to their provincial government and have no formal contact with the federal government. Southern Ontario and southern Quebec are divided into counties, which comprise a number of municipalities.

Voting

You must be a Canadian citizen, aged over 18 and on the list of electors in order to vote in Canada. The 'electoral roll' used to be compiled by enumerators who called on households to check who was eligible to vote, but it's now up to individuals to ensure that they're on the list and receive their 'elector information card' (which confirms that a person is on the list of electors and tells him where and when to vote). If you haven't been given a card or if there are errors on it, you should contact your local Elections Canada office or phone (☎ 1-800-463-6868). On polling day you simply take your card to your local polling station, obtain a voting paper from the polling officer and cast your vote by placing an X in the box next to the name of your favoured candidate, before putting the paper in the ballot box. Voting in Canada is by secret ballot.

National Anthem & Flag

The National Anthem, 'O Canada', was composed in 1880 by Calixa Lavallée (the French lyrics were written by Sir Adolphe-Basile Routhier). The English lyrics were originally composed by Mr. Justice Robert Stanley Weir in 1908, but there have been many versions over the years. The latest official English version was agreed in 1968 by a special joint committee of the Senate and the House of Commons. The national flag of a red maple leaf on a white background with red sidebars (representing the two ocean boundaries) was instituted in 1965 after a design competition. The sidebars are red, rather than blue, because part of the reason for the new flag was to show independence from both Britain and France, both of which have red, white and blue in their national flags. Each province and territory also has its own flag.

LEGAL SYSTEM

The Canadian legal system is based on federal law, augmented by provincial laws and local by-laws. Most rights and freedoms enjoyed by Canadians are enshrined in the Canadian Charter of Rights and Freedoms (which became part of the constitution in 1982). Canadian law and the constitution apply to everyone in Canada, irrespective of citizenship or immigration status, and even illegal immigrants have the same basic legal rights as a Canadian citizen. Under the Canadian constitution, each province has the right to make its own laws in certain areas and you shouldn't automatically assume that the law is the same in different provinces. In most of Canada (Quebec being, as usual, the exception) laws are a mixture of statute and common laws. Common law is particularly valid in the case of civil law which is based on precedent and deals with private matters between individuals, such as property disputes or business transactions. In Quebec there's a written *Code Civil* (based on the French Napoleonic Law) that contains general principles and rules for different types of cases. Unlike common law, the judge looks at this written code for guidance before considering precedents set by earlier judgements. At the end of the day, although the principles are different, the decisions reached are generally much the same.

Provincial courts deal with most types of criminal offence, small claims (private disputes involving limited amounts of money) and youth and family courts. Judges at this level are appointed by the province. The next highest level is the superior court, with judges appointed by the federal government, which handle serious criminal and civil cases. Above this level is the provincial court of appeal. A separate system of federal courts operates alongside provincial courts and deals with cases arising under the Canadian constitution or any law or treaty. These include claims against the federal government and such matters as patents, copyright and maritime law. The federal court system is based in Ottawa, but judges may sit across the country. Federal court judges may also act as arbitrators under the Unemployment Insurance Act and in certain cases involving agriculture.

At the top of the legal system is the Supreme Court of Canada, which consists of a Chief Justice and eight other judges appointed by the federal cabinet. Three of these judges must come from Quebec and three traditionally also come from Ontario, two from Western Canada and one from the Atlantic provinces. Cases may be referred to the supreme court only if the court itself agrees (although this doesn't apply to certain cases, such as criminal cases where an acquittal has been set aside by a provincial court of appeal), the idea being to restrict its deliberations to matters of public importance or those that raise important questions of law. The supreme court sits for three sessions per year (winter, spring and autumn) in Ottawa and has recently begun to use tele-conferencing to permit presentations from other parts of the country. Information about the Supreme Court of Canada is available on the Internet (🖥 www.scc-csc.gc.ca). There's also a Tax Court of Canada that sits in major cities across the country.

The courts are administered by an official who's known variously as the 'registrar', 'clerk' or 'administrator of the court'. His duties include informing the legal profession of court procedures, signing orders and judgements, issuing summonses and collecting court costs. Jury management is usually dealt with by a sheriff or bailiffs. In addition to formal courts, some minor matters are heard by a judge sitting 'in chambers', and in Ontario, Family Law Commissions deal with some divorce cases and other family law matters. In some cities there are judicial officers who can act as judges in certain circumstances, such as assessing penalties under summary convictions on criminal code offences or issuing search warrants. In the north and in some provinces, official judges take part in 'circle courts', where the judge, police, social workers, tribal officials, victims and the convicted person sit in a circle to consider an appropriate sentence and restitution.

There's no Canadian equivalent of the US 'Miranda' law that requires arresting officers to recite your rights to you. **You do, however, have the right to remain silent, the right to have a lawyer present during questioning and the right to have a free legal aid lawyer if you cannot afford one.** It's wise to say nothing until you've spoken with a lawyer. If you're arrested, you're entitled to call your lawyer and if you don't have one the police officer must give you the number of the legal aid office and allow you to call them. You must be allowed to talk to your lawyer alone and must be taken before a court within 24 hours or released.

Another area where Canada differs considerably from its US neighbour is in the matter of private litigation. Obviously people and companies do go to court to settle their differences, but suing large corporations in the hope that a sympathetic jury will award a plaintiff millions of dollars is rare in Canada.

Many social service agencies provide free legal assistance to immigrants, although some may serve the nationals of a particular country or religion only. There are help lines and agencies offering free legal advice in most towns and cities, many working with legal aid societies (offering free advice and referral on legal matters), Better Business Bureaux (dealing with consumer-related complaints, shopping services, etc.) and departments of consumer affairs (which also handle consumer complaints).

MARRIAGE & DIVORCE

In order to get married in Canada the bride and groom must usually be aged at least 18, or 16 if they have parental consent, although ages vary depending on the province. In most provinces marriage licences are issued by local city or county clerks and an application must usually be made in the municipality where the woman lives. Common law marriages don't require a licence and carry the same legal status as official marriages after six months. They basically consist of a man and woman living together as man and wife sharing a common name. Gay common law marriages are quite common and in 1999 the supreme court ruled that 'a same sex couple is still a couple', thus giving them full legal status.

Canada has a high divorce rate, with some 70,000 couples getting divorced every year (about half the marriage rate). Once you've been separated from your spouse for a year, you can file (petition) for a divorce and if your spouse doesn't raise any objection within one month, the petition is rubber-stamped and you're free to marry again (this is known as an 'uncontested divorce'). If you anticipate any objections, you should consult a divorce lawyer. Due to the high probability of divorce in Canada, many potential marriage partners insist on a (decidedly unromantic) marriage contract or prenuptial agreement, limiting a spouse's claims in the event of a divorce. Foreigners living in Canada who are married, divorced or widowed should have a valid marriage licence, divorce papers or death certificate. These are necessary to confirm your marital status with the authorities, e.g. to receive certain legal or social insurance benefits. Foreigners married abroad come under the marriage laws of the country where they were married.

Like most things in Canada, marriage and divorce laws vary from province to province. If you're contemplating either and need to know the law, a series of books covering a number of provinces (including Alberta, British Columbia and Ontario) is published by Self Counsel Press Inc.

MILITARY SERVICE

There's no draft (conscription) in Canada and no requirement to register for military service, as all members of the armed forces are volunteers. Canada has a relatively small number of armed forces, which has fallen from a high of 112,000 in 1986 to the current level (2003) of 60,000 regulars and 20,000 reserves. Women are allowed to serve in combat roles in the military, although prejudice is rife, which has been highlighted in recent years by a number of high-profile lawsuits against the military for sexual harassment and other abuses.

PETS

All animals and birds imported into Canada are subject to health, quarantine, agriculture, wildlife, and customs requirements and prohibitions, as are pets taken out of Canada and returned. Pets excluded from entry must be exported or destroyed. Dogs and cats under three months of age can be imported from the US without documentation, as can 'seeing eye' and other trained dogs from any country, provided that they accompany you on arrival and are in good health. Dogs and cats over three months old can be imported from the US provided that you obtain a certificate signed and dated by a veterinarian showing that the animal has been vaccinated against rabies not less than 30 days or more than 180 days prior to its importation. The certificate must identify the animal by breed, age, sex, colouring and any distinguishing marks.

For animals other than dogs and cats from the US and animals of any kind from other countries, you should check the regulations with the Animal Health Division, Agriculture Canada, Ottawa ON K1A 0Y9 (☎ 613-952-8000). However, if cats or dogs are imported from countries considered by the veterinary Director General of Canada to be rabies-free (such as the UK), either originating from that country or having been quarantined in that country for at least six months, they may not require a rabies certificate, provided that they have a general health certificate. If you're coming to Canada from outside North America it's wise to consult a company that's experienced in exporting and transporting animals abroad. Note also the following:

- Don't let your pets run free and don't allow your children to play with or approach strange or wild animals as they could have rabies. If a child is bitten by an unknown animal, he may require a series of anti-rabies injections.

- Always shop around and compare veterinarian fees. You can take out health insurance for less than $1 per day for a dog and under 50¢ per day for a cat, which covers veterinary bills and replacement of your pet due to its death from accident or illness.

- In most municipalities dogs must have licences and some also require cats to be licensed. Some communities levy a higher licence fee for un-neutered animals and may require you to hold a breeder's licence if an animal isn't neutered. In some municipalities, animals must be tattooed or have a microchip inserted under their skin so that they can be traced when lost. Proof of vaccination against rabies may be required in order to obtain a licence. Check with your local town hall or city clerk.

- Most communities require dogs to be kept on leads in municipal parks and for the owner to clear up after them. Take a 'poop-scoop' and a plastic bag with you when walking your dog and 'stoop and scoop' when your dog does his business. This is taken seriously and there are large fines for those who don't comply (which accounts for the lack of 'canine waste' on the streets).

- There are severe penalties for cruelty to animals and plans to increase the maximum penalty to five years in jail.

- With the exception of seeing eye and hearing-guide dogs (which may travel on trains and buses free of charge), dogs aren't allowed on public transport or in most restaurants and shopping malls.

- Your vet will arrange to collect and cremate the body of a dead pet (for a fee), although you can bury a dead pet in your garden (yard) in some areas. There are many commercial pet cemeteries in Canada, where the pets of the rich and famous are given a send-off befitting their pampered position in life.

- Many apartments and rented accommodation have regulations forbidding the keeping of dogs and other animals (cats are usually okay) and finding accommodation that accept dogs is difficult in most cities. The number of cats and dogs per residence may also be limited and large animals such as horses may be prohibited (particularly in condos).

Most major cities and towns have animal hospitals and clinics, and individuals and humane societies in many areas run sanctuaries for injured or orphaned wild animals and abandoned pets. Many cities and towns have animal shelters where you can obtain a stray dog or cat free of charge. Their policy is to retain all animals for adoption for as long as it takes to find them a new home. For further information about keeping pets in Canada contact the Canadian Society for the Prevention of Cruelty to Animals (CSPCA) at its head office at 5215 Jean-

Talon W, Montreal PQ H4P 1X4 (☎ 514-735-2711, ▣ www.spca.com). Dog owners may be interested in *Dogs in Canada* magazine, Apex Publishing Limited, 89 Skyway Avenue, Suite 200, Etbicoke ON M9W 6R4 (☎ 416-798-9778, ▣ www.dogs-in-canada.com).

POLICE

Canada's national police force is the world-famous Royal Canadian Mounted Police (RCMP), affectionately known as the Mounties. Its motto isn't, as many people think, 'they always get their man', but *'Maintiens le Droit'* (uphold the right). The distinguished uniform of red jacket, breeches and broad hat is now used just for ceremonial purposes and the only horses in use these days are those employed by the 32-strong musical riding team based at its headquarters in Rockliffe, Ottawa. There are no physical limitations for recruits, who no longer need to be at least 5ft 10in (1.78m) tall and have perfect vision. The only requirement is passing some physical tests and being in good mental health. As in many police forces, the pay isn't exceptional and a recent pay freeze has led to many officers defecting to municipal police forces or private security companies. One benefit of being in the RCMP is that when you're in ceremonial uniform you get your photograph taken a lot and if you're a man, you will apparently be in great demand from women suffering from what's known as 'scarlet fever'.

With the exception of Ontario and Quebec, the RCMP is the only provincial/territorial police force. Large cities in other provinces have their own regional forces and smaller communities have a local police force that's responsible for crime and road traffic offences. Canada also has an anti-terrorist force, the Canadian Security and Intelligence Service (CSIS).

All police are armed, and in crime-prone, inner-city areas they wear bullet-proof vests and carry pepper sprays (they also use rubber bullets in riot situations). In general, Canadian police officers are civil and polite. However, if you're stopped by a policeman, either in a car or when walking, don't make any sudden movements and keep your hands where they can be seen. Some policemen may interpret any movement as an attempt to reach a concealed weapon. Always remain courteous and helpful. It may not do any harm to emphasise that you're a foreigner or to tell the officer you're a visitor or newcomer. See also **Crime** on page 381 and **Legal System** on page 387.

POPULATION

The population of Canada in January 2003 was estimated at being around 31.5 million, over double what it was in 1951, with those of British origin accounting for nearly a third of the total. Around a quarter of Canadians are descendants from the original French settlers, most of whom live in Quebec, although there are also large numbers in New Brunswick (which is officially bi-lingual), Ontario and Manitoba. There are also some 49 per cent of Canadians with an ethnic origin other than British or French. Canada's third-largest ethnic group is German, while other major groups include Italian, Ukrainian, Dutch, Greek, Polish and Scandinavian. In recent decades there has been an influx of immigrants from Asia, particularly Chinese from Hong Kong, and to a lesser extent Latin Americans and people from the Caribbean. Toronto and Vancouver are among world's most cosmopolitan cities with large Chinese communities, while in other areas there are German, East European, African and Caribbean communities.

There are also around 350,000 'Native Indians', 30,000 Inuit and some 400,000 *Métis*, the name used to denote those of mixed native American and European blood. Collectively they're termed 'Native Canadians' or 'First Nations', and together they comprise around 4 per cent of the population. The majority of Native Canadians live in the Yukon, Northwest Territories, Nunavut and Ontario, although each province has some Native Canadian communities.

Ontario is the most populous province in Canada and is home to almost 40 per cent of Canadians, over 80 per cent of whom live in the urban areas between Kingston and Windsor (along the Great Lakes that make up the southern border). From 1951 to 1996 the population of Quebec fell from 29 to 25 per cent of Canada's total, during which period the fastest growing provinces were British Columbia and Alberta, which increased their share of the population from 15 to 22 per cent, while the population of the Atlantic provinces fell from 12 to 8 per cent. Some three-quarters of Canadians live in an urban area, around a third in the major cities and their suburbs, while only some two million (around 7 per cent) live in genuine rural areas. Canada's largest cities are Toronto with 4.2 million inhabitants, Montreal (3.3 million), Vancouver (1.8 million), Ottawa, the capital, (1 million), Edmonton (900,000), Calgary (800,000), Winnipeg (675,000) and Quebec City (650,000). The population density is one of the lowest in the world, with just three people per square kilometre (or just over one person per square mile).

RELIGION

There's no official religion in Canada and religion doesn't play a large part in Canadian life. Most Canadians are Christian, fairly evenly divided between Roman Catholics (of French descent) and Protestants (of British descent), but many other religions are also represented. There are many Jewish people in Montreal, Toronto and Winnipeg, and Vancouver has the highest concentration of Sikhs outside the Punjab. The large Chinese population in Toronto is mainly Buddhist and there are also small pockets of rural traditional sects such as Mennonites, Hutterites and Doukhobors. However, religion isn't significant in Canadian life and church attendance has steadily diminished since the 1950s, and a general lack of interest in religion by the children of immigrant families has lead to some domestic strife. Most of the First Nations population list themselves as Catholic thanks to Jesuit missionaries, although there has been something of a revival of ancient customs and beliefs in recent years, with many native Americans (and immigrants) turning to belief systems based on the natural world and the legends of their ancestors (as evidenced by the huge popularity of the fantasy books written by the Canadian author Charles de Lint).

Although the influence of religion has declined in most western societies in the latter part of the 20th century and the early 21st century (the US is a notable exception), churches and religious meeting places representing a multitude of faiths can be found throughout Canada. In smaller towns and communities, churches are often the main centres of social and community life and most churches organise a wide range of social activities, including sports events, dances, coffee hours, dinners and suppers, discussion groups and outings. Many also run nursery schools and after-school and youth programmes for older children. Many charities and social activities are also administered by church and religious groups, including homeless shelters, canteens, workshops for the disabled, youth centres, special schools, and many other projects. If you want to know how poorer people live, you need only ask a minister in any major city.

For information about local religious centres and service times, contact your local library or phone religious centres for information (listed in the yellow pages under 'religious organisations' or 'churches'). Some religious centres conduct services in a number of languages. In some areas a church directory is published and local religious services are usually listed in tourist guides and published in local newspapers, where a whole page may be devoted to church and religious news.

SOCIAL CUSTOMS

All countries have their own particular social customs and Canada is no exception. Good manners, politeness and consideration for others are considered important by Canadians, although they're generally informal in their relationships and won't be too upset if you break the social rules – provided that your behaviour isn't too outrageous. As a foreigner you may be forgiven if you accidentally insult your host, but may not be invited again! The following are a few common Canadian social customs:

- Canadians often greet total strangers, particularly in small towns and communities. This may vary from a formal "good morning" to a more casual "hi"; it's considered polite to respond likewise. Canadians often reply "You're welcome" or something similar when somebody thanks them and they may think you're impolite if you don't do likewise.

- It isn't usual to ask people personal questions such as their age or how much they paid for things – both are considered rude (unlike in the US, where such questions are commonplace).

- Don't ask Canadians if they're American, which is the ultimate insult, as many people have disdain for the US. They also don't refer to the US as America (as in North America), but call it the States.

- When introduced to someone, it's common to follow the cue of the person performing the introduction, e.g. if someone is introduced as Bill, you can usually call him Bill. Canadians generally dislike formality or any sort of social deference due to age or position, and most quickly say "Please call me Paul (or Paula)". To Canadians, informality shows no lack of respect. Due to the rise of women's liberation in Canada (which inevitably found its way over the US border), women may be introduced with the title 'Ms' (pronounced 'Mizz') and some women object to the title 'Miss' or 'Mrs'. However, in conversation most Canadians don't use names or titles at all. As a consequence of the diverse religions in Canada, Canadians refer to 'first' or 'given' names, rather than 'Christian' names.

  After you've been introduced to someone, you usually say something like, "Pleased to meet you" or "My pleasure." and shake hands with a firm grip (although more common among men). If someone asks "How are you?", it's normal to reply "Fine thanks" (even if you feel dreadful). When saying goodbye, it isn't customary in Canada to shake hands again, although some people do. Among friends in Quebec, it's common for men to kiss ladies on one or both cheeks. Men don't usually kiss or embrace each other in Canada, although this depends on their nationality or ethnic origin (or sexual orientation).

- Canadians don't have status or inherited titles (e.g. Sir or Lord) but do defer to people with a professional title that has been earned. These include foreign diplomats (e.g. Sir), members of the Senate (Senator), judges, medical doctors and others with a doctorate, military officers (e.g. General, Colonel, even when retired), professors, priests and other religious ministers (e.g. Father, Rabbi, Reverend).

- If you're invited to dinner, it's customary to take along a small present of flowers, a plant, chocolates or a bottle of wine (but nothing extravagant or ostentatious). Flowers can be tricky, as to some people carnations mean bad luck, chrysanthemums are for cemeteries and roses signify love. If you stay with someone as a house guest for a few days, it's customary to give your host or hostess a small gift when you leave. Pot-luck suppers are popular in some parts of Canada, where each guest or couple brings enough food to feed themselves and all the dishes are then placed on a large table and you help yourself to whatever you fancy. **If you bring something unusual or extra spicy, you should tell your hostess so that other people can be warned.**

- Many Canadians don't smoke and smoking without asking permission is considered rude in confined public places and totally unacceptable in someone's home.

- Although many foreigners have the impression that Canadians are relaxed and casual in their dress, they often have strict dress codes, particularly in the workplace. Some offices have introduced a 'dress-down' day on one day per week (usually Friday), when employees may wear casual attire (presentable blue jeans are permissible, but shorts or anything scruffy aren't). Formal social invitations usually state what dress is appropriate ('business attire' means jacket and tie for men and a dress or business suit for women). If you're in any doubt, it's perfectly acceptable to ring your hostess and ask what you should wear. Black or dark clothes are usually worn at funerals in Canada.

● Guests are normally expected to be punctual, with the exception of certain society parties, when late arrival is *de rigueur* (provided that you don't arrive after the celebrity guest). It's usual to arrive half an hour to an hour after the official start of a dance. You should, however, never be late for funerals, weddings, the theatre and other public performances, sports events, lectures and business appointments, to name but a few.

Invitations to cocktail parties or receptions may state 5 to 7pm, in which case you may arrive at any time between these hours. Dinner invitations are often phrased as 8 for 8.30pm. This means you should arrive at 8pm for drinks and dinner will be served (usually promptly) at 8.30pm. Arriving late for dinner is considered very impolite, although you must also *never* arrive early (unless you plan to help with the cooking).

● Some families say grace before meals, so you should follow your host's example before tucking in. If you're confused by a multitude of knives, forks and spoons, don't panic but just copy what your neighbour is doing (the rule is to start at the outside and work in).

● Don't overstay your welcome. This becomes obvious when your host starts looking at his watch, talking about his early start the next day, yawning, or in desperation, falling asleep.

TIME DIFFERENCE

Canada has six time zones, shown on the map below. The following table shows the time in each zone when it's noon in Vancouver.

Zone/Province	Time
Pacific Standard Time (PST)	noon
Mountain Standard Time (MST)	1pm
Central Standard Time (CST)	2pm
Eastern Standard Time (EST)	3pm
Atlantic Standard Time (AST)	4pm
Newfoundland Standard Time	4.30pm

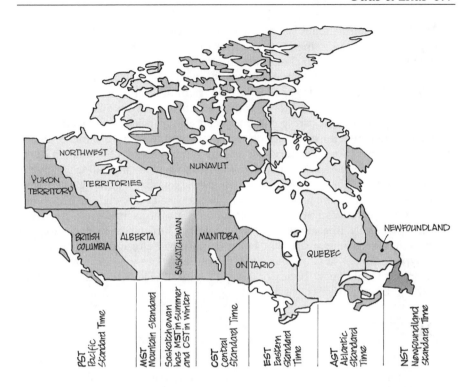

Canada operates a 'daylight saving' scheme, when every province except Saskatchewan moves its clocks forward one hour on the last Sunday in April and returns them to standard time on the last Sunday in October. When telling the time, Canadians say 'twenty to three', while 'twenty after three' is 'twenty minutes *past* three' or 3.20. Times are commonly written with a colon, e.g. 2:40 or 3:20. Canadians don't generally use the 24-hour clock.

TIPPING

Many Canadians don't tip (or tip very little) and don't mind being thought cheap – they like to think they're being thrifty (there's a local joke that goes "What's the difference between a canoe and a Canadian? A canoe tips!"). In Canada, tips are given only to people in service jobs such as bar-keepers, restaurant staff, cab drivers and redcaps. Many restaurant owners and other employers exploit the practice of tipping by paying starvation wages in the certain knowledge that employees can supplement their wages with tips. If you don't tip a waiter he may not starve, but he'll certainly struggle to survive on his meagre salary. In general a service charge isn't included in the bill in restaurants and you're expected to tip the waiter, waitress and barkeeps around 15 per cent, depending on the class of establishment.

Don't be bashful about asking whether service is included, although it should be shown on the menu. Restaurant tips can be included in credit card payments or given as cash. The total on credit card counter-foils is often left blank (even when service is included in the price) to encourage you to leave a tip. Some bills even include separate boxes for gratuities, but don't forget to fill in the total before signing it. Most restaurant staff prefer you to leave a cash tip as tips included in credit card payments aren't always passed onto staff.

Most people give the doorman or superintendent of their apartment block a tip (or 'sweetener') for extra services, usually ranging from a few dollars up to $10, depending on the service provided. Christmas is generally a time for giving tips to all and sundry, e.g. your doorman, newspaper boy, parking attendant, hairdresser, laundryman, handyman, etc. The size of a tip depends on how often someone has served you, the quality and friendliness of service, and how rich you are. Generally tips range from a few dollars up to $20 or more for the superintendent of your apartment block (it pays to be nice to him), which is usually placed inside a Christmas card. If you're unsure who or how much to tip, ask your neighbours, friends or colleagues for advice (who will all tell you something different!).

TOILETS

Some Canadians find the word 'toilet' distasteful and use a myriad of 'genteel' terms such as restroom, powder room, washroom, bathroom, ladies' or men's room, and even 'comfort station' to refer to their toilets (never 'water closet'). When inquiring about a toilet, most people ask for the restroom/bathroom or the men's or ladies' room. **Take care when using public toilets, as it isn't always easy to tell from the sign on the door whether it's the ladies' or men's room.** Public toilets can be found in most public buildings, restaurants and other public places. Separate toilets are usually provided for men and women. There is usually no charge for using them, although it isn't always easy to stroll in off the street and use a restroom in a private building such as an office block, and it helps if you look the part. Bars and restaurants may try to deter non-customers with intimidating signs such as 'Restrooms for Patrons Only', although you can usually get away with using the toilet in a busy bar and many people use the facilities in large hotels. Some toilets in large hotels and restaurants have an attendant, when it's customary to 'tip' around 50¢. Some toilets provide nappy (diaper) changing facilities or facilities for nursing mothers (nursing isn't usually performed in public in Canada). Many shopping centres (malls) have special toilets for the disabled, as do airports and major railway stations, although most public toilets for motorists aren't accessible to disabled drivers.

19.

THE CANADIANS

Who are the Canadians? What are they like? Let's take a candid and totally prejudiced look at the Canadian people, tongue firmly in cheek, and hope they forgive my flippancy or that they don't read this bit (which is why it's hidden away at the back of the book!). The typical Canadian is polite, hard-working, law-abiding, classless, unpretentious, generous, friendly, independent, liberal, cheerful, a good skier, proud, compassionate, an animal lover, reserved, dull, helpful, practical, introverted, conservative, a city dweller, talkative, fair, prosperous, a nice guy, peace-loving, an environmentalist, indefinable, honest (except with regard to taxes), an immigrant, polite, respectful, a humanitarian, healthy, unassuming, an outdoors man, cautious, democratic, modest, boring, loyal, relaxed, convivial, honourable, informal, tolerant, decisive, tough, pragmatic, well-educated, determined, sporting, hospitable, cosmopolitan, patriotic, mean, stoic, a hockey fan and definitely **NOT** an American.

You may have noticed that the above list contains 'a few' contradictions, which is hardly surprising as there's no such thing as a typical Canadian and few people conform to the popular stereotype (whatever that is). Canada is one of the most cosmopolitan and multi-cultural countries in the world (Toronto and Vancouver are among the world's most cosmopolitan cities) and a nation of foreigners (except for a few hundred thousand native Americans and Inuit) who often have little in common with one another. However, despite its diverse racial mix, Canada isn't a universal melting pot and has been called a cultural mosaic, where the country's multi-cultural approach emphasises the different backgrounds and cultures of its people. Canadians are one of the most difficult peoples to categorise and the country has been described as not so much a nation as a collection of different peoples on a continental scale. For a nation that's made up almost entirely of immigrants, it's hardly surprising that many Canadians have an identity crisis and spend a lot of time pondering 'The Canadian Question'. (As good an answer as any to the eternal question "What is a Canadian?" is probably "A person who knows how to make love in a canoe.").

Canadians pride themselves on their lack of class-consciousness and don't have the same caste distinctions and pretensions common in the old world. Canada isn't, however, a classless society and status is as important there as it is anywhere else, although it's usually based on money and character rather than birthright. Canada generally has no class or 'old school tie' barriers to success and almost anyone, however humble his origins, can fight his way to the top of the heap (although colour barriers aren't always so easy to overcome). However, although it doesn't have an aristocracy, old money and political alliances are important, and there are still a number of barriers that even vast amounts of new money cannot breach. Despite the fact that the vast majority of Canadians are misplaced Britons and assorted Europeans on the wrong side of the Atlantic, modern Canada has (not surprisingly) more in common with the US in lifestyle than with Britain or Europe.

However, apart from lifestyle, Canadians have little in common with Americans and, indeed, are at pains to emphasise the differences between themselves and their southern neighbours ('south of the border' in Canada means the US, not Mexico). Canadians *don't like* being mistaken for Americans, who they see as arrogant, brash and vulgar. It doesn't help that the US is Canada's biggest trading partner and has a huge influence on the Canadian economy; in a much quoted speech in 1969, the then Prime Minister Pierre Trudeau remarked that "Living next to the US is like sleeping with an elephant. No matter how friendly and even-tempered the beast, one is affected by every twitch and grunt". One sure way of making yourself unpopular with Canadians is to call them Americans or refer to 'America' when you mean the US (usually referred to as the States). Canada is part of 'the Americas' and therefore Canadians don't want that lot below the border to claim the title. So as not to be confused with Yanks when travelling, Canadians often wear a maple leaf badge or stick huge Canadian flags on their luggage to let people know where they are from.

Although they're often assumed to be Americans, many Canadians enjoy (or have enjoyed) world-wide fame, including Dan Ackroyd, Bryan Adams, Paul Anka, Elizabeth Arden, Margaret Atwood, Saul Bellow, Raymond Burr, John Candy, Jim Carrey, Leonard Cohen, Michael J. Fox, Glenn Gould, Lorne Greene, Wayne Gretsky, Arthur Hailey, Jack Kerouac, K. D. Lang, Gordon Lightfoot, Raymond Massey, Joni Mitchell, Anne Murray, Mike Myers, Mary Pickford, Christopher Plummer, William Shatner, David Steinberg, Donald Sutherland and Neil Young, most of whom don't (or didn't) complain too vociferously when being taken for Americans as it's good for business and helps to be accepted in the US. Canada also gave the world Trivial Pursuit (not many people know that), instant mashed potatoes, the gas mask, the parka, baby cereal, the electron microscope, the (zip) zipper, the snowmobile (no surprise there), the paint roller, Greenpeace (founded in Vancouver in 1970), the push-up bra, insulin, the chocolate bar, Ghostbusters, the paint roller, ice hockey and basketball (a real surprise – and a sore point with the Americans). The world would be a much poorer place without Canadians.

You may have noticed that Canada is a *very* large country (it takes a week just to drive across it); so large in fact that Canadians coined a new word to describe it: HUMONGOUS. It's the second-largest country in the world (after China) and almost as large as the whole of Europe, with six different time zones. The more you see of Canada the bigger it gets and in rural areas your nearest neighbours are likely to be miles away. The interior plains or the prairies are Canada's (and the world's) bread basket, consisting of hundreds of miles of wheat fields interspersed with vast forests and a few scattered towns. Despite it huge size, Canada has a small population of just over 30 million people, largely due to its inhospitable climate.

The weather is a topical subject of conversation in Canada, which is surprising considering that most of the year it's either bloody freezing or as hot as hell, with little in between these extremes (which the exception of Vancouver, which is really part of the US). For most of the year much of Canada is frozen solid and most of the time is spent indoors trying to keep warm or cool (which is why they invented Trivial Pursuit). However, unlike the Americans,

Canadians revel in their winters and turn (and tame) the weather to their advantage. They love the outdoor life and have a thriving winter sports industry, and spend the summers hiking, camping, hunting, fishing and boating (and trying to avoid being eaten by bears). The outdoors has a major influence on the lives of most Canadians, although most live in cities. They are passionate conservationists and schemes to protect the environment and recycling abound.

If you wonder what Canadians get up to during the long winters, judging by the low birth-rate it isn't sex (high immigration numbers are largely to compensate for the low birth-rate). Canadians are fairly broad-minded when it comes to sex and nudity, and some provinces have 'topless' laws which make it discriminatory to forbid women to go topless in any place where men can go without a shirt. This hasn't, however, led to a surfeit of ladies baring their breasts in public, but simply to many places (such as sports stadiums) banning topless men (and hence women). While on the subject of sex, you may be interested to know that (according to a recent survey) the average Canadian makes love 102 times per year (how do they know these things – surely they don't believe what people tell them?). Canadians are apparently thoughtful lovers and rate highest in the league for considering their partner's satisfaction more important than their own and ninth in the list of countries considered good lovers. Naturally the French are top in this respect – the statistics don't mention French Canadians, who no doubt consider themselves French in this regard! Like Americans, Canadians are tolerant of homosexuals and many cities have 'Gay Pride' days, when parades and other celebrations attract large crowds, including straights (or as they're called by gays, 'breeders').

Life in Canada isn't always a bed of roses, however, and it has a 'few' problems, although they're minor compared with those faced by most other countries. One festering sore is the treatment and rights of its indigenous peoples such as the Inuit (also known as Eskimos) and native Americans, who are now collectively referred to in politically correct terms as 'First Nation' people. Like the natives of all countries 'discovered' by Europeans, First Nation peoples were treated abominably, 'persuaded' first to part with their land, then their traditions and finally their lifestyle. In return they received the dubious benefits of Christianity and European diseases (such as measles, smallpox and tuberculosis) that killed them off like flies and the joys of alcoholism. In recent years the Canadian government has moved away from its paternalistic attitude and in 1999 granted the Inuit almost two million square kilometres (770,000mi2) of the Northwest Territories as a separate and autonomous territory called Nunavut ('our land').

However, although the deal included the eviction of all non-Inuit-owned businesses, put federal agencies under Inuit control and included payments totalling $500 million plus interest, it isn't as generous as it seems. In return the Inuit had to renounce claims of direct ownership of most of the territory, especially the main offshore gas and oil exploration areas (as John Paul Getty said, "The meek shall inherit the earth, but not the mineral rights"). This agreement has opened a can of worms, with other native groups now pressing for similar deals, and what started out as orderly protests have become barricaded roads and armed confrontations in some areas.

Canada's other major concern is the acrimonious debate over the future of Quebec. There's an ancient animosity between French-Canadians and English speakers dating back to the beginning of the 17th century, when the French were instrumental in opening up most of North America. They were involved in a running war with the British that culminated in the defeat of the French forces at Quebec City in 1759, following which 'New France' was ceded to Britain in 1763. Despite its defeat, the province of Quebec remained a stronghold of French nationalism and some 200 years later in the early 1960s the French-Canadians, fed up with their almost second-class citizen status in a country dominated by Anglo-Saxons, formed a separatist movement to demand that Quebec become a separate state. The campaign forced referendums (or 'neverendums' as they're frequently called) on the question of Quebec separation in 1980 and 1995, both of which were only narrowly defeated (in 1995, just 52 per cent voted to remain part of Canada), although a recent poll of *Québécois* showed that over 75 per cent want to remain part of Canada.

The average English-speaking Canadian has a jaundiced view of the *Québécois* and the French language, which many believe has more influence than it merits. In an effort to appease French-Canadians, the French language has become the first language of Quebec and Canada has become officially bi-lingual. To the immense irritation of the rest of Canada, all official documents and much other printed matter must be dual-language, most of the civil service speaks French only, and the dreaded 'language police' have garnered the sort of power that enables them to force Chinese businesses in Chinatown to take down their Chinese signs. Outside Quebec, many Canadians cannot wait to see the back of the *Québécois*, if only "so we won't need to have our soup can labels printed in French". Of one thing you can be sure, the separation issue is unlikely to go away and it seems inevitable that the *Québécois'* irreconcilable differences will eventually end in some form of separation.

Now for the good bit. Canada is one of the most open, liberal, stable and tolerant societies in the world. It has a thriving economy with political stability, abundant natural resources, a skilled workforce, steady population growth, and substantial domestic and foreign capital investment. It's renowned for its beauty, outdoor lifestyle, unspoilt environment, rich flora and fauna, healthy diet, friendly people, creativity, open spaces, sports facilities, cultural diversity, freedom, good transportation, education, health care, excellent local government and things that work. Canadians have more freedom from government interference than the people of most countries, to do, say and act any way they like. They place a high value on hard work, fairness, honesty and order, which help make Canada one of the least corrupt, safest (deaths from hand guns number in single digits, while in the US they run into thousands) and most civilised countries in the world. Canadians are very family oriented, which is one of the most important foundations of their lives, and it's a caring society where the community comes before the individual. This is highlighted by the abundance of charitable and voluntary organisations in Canada that do invaluable work (both nationally and internationally) and are supported by a veritable army of some five million voluntary workers.

Despite the shock and lingering memories of the crippling recession in the early 1990s, Canadians have strong faith in themselves and are optimistic about the future. Although immigrants may criticise some aspects of Canadian life, most feel privileged to live there and are proud to call themselves Canadian, and very few seriously consider leaving. In fact, immigrants from a vast range of backgrounds firmly believe that Canada is the promised land and a great place to live and raise a family. This is borne out by the United Nations' 'quality of life' survey that consistently ranks Canada in the number one position, based on such things as the standard of healthcare, educational achievement, wealth, life expectancy and standard of living. It may not be everyone's idea of paradise (particularly if you hate the cold), but Canada certainly has a good claim to be the best country in the world. For vitality and *joie de vivre* Canada has few equals, and for those fortunate enough to secure a residence permit it's a land where you can turn your dreams into reality.

Long Live Canada! *Vive le Canada! O Canada!*

20.

MOVING HOUSE OR LEAVING CANADA

When moving house or leaving Canada there are many things to be considered and a 'million' people to inform. The checklists contained in this chapter make the task easier and hopefully help prevent an ulcer or nervous breakdown (only divorce or a bereavement cause more stress than moving house), provided of course that you don't leave everything to the last minute. See also **Moving House** on page 119 and **Relocation Consultants** on page 109.

MOVING HOUSE

When moving house within Canada, particularly when changing province, the following matters should be considered:

- Give notice to your employer or inform him of your new address.
- If you live in rented accommodation you must give your landlord the necessary notice, as specified in your lease. If you don't give sufficient notice, you must pay the rent until the end of your lease or for the full notice period.
- If you aren't moving into permanent accommodation, book temporary accommodation and have them confirmed in writing.
- Inform the following:
  - Your utility companies, e.g. electricity, gas and water companies. Make sure any security deposits are returned if you're moving to a new area.
  - Your phone company, preferably at least two weeks in advance. If you're moving home and remaining within the same code area you may be able to retain your existing number. Don't forget to have your phone line disconnected when moving, otherwise the new owners or tenants will be able to make calls at your expense.
  - Your insurance companies (for example health, car, homeowner's, life, etc.), banks, stockbroker and other financial institutions, credit card and loan companies, lawyer and accountant, and local businesses where you have accounts. Make sure you have valid insurance if you're moving to another province.
  - Your doctor, dentist and other health practitioners. Health records should be transferred to your new doctor and dentist, if applicable. Contact your vet for information and health records for your pets and any special transportation requirements.
  - Your family's schools. If applicable, arrange for schooling in your new community. Try to give a term's notice and obtain a copy of any relevant school reports or records from your children's current schools.
  - Give or send all regular correspondents your new address and phone number. These may include subscriptions, social and sports clubs, church

and other organisations, professional and trade journals, not forgetting your friends and relatives.

- Arrange to have your post redirected by Canada Post (see **Change of Address** on page 138). This should be arranged two to four weeks before moving.

- If you're moving to another province and have a Canadian driver's licence or Canadian registered car, inform your local motor licence office as soon as possible after moving. Give your automobile association (club) (see page 233) your new address.

● Return any library books or anything borrowed.

● Book a moving company (see page 109) well in advance to transport your furniture and personal effects to your new home. If you have just a few items of furniture to move you may prefer to do your own move, in which case you may need to rent a vehicle or trailer. Keep a record of all moving expenses for tax purposes.

● Arrange for a cleaning or decorating company for rented accommodation, if necessary.

● If renting, contact your landlord or the letting agency to have your security deposit returned.

● Cancel newspaper and other regular home deliveries.

● If necessary, arrange for someone to look after your children and pets during the move.

● Ask yourself (again): 'Is it really worth all this trouble?'.

LEAVING CANADA

Before leaving Canada permanently or for an indefinite period, the following matters should be considered *in addition* to those listed above under **Moving House**:

● Check that your family's passports are valid.

● Check whether there are any special requirements (e.g. visas, permits or inoculations) for entry into your destination country by contacting the local embassy or consulate in Canada. An exit permit or visa isn't required to leave Canada.

● If you're shipping household and personal effects, find out the exact procedure from the local embassy of your destination country. Special forms may need to be completed before arrival. If you've been living in Canada for less than a year you're required to re-export all imported personal effects, including furniture and vehicles (if you sell them you should pay duty). Contact an international shipping company (see page 109) well in advance to arrange shipment of your furniture and personal effects.

- Notify any utility companies well in advance if you need to get a security deposit returned.

- You must pay your federal and provincial taxes for the current year in the normal way before leaving Canada (see page 300). If you're leaving Canada permanently and are a member of a company pension plan (or have a private pension plan), you should receive a lump sum payment in lieu of a pension. Contact your company personnel office, local Canada Customs and Revenue Agency office or pension company for information. **As a non-resident, a withholding tax of 25 per cent is levied on interest, dividends, rents, royalties, alimony, pension benefits and certain payments from retirement savings plans, old age social insurance benefits and the net income from a business in Canada.** If you've been employed temporarily in Canada, you must ensure that Canada Customs and Revenue Agency is aware that you're no longer a resident, otherwise you could continue to receive tax demands.

- Arrange to sell anything you aren't taking with you (home, car, furniture, etc.). If you have a Canadian registered car that you're exporting, check the procedure and cost (e.g. shipping, tax and import duty) of exporting it and make arrangements for its shipment.

- Depending on your destination, your pets may require special inoculations or may be required to go into quarantine for a period. Make arrangements well in advance.

- Arrange health, travel and other insurance as necessary (see **Chapter 13**).

- Depending on your destination, arrange health and dental check-ups for your family before leaving Canada. Obtain a copy of your family's health and dental records and a statement from your health insurance company stating your present level of cover.

- Settle any loans, leases or instalment contracts and pay all outstanding bills (allow plenty of time as some companies may be slow to respond).

- Check whether you're entitled to a rebate on your car registration and car and other insurance. Obtain a letter from your Canadian car insurance company stating your number of years 'good-driver' discount.

- Sell your house, apartment or other property, or arrange to let it through a friend or an agent (see **Chapter 5**).

- Check whether you require an international driver's permit or a translation of your Canadian or foreign driver's licence for your country of destination.

- Give friends and business associates a temporary address and phone number where you can be contacted abroad.

- If you're travelling by air, allow yourself plenty of time to get to the airport, register your luggage, and clear security and immigration.
- Buy a copy of *Living and Working in ********* by Survival Books before leaving Canada. If we haven't published it yet, drop us a line and we'll get started on it right away!

Have a safe journey!

APPENDICES

Appendix A: Useful Addresses

Embassies & High Commissions

The list below includes the majority of foreign embassies and High Commissions (for Commonwealth countries) in the capital, Ottawa. Many countries also have consulates in other cities (e.g. Montreal, Toronto and Vancouver), which are listed in phone books. For countries that don't have representation in Canada contact the embassy in Washington DC, USA.

Algeria: 435 Daly Avenue, Ottawa ON K1N 6H3 (☎ 613-789-8505/0282).

Argentina: 90 Sparks Street, Suite 910, Ottawa ON K1P 5B4 (☎ 613-236-2351).

Australia: 50 O'Connor Street, Suite 710, Ottawa ON K1P 6L2 (☎ 613-236-0841).

Austria: 445 Wilbrod Street, Ottawa ON K1N 6M7 (☎ 613-789-1444/3429/3430).

Bangladesh: 275 Bank Street, Suite 302, Ottawa ON K2P 2L6 (☎ 613-236-0138/9).

Barbados: 130 Albert Street, Suite 600, Ottawa ON K1P 5G4 (☎ 613-236-9517/9518).

Belgium: 80 Elgin Street, 4th Floor, Ottawa ON K1P 1B7 (☎ 613-236-7267/68/69).

Bolivia: 130 Albert Street, Suite 416, Ottawa ON K1P 5G4 (☎ 613-236-5730).

Chile: 50 O'Connor Street, Suite 1413, Ottawa ON K1P 6L2 (☎ 613-235-4402).

China: 515 St Patrick Street, Ottawa ON K1N 5H3 (☎ 613-789-3434).

Colombia: 360 Albert Street, Suite 1002, Ottawa ON K1R 7X7 (☎ 613-230-3760).

Cote D'Ivoire: 9 Marlborough Avenue, Ottawa ON K1N 8E6 (☎ 613-236-9919).

Croatia: 229 Chapel Street, Ottawa ON K1N 7Y6 (☎ 613-562-7820).

Czech Republic: 251 Cooper Street, Ottawa ON K2P 0G2 (☎ 613-562-3875).

Denmark: 47 Clarence Street, Suite 450, Ottawa ON K1N 9K1 (☎ 613-562-1811).

Ecuador: 50 O'Connor Street, Suite 113, Ottawa ON K1P 6L2 (☎ 613-563-8206).

Egypt: 454 Laurier Avenue East, Ottawa ON K1N 6R3 (☎ 613-234-4931/4935/4958).

Ethiopia: 151 Slater Street, Suite 210, Ottawa ON K1P 5H3 (☎ 613-235-6637).

Finland: 55 Metcalfe Street, Suite 850, Ottawa ON K1P 6L5 (☎ 613-236-2389).

France: 42 Sussex Drive, Ottawa ON K1M 2C9 (☎ 613-789-1795).

Germany: 1 Waverley Street, Ottawa ON K2P 0T8 (☎ 613-232-1101).

Hungary: 299 Waverley Street, Ottawa ON K2P 0V9 (☎ 613-230-2717).

India: 10 Springfield Road, Ottawa ON K1M 1C9 (☎ 613-744-3751/3752/3753).

Indonesia: 55 Parkdale Avenue, Ottawa ON K1Y 1E5 (☎ 613-724-1100).

Iran: 245 Metcalfe Street, Ottawa ON K2P 2K2 (☎ 613-235-4726).

Israel: 50 O'Connor Street, Suite 1005, Ottawa ON K1P 6L2 (☎ 613-567-6450).

Japan: 255 Sussex Drive, Ottawa ON K1N 9E6 (☎ 613-241-8541).

Kenya: 415 Laurier Avenue East, Ottawa ON K1N 6R4 (☎ 613-563-1773/1776/1778).

Korea: 150 /Boteler Street, 5th Floor, Ottawa ON K1N 5A6 (☎ 613-244-5010).

Latvia: 280 Albert Street, Suite 300, Ottawa ON K1P 5G8 (☎ 613-238-6868).

Lebanon: 640 Lyon Street, Ottawa ON K1S 3Z5 (☎ 613-236-5825/5855).

Malaysia: 60 Botelar Street, Ottawa ON K1N 8Y7 (☎ 613-241-5182).

Mexico: 45 O'Connor Street, Suite 1500, Ottawa ON K1P 1A4 (☎ 613-233-8988).

Morocco: 38 Range Road, Ottawa ON K1N 8J4 (☎ 613-236-7391/7392/7393).

New Zealand: 99 Bank Street, Suite 727, Ottawa ON K1P 6G3 (☎ 613-238-5991).

Norway: Royal Bank Centre, 90 Sparks Street, Suite 532, Ottawa ON K1P 5B4 (☎ 613-238-6571).

Paraguay: 151 Slater Street, Suite 401, Ottawa ON K1P 5H3 (☎ 613-567-1283).

Peru: 130 Albert Street, Suite 1901, Ottawa ON K1P 5G4 (☎ 613-238-1777).

Philippines: 130 Albert Street, Suite 606, Ottawa ON K1P 5G4 (☎ 613-233-1121).

Poland: 443 Daly Avenue, Ottawa ON K1N 6H3 (☎ 613-789-0468).

Russia: 285 Charlotte Street, Ottawa ON K1N 8L5 (☎ 613-235-4341).

Slovakia: 50 Rideau Terrace, Ottawa ON K1M 2A1 (☎ 613-749-4442).

South Africa: 15 Sussex Drive, Ottawa ON K1M 1M8 (☎ 613-744-0330).

Spain: 74 Stanley Avenue, Ottawa ON K1M 1P4 (☎ 613-747-2252/7293).

Sri Lanka: 333 Laurier Avenue West, Suite 1204, Ottawa ON K1P 1C1 (☎ 613-233-8449).

Thailand: 180 Island Park Drive, Ottawa ON K1Y 0A2 (☎ 613-722-4444).

Trinidad and Tobago: 200 First Avenue, 3rd Level, Ottawa ON K1S 2G6 (☎ 613-232-2418/2419).

Ukraine: 310 Somerset Street, Ottawa ON K2P 0J9 (☎ 613-230-2961).

United Kingdom: 80 Elgin Street, Ottawa ON K1P 5K7 (☎ 613-237-1303).

United States of America: 490 Sussex Drive, Ottawa ON K1N 1G8 (☎ 613-238-5335)

Uruguay: 130 Albert Street, Suite 1905, Ottawa ON K1P 5G4 (☎ 613-234-2727).

Other Addresses

Association of Canadian Travel Agents (ACTA), 130 Albert Street, Suite 1705, Ottawa ON K1P 5G4 (☎ 613-237 3657, 🖳 www.acta.net).

Association of Professional Placement Agencies and Consultants, 114 Richmond Street E, Suite L-109, Toronto ON M5C 1P1 (☎ 416-362-0983).

Association of Universities and Colleges of Canada, 350 Albert Street, Suite 600, Ottawa ON K1R 1B1 (☎ 613-563-1236, 💻 www.aucc.ca).

Canadian Association of Independent Schools, 13425 Dufferin Street, King City ON L7B 1K5 (☎ 905-833-3385, 💻 www.cais.ca).

Canadian Automobile Association (CAA), 1145 Hunt Club Road, Suite 200, Ottawa ON K1V 0Y3 (☎ 613-247-0117, 💻 www.caa.ca).

Canadian Council of Better Business Bureaus, 44 Byward Market Square, Suite 220 Ottawa ON K1N 7A2 (☎ 613-789-5151, 💻 www.canadiancouncilbbb.ca).

Canada Customs and Revenue Agency, 2265 St. Laurent Boulevard, 1st Floor, Ottawa ON K1G 4K3 (☎ 1-800-461-9999, 💻 www.ccra-adrc.gc.ca).

Canadian Real Estate Association (CREA), Suite 1600, 344 Slater Street, Canada Building, Ottawa ON K1R 7Y3 (☎ 613-237-7111, 💻 www.crea.ca).

Consumers Association of Canada, Suite 404, 267 O'Connor Street, Ottawa ON K2P 1V3 (☎ 613-238-2533, 💻 www.consumer.ca).

Consumers Council of Canada, 35 Madison Avenue, Suite 100, Toronto ON M5R 2S2 (☎ 416-961-3487, 💻 www.consumerscouncil.ca).

Employment and Immigration Canada, Public Enquiries Centre, 140 Promenade du Portage, Phase IV, Hull PQ K1A 0JA (☎ 819-994-6313).

Forum for International Trade Training (FITT), 30 Metcalfe Street, Ottawa ON K1P 5L4 (☎ 613-230-3553, 💻 www.fitt.ca).

Human Resources Development Canada (HRDC), Public Inquiries Centre, 140 Promenade du Portage, Hull Qc K1A 0J9 (✆ 819-953-7260, 💻 www.hrdc-drhc.gc.ca).

Insurance Bureau of Canada, 151 Yonge Street, Suite 1800, Toronto ON M5C 2W7 (☎ 416-362-2031).

Motor Vehicle Regulations Directorate, Transport Canada, 330 Sparks Street, Ottawa ON K1A 0N5 (☎ 613-990-2309, 💻 www.tc.gc.ca).

Organization of Professional Immigration Consultants, PO Box 63563, Woodside Square, 1571 Sandhurst Circle, Toronto ON M1V 1VO (☎ 416-483 7044).

APPENDIX B: **FURTHER READING**

Newspapers & Magazines

Beautiful British Columbia, #302, 3939 Quadra Street, Victoria BC V8X 1J5 (☎ 250-380-7611, 💻 www.beautifulbc.ca). Quarterly travel magazine.

The Calgary Herald, 16 Street SE, Suite 215, Calgary AB T2P 0W8 (☎ 403-235-7100, 💻 www.calgaryherald.com). Daily newspaper.

The Calgary Sun, 2615 12 Street NE, Calgary AB T2E 7W9 (☎ 403-250-4300, 💻 www.fyicalgary.com/calsun.shtml). Daily newspaper.

Canada News, Outbound Newspapers, 1 Commercial Road, Eastbourne, East Sussex BN21 3XQ, UK (☎ +44-(1)-323-726-040, 💻 www.outbound-newspapers.com). Monthly newspaper for immigrants.

Canada Employment Weekly, 21 New Street, Toronto ON M5R 1P7 (☎ 416-964-6069, 💻 www.mediacorp2.com).

Canadian Business, 777 Bay Street, 5th Floor, Toronto ON M5W 1A7 (☎ 416-596-5523, 💻 www.canadianbusiness.com). Monthly business magazine.

Canadian Living, Transcontinental Publications Inc., 25 Sheppard Avenue West, Suite 100, Toronto ON M2N 6S7 (☎ 416-733-7600, 💻 www.canadianliving.com). Monthly women's home and lifestyle magazine.

The Edmonton Journal, 10006-101 Street, Edmonton AB T5J 0S1 (☎ 780-429-5100, 💻 www.edmontonjournal.com). Daily newspaper.

The Globe and Mail, 444 Front Street, Toronto ON M5V 2S9 (☎ 416-585-5000, 💻 www.theglobeandmail.com). Daily newspaper.

The Halifax Daily News, PO Box 8330, Station A, Halifax NS B3K 5M1 (☎ 902-468-1222, 💻 www.hfxnews.southam.ca). Daily newspaper.

Maclean's, 777 Bay Street, Toronto ON M5W 1A7 (☎ 416-596-5386, 💻 www.macleans.ca). Weekly current affairs magazine.

The Montréal Gazette, 250 St Antoine W, Montreal PQ H2Y 3R7 (☎ 514-987-2222, 💻 www.montrealgazette.com). Daily newspaper.

Moving Publications Ltd., 178 Main Street, Unionville ON L3R 2G9 (☎ 905-479-0641, 💻 www.movingto.com). Home moving guides to Alberta, SW Ontario, Ottawa/Hull, Manitoba, Montreal & Area, Saskatchewan, Toronto & Area, and Vancouver & BC.

The National Post, 300-1450 Don Mills Road, Don Mills ON M3B 3R5 (☎ 416-383-2300, 🖳 www.nationalpost.com). Daily newspaper.

The Ottawa Citizen, 1101 Baxter Road, Box 5020, Ottawa ON K2C 3M4 (☎ 613-829-9100, 🖳 www.ottawacitizen.com). Daily Newspaper.

The Province, 200 Granville Street, Suite 1, Vancouver BC V6C 3N3 (☎ 604-605-2222, 🖳 www.vancouverprovince.com). Daily newspaper.

Toronto Life, 59 Front Street E, Toronto ON M5E 1B3 (☎ 416-364-4433, 🖳 www.torontolife.com). Monthly lifestyle magazine.

Vancouver Magazine, Suite 300, East Tower, 555 West 12th Avenue, Vancouver BC V5Z 4L4 (☎ 604-877-7732, 🖳 www.vanmag.com). Monthly lifestyle magazine.

The Vancouver Sun, 200 Granville Street, Suite 1, Vancouver BC V6C 3N3 (☎ 604-605-2111, 🖳 www.vancouversun.com). Daily newspaper.

The Windsor Star, 167 Ferry Street, Windsor ON N9A 4M5 (☎ 519-255-5711, 🖳 www.canada.com/windsor). Daily newspaper.

The Winnipeg Free Press, 1355 Mountain Avenue, Winnipeg MA R2X 3B6 (☎ 204-697-7000, 🖳 www.winnipegfreepress.mb.ca). Daily newspaper.

Books

In the list below, the publication title is followed by the author's name and the publisher (in brackets). All books prefixed with an asterisk (*) are recommended by the author. Some titles may be out of print, but you may still be able to find a copy in a book shop or library.

General Reference

Canada Year Book (Statistics Canada)

Canadian Encyclopaedia (McClelland & Stewart)

Canadian World Almanac and Book of Facts (Global Press)

Tourist Guides

In addition to the national tourist guides listed below, there are numerous regional, provincial and city guides.

*****Baedeker Canada** (AA/Baedeker)

*****Birnbaum's Canada**, Alexandra Mayes Birnbaum (Harper-Perennial)

*Blue Guide Canada (A & C Black)

*Canada: The Rough Guide, Tim Jepson, Phil Lee & Tania Smith (Rough Guides)

Discover Canada (Berlitz)

*Explorer Guide: Canada (AA Publishing)

Exploring Canada (Fodor's Travel Publications)

*Fodor's Canada (Hodder & Stoughton)

Frommer's Dollarwise Guide to Canada (Frommer)

A Handbook of the Canadian Rockies, Ben Gadd (Corax)

*Insight Guide: Canada (APA Publications)

*Let's Go: USA and Canada (Pan)

*Lonely Planet: Canada, Mark Lightbody, Jim DuFresne & Dorinda Talbot (Lonely Planet)

*Michelin Green Guide Canada (Michelin)

*The National Geographic Traveller Canada (AA Publishing)

*The Outdoor Traveller's Guide to Canada, David Dunbar (Stewart, Tabori & Chang)

Immigration, Living & Working

Canada and Immigration, Freda Hawkins (McGill-Queen's UP)

*Canadian Experience Handbook (Hongkong Bank of Canada)

Finding a Job in Canada, Valerie Gerrard (How To)

*Immigrating to Canada, Gary Segal (Self Council Press)

Migrating to Canada, Martin J. Bjarnason (How To)

*Migration Canada, H. Arnold Sherman & Jeffrey D. Sherman (Kluwer Law International)

Working in Canada, Walter Johnson (Black Rose)

Miscellaneous

1001 Questions about Canada, John R. Colombo (Doubleday)

The Adventure Guide to Canada, P. Hobbs (Hunter Publishing)

The Big Picture: What Canadians Think About Almost Anything, Allan R. Gregg (Macfarlane, Walter & Ross)

*Canada 2002, Wayne C. Thompson (Stryker-Post)

Brain Quest Canada; 1,000 Questions & Answers, Linda Granfield (Workman)

*Canada – A Portrait (Statistics Canada)

Canada – the Culture, Bobby D. Kalman (Crabtree)

Canada from A to Z, Bobby D. Kalman (Crabtree)

Canada – the People, Bobby D. Kalman (Crabtree)

Canada in World Affairs, Canadian Institute of international Affairs (Oxford University Press, Toronto)

*The Canadians, George Woodcock (Fitzhenry & Whiteside)

*City to City (also called 'O Canada! Travels in an Unknown Country'), Jan Morris (Harper Collins)

*The Complete Canadian Small Business Guide, Douglas A. Gray (McGraw Hill & Ryerson)

A Concise History of Business in Canada, Graham D. Taylor & Peter A. Baskerville

*A Day in the Life of Canada, Rick Smolen (Collins)

Destination Canada, Harald Mante (Windsor Books)

*The Eskimos and Aleuts, Don Dumond (Thames & Hudson)

Government of Canada, Robert MacGregor Dawson (University of Toronto Press)

A History of the Peoples of Canada, J. M. Bumstead (OUP)

How Canadians Govern Themselves, Eugene Forsey (Supply & Services Canada)

*The Illustrated History of Canada, Robert Craig Brown (Lester)

Language, Culture and Values in Canada at the Dawn of the 21st Century, André LaPierre (Carleton University Press)

*The Last Wilderness, P. Browning (Hutchinson)

The New Canadian Basics Cookbook, Carol Ferguson & Murray McMillan (Penguin)

*The Penguin History of Canada, Kenneth McNaught (Penguin)

In Search of Canada, S. Graubard (Transaction Publications)

A Short History of Canada, Desmond Morton (McClelland & Stewart)

*A Social History of Canada, George Woodcock (Penguin)

*The Story of Canada**, Janet Lunn & Christopher Moore (Lester Publishing)

Symbols of Nationhood (Canada Communications Group)

*Why We Act Like Canadians**, Pierre Berton (McClelland & Stewart)

*Writing Hone: A PEN Anthology**, Constance Rooke (McClelland & Stewart)

APPENDIX C: USEFUL WEBSITES

There are dozens of expatriate websites and, as the Internet increases in popularity, the number grows by the day. Most information is useful, and websites generally offer free access, although some require a subscription or payment for services. Relocation and other companies specialising in expatriate services often have websites, although these may provide only information that a company is prepared to offer free of charge, which may be rather biased. However, there are plenty of volunteer sites run by expatriates providing practical information and tips.

A particularly useful section found on most expatriate websites is the 'message board' or 'forum', where expatriates answer questions based on their experiences and knowledge and offer an insight into what living and working in Canada (or in a particular province or town) is **really** like.

Note that websites listed below are under headings in alphabetical order and the list is by no means definitive.

Canadian Websites

Bank of Canada (🖥 www.bankofcanada.ca): Contains plenty of financial information, including exchange rates.

BuyitCanada.com (🖥 www.buyitcanada.com): A directory, divided into provinces and cities, with links to websites about everything from apartment rentals and the arts to immigration lawyers and utilities.

CampSource (🖥 www.campsource.com): A guide to camping resources in Canada.

Canada.com (🖥 www.canada.com): A comprehensive network, with news and information about everything Canadian, from careers to shopping.

Canada Immigration Research Institute (🖥 www.immigrationvisa. org/index.html): Information about Canada and its immigration laws.

Canada International (🖥 www.canadainternational.gc.ca): Contains links to government services, information and resources, aimed at citizens of other countries.

Canada Post (🖥 www.canadapost.ca): Comprehensive information about Canada's postal services and prices.

Canadian Broadcasting Corporation (⌨ www.cbc.ca): Details of CBC's radio and TV output as well as coverage of news, sports, business, the arts and much else.

Canadian Passport Office (⌨ www.ppt.gc.ca): Information about passports.

Canadian Relocation Systems (⌨ http://relocatecanada.com): A guide for people relocating within or moving to Canada, with plenty of details about life, services and prices throughout the country.

Canadian Tourism Commission (⌨ www.travelcanada.ca): Contains comprehensive information and links about all aspects of Canada.

Citizenship and Immigration Canada (⌨ www.cic.gc.ca): Government information about immigration to Canada.

Citizine (⌨ www.citizine.ca): A government website aimed at younger people, 'designed to broaden the views of its users ... about Canadian issues, persons and products'.

Environment Canada (⌨ www.ec.gc.ca): Government information about the environment.

FactsCanada.ca (⌨ www.factscanada.ca): Contains information and news about all aspects of Canada.

Government of Canada (⌨ http://canada.gc.ca): Details the services offered by the government to Canadians, non-Canadians and businesses.

Health Canada (⌨ www.hc-sc.gc.ca): Government information on all aspects of healthcare.

Moving in Canada (⌨ www.movingincanada.com): A comprehensive guide to life in Canada's various provinces, cities and towns.

National Research Council Canada (⌨ www.nrc-cnrc.gc.ca): The website of the government's organisation for research and development in science, industry and technology.

Rural Living Canada (⌨ http://members.attcanada.ca): A wide-ranging compendium of links for those wanting to live out of Canada's cities and towns.

School Net (⌨ www.schoolnet.ca): Government information about education.

Skinet Canada (⌨ www.skinetcanada.com): Information about skiing conditions, weather, prices and other facts and figures for skiers in Canada and the USA.

SOS Canada 2000 (🖥 http://soscanada2000.com): A country and migration guide to Canada.

Statistics Canada (🖥 www.statcan.ca): Government statistics on all aspects of Canada and Canadian life.

The Weather Network (🖥 www.theweathernetwork.com): 'Voted number one for best forecast by Canadians'. (With luck their forecasting is better than their grammar!)

General Websites

Australia Shop (🖥 www.australia.shop.com): Expatriate shopping for homesick Australians.

British Expatriates (🖥 www.britishexpat.com and www.ukworld wide. com): Two sites designed to keep British expatriates in touch with events in and information about the UK.

Direct Moving (🖥 www.directmoving.com): General expatriate information, tips and advice, and numerous links.

Escape Artist (🖥 www.escapeartist.com): One of the most comprehensive expatriate sites, including resources, links and directories covering most expatriate destinations. You can also subscribe to the free monthly online expatriate magazine, Escape from America.

ExpatAccess (🖥 www.expataccess.com): Aimed at those planning to move abroad, with free moving guides.

ExpatBoards (🖥 www.expatboards.com): A comprehensive site for expatriates, with popular discussion boards and special areas for Britons and Americans.

Expat Exchange (🖥 www.expatexchange.com): Reportedly the largest online 'community' for English-speaking expatriates, including articles on relocation and a question and answer facility.

Expat Forum (🖥 www.expatforum.com): Provides cost of living comparisons as well as over 20 country-specific forums.

Expat Mums (🖥 www.expat-moms.com): Information for expatriate mothers.

Expat Network (🖥 www.expatnetwork.com): The UK's leading expatriate website, which is essentially an employment network for expatriates, although it also includes numerous support services and a monthly online magazine, Nexus.

Expat Shopping (💻 www.expatshopping.com): Order your favourite foods from home.

Expat World (💻 www.expatworld.net): Information for American and British expatriates, including a subscription newsletter.

Expatriate Experts (💻 www.expatexpert.com): Run by expatriate expert Robin Pascoe, providing advice and support.

Global People (💻 www.peoplegoingglobal.com): Includes country-specific information with a particular emphasis on social and political issues.

Living Abroad (💻 www.livingabroad.com): Includes an extensive list of country profiles, which are available only on payment.

Outpost Information Centre (💻 www.outpostexpat.nl): Contains extensive country-specific information and links operated by the Shell Petroleum Company for its expatriate workers, but available to everyone.

Real Post Reports (💻 www.realpostreports.com): Includes relocation services, recommended reading lists and 'real-life' stories written by expatriates in cities throughout the world.

Save Wealth Travel (💻 www.savewealth.com/travel/warnings): Travel information and warnings.

Trade Partners (💻 www.tradepartners.gov.uk): A UK government-sponsored site providing trade and investment (and general) information about most countries, including the USA.

The Travel Doctor (💻 www.tmvc.com.au/info10.html): Includes a country by country vaccination guide.

Travelfinder (💻 www.travelfinder.com/twarn/travel_warnings.html): Travel information with warnings about danger areas.

World Health Organization (💻 www.who.int): Health information.

The World Press (💻 www.theworldpress.com): Links to media sites in practically every country in the world's media.

World Travel Guide (💻 www.wtgonline.com): A general website for world travellers and expatriates.

Yankee Doodle (💻 www.yankeedoodleiow.com): Import American products.

Websites for British Expatriates

British Expatriates (⌨ www.britishexpat.com and www.ukworld wide. com): These websites keep British expatriates in touch with events and information in the United Kingdom.

Trade Partners (⌨ www.tradepartners.gov.uk): A government-sponsored website whose main aim is to provide trade and investment information for most countries. Even if you aren't intending to do business, the information is comprehensive and up to date.

Websites for Women

Career Women (⌨ www.womenconnect.com): Contains career opportunities for women abroad plus a wealth of other useful information.

Expatriate Mothers (⌨ http://expatmoms.tripod.com): Help and advice on how to survive as a mother on relocation.

Spouse Abroad (⌨ www.expatspouse.com): Information about careers and working abroad. You need to register and subscribe.

Third Culture Kids (⌨ www.tckworld.com): Designed for expatriate children.

Women Abroad (⌨ www.womanabroad.com): Advice on careers, expatriate skills and the family abroad. Opportunity to subscribe to a monthly magazine of the same name.

Worldwise Directory (⌨ www.suzylamplugh.org/worldwise): Run by the Suzy Lamplugh charity for personal safety, the site provides practical information about a number of countries with special emphasis on safety, particularly for women.

APPENDIX D: WEIGHTS & MEASURES

Canada offically converted to the international metric system of measurement in 1970, although even today both metric and Imperial measures are used (e.g. fuel is sold by the litre, while most food is sold by the pound). Those who are unfamiliar with either system will find the tables on the following pages useful. Some comparisons shown are only approximate, and clothes sizes often vary considerably with the manufacturer (as we all know only too well). Try all clothes on before buying and don't be afraid to return something if, when you try it on at home, you decide it doesn't fit (most shops will exchange goods or give a refund).

Women's Clothes

Continental	34 36 38 40 42 44 46 48 50 52
UK	8 10 12 14 16 18 20 22 24 26
USA	6 8 10 12 14 16 18 20 22 24

Pullovers

	Women's	Men's
Continental	40 42 44 46 48 50	44 46 48 50 52 54
UK	34 36 38 40 42 44	34 36 38 40 42 44
USA	34 36 38 40 42 44	sm med lar xl

Men's Shirts

Continental	36 37 38 39 40 41 42 43 44 46
UK/USA	14 14 15 15 16 16 17 17 18 -

Men's Underwear

Continental	5	6	7	8	9	10
UK	34	36	38	40	42	44
USA	sm	med		lar	xl	

Note: sm = small, med = medium, lar = large, xl = extra large

Children's Clothes

Continental	92	104	116	128	140	152
UK	16/18	20/22	24/26	28/30	32/34	36/38
USA	2	4	6	8	10	12

Children's Shoes

Continental	18 19 20 21 22 23 24 25 26 27 28 29 30 31 32
UK/USA	2 3 4 4 5 6 7 7 8 9 10 11 11 12 13
Continental	33 34 35 36 37 38
UK/USA	1 2 2 3 4 5

Shoes (Women's and Men's)

Continental	35	36	37	37	38	39	40	41	42	42	43	44
UK	2	3	3	4	4	5	6	7	7	8	9	9
USA	4	5	5	6	6	7	8	9	9	10	10	11

Weight

Avoirdupois	Metric	Metric	Avoirdupois
1oz	28.35g	1g	0.035oz
1lb*	454g	100g	3.5oz
1cwt	50.8kg	250g	9oz
1 ton	1,016kg	500g	18oz
2,205lb	1 tonne	1kg	2.2lb

Length

British/US	Metric	Metric	British/US
1in	2.54cm	1cm	0.39in
1ft	30.48cm	1m	3ft 3.25in
1yd	91.44cm	1km	0.62mi
1mi	1.6km	8km	5mi

Capacity

Imperial	Metric	Metric	Imperial
1 UK pint	0.57 litre	1 litre	1.75 UK pints
1 US pint	0.47 litre	1 litre	2.13 US pints
1 UK gallon	4.54 litres	1 litre	0.22 UK gallon
1 US gallon	3.78 litres	1 litre	0.26 US gallon

Note: An American 'cup' = around 250ml or 0.25 litre.

Area

British/US	Metric	Metric	British/US
1 sq. in	0.45 sq. cm	1 sq. cm	0.15 sq. in
1 sq. ft	0.09 sq. m	1 sq. m	10.76 sq. ft
1 sq. yd	0.84 sq. m	1 sq. m	1.2 sq. yds
1 acre	0.4 hectares	1 hectare	2.47 acres
1 sq. mile	2.56 sq. km	1 sq. km	0.39 sq. mile

Temperature

°Celsius	°Fahrenheit	
0	32	(freezing point of water)
5	41	
10	50	
15	59	
20	68	
25	77	
30	86	
35	95	
40	104	
50	122	

Notes: The boiling point of water is 100°C / 212°F.

Normal body temperature (if you're alive and well) is 37°C / 98.4°F.

Temperature Conversion

Celsius to Fahrenheit: multiply by 9, divide by 5 and add 32. (For a quick and approximate conversion, double the Celsius temperature and add 30.)

Fahrenheit to Celsius: subtract 32, multiply by 5 and divide by 9. (For a quick and approximate conversion, subtract 30 from the Fahrenheit temperature and divide by 2.)

Oven Temperatures

Gas	Electric	
	°F	°C
-	225–250	110–120
1	275	140
2	300	150
3	325	160
4	350	180
5	375	190
6	400	200
7	425	220
8	450	230
9	475	240

Air Pressure

PSI	Bar
10	0.5
20	1.4
30	2
40	2.8

APPENDIX E: MAP

The map of Canada opposite shows the ten provinces and three territories (Northwest, Nunavut and Yukon), which are listed below with their official abbreviations and capital cities.

Province/Territory	Abbreviation	Capital
Alberta	AB	Edmonton
British Columbia	BC	Victoria
Manitoba	MB	Winnipeg
New Brunswick	NB	Fredericton
Newfoundland	NF	St John's
Northwest Territories	NT	Yellowknife
Nova Scotia	NS	Halifax
Nunavut	NT	Iqualuit
Ontario	ON	Toronto
Prince Edward Island	PE	Charlottetown
Quebec	PA	Quebec City
Saskatchewan	SK	Regina
Yukon Territory	YT	Whitehorse

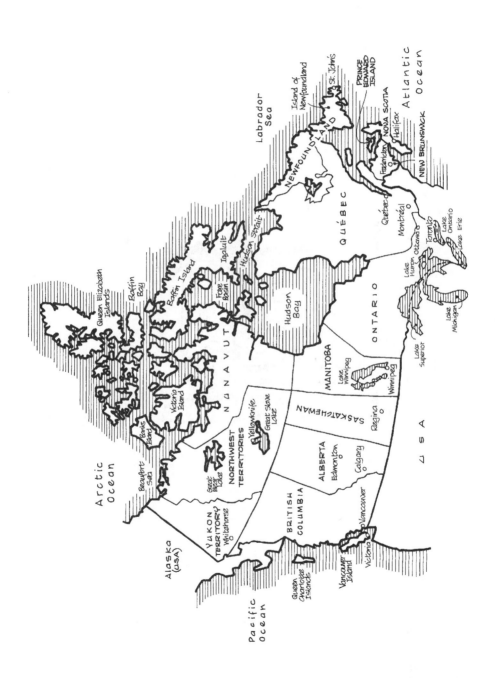

INDEX

A

Accidents 228
  Roads 224
Accommodation 101
  Air-Conditioning 126
  Buying A Home 112
  Canadian Homes 110
  Estate Agents 115
  Heating 126
  Holiday Homes 114
  Keys & Security 121
  Moving House 119
  Relocation Consultants 109
  Rental 117
  Temporary 102
  Utilities 122
Aerial Sports 331
Air-Conditioning 126
Airline Services 198
  Airports 199
  Domestic Fares 201
  International Fares 200
Alcohol 369
Amusement Parks 317
Appendices
  Appendix A: Useful Addresses 416
  Appendix B: Further Reading 420
  Appendix C: Useful Websites 425
  Appendix D: Metric System 430
  Appendix E: Map 434
Arrival 87
  Checklists 97
  Customs 89
  Finding Help 95
  Immigration 88
  Record 88
Art Galleries 318
Au Pairs 29

B

Ballet 321
Banks 287
  Accounts 289
  Cards 292
  Credit & Charge Cards 293
  Hours 288
Bars 325
Baseball 332
Bed & Breakfast (B&B) 106
Books 367
Buses 195
Buying
  A Car 211
  A Home 112

C

Camping & Caravanning 316
Canadian
  Citizenship 378
  Currency 283
  Football 333
  Homes 110
  National Anthem & Flag 387
  People 401
  Social Customs 394
Capital Gains Tax 306
Cars. See Motoring
Chain Stores 361
Checklists 60, 97, 410
Cinema 319
Citizenship 378
  Passports 379
Climate 379
Climbing 334
Clothing 364

Consumer Associations 375
Cost Of Living 309
Counselling 250
Credit Rating 286
Crime 381
    Guns & Other Weapons 382
    Prevention & Safety 381
Currency 283
Customs 89
    Drugs & Syringes 93
    Permanent Residence 90
    Restricted Goods 93
    Returning Residents 92
    Seasonal Residents 92
    Temporary Residence 90
    Visitors 92
Cycling 334

D

Death 253
Dentists 248
Department Stores 361
Disability Insurance 271
Divorce 389
Doctors 243
Driving. See Motoring
Drugs 252
Dry Cleaning 370
Duty-Free Allowances 372

E

Education 23, 167
    Adult & Further 182
    Higher 179
    Language Schools 183
    Private 177
    Public Or Private School? 169
    Public Schools 171
Embassies & Consulates 416
Emergency Numbers 155

Employment. See also Finding A Job
    Agencies 23
    Services 22
Employment Conditions 41
    Authorisation 81
    Checklists 60
    Contract 43
    Disability Benefit 54
    Discrimination 42
    Health & Safety 58
    Holidays & Leave 48
    Insurance 53
    Other Conditions 56
    Place Of Work 44
    Retirement & Pensions 55
    Salary & Benefits 44
    Sick Pay 54
    Travel & Relocation Expenses 47
    Union Membership 55
    Working Hours 48
Estate Agents 115
Exporting Money 284

F

Ferries 203
Finance 281
    Banks 287
    Canadian Currency 283
    Capital Gains Tax 306
    Cost Of Living 309
    Credit Rating 286
    Exporting Money 284
    Importing Money 284
    Income Tax 297
    Inheritance & Gift Tax 307
    Mortgages 295
    Property Tax 305
    Wills 307
Finding A Job 19
    Contract Jobs 25
    Employment & Job Services 22
    Employment Agencies 23

Holiday & Short-Term Jobs 27
HRCCs 22
HRDC 22
Illegal Working 37
Job Seeking 31
Language 38
Nannies & Au Pairs 29
Part-Time 26
Salary 33
Self-Employment 34
Temporary & Casual Work 26
Trainees & Work Experience 29
Training & Education 23
Voluntary Work 27
Working Women 30
Finding Help 95
Fishing 336
Food Shops 362
Fuel 232
Furniture & Furnishings 365
Further Reading 420

G

Gambling 323
Geography 382
Arctic 383
Atlantic Provinces 383
Canadian Shield 383
Cordillera 384
Great Lakes 384
Great White North 383
Pacific Coast 384
Prairies 384
St Lawrence Lowlands 384
Golf 336
Government 385
Local 386
National Anthem & Flag 387
Provincial & Territorial 386
Voting 387
Guns & Other Weapons 382
Gymnasiums 331

H

Health 239
Childbirth 247
Counselling 250
Death 253
Dentists 248
Doctors 243
Drugs 252
Emergencies 242
Hospitals & Clinics 246
Medicines 245
Opticians 249
Pharmacies 245
Service 241
Smoking 251
STDs 253
Health Clubs 331
Heating 126
Help 95
Hiking 337
Holiday & Short-Term Jobs 27
Holidays & Leave 48
Annual Holidays 48
Compassionate & Special Leave 52
National & Provincial Holidays 49
Pregnancy 52
Sickness Or Accident 53
Hospitals & Clinics 246
Hostels 108
Hotels 103
Household Goods 366
HRCCs 22
HRDC 22
Hunting 339

I

Ice Hockey 339
Illegal Working 37
Immigration 88
Importing Money 284

Income Tax 297
   Credits & Deductions 301
   Federal 300
   Provincial 301
   Residence 299
   Return 302
Inheritance & Gift Tax 307
Insurance 53, 257
   Car 218
   Companies & Agents 258
   Compensation 53
   Contents 276
   Contracts 259
   Dental 269
   Disability 271
   Employment 54, 265
   Health 53
   Holiday & Travel 277
   Household 272
   Liability 277
   Long-Term Health Care 270
   Medicare 266
   Private Health 266
   Private Pension Plans 272
   Social 53, 260
International Calls 148
Internet 154
   Shopping 371

J

Jobs. See also Finding A Job
   Contract 25
   Holiday & Short-Term 27
   Part-Time 26
Jogging & Running 341

L

Lacrosse 341
Language 38, 183
Laundry 370

Leaving Canada 411
Legal System 387
Leisure 311
   Amusement Parks 317
   Art Galleries 318
   Ballet 321
   Bars 325
   Camping & Caravanning 316
   Cinema 319
   Gambling 323
   Libraries 327
   Museums 318
   Music 321
   Night-Life 323
   Parks 314
   Restaurants 326
   Social Clubs 322
   Theatre 320
   Tourist Information 313
Libraries 327

M

Magazines 367
Mail-Order Shopping 370
Map 434
Markets 361
Marriage 389
Medicare 241, 266
Medicines 245
Military Service 390
Mobile Phones 152
Mortgages 295
   Getting The Best Deal 297
   Types 296
Motels 105
Motor Sports 342
Motoring 207
   Accidents 228
   Automobile Clubs 233
   Buying A Car 211
   Canadian Roads 224
   Car Insurance 218

Car Rental 233
Car Theft 231
Drinking & Driving 230
Driving Licence 216
Fuel 232
General Road Rules 220
Motorcycles 227
Parking 235
Safety & Emission Inspection 215
Speed Limits 220
Traffic Police 226
Vehicle Importation 208
Vehicle Registration 210
Winter Driving 225
Moving House 119, 410
What to Take With You? 120
Museums 318
Music 321

N

Nannies 29
Newspapers 367
Night-Life 323
Non-Immigrant Visas 79
Student Authorisation 80
Visitor 79
Work Permits 81
Work Programmes for Students 84

O

Opticians 249
Order Forms 446

P

Parking 235
Parks 314
Wildlife 315

Pensions 55, 272
Permits & Visas 67
Applications 70
Categories 70
Fees 74
Forms & Documentation 74
Immigrant 69
Interviews 77
Non-Immigrant Visas 79
Points System 75
Priority System 76
Quebec 77
Pets 390
Pharmacies 245
Police 226, 392
Population 392
Post Office Services 129
Business Hours 131
Change of Address 138
Important Documents 136
Letters & Letter Packages 131
Parcels & Packages 135
Valuables 136
Pregnancy 52, 247
Property Tax 305
Provinces & Territories 434
Public Transport 187
Airline Services 198
Ferries 203
Long-Distance Buses 195
Taxis 197
Trains 189
Travellers with Disabilities 188
Urban Transit Systems 193

R

Racquet Sports 342
Radio 163
Receipts & Warranties 374
Religion 393
Relocation
Consultants 109
Expenses 47

Rental
  Accommodation 117
  Cars 233
Restaurants 326
Roads 224

S

Salary & Benefits 33, 44
  Commission & Bonuses 45
  Company Cars 47
  Education & Training 46
  Expenses 46
  Overtime 45
  Redundancy Pay 59
  Sick Pay 54
Sales Taxes 358
Schools
  Language 183
  Private 177
  Public 171
Secondhand Goods 358
Security 121, 231, 381
Self-Catering 107
Self-Employment 34
Shopping 353
  Alcohol 369
  Bargain 355
  Books 367
  Centres 360
  Chain Stores 361
  Clothing 364
  Consumer Associations 375
  Department Stores 361
  Dry Cleaning 370
  Duty-Free Allowances 372
  Food Shops 362
  Furniture & Furnishings 365
  Hours 360
  Household Goods 366
  Magazines 367
  Mail-Order 370

  Markets 361
  Newspapers 367
  Receipts & Warranties 374
  Sales Taxes 358
  Secondhand Goods 356
  Supermarkets 362
  Tobacco 369
Skiing 343
  Cross-Country 346
Smoking 251
Snow Sports 343
  Dog-Sledding 347
  Snowmobiling 346
Social Clubs 322
Social Customs 394
Sports 329
  Aerial Sports 331
  Baseball 332
  Canadian Football 333
  Climbing 334
  Cycling 334
  Fishing 336
  Golf 336
  Hiking 337
  Hunting 339
  Ice Hockey 339
  Jogging & Running 341
  Lacrosse 341
  Motor Sports 342
  Other Snow Sports 343
  Other Sports 350
  Racquet Sports 342
  Skiing 343
  Swimming 347
  Watersports 348
Starting A Business 34
  Business Structures 35
  Business Visas 35
  Information 36
  Professional Advice 36
STDs 253
Supermarkets 362
Swimming 347

T

Tax
    Capital Gains 306
    Income 297
    Inheritance & Gift 307
    Property 305
    Sales 358
Taxis 197
Telephone 141
    Billing & Payment 148
    Charges 147
    Choosing A Telephone 143
    Custom Services 146
    Directories 151
    Emergency Numbers 155
    Entertainment 145
    Information 145
    Installation 142
    International Calls 148
    Internet 154
    Mobile Phones 152
    Operator Services 146
    Optional Services 146
    Public Service Numbers 155
    Public Telephones 149
    Registration 142
    Telegrams 153
    Telex & Fax 153
    Toll-Free Numbers 145
    Using The Telephone 143
Television 157
    Cable 160
    Satellite 161
    Standards 158
    Stations & Programmes 159
    Videos 162
Temporary & Casual Work 26
Theatre 320
Time Difference 396
Tipping 397
Tobacco 369
Toilets 398
Tourist Information 313

Training 23
Trains 189
    Accommodation 193
    Tickets 191

U

Union Membership 55
Urban Transit Systems 193
Useful Addresses 416
Useful Websites 425
Utilities 122
    Electricity 123
    Gas 125
    Water 125

V

Vehicles. See Motoring
Visas. See Permits & Visas
Voluntary Work 27

W

Watersports 348
    Canoeing & Kayaking 349
    Sailing 349
    Sub-Aqua 349
    Surfing 348
    Whitewater Rafting 350
Websites 427
Weights & Measures 430
Wills 307
Work Permits 81
Working. See Finding A Job

Y

YMCAs/YWCAs 108

LIVING AND WORKING SERIES

Living and Working books are essential reading for anyone planning to spend time abroad, including holiday-home owners, retirees, visitors, business people, migrants, students and even extra-terrestrials! They're packed with important and useful information designed to help you **avoid costly mistakes and save both time and money.** Topics covered include how to:

- Find a job with a good salary & conditions
- Obtain a residence permit
- Avoid and overcome problems
- Find your dream home
- Get the best education for your family
- Make the best use of public transport
- Endure local motoring habits
- Obtain the best health treatment
- Stretch your money further
- Make the most of your leisure time
- Enjoy the local sporting life
- Find the best shopping bargains
- Insure yourself against most eventualities
- Use post office and telephone services
- Do numerous other things not listed above

Living and Working books are the most comprehensive and up-to-date source of practical information available about everyday life abroad. They aren't, however, boring text books, but interesting and entertaining guides written in a highly readable style.

Discover what it's *really* like to live and work abroad!

Order your copies today by phone, fax, mail or e-mail from: Survival Books, PO Box 146, Wetherby, West Yorks. LS23 6XZ, United Kingdom (☎/▤ +44 (0)1937-843523, ✉ orders@ survivalbooks.net, 💻 www.survivalbooks.net).

BUYING A HOME SERIES

Buying a Home books are essential reading for anyone planning to purchase property abroad and are designed to guide you through the jungle and make it a pleasant and enjoyable experience. Most importantly, they're packed with vital information to help you **avoid the sort of disasters that can turn your dream home into a nightmare!** Topics covered include:

- Avoiding problems
- Choosing the region
- Finding the right home and location
- Estate agents
- Finance, mortgages and taxes
- Home security
- Utilities, heating and air-conditioning
- Moving house and settling in
- Renting and letting
- Permits and visas
- Travelling and communications
- Health and insurance
- Renting a car and driving
- Retirement and starting a business
- And much, much more!

Buying a Home books are the most comprehensive and up-to-date source of information available about buying property abroad. Whether you want a detached house, townhouse or apartment, a holiday or a permanent home, these books will help make your dreams come true.

Save yourself time, trouble and money!

Order your copies today by phone, fax, mail or e-mail from: Survival Books, PO Box 146, Wetherby, West Yorks. LS23 6XZ, United Kingdom (☎/▤ +44 (0)1937-843523, ✉ orders@ survivalbooks.net, 💻 www.survivalbooks.net).

ORDER FORM

ALIEN'S GUIDES / BEST PLACES / BUYING A HOME / DISASTERS / WINES

Qty.	Title	Price (incl. p&p)*			Total
		UK	**Europe**	**World**	
	The Alien's Guide to Britain	£5.95	£6.95	£8.45	
	The Alien's Guide to France	£5.95	£6.95	£8.45	
	The Best Places to Buy a Home in France	£13.95	£15.95	£19.45	
	The Best Places to Buy a Home in Spain	£13.45	£14.95	£16.95	
	Buying a Home Abroad	£13.45	£14.95	£16.95	
	Buying a Home in Britain	£11.45	£12.95	£14.95	
	Buying a Home in Florida	£13.45	£14.95	£16.95	
	Buying a Home in France	£13.45	£14.95	£16.95	
	Buying a Home in Greece & Cyprus	£13.45	£14.95	£16.95	
	Buying a Home in Ireland	£11.45	£12.95	£14.95	
	Buying a Home in Italy	£13.45	£14.95	£16.95	
	Buying a Home in Portugal	£13.45	£14.95	£16.95	
	Buying a Home in Spain	£13.45	£14.95	£16.95	
	How to Avoid Holiday & Travel Disasters	£13.45	£14.95	£16.95	
	Renovating & Maintaining Your French Home	Autumn 2003			
	Rioja and its Wines	£11.45	£12.95	£14.95	
	The Wines of Spain	£15.95	£18.45	£21.95	
				Total	

Order your copies today by phone, fax, mail or e-mail from: Survival Books, PO Box 146, Wetherby, West Yorks. LS23 6XZ, UK (☎/▤ +44 (0)1937-843523, ✉ orders@ survivalbooks.net, 💻 www.survivalbooks.net). If you aren't entirely satisfied, simply return them to us within 14 days for a full and unconditional refund.

Cheque enclosed/please charge my Amex/Delta/MasterCard/Switch/Visa* card

Card No.   _ _ _ _   _ _ _ _   _ _ _ _   _ _ _ _

Expiry date _____   Issue number (Switch only) _____

Signature _____   Tel. No. _____

NAME _____

ADDRESS _____

_____

_____

* Delete as applicable (price includes postage – airmail for Europe/world).

ORDER FORM

LIVING & WORKING SERIES / RETIRING ABROAD

Qty.	Title	Price (incl. p&p)*			Total
		UK	**Europe**	**World**	
	Living & Working Abroad	£16.95	£18.95	£22.45	
	Living & Working in America	£14.95	£16.95	£20.45	
	Living & Working in Australia	£14.95	£16.95	£20.45	
	Living & Working in Britain	£14.95	£16.95	£20.45	
	Living & Working in Canada	£16.95	£18.95	£22.45	
	Living & Working in the Far East	Winter 2003			
	Living & Working in France	£14.95	£16.95	£20.45	
	Living & Working in Germany	£16.95	£18.95	£22.45	
	Living & Working in the Gulf States & Saudi Arabia	£16.95	£18.95	£22.45	
	Living & Working in Holland, Belgium & Luxembourg	£14.95	£16.95	£20.45	
	Living & Working in Ireland	£14.95	£16.95	£20.45	
	Living & Working in Italy	£16.95	£18.95	£22.45	
	Living & Working in London	£11.45	£12.95	£14.95	
	Living & Working in New Zealand	£14.95	£16.95	£20.45	
	Living & Working in Spain	£14.95	£16.95	£20.45	
	Living & Working in Switzerland	£14.95	£16.95	£20.45	
	Retiring Abroad	£14.95	£16.95	£20.45	
				Total	

Order your copies today by phone, fax, mail or e-mail from: Survival Books, PO Box 146, Wetherby, West Yorks. LS23 6XZ, UK (☎/▤ +44 (0)1937-843523, ✉ orders@ survivalbooks.net, ▣ www.survivalbooks.net). If you aren't entirely satisfied, simply return them to us within 14 days for a full and unconditional refund.

Cheque enclosed/please charge my Amex/Delta/MasterCard/Switch/Visa* card

Card No. _ _ _ _   _ _ _ _   _ _ _ _   _ _ _ _

Expiry date _____   Issue number (Switch only) _____

Signature _____   Tel. No. _____

NAME _____

ADDRESS _____

_____

_____

* Delete as applicable (price includes postage – airmail for Europe/world).

OTHER SURVIVAL BOOKS

Survival Books publishes a variety of books in addition to the *Living and Working* and *Buying a Home* series (see previous pages). These include:

The Alien's Guides: *The Alien's Guides to Britain* and *France* provide an 'alternative' look at life in these popular countries and will help you to avoid the most serious gaffes and to appreciate more fully the peculiarities (in both senses) of the British and French.

The Best Places to Buy a Home: *The Best Places to Buy a Home in France* and *Spain* are the most comprehensive and up-to-date sources of information available for anyone wanting to research the property market in France and Spain and will save you endless hours choosing the best place for your home.

How to Avoid Holiday and Travel Disasters: This book is essential reading for anyone planning a trip abroad and will help you to make the right decisions regarding every aspect of your travel arrangements and to avoid costly mistakes and the sort of disasters that can turn a trip into a nightmare.

Renovating & Maintaining Your French Home: New for 2003 is the ultimate guide to renovating and maintaining your dream home in France, including essential information, contacts and vocabulary and time and cost-saving tips.

Retiring Abroad: This is the most comprehensive and up-to-date source of practical information available about retiring to a foreign country and will help to smooth your path to successful retirement abroad and save you time, trouble and money.

Wine Guides: *Rioja and its Wines* and *The Wines of Spain* are required reading for lovers of fine wines and are the most comprehensive and up-to-date sources of information available on the wines of Spain and of its most famous wine-producing region.

Broaden your horizons with Survival Books!

Order your copies today by phone, fax, mail or e-mail from: Survival Books, PO Box 146, Wetherby, West Yorks. LS23 6XZ, United Kingdom (☎/▤ +44 (0)1937-843523, ✉ orders@ survivalbooks.net, ▢ www.survivalbooks.net).